AA

Ireland

AA Publishing

Written by Julia Hynard

Edited and produced by AA Publishing

Regional Map produced by AA Cartographic Department of the Automobile Association.

The contents of this publication are believed correct at the time of printing. Nevertheless, the publishers cannot be held responsible for any errors or omissions or for changes in the details given in this guide or for the consequences of any reliance on the information provided by the same. Assessments of AA inspected establishments are based on the experience of the Hotel, Restaurant and Camping & Caravanning Inspectors on the occasion of their visit(s) and therefore descriptions given in this guide necessarily contain an element of subjective opinion which may not reflect or dictate a reader's own opinion on another occasion. We have tried to ensure accuracy in this guide but things do change and we would be grateful if readers would advise us of any inaccuracies they may encounter.

Typeset by Microset Ltd, Basingstoke, England
Printed and bound by G Canale & C. S.P.A., Torino, Italy
Cover design by Mike Ballard, Twyford, England
Internal design by PPD, Basingstoke, England

Advertisement Sales Head of Advertisement Sales:
Christopher Heard, ☎ 01256 491544
Advertisement Production:
Karen Weeks, ☎ 01256 491545

A CIP catalogue record for this book is available from the British Library

ISBN 0-7495-1764 5

AA Ref. 10126

Published by AA Publishing, which is a trading name of Automobile Association Developments Limited, whose registered office is Norfolk House, Priestley Road, Basingstoke, Hampshire RG24 9NY.
Registered number 1878835

All pictures are held in the Association's own library (AA Photo Library) with the exception of pages 56, 92/3 (Robert Harding Picture Library), 126/7 (Spectrum Colour Library), 153 (Pictures Colour Library), 168 (Bord Failte)

CONTENTS

IRELAND
Regions and Historic Towns

EASTERN COUNTIES
County Dublin
County Kildare
County Louth
County Meath
County Wicklow

SOUTHEASTERN COUNTIES
County Carlow
County Kilkenny
County Tipperary
County Waterford
County Wexford

SOUTHWESTERN COUNTIES
County Cork
County Kerry
County Limerick

WESTERN COUNTIES
County Clare
County Galway
County Mayo

NORTHWESTERN COUNTIES
County Donegal
County Leitrim
County Sligo

NORTHERN IRELAND
County Antrim
County Armagh
County Down
County Fermanagh
County Londonderry
County Tyrone

LAKELAND COUNTIES
County Cavan
County Laois
County Longford
County Monaghan
County Offaly
County Roscommon
County Westmeath

Donegal Coast
North Channel
GB
Buncrana
Portrush
Portstewart
Ballycastle
Coleraine
Limavady
Ballymoney
Londonderry
Letterkenny
DONEGAL
LONDONDERRY
ANTRIM
Larne
Ballymena
Ballyclare
Strabane
NORTHERN IRELAND
Carrickfergus
Bangor
Holywood
Donaghadee
Cookstown
BELFAST
Newtownards
Omagh
TYRONE
Lisburn
Ballyshannon
Dungannon
Craigavon
Dromore
Portadown
Armagh
Downpatrick
FERMANAGH
Enniskillen
Banbridge
DOWN
Monaghan
ARMAGH
Sligo
Newcastle
MONAGHAN
Newry
Mourne Mountains
Clones
Castleblayney
Warrenpoint
Kilkeel
LEITRIM
CAVAN
Dundalk
Cavan
LOUTH
REPUBLIC
Ardee
IRISH SEA
ROSCOMMON
LONGFORD
Strokestown
Kells
Longford
Drogheda
Navan
Balbriggan
MEATH
Skerries
Mullingar
Trim
WESTMEATH
Athlone
OF
Malahide
DUBLIN
Ballinasloe
Clara
Edenderry
DUBLIN
Tullamore
KILDARE
Dun Laoghaire
OFFALY
Newbridge (Droichead Nua)
Naas
Dalkey
Bray
Loughrea
Kildare
Birr
Mountmellick
Portlaoise
WICKLOW
Athy
Wicklow
Abbeyleix
Wicklow Mountains
Roscrea
LAOIS
Nenagh
Carlow
IRELAND
Arklow
Thurles
CARLOW
Kilkenny
Gorey
TIPPERARY
KILKENNY
WEXFORD
Cashel
Tipperary
Enniscorthy
New Ross
Clonmel
Carrick-on-Suir
Cahir
Waterford
Wexford
WATERFORD
Fermoy
Tramore
Lismore
Dungarvan
St George's Channel
Youghal
Cork
Midleton
GB
Cobh
Kinsale
Heritage Towns of Ireland
0 20 40 60 80 km
0 10 20 30 40 50 miles

WELCOME TO THE GUIDE

HOW THE GUIDE IS DIVIDED
For the purposes of this guide Ireland has been divided into seven regions:

Dublin and the Eastern Counties:
(Counties Dublin, Kildare, Louth, Meath, Wicklow)

The Southeastern Counties:
(Counties Carlow, Kilkenny, Tipperary, Waterford, Wexford)

Cork and the Southwestern Counties:
(Counties Cork, Kerry, Limerick)

The Western Counties:
(Counties Clare, Galway, Mayo, Aran Islands)

The Northwestern Counties:
(Counties Donegal, Leitrim, Sligo)

The Lakeland Counties:
(Counties Cavan, Longford, Laois, Monaghan, Offaly, Roscommon, Westmeath)

Belfast and Northern Ireland:
(Counties Antrim, Armagh, Down, Fermanagh, Londonderry, Tyrone)

REGIONAL DIVISIONS
Each region starts with a brief description of the region, followed by events and festivals taking place there throughout the year. Each region is then divided into counties.

COUNTY DIVISIONS
Each county begins with a brief description and the principal town or towns within it. Information is divided into the following sections:

WHERE TO GO AND WHAT TO DO
Our intention has been to include as many attractions possible to reflect the widest range of interests for the benefit of the reader. To do this entries are necessarily brief, but do include location, a telephone contact number and directions (if applicable and supplied)
The Must See section is generally more informative than the subsequent headings and is intended to give an good overall tourist attraction picture of the county.

Other interests (see below) have been divided into lists for ease of use. Their descriptions may not be so long , but will always incorporate the address and/or directions and a telephone number (if supplied or applicable). For example, if you are on holiday with the children, the Great for Kids section incorporates everything in the area to do. If you prefer stately homes, gardens, castles, churches and sites of architectural then the Homes & Gardens or Historic & Ancient Sites sections may appeal. If an activity holiday is what you are looking for then our Sports & Leisure section in the Essential Information section holds a wealth of sporting information.

MUST SEE
BIG OUTDOORS
GREAT FOR KIDS
HISTORIC & ANCIENT SITES
HOMES & GARDENS
(in main cities Gardens appear separately)
MUSEUMS & ART GALLERIES
(which may be split if the number of entries merits it)

Must See
Entries include the very best or most interesting places to go in the county. These could include any of the Where to See and What to Do

ategories. The entries could range from the ıost famous tourist attraction - for example, The 3larney Stone - to something small that captures ıe essence of the area.

ig Outdoors
ntries include beaches, nature parks, scenic laces, bird reserves

reat for Kids
Many of the big tourist attractions are geared up o children with special exhibitions, audio-visual resentations and the like. The entries in this eading may include some, or none of these, epending on what else is available in the area. xpect to find children's farms, beaches, local ctivities, leisure centres.

istoric & Ancient Sites
reland is rich in castles, churches and sites such s ancient crosses, standing stones and prehistoric emains

omes & Gardens
tately and not so stately homes and their ardens and grounds; plus the many fascinating ardens of every style and size which are open to ıe public Note: In cities only you will find the tle will have changed to Parks & Gardens.

useums & Art Galleries
Museums of every type and size plus art alleries.

SSENTIAL INFORMATION

ourist Information
Main tourist information offices have been listed rst. Full addresses, telephone and fax numbers re given, where they have been provided. (See Dublin for an Internet address)

ccess
Main air and sea ports of entry are listed

Transport
Information on buses, trains as applicable, plus car hire, cycle hire

Crafts
Names, addresses and telephone numbers are listed, usually with a brief description. Please note: it is often advisable to telephone first to make an appointment or to find out opening times to save a disappointing journey.

Local food & drink
Any local specialities to look out for are noted.

Shopping
In larger towns, information on shopping areas and what you will find there.

Sport & Leisure
A vast array of activities is listed and these depend on what is on offer in the area. Where applicable we give the activity title, name, address, telephone number and sometimes a brief description.

Activity centres, angling, boating & cruising, cycling, equestrian centres, greyhound racing, horse racing, leisure centres, swimming pools, scenic drives, walking (including walking tours and guided walks) are among a selection listed.

WHERE TO STAY

Wide range of accommodation
All AA recommended accommodation from 5-star hotels to camping and caravanning sites is included in this guide and details were correct at the time of going to press.

Quality Assured
When hotels and other guest accommodation apply to join the AA scheme they are visited anonymously by the AA's professional Hotel Inspectorate and are inspected and assessed for facilities and the quality of what they provide. This assessment reflects the quality of the accommodation and services provided by each

establishment. Hotels are awarded from one to five stars on a rising scale, and other accommodation is awarded from one to five Qs for its quality.

Only after testing the accommodation and services and having paid their bill do inspectors introduce themselves in order to make a thorough inspection of the entire premises. Camping and caravanning sites are also regularly inspected by the Hotel Inspectorate in the Republic, and in Northern Ireland by an experienced Campsites Inspector.

PRICE SYMBOLS

The £ symbol has been used as a price guide and in the Republic equates to Irish Punts but in Northern Ireland to pounds sterling. The following categories indicate the price of a single room prices per night and are indications only. If the establishment is in the Bed & Breakfast Accommodation section, then the room price will almost certainly include breakfast. Some establishments offer free accommodation to children up to a certain age, provided they share the parents' room. Check for availability of family rooms and terms and conditions prevailing. Check current prices before booking.

£	**up to £30**
££	**£31 - £50**
£££	**£51 - £70**
££££	**£71 and over**

THE RATING SYMBOLS

The Hotel Star-Rating

★ Usually privately owned and run, one-star hotels tend to be small, with a more personal atmosphere than larger ones. Furnishings and services will be good but simple; not all bedrooms may have en suite facilities. Some hotels may not offer all the expected hotel services - e.g. lunch service may be limited.

★★ May include group-owned as well as proprietor-owned hotels. At this star rating they are usually small to medium sized. At least half the bedrooms will have en suite bath/shower rooms. and may also have phones and TVs.

★★★ Three-star hotels offer a greater range of facilities and services, including full reception service as well as more formal restaurant and bar arrangements. Bedrooms should all have en suite facilities, mostly with baths.

★★★★ Usually large hotels with spacious accommodation, offering high standards of comfort and food. All bedrooms will have en suite bathrooms with bath and shower and private suites will usually also be available. The range of services should include porterage, room service, formal reception and probably a choice of styles of restaurant.

★★★★★ Five stars denote large, luxury hotels offering the highest international standards of accommodation, facilities, services and cuisine.

RED STAR HOTELS

These awards are made annually to a select number of hotels as a recognition of excellence within their star rating. This is the AA's supreme award for hotels and to earn it, they must consistently provide outstanding levels of hospitality, service, food and comfort.

LODGES

Useful budget accommodation for an overnight stay. They have rooms suitable for family use which are often charged at a flat rate regardless of number of occupants. They are usually found conveniently next to main roads and motorways.

THE GUEST ACCOMMODATION SYMBOLS

(Guest Houses, Private Hotels, Town & Country, Farmhouses and Inns)

Q Recommended This assessment indicates an establishment with simple accommodation and adequate bathroom facilities.

QQ Recommended This assessment indicates a sound standard of accommodation offering more in terms of decor and comfort and likely to have some bedrooms with en suite bath or shower rooms

QQQ Recommended This assessment indicates well appointed accommodation and a wider range of facilities than a one or two Q establishment. Bedrooms may have en suite bath/shower rooms.

QQQQ Selected This assessment indicates that the accommodation will be comfortable and well appointed, that hospitality and facilities will be of high quality, and that a reasonable proportion of bedrooms will have en suite bath or shower rooms

QQQQQ Premier Selected This is the AA's highest assessment for guest houses, farmhouses or inns. It has been introduced in response to the rapidly growing number of really excellent establishments. It indicates an outstanding level of accommodation and service, with an emphasis on quality, good facilities for guests and an exceptionally friendly and hospitable atmosphere. The majority of bedrooms will have en suite bath or shower rooms.

HOW TO READ EACH ENTRY

Towns are listed in alphabetical order under each county within their designated region.

Quality rating: all accommodation is rated for quality on a scale of one to five, denoted by the appropriate symbol (see previous pages)
Name, address, postal code of establishment
Telephone numbers may be changed during the currency of this book in some areas. In case of difficulty, check with the operator.
Fax numbers are given when supplied.
Directions are given wherever they have been supplied by the proprietor and are shown in italics.
Opening details - unless otherwise stated, the establishments are open all year, but where dates are shown they are inclusive: e.g. 'Apr-Oct' indicates that the establishment is open from the beginning of April to the end of October. Some places are open all year, but offer a restricted service off season. The abbreviation 'Res' indicates this. It may mean either that evening meals are not served or that other facilities listed are not available. If the text does not say what the restricted services are, you should check before booking.

DESCRIPTION OF THE PROPERTY

Establishments have been described very briefly, but the facilities are shown in italics at the end of each description

Accommodation details

The first figure shows the number of letting bedrooms.
Annexe - shows that bedrooms are available in separate building. The standard is acceptable, but it is advisable to check the nature of the accommodation and tariff before making a reservation.
fmly - indicates family bedrooms.
No smoking - if the establishment is only partly no-smoking, the areas where smoking is not permitted are shown
No children - indicates that children cannot be accommodated. A minimum age may be specified (e.g. No children under 4 yrs = no children under four years old). Although establishments may accept children of all ages they may not necessarily be able to provide special facilities. If you have very young children, check before booking about provisions like cots and high chairs, and any reductions made.
Children's Facilities - indicates establishments with special facilities for children, which will include baby-sitting service or baby intercom system, playroom or playground, laundry facilities, drying and ironing facilities, cots, high chairs and special meals.
Additional facilities - such as lifts, leisure activities, conference and/or banqueting facilities. In the case of farmhouses, number of acres and type of farming eg dairy, poultry etc.
Leisure activities - could encompass tennis, croquet, cycle hire, fishing, golf, sauna, jacuzzi, spa, beauty therapy, horse-riding,swimming pool, snooker.
Parking - denotes on-site car parking.
Credit and Charge card symbols - the following cards may be accepted, but check current details when booking:

- Mastercard
- Visa
- Connect
- Switch
- American Express
- Diners
- Delta

GUESTS WITH DISABILITIES

Guests with any form of disability should notify proprietors, so that arrangements can be made to minimise difficulties, particularly in the event of an emergency.

NOTES ABOUT ACCOMMODATION

Common to all

Whatever the type of establishment, there are certain requirements common to all, including a well-maintained exterior, clean and hygienic kitchens; good standards of furnishing; friendly and courteous service; access to the premises at reasonable times; the use of a telephone; and a full, cooked breakfast in the Irish tradition.

Bedrooms should be equipped with comfortable beds, a wardrobe, a bedside cabinet, a washbasin (unless there is an en suite or private bath/shower room) with soap, towel, mirror and shaver socket and at least a carpet beside the bed. There should not be an extra charge for the use of baths or lavatories, and heating should not be metered.

CANCELLATION

If you find that you must cancel a booking, let the proprietor know at once, because if the room you booked cannot be re-let, you may be held legally responsible for partial payment. Whether it is a matter of losing your deposit, or of being liable for compensation, you should seriously consider taking out cancellation insurance, such as AA Travelsure.

COMPLAINTS

Readers who have any cause to complain are urged to do so on the spot. This should provide an opportunity for the proprietor to correct matters. If a personal approach fails, readers should inform: AA Hotel Services, Fanum House, Basingstoke, Hants, RG21 4EA.

FOOD AND DRINK

If you intend to take dinner at an establishment, note that sometimes the meal must be ordered in advance of the actual meal time. In some cases, this may be at breakfast time, or even on the previous evening. If you have booked on bed, breakfast and evening meal terms, you may find that the tariff includes only the set menu, but, if there is one, you can usually order from the à la carte menu and pay a supplement. On Sundays, many establishments serve the main meal at midday, and provide only a cold supper in the evening.

Payment

Most proprietors will only accept cheques in payment of accounts if notice is given and some form of identification (preferably a cheque card) is produced. If a hotel accepts credit or charge cards, this is shown by a global credit card symbol in its directory entry. Please contact establishments directly to check which are accepted.

Prices

Hotels must display tariffs, either in the bedrooms or at reception. Application of VAT and service charges varies, but all prices quoted must be inclusive of VAT.

Telephone Numbers

Area codes shown against the numbers in the Republic of Ireland are applicable only within the Republic. If dialling from outside, you will need to check with the telephone directory. The area codes shown for Britain and Northern Ireland cannot be used directly from the Republic.

FIRE PRECAUTIONS

Northern Ireland: The Fire Services (NI) Order 1984 covers establishments accommodating more than 6 persons, and they must have a fire certificate issued by the Northern Ireland Fire Authority. Places accommodating fewer than 6 persons must have adequate exits.

Republic of Ireland: safety regulations are a matter for local authority regulations, but AA officials inspect emergency notices, fire-fighting equipment and fire exits.

For your own and others' safety, you must read the emergency notices displayed and be sure you understand them.

LICENSING REGULATIONS

Northern Ireland: public houses open from 11.30 - 23.00, and on Sun 12.30 - 14.30 and 19.00 - 22.00. Hotels can serve residents without restriction. Non-residents can be served from 12.30 - 22.00 on Christmas Day. Children under 18 are not allowed in the bar area and may neither buy nor consume liquor in hotels.

Republic of Ireland: general licensing hours at present are 10.30 - 23.00 (23.30 in summer), Mon - Sat. On Sun and St Patrick's Day (17 March) 12.30 - 14.00 and 16.00 - 23.00.

Hotels can serve residents without restriction. There is no service on Christmas Day or Good Friday.

CODES OF PRACTICE

The Hotel Industry Voluntary Code of Booking Practice was revised in 1986, and the AA encourages its use in appropriate establishments. Its prime object is to ensure that the customer is clear about the precise services and facilities s/he is buying and what price will have to be paid, before entering into a contractually binding agreement. If the price has not been previously confirmed in writing, the guest should be handed a card at the time of registration, stipulating the total obligatory charge.

Some guest houses offer bed and breakfast only, so guests must go out for the evening meal. It is also wise to check when booking if there are any restrictions to your access to the house, particularly in the late morning and during the afternoon.

However, many guest houses do provide an evening meal. They may only be able to offer a set meal, but many offer an interesting menu and a standard of service that one would expect in a good restaurant. You may have to arrange dinner in advance, so you should ask about the arrangements for evening meals when booking. Many places have a full licence, or at least a table licence and wine list.

FARMHOUSES

Farmhouses particularly noted for being inexpensive and cosy. Those listed in our book are generally working farms, and some farmers are happy to allow visitors to look around, or even to help feed the animals. However, we must stress that the modern farm is a potentially dangerous place, especially where machinery and chemicals are concerned, and visitors must be prepared to exercise care, particularly if they bring children.

NEVER LEAVE CHILDREN UNSUPERVISED AROUND THE FARM.

Sometimes, guest accommodation is run as a separate concern from the farm, and visitors are discouraged from venturing on to the working land. In other cases, the land has been sold off and only the house remains. Although the directory entry states the acreage and the type of farming carried out, you should check when booking to make sure that it matches your expectations.

Some of our farmhouses are grand ex-manor houses furnished with antiques and offering a stylish way of life, whereas others offer more simply furnished accommodation, and in others guests may have to share the family bathroom and sitting/dining room.

OFF THE BEATEN TRACK

All of the farmhouses are listed under town or village names, but obviously many will be some distance from any other habitation. Directions may be given as part of the entry, but DO ask the owners if the property is hard to find and ask for supplementary directions when you book.

INNS

We all know what we can expect to find in a traditional inn - a cosy bar, a convivial atmosphere, good beer and pub food.

In this guide, a number of small, fully licensed hotels are classified as inns, and the character of the properties will vary according to whether they are traditional country inns or larger establishments in towns. Again it is important to check details before you book, and also remember to ask if you can arrive at any time of the day or only during opening hours.

BOOKING

Book as early as possible, particularly for the peak holiday period from the beginning of June to the end of September, and may also include Easter and other public holidays.

Although it is possible for chance callers to find a night's accommodation, it is by no means a certainty, especially at peak holiday times and in popular areas, so it is always advisable to book as far in advance as possible. Some may only accept weekly bookings from Saturday. Some establishments will require a deposit on booking.

Only brief descriptions appear about each establishment, so if you require further information, write to, telephone or fax the establishment itself. Do remember to enclose a stamped addressed envelope, or an international reply-paid coupon if writing from overseas, and please quote this publication in any enquiry. Although we try to publish accurate and up to date information, please remember that any details, and particularly prices, are subject to change without notice and this may happen during the currency of the guide.

CAMPING AND CARAVANNING

Whether you are newcomer to camping and caravanning or an old hand, it is probable that what attracted you in the first place to the freedom of going where you please. However, in practice, especially during holiday periods, parks in popular parts of Ireland get dreadfully crowded, and if you choose somewhere off the beaten track, you may go for miles without finding anywhere.

Telephone the park before you travel. In the caravan and camping world there may be some restrictions and some categories of visitor e.g. single sex groups, unsupervised groups of young people, and motorcycle clubs are banned altogether.

HOW THE PENNANT RATING WORKS

The AA pennant-rating scheme is based on regular inspections and classification of facilities. The system emphasises quality as much as quantity, and the higher-rated sites are of a very high all-round standard indeed.

The scheme is designed for touring holidaymakers who travel with their own caravans, motor caravans, or tents. Our officers visit camping and caravanning parks to assess their touring facilities, but do not inspect any static caravans, chalets or ready-erected tents available for hire. All such accommodation is outside the scope of the scheme.

As the pennant rating increases, so the quality and variety of facilities will be greater. The basic requirement of the scheme is that the camping and caravanning parks reserve an acceptable number of pitches for the use of touring caravanners and campers, and that the facilities provided for tourers are well maintained and clean, and comply with our standards of classification. Many parks in the AA scheme display a yellow and black sign showing their pennant rating, but not all parks choose to have one, and some local authorities prohibit the display of signs.

Basic Requirements

All parks must have a local authority site licence (unless specially exempted) and must have satisfied local authority fire regulations. Parks at the higher pennant rating must also comply with the basic requirements, and offer additional facilities according to their classification.

Please note that campsites are legally allowed to use an overflow field which is not normally part of their camping areas for up to 28 days in any one year as an emergency method of coping with additional numbers at busy periods.

When this 28 day rule is being invoked site owners should increase the numbers of sanitary facilities accordingly when the permanent facilities become insufficient to cope with the extra numbers.

Town & Country Pennant Parks

These may offer a simple standard of facilities, and sometimes only drinking water and chemical waste disposal for the really self contained tourer. Do check with individual sites at the time of booking to make sure they satisfy you own personal requirements. All the following should be offered.

- Maximum 30 pitches per campable acre
- At least 10 feet between units
- Urgent telephone numbers signed
- Whereabouts of an emergency telephone shown
- First aid box

►►► 3-Pennant Family Parks

In addition to the above, these parks guarantee a greater degree of comfort, with modern or modernised toilet blocks offering an ideal minimum of two washbasins and two toilets per 30 pitches per sex.
Toilet facilities should include:

- Hot water to wash basins and showers
- Mirrors, shelves and hooks
- Shaver/hairdryer points
- Soap and hand dryer/towels
- A reasonable number of modern cubicled showers
- All-night internal lighting

Family parks should also have:

- Evenly surfaced roads and paths
- Some electric hook-ups
- Some level ground suitable for motor caravans

►►►► 4 - Pennant De-Luxe Parks

As well as all of the above, these parks are of a very high standard, with good landscaping, natural screening and attractive park buildings. Toilets are smartly modern and well maintained, plus the following:

- Spacious vanitory-style washbasins
- Fully-tiled shower cubicles with dry areas, shelves and hooks, at least one per 30 pitches per sex.

Other requirements are:

- Shop on site, or within reasonable distance
- Warden available 24-hours
- Reception area open during the day
- Internal paths, roads and toilet blocks lit at night
- electric hook-ups
- hardstandings where necessary

These parks should also ideally offer a late arrivals enclosure, and some fully-serviced toilet cubicles.

►►►►► 5-Pennant Premier Parks

All parks in this category are of an award-winning standard, and are set in attractive surroundings with superb landscaping. They must offer some fully-serviced pitches or first-class cubicled washing facilities; most pitches should also offer electric hook-ups. Ideally, but not necessarily there may be in addition to the above:

- a heated swimming pool (outdoor, indoor or both)
- a clubhouse with some entertainment
- a well-equipped shop
- a café or restaurant and a bar
- decent indoor and outdoor leisure facilities for young people
- a designated dog-walking area if dogs accepted

Electrical Hook-up

This is becoming more generally available at parks with three or more pennants, but if it is important to you, you must check before booking. The voltage is generally 240v AC, 50 cycles, although variations between 200v and 250v may still be found. All parks in the AA scheme which provide electrical hook-ups do so in accordance with International Electrotechnical Commission regulations.

Outlets are coloured blue and take the form of a lidded plug with recessed contacts, making it impossible to touch a live point by accident. They are also waterproof. A similar plug, but with protruding contacts which hook into the recessed plug, is on the end of the cable which connects the caravan to the source of supply, and is dead.

Motor Caravans

At some parks motor caravans are only accepted if they remain static throughout the stay. Also check that there are suitable level pitches at the parks where you intend to stay.

Parking

Some park operators insist that cars be put in a parking area separate from the pitches; others will allow more than one car for each caravan or tent.

Park rules

Most parks display a set of rules which you should read on your arrival. Dogs may or may not be accepted on parks, and this is entirely at the owners' or wardens' discretion. We most strongly advise that you check when you book.

Most parks will not accept the following categories of people: single-sex groups, unsupervised youngsters, motorcyclists whether singly or in groups, sometimes even adults travelling on their own are barred. If you are not a family group or a conventional couple, you would be well advised to make sure what rules apply before you book.

Restricted service

This means that full amenities and services are not available during the period stated - e.g. a swimming pool or bar/restaurant may be open only in the summer. Restrictions vary greatly from park to park, so you must check before setting off.

Signposted

This does not refer to AA signs, but indicates that there is an International Direction sign on the nearest main road.

Static van pitches

We give the number of static van pitches available, in order to give a picture of the size and nature of the park. The AA pennant rating system is based on an inspection of the touring pitches and facilities only. AA inspectors do not visit or report on fixed types of accommodation. The AA takes no responsibility for the condition of rented caravans or chalets and can take no action whatsoever about complaints relating to them.

Supervised
This means that the park has someone in attendance 24 hours a day. Other parks may have less comprehensive cover.

WHERE TO EAT

There are two distinct sections in the Where to Eat section.

AA Recommended Restaurants
The first is AA recommended restaurants and hotel restaurants; these are awarded rosettes for the standard of cooking, the highest being five rosettes.

Pubs, Inns & Other Places
The second section includes a range of pubs, country inns, village restaurants and quick bite places. Names, addressess and telephone numbers are supplied, plus a short description. These do not have a price guide.

HOW AA ROSETTES ARE AWARDED

The AA makes annual rosette awards on a rising scale of one to five for the quality of food served in restaurants. Every restaurant awarded AA rosettes has had at least one anonymous meal visit from an AA inspector. Many, especially at the higher award levels, have been visited more than once by different inspectors at different times. AA inspection visits are anonymous; no favours are accepted.

All the entries have been written from reports filed by AA inspectors. Although our inspectors are a highly trained and very experienced team of professional men and women, it must be stressed that the opinions expressed are only opinions, based on the experience of one or more particular occasions. Assessments are therefore to some extent necessarily subjective. AA inspectors are experienced enough to make a balanced judgement, but they are not omniscient.

Vegetarian: almost all restaurants featured will prepare a vegetarian dish or accommodate a special diet if given prior notice

Smoking: establishments that do not allow smoking in the dining room may allow it elsewhere, in a lounge of bar, for instance. If you are a smoker, it is worth checking beforehand.

What the rosettes signify:

✿ One rosette denotes simple, carefully prepared food, based on good quality, fresh ingredients, cooked in such a way as to emphasise honest flavours. Sauces and desserts will be home-made and the cooking will equate to first-class home cooking.

✿✿ Two rosettes denote cooking that displays a high degree of competence on the part of the chef. The menus should include some imaginative dishes, making use of very good raw ingredients, as well as some tried and tested favourites. Flavours should be well balanced and complement or contrast with one another, not over-dominate.

✿✿✿ Only cooking of the highest national standard receives three or more rosettes. Menus will be imaginative; dishes should be accurately cooked, demonstrate well developed technical skills and a high degree of flair in their composition. Ingredients will be first-class, usually from a range of specialist suppliers, including local produce only if its quality is excellent. Most items - breads, pastries, pasta, petits fours - will be made in the kitchens, but if any are bought in, for example, breads, the quality will be excellent.

✿✿✿✿ At this level, cuisine should be innovative, daring, highly accomplished and achieve a noteworthy standard of consistency, accuracy and flair throughout all the elements of the meal. Excitement, vibrancy and superb technical skill will be the keynotes.

✿✿✿✿✿ Five rosettes is the supreme accolade, made to chefs at the very top of their profession. This award recognises superlative standards of cuisine at an international level, evident at every visit in every element of the meal. Creativity, skill and attention to detail will produce dishes cooked to perfection, with intense, exciting flavours in harmonious combinations and faultless presentation. Menus may be innovative or classical, and may use luxury ingredients like lobster, truffles, foie gras, etc., often in unexpected combinations and with secret ingredients that add an extra dimension of taste and interest.

Price Guidelines For AA Recommended Restaurants
ALC is the cost of an à la carte meal for one person, including coffee and service but not wine. **Fixed L** or **Fixed D** shows the approximate price guide for a fixed-price lunch or dinner. The prices quoted are a guide only, and are subject to change without notice.

£	**up to £15**
££	**£16 - £25**
£££	**£30 and upwards**

THE BEST OF EQUESTRIAN IRELAND

THE EVENTS NOT TO MISS

CLIFDEN PONY SHOW

Run by the Connemara Pony Society, founded in 1923, this is the premier Connemara pony show with championships for riding ponies, led ponies and young stock. Clifden attracts buyers from around the world for Connemara ponies, and can be combined with a trip to Maam Cross. Further information from the Connemara Pony Society Tel 095 21863.

THE DUBLIN SHOW

The highlight of the showing year is organised by the Royal Dublin Society and is held during the first week in August - Wednesday to Sunday. It is the week when the country comes to the city, bringing many contestants for the coveted Supreme Champion Hunter title held on the Friday morning. The best of the country's horses come to compete in national showjumping classes, while in the main arena top international riders battle it out in a number of competitions, including the Puissance (Saturday) and the Grand Prix (Sunday). The Aga Khan Nations Cup (Friday) is an event of some ceremony, attended by the President of Ireland and introduced with appropriate fanfare from the army band. For glamour, Ladies' Day on Thursday is a must, and don't miss the Antique Fair held in the main building. There's plenty for children too - a crêche, play area and Punch and Judy show. For evening entertainment during show week, you can start with at drink at Horse Show House, enjoy a meal at Jurys Hotel and then dance the night away at the Horse Show Ball. For further information contact the RDS Events Department Tel 01 6604014.

GALWAY RACING FESTIVAL

An annual pilgrimage for all those interested in Irish racing, the festival is held during the last week in July at the Ballybrit track just outside Galway City. Feature events include the Galway Plate (Wednesday) and the Galway Hurdle (Thursday). A funfair helps to amuse the kids and Ladies' Day on Thursday is a focus for the fashion conscious. Make sure you arrive early to guarantee entry. At night, head for Salthill where the horsey folk gather to discuss the horses and the form for the next day. For more information Tel 091 735870.

THE IRISH DERBY

Held at the Curragh in Co Kildare on the last weekend in June, this festival of racing is de rigeur in the best social circles. An evening meeting is held on Friday, with afternoon meetings on Saturday and Sunday. The main event, attended by the rich and famous, is theIrish Derby held on the Sunday afternoon. This is your opportunity to mingle with the stars. A tented village offers a funfair and a variety of bars and restaurants. Further enquiries Tel 045 441205 or 441105.

KINSALE POINT-TO-POINT

Point-to-points are very much part of the rural way of life, especially in the Cork area where a meeting is held every Sunday from Lisgoold on the first Sunday in January to the two-day International Festival held in the pretty village of Kinsale during the last weekend in May. Many great horses start their careers in the point-to-point, including such as The Thinker, Imperial Call and One Man. The Kinsale Festival, which draws entries from the UK and France, has a great holiday spirit about it, with plenty of good racing, food and drink. It is advisable to book a bed early if you are going to stay locally for the weekend. Dates and information from Brian Gleeson Racing Promotions Tel 024 94134.

MILLSTREET

Two international show jumping event are held each year at Millstreet, outdoor in August and indoor in October. Top riders from around the globe compete in the Irish equivalent of Hickstead's Derby and in the Volvo World Cup qualifiers. Set in a picturesque area of County Cork, Millstreet is a family-run show which continues to grow annually. It is also

home to top national competitions, including the Boomerang for four-year-olds, and the Young Irelander for three-year-olds; whilst the pony jumping provides some exciting moments. For refreshment and recuperation during the show, head for the Millstreet bar, reputed to be the longest in Ireland. Further information from Green Glens Equestrian Centre Tel 029 70707.

PUNCHESTOWN THREE-DAY EVENT

Held during May near Naas in Co Kildare, this is the main Irish three-day event. The international competition has a FEI three-star rating and so attracts many top international competitors. Dressage is held on Friday and Saturday, with the exciting cross country phase on Sunday, and show jumping on Monday. Information from the IHTS office Tel 045 886674

IRISH HORSE SALES

BALLINASLOE FAIR

Held in early October, at Ballinasloe, Co Galway, this is the biggest of the Irish fairs. It is a step back into the old Irish way of life, with fair fields, and hundreds of horses lining the streets. Take care that you don't find yourself buying a horse that you'd never intended to! Further details from any Irish Tourist Office.

GOFF'S BLOODSTOCK SALES

Rub shoulders with the rich and famous at the big flat-bred yearling sales held in October, at Kill, Co Kildare. Millions of pounds are paid for horses at this sale and even if you can't afford to buy, it is fascinating to watch the bidding - you might even pick out a future Irish Derby winner. Tel 045 877211

GORESBRIDGE SPORT HORSE SALES

If you are looking to buy a sport horse, or just want to see what's on offer, pay a visit to Donohoe's of Gorebridge in Co Kilkenny. They hold a monthly sale, and a Special Sale in September, when there will be around 1800 horses for sale. Donohoe's was the first sport horse sale to be established in Ireland and always offers a good choice. While there, be sure to visit the antique shop, just outside the gate, run by the same family. For sale dates Tel 0503 75265.

A LITTLE BIT DIFFERENT

BEACH RACING

Racing started on the strand at Laytown in Co Meath in 1876. This one evening event, usually held in early June, is the only meeting run on the beach under the Rules of Racing in Ireland or England. Laytown is just 23 miles from Dublin, and you can take the train directly to Laytown station. This is a very different racing event from anything else you will experience. For dates and further information Tel 041 23425.

BEACH TREKKING

Ireland's unspoilt coastline provides the perfect setting for riding on the beach, with only the Atlantic Ocean between you and America. Monatrea Equestrian Centre, situated near historic Ardmore in Co Waterford, provides horses and can share knowledge about the area and its history. Tel 024 94550 for information. For details of other equestrian centres see Essential Information for each county.

STUD VISIT

For horse-lovers, a visit to the palatial National Stud in Kildare town is a must. Set up in 1902 by a Scot, William Hall-Walker, whose breeding methods were somewhat eccentric. Stallions and mares were paired according to their signs of the zodiac, and a horoscope drawn up for each foal. If the omens were inauspicious, the foal was sold. William Hall-Walker passed the stud to the British Government in 1915, who in turn passed it to the Irish Government in 1943.

You can take a guided tour of some of the world's finest stallions and horses, including Vintage Crop, winner of the prestigious Melbourne Cup in 1993. There are plenty of beautiful Thoroughbred mares and their precious offspring to see. You can also visit the Falabellas, perfectly proportioned tiny little horses bred in Argentina. Confusingly, these are classed as horses even though they are much smaller than the average pony.

There's also plenty of interest in the Irish Horse Museum, which houses the skeleton of the legendary steeplechaser Arkle, winner of three Cheltenham Gold Cups. The traditional crafts of saddlery and farriery are also on display here. For further information Tel 045 521617.

Dublin & The Eastern Counties

COUNTIES DUBLIN, KILDARE, LOUTH, MEATH AND WICKLOW

THE EASTERN COUNTIES

The counties dotted around Dublin are known as The Pale, historically influenced by English rule since Norman times. The area beyond The Pale eluded English control, and was seen as a threat to English interests - hence the expression 'beyond the pale'. Apart from the obvious attractions of the capital, the eastern counties have much to engage the visitor. The area is immensely rich in significant ancient sites, including the passage graves at Newgrange - Ireland's best-known Neolithic site - some extremely well preserved Celtic High Crosses, and the monastic settlement at Glendalough. You can also see some of Ireland's grandest houses and gardens; racing afficionados will want to visit The Curragh and the nearby National Stud, and for fine scenery and good walking country, the Wicklow mountains are hard to beat

EVENTS & FESTIVALS

February

Goff's Bloodstock Sales,
Kill, Co Kildare

International Film Festival,
Dublin, Co Dublin

March

Arklow Music Festival,
Arklow, Co Wicklow

Dublin Film Festival,
Dublin, Co Dublin

St Patrick's Day celebrations (17th March)
throughout the region

Temple Bar Fleadh Festival of Traditional Music,
Dublin, Co Dublin

Easter Racing Festival,
Fairyhouse Racecourse, Co Meath

April

Gaelic Football League Final,
Dublin, Co Dublin

Irish National Hunt Festival,
Punchestown Racecourse, Naas, Co Kildare

Irish Grand National,
Fairyhouse Racecourse, Co Meath

Dublin Grand Opera Society Spring Season,
Dublin, Co Dublin

May

International Music Festival,
Dublin, Co Dublin

1,000 & 2,000 Guineas Race Meeting,
the Curragh Racecourse, Co Kildare

Evening Race Meeting,
Fairyhouse Racecourse, Co Meath

Bank of Ireland Proms at the Royal Dublin Society,
Dublin, Co Dublin

Garden Festival at Royal Hospital,
Kilmainham, Co Dublin

Dublin Maritime Festival,
Dublin, Co Dublin

East Coast Classic Golf Tournament,
Drogheda, Co Louth

Spring Show,
Royal Dublin Society Showgrounds, Co Dublin

June

Music in Great Irish Houses Festival
throughout the region

Bloomsday Celebrations, (16th June)
Dublin, Co Dublin

Irish Derby Weekend,
the Curragh Racecourse, Co Kildare

Dublin Organ & Choral Festival,
Dublin, Co Dublin

County Wicklow Gardens Festival,
throughout Co Wicklow

Celtic Inishowen Golf Classic,
Drogheda, Co Louth

July

Irish Open Golf Championship,
Druid's Glen, Co Wicklow

Irish Oaks
The Curragh Racecourse, Co Kildare

Temple Bar Blues Festival,
Dublin, Co Dublin

Garden of Ireland Festival,
Arklow, Co Wicklow

August

Evening Race Meeting,
Fairyhouse Racecourse, Co Meath

Irish Antique Dealers Fair,
Dublin, Co Dublin

River Liffey Powerboat Race,
Dublin Regatta, Co Dublin

Royal Dublin Horse Show,
Dublin, Co Dublin

Wicklow Regatta Festival,
Co Wicklow

Goff's National Hunt Sales,
Kill, Co Kildare

Father & Son World Invitational Golf Tournament,
Dublin, Co Dublin

European Golf Tournament,
K Club, Co Kildare

September

All Ireland Hurling Championship Final,
Croke Park, Dublin, Co Dublin

Irish St Leger Race Meeting,
The Curragh Racecourse, Co Kildare

All Ireland Football Championship Final,
Croke Park, Dublin, Co Dublin

International Puppet Festival,
Dublin, Co Dublin

South East Classic Golf Tournament,
Drogheda, Co Louth

October

Dublin Theatre Festival,
Dublin, Co Dublin

Irish Cesarewitch Race Meeting,
The Curragh Racecourse, Co Kildare

Goff's Bloodstock Sales,
Kill, Co Kildare

Irish Whiskey International Golf Challenge,
Dublin, Co Dublin

Dublin Marathon, last Monday of the month,
Dublin, Co Dublin

November

Goff's Bloodstock Sales,
Kill, Co Kildare

Intervarsity Race Day,
Leopardstown Racecourse, Stillorgan, Dublin, Co Dublin

Irish National Stamp Exhibition,
Dublin, Co Dublin

December

Christmas Racing Festival,
Leopardstown Racecourse, Stillorgan, Dublin, Co Dublin

Dublin Grand Opera Society Winter Season,
Dublin, Co Dublin

Goff's Bloodstock Sales,
Kill, Co Kildare

THE CITY OF DUBLIN

Dublin is a colossally entertaining city full of paradox and whimsy. It has bred and inspired many literary giants, such as Shaw, Sheridan, Swift, Joyce, Wilde and Yeats. Indeed it is said that every drinker in Dublin has a novel waiting to be finished at home. Its stately institutions, fine Georgian architecture and broad avenues recall its heyday as one of Europe's foremost cities, though Dublin is maybe better known these days for the wit and loquacity of its pub life.

The name dubh linn, (dark pool) derives from the joining of the River Poddle with the peat-coloured water of the River Liffey, so a good place to begin a tour of city is the O'Connell Bridge. This leads to the city's main shopping area, O'Connell Street, where the best buys are local products, such as Dublin crystal, linen and lace, homespun tweeds and knitwear. The central areas are compact and can be explored on foot, with several interesting guided walks on offer.

Cultural Dublin is centred in the cobbled streets around Temple Bar, close to the banks of the River Liffey, where there is an abundance of small art galleries, theatres, cafés, colourful restaurants and shops.

No visit to Dublin would be complete without acquiring some understanding of the struggle for Irish independence. Although the 1916 Easter Rising was a flashpoint, it was hastily organised and commanded little support at the time. However, its heroes quickly achieved martyrdom status in the struggle against the British. Exhibitions at Kilmainham Gaol, the Pearse and National museums explain the events leading to the declaration of independence and the formation of the Irish Republic in 1918.

MUST SEE

USTOM HOUSE VISITOR CENTRE
ustom House Quay, Dublin 1
.5km from O'Connell Bridge. Near Busarus.
01 8787660
loating on a fragile platform of pine lanks near the River Liffey, this grand ıasterpiece of neo-classic architecture vas designed by James Gandon in 1791, lany of original architectural features and xhibitions of the history of the house om its inception to its restoration after ıe 1921 fire, the important characters ssociated with it, and the architect imself plus his other major works.

THE GENERAL POST OFFICE,
O'Connell Street, Dublin 1
Long associated with the struggle for Irish independence, the General Post Office, dating from 1818, was the focus of the 1916 Easter Rising. Patrick Pearse, James Connolly and co-read their proclamation from its front steps. In the siege that followed, the building was gutted by fire, and the façade, with its Ionic portico, remains scarred. The building was further damaged at the outset of Civil War in 1922 and did not re-open until 1929. It remains a favoured point of protest.

HOENIX PARK
nity College, Dublin 7
01 6770095 (Visitor Centre)
the west end of the city, stretching ong the Liffey for about 3 miles/5km, e Phoenix Park covers 1,760 acres/712 and includes lakes, gardens, woods, a erd of deer, a race course, sports grounds d Dublin Zoo. The headquarters of the arda is here, plus a police museum. The entre has a historical interpretation of the rk (from 3500BC onwards) through ractive displays. Exhibition area, audio-sual room. Restaurant. Ashtown Castle stored 17th-century tower house.

TRINITY COLLEGE,
College Green, Dublin 2 **01 6082286**
The oldest university in Ireland, set amidst gardens, was founded in 1592 by Queen Elizabeth 1, to 'civilise Ireland with both learning and the Protestant religion'. (Until 1966 Catholics could only attend by special dispensation.) The Dublin Experience video gives a history of the city and is screened in the Arts Building. The library houses over three million volumes, including the superb Book of Kells, work of 9th century monks from the Scottish island of Iona, fleeing from the Vikings. The book was taken from Kells to Trinity College during the Cromwellian wars, and is still there.

DUBLIN WRITERS MUSEUM
18 Parnell Square North, Dublin 1
T 01 8722077 F 01 8722231
Dublin's rich literary heritage is celebrated in the magnificent setting of a restored Georgian house. Written tradition in Ireland is traced from the 8th century to the present day. Among those featured through their books, letters, portraits and personal property areSwift, Sheridan, Shaw, Wilde, Yeats, Joyce and Beckett. Events, exhibitions and readings. Room devoted to children's literature. Tara's Palace, one of Ireland's largest doll houses is here.

DUBLIN'S VIKING ADVENTURE,
Essex Street West, Temple Bar, Dublin 2
T 01 6796040/6057777 F01 6796033
An exciting, interactive simulation of life in Viking Dublin, located close to Wood Quay, at the heart of the 9th and 10th-century Viking settlement. You can walk the narrow street of 'Dyflin', chat to the locals, watch them at work and experience authentic sounds and smells. There is also an extensive display of Viking artefacts from excavations in the city.

DUBLIN'S VIKING FEAST
Essex Street West, Temple Bar, Dublin 2
T 01 6796040/6057777 F 01 6796033
A chance to dine in style with Dublin's most colourful ancestors in the impressive surroundings of the Dyflin Feasting Hall. Diners sit down to a four-course meal, while the cast of Vikings entertain them with music, song and dance. Advance booking essential.

GUINNESS HOP STORE,
Crane Street, Dublin 8
T 01 536700 F 01 533631
Way upstream of most of the central sites, in a less than salubrious area, is the legendary Guinness Brewery. You can't visit the brewery itself, but there is a visitor's centre nearby at The Hop Store. You are guided through the brewery's history by exhibits and audio-visual presentations. Comprehensive collection of coopers' tools and oak casks displayed in an authentic brewery setting. Thrown in with the tour ticket is a half pint or so of the famous brew in the Sample Bar.

IRISH WHISKEY CORNER,
Bow Street, Dublin 7
T 01 4536700 F 01 4084965
An old bonded warehouse, used to mature whiskey, is the setting for this exhibition, which includes an audio-visual show and a model of an old distillery explaining the history of distilling in Ireland. The experience ends with a tasting to establish the difference between Scotch, Irish and Bourbon.

NUMBER TWENTY-NINE,
Lower Fitzwilliam Street, Dublin 2
T 01 7026165 F 01 6615376
A completely restored late 18th-century house, presented as a museum by the Electricity Supply Board (who built their headquarters here in the 1960s) and the National Museum of Ireland. The house is furnished in period style (around 1790-1820), and demonstrates the best of Irish craftwork plus a collection of artefacts and works of art. The life of an 18th-century middle-class merchant's family is described in an audio-visual presentation. Guided tours, a tea room and gift shop.

ART GALLERIES

BANK OF IRELAND ARTS CENTRE
Foster Green (off College Green), Dublin 2
T 01 6711488
Interactive museum exploring both banking and Irish history over the past 200 years.

CHESTER BEATTY LIBRARY,
20 Shrewsbury Road, Ballsbridge, Dublin 4
T 01 692386
Astonishing display of oriental and Middle Eastern fine art collected by an American mining engineer of Irish ancestry (1875-1968).

HUGH LANE MUNICIPAL GALLERY OF MODERN ART
Charlemont House, Parnell Square, Dublin 1
T 01 536700 F01 533631
Lovely Georgian mansion housing collections of Irish works, and art from the modern French and British schools. Exhibitions.Children's workshops.

IRISH MUSEUM OF MODERN ART,
Royal Hospital, Kilmainham, Dublin 8
T 01 6718666
Interesting exhibits in a fine 17th-century building. Temporary exhibitions plus educational and community programmes of music, theatre and visual arts.

NATIONAL GALLERY
Merrion Square West, Dublin 1
T 01 6615133
Fine collection of some 2,000 works of Irish, US and all the major European schools of art up to the 19th-century.

BIG OUTDOORS

NORTH BULL ISLAND NATURE RESERVE
A peaceful nature reserve on a magnificent stretch of sand reached from the Howth road. Guided tours are available from the information centre.

ENTERTAINMENT

CINEMAS

AMBASSADOR *(1-screen)*
Parnell Street, Dublin 1 **T 01 8727000**

IRISH FILM CENTRE *(2-screen)*
6 Eustace Street, Temple Bar, Dublin 2
T 01 6795744

PARNELL CENTRE
Parnell Street, Dublin 1 **T 01 8727333**
Urban entertainment complex including a 9-screen Virgin cinema; Virtual Voyages, a 24-seat simulation with graphics and movement; and Imax 3D theatre.

SAVOY *(6-screen)*
Upper O'Connell St, Dublin 1
T 01 8748487

THEATRES

ABBEY THEATRE
Lower Abbey Street, Dublin 1
T 01 8787222
The Abbey is the heart of Dublin's great theatrical tradition.

THE PEACOCK
Lower Abbey Street, Dublin 1
T 01 8787222
Annexe to the Abbey Theatre, specialising in avant-garde and experimental work.

CITY ARTS CENTRE
23-25 Moss Street **T 01 6770643**

GAIETY THEATRE
South King Street, Dublin 2 **T 01 6771717**

GATE THEATRE
Parnell Square, Dublin 1 **T 01 8744045**

NATIONAL CONCERT HALL
Earlsfort Terrace, Dublin 2 **T 01 711888**

OLYMPIA THEATRE
72 Dame Street, Dublin 2 **T 01 6778962**

PROJECT ARTS CENTRE
39 Essex Street East, Temple Bar, Dublin 2
T 01 6712321

TIVOLI THEATRE
135 Francis St, Dublin 8 **T 01 4544472**

GREAT FOR KIDS

THE ARK
Eustace Street, Temple Bar, Dublin 2
T 01 6707788 F 01 6707758
Cultural centre for children with a regularly changing programme of plays, exhibitions, workshops, concerts, etc.

DUBLINIA
St Michael's Hill, Dublin 8 **T 01 6794611**
Multi-media presentation of life in medieval Dublin, featuring a model of Dublin c1500, a display of artefacts and a medieval maze.

DUBLIN ZOO
Royal Zoological Society of Ireland, Phoenix Park, Dublin 7
T 01 6771425 F 01 6771660
The third oldest zoo in the world, with many birds and mammals and successful breeding programmes for endangered species, including lions.

EISUREPLEX
Malahide Road, Coolock, Dublin 17
T 01 8485722
pen 24 hours, seven days a week, ncluding Bowler Vision, Quasar, nooker/pool, children's play area, video ames and restaurant.

MUSEUM OF CHILDHOOD
ne Palms, 20 Palmerston Park, Rathmines, ublin 6 T 01 4973223
eatures a collection of dolls, some dating ack 300 years. Open Sunday.

ATIONAL WAX MUSEUM
arnell Square, Dublin 1 T 01 8726340
ncluding Children's World of Fairytale and antasy, life-size rock stars, Irish historical gures, the Chamber of Horrors, and the dventure Tunnels.

HISTORIC & ANCIENT SITES

UBLIN CASTLE
ame Street, Dublin 2 T 01 6777129
ating from 988AD; the centre of English ower in Ireland for centuries, and the ost heavily guarded fortress in the ountry. Now an assembly of courts, fices and state apartments.

LITERARY DUBLIN

RCHBISHOP MARSH'S LIBRARY
Patrick's Close, Dublin
01 4543511 F 01 4543511
e first public library in Ireland, founded 1701, the library contains nearly 25,000 lumes from the16th to the 18th-century.

EORGE BERNARD SHAW HOUSE
Synge Street, Dublin
014750854 & 8722077 F 01 8722231
thplace of the playwright George rnard Shaw, restored to recreate the mosphere of his childhood home.

MES JOYCE CENTRE
North Great Georges Street
01 8788547 F 01 8788488
popular centre dedicated to the life and rks of James Joyce

WMAN HOUSE
iversity College Dublin, 86 St Stephen's een
01 7067422 & 4757255 F 01 7067211
e founding home of University College blin in 1854, a superb Georgian ilding, associated with James Joyce, rard Manley Hopkin and Cardinal wman.

MUSEUMS

IC MUSEUM
South William Street, Dublin 2
01 6794260
e history of the city since Viking times, the old City Assembly House.

HERALDIC MUSEUM
2 Kildare Street, Dublin 2 T 01 618811
Display of banners, crests and coats of arms, likely to be of interest to those researching their roots.

IRISH JEWISH MUSEUM
3-4 Walworth Road, Portobello, Dublin 8
T 01 4531797

KILMAINHAM GAOL
Inchicore Road, Kilmainham, Dublin 8
T 01 4535984
Last used as a prison in 1924, the museum documents the Irish struggle for independence.

NATURAL HISTORY MUSEUM & EARTH SCIENCE MUSEUM
Merrion Street, Dublin 2
T 01 677444 F 01 6766116
Museum and research institute with exhibitions ranging from Irish fauna to all the major animal groups. Plus the Blaschka glass models of marine animals.

NATIONAL MUSEUM
Kildare Street, Dublin 2 T 01 6777444
Displays many of the finest masterpieces of Irish Celtic art from the Bronze Age to the Middle Ages, including the Tara brooch. Also mementoes of the Easter Rising and the Civil War.

PEARSE MUSEUM
St Enda's Park, Rathfarnham, Dublin 14
T 01 934208
Once run by Padraic Pearse as a boys' school; the museum is devoted to memorabilia connected with his life and the events that led to his death in the Easter Rising.

WATERWAYS VISITOR CENTRE
Grand Canal Basin, Grand Canal Quay, Dublin 4 T 01 6777510 F 01 6777514
The Visitor Centre, which actually floats in the canal basin, houses an exhibition on Ireland's inland waterways, their history and current uses, includes working models.

PARKS & GARDENS

ARBOUR HILL CEMETERY
Arbour Hill, Dublin 7
A quiet memorial garden where the leaders of the Easter Rising are buried, their names carved in stone beside a copy of the proclamation of independence.

DILLON GARDEN
45 Sandford Road, Ranelagh, Dublin 6
T 01 4971308 F 01 4971308
An urban setting for a series of cleverly designed little gardens around a central lawn. An extensive range of plants is used in the themed areas.

IVEAGH GARDENS
Earlsfort Terrace, Dublin 2 T 01 4757816
This haven of tranquillity is a little known treasure among the city's gardens. Designed by Ninian Niven in 1863, it features a grotto, fountains, a maze, wilderness area and woodlands.

NATIONAL BOTANIC GARDENS
Glasnevin, Dublin 9
T 01 8374388
Dating from 1795, with some 20,000 species of plants and trees. There are ornate 19th-century glasshouses, and riverside walks lead through bog and peat gardens and the aboretum.

ST STEPHEN'S GREEN
Dublin 2
Dublin's most notable Georgian square, with lawns, flower beds, paved walks, shrubberies and an ornamental lake with wildfowl. Monuments include Henry Moore's memorial to Yeats.

71 MERRION SQUARE
Dublin 2 T 01 6767281
Town garden with an extensive collection of plants, including some rarities.

WAR MEMORIAL GARDENS
South Circular Road, Islandbridge, Dublin 8
T 01 6770236
Designed by Sir Edwin Lutyens, these dignified gardens commemorate 49,000 Irish soldiers who died in World War One

RELIGIOUS DUBLIN

CHRIST CHURCH CATHEDRAL
Lord Edward Street, Dublin 8
The official state church until 1871, founded by Sitric Silkenbeard, the first Viking Christian King of Dublin.

ST MARY'S PRO-CATHEDRAL
Marlborough Street, Dublin 1
Dublin's most significant Catholic church, though it has never been granted full cathedral status.

ST MICHAN'S CHURCH
Church Street, Dublin 8
Mummified corpses in the vaults can be inspected by anyone who cares to peer through a hatch. The church dates from 1095.

ST PATRICK'S CATHEDRAL
Patrick Street, Dublin 2
The national cathedral, Ireland's largest church, and Ireland's first university (1320-1520). The most famous incumbent was Dean Jonathan Swift, author of Gulliver's Travels.

Also worth a look:

CARMELITE CHURCH, 57 Aungier Street

ST ANN'S, Dawson Street, Dublin 2

ST FRANCIS XAVIER'S, Upper Gardiner Street, Dublin 1

ST MARY'S ABBEY, off Capel Street

SHOPPING

GRAFTON STREET/O'CONNELL STREET
The main areas for the serious shopper, with a cosmopolitan array of shops and cafés, ranging from exclusive boutiques to department stores, with street buskers adding to the atmosphere.

FRANCIS STREET
(in the Liberties beyond Christ Church)
This is the place for antiques.

MOORE STREET
Where street vendors maintain the tradition of Molly Malone.

NASSAU STREET
Specialises in quality woollens and hand woven Donegal tweeds. Many shops are still in the hands of the founding families

TEMPLE BAR
An area with its own unique character: trendy, chic and a little alternative.

SHOPPING PRECINCTS

POWERSCOURT TOWNHOUSE
(off Grafton Street),
Reconstructed shell of an 18th-century building, with splendid façade.

ST STEPHEN'S GREEN
Another central shopping mall, an unmissable, modern greenhouse-like structure with yet more shops and cafés.

ST STEPHEN'S GREEN/COLLEGE GREEN & THE QUAYSIDES
As one might expect in such a literary city, there are plenty of bookshops, and this is where you'll find most of them.

GEORGIAN DUBLIN

The 18th-century was a time of comparative peace and prosperity in the English Pale, bringing a flowering in architecture, philosophy and the arts. Fine terraces, parks, squares, imposing monuments and dignified townhouses appeared throughout the centre of Dublin.

CUSTOM HOUSE
A grand building dating from 1791 designed by James Gandon, floating on a fragile platform of pine planks on swampy land on the north side of the River Liffey.

THE FOUR COURTS
Another James Gandon building (1785); the seat of the High Court of Justice for Ireland.

GUINNESS BREWERY
St James's Gate, in the Liberties
Established 1759, the oldest parts are on the south side of James's St. It was once the largest brewery in the world.

KING'S INNS
Another Gandon building (1795-1827); Dublin's Inns of Court, where budding barristers lived and studied.

ROTUNDA MATERNITY HOSPITAL
Often overlooked, the first purpose-built maternity hospital in Europe has some fine stucco work in its chapel.

LEINSTER HOUSE
Constructed for the Duke of Leinster in 1745, the oppulent building caused a shift in popularity towards the south side of the Liffey. It is now The Dáil, Ireland's parliament building

MERRION SQUARE
An attractive open space dating from the Georgian era, including the restored Rutland Fountain.

ESSENTIAL INFORMATION

ACCESS

AIR ACCESS

DUBLIN INTERNATIONAL AIRPORT,
8 miles/12km from city centre

SEA ACCESS

THE PORTS OF DUBLIN AND DUN LAOGHAIRE

TRANSPORT

Irish Bus Bus Eireann has a nationwide network of buses serving cities, towns and villages outside the Dublin area. The Busàras, central bus station, is on Store Street **T 01 8366111** *(buses are generally much cheaper than regular trains)*

Irish Rail, Iarnród Eireann, operates services to most major towns and cities **T 01 836 6222**

TOURIST INFORMATION

Irish Tourist Board - Bord Fáilte
DUBLIN TOURISM CENTRE Suffolk St, Dublin 2 **T 01 6057777 F 01 6057787**

DUBLIN 24-HOUR VISITOR INFORMATION
T 1550-11-2233 F 1550-11-4400 -*calls charged at premium rates*
Located in the former church of St Andrews, the Centre offers an all Ireland information service, accommodation & ticket reservation service, tourist literature and book shop, 'Exclusively Irish' gift shop, Dublin Bus day tours, bus information, bureau de change, Bus Éireann Tours, Grayline Tours, Argus Rent-A-Car. Café

Also at:
ARRIVALS HALL Dublin Airport

FERRY TERMINAL Dun Laoghaire Port, Baggot Street Bridge, Dublin 2

TOURIST BOARD INTERNET SITE: Internet http://www.visit.ie

TELEPHONE

The area code for Dublin is 01. International dialling code 00 353 then 1 for Dublin.

LOCAL FOOD & DRINK

DUBLIN CODDLE a type of stew made with bacon, sausages, onions, potatoes and water. Dublin Bay prawns - originally from Dublin Bay, now often from other parts of the country.

GUINNESS the renowned local stout; a dark brew made with roasted barley. The brewery was founded in 1759 at St James' Gate on the Liffey, and has a nearby visitor centre (see page 00).

CAR HIRE

ARGUS 59 Terenure Road East, Dublin 6 **T 01 4904444**

AVIS 1 Hanover Street East, Dublin 2 **T 01 6774010 & Dublin Airport T 01 6057500**

BUDGET 151 Drumcondra Road, Ferry Port, Dublin 9 **T 01 8379611 & Dublin Airport T 01 8445919**

DAN DOOLEY CAR & VAN RENTALS 42 Westland Row, Dublin 2 **T 01 6772723**

HERTZ 149 Leeson Street Upper, Dublin 2 **T 01 6604504**

MURRAYS EUROPCAR Baggot Street Bridge, Dublin 4 **T 01 668 1777**

PAYLESS CAR RENTAL Dublin Airport, Dublin 9 **T 01 8444092**

PRACTICAL CAR RENTAL St Stephen's Green, Dublin 2 **T 01 671554[illegible]**

THRIFTY RENT-A-CAR 14 Duke Street, Dublin 2 **T 01 6799420**

WINDSOR CAR RENTALS Rialto, Dublin 8 **T 01 4540800**

CAR PARKING

There are multi-storey car parks throughout the city, plus parking meters and disc parking (discs can be purchased from local shops). Electronic signs on some streets indicate the location of the nearest car park and the spaces available. Although parking in the city centre is expensive, it is best to avoid quiet back streets as the incidence of theft and vandalism is high.

COACH TOURS

A number of bus companies organise tours around Dublin, and attractions further afield. For further details contact Bus Eireann, Dublin Bus or the Tourist Board.

CYCLE HIRE

C HARDING 30 Bachelor's Walk, Dublin 1 **T 01 8732455**

T HOLLINGSWORTH 14/54 Templeogue Road, Dublin 6 **T 01 4905090/4920026**

HOLLINGSWORTH BIKES 1 Drummartin Road, Stillorgan, Dublin 14 **T 01 2960255**

JOE DALY Lower Main Street, Dundrum, Dublin 14 **T 01 2981485**

LITTLE SPORT 3 Marville Avenue, Fairview, Dublin 3 **T 01 8330044**

MCDONALD'S CYCLES 1 Orwell Road, Rathgar, Dublin 2 **T 01 4979636**

RALEIGH IRELAND Raleigh House, Kylemore Road, Dublin 10 **T 01 6261333**

RENT A BIKE 58 Lower Gardiner Street, Dublin 1 (beside Central Bus Station) **T 01 8725399 F 01 836 4763**

DART

Dublin Area Rapid Transit (DART) railway runs along Dublin Bay, from Howth (north) to Bray (south). Unlimited travel tickets available.

DUBLIN BUS

Dublin Bus or Bus Atha Cliath, operates from 6am-11pm. Limited late night bus service on Thursday, Friday and Saturday, 59 Upper O'Connell Street **T 01 8734222**

TRAINS

CONNOLLY STATION *(Destinations north)* **T 01 8363333**

HEUSTON STATION *(Destinations, south, west and south-west)* **T 01 836 5241**

Eireann Travel Centre, 35 Abbey Street Lower **T 01 8366222** *for information*

CRAFTS

DESIGN YARD ...

IQ GALLERY *(Crafts Council of Ireland)* The Powerscourt Townhouse Centre, South William Street, Dublin 2 **T 01 6797368** Best of Irish craft design. Open Mon-Sat.

MARLEY PARK CRAFT COURTYARD Rathfarnham, Dublin 16 **T 01 942083** Pottery, glass, woodwork and assorted crafts. Coffee shop. Open 7 days.

TOWER DESIGN GUILD IDA Enterprise, Pearse St, Dublin 2 **T 01 775655** Heraldic artistry, jewellery, pewter, silk painting, designer knitting, etching, woodwork and pottery. Open Mon-Fri.

GAELIC DESIGN SWEATER & GIFT SHOP Asdills Row, Temple Bar, Dublin 2 **T 01 6711146** A plethora of souvenirs including bodhrans (small, single-skin drums) plus classy knitwear, cottons and tweeds.

MOTHER REDCAP'S INDOOR MARKET Back Lane, Christchurch, Dublin 8 Crafts, paintings and antiques.

SPORT & LEISURE

ANGLING

For information on coarse, game and sea angling: **EASTERN REGIONAL FISHERIES BOARD, MOBHI BOREEN,** Glasnevin, Dublin 9 **T 01 379209 F 01 360060**

EQUESTRIAN CENTRES

ASHTON EQUESTRIAN CENTRE Ashton House, Castleknock, Dublin 15 **T 01 8387611 F 01 8382051**

BALLYCULLEN Ballycullen Rd, Dublin 16 **T/F 01 4945415**

CARRICKMINES Glenamuck Rd, Dublin 18 **T 01 2955990 F 01 2955934**

GOLF COURSES

CLONTARF GOLF CLUB Donneycarney House, Malahide Road, Dublin 3 **T 833 1892**

Edmondstown Golf Club

EDMONDSTOWN Rathfarnham, Dublin 16 **T 01 4931082 F 01 4933152** Mature golf course, not too taxing, less than 7 miles/11km south of Dublin.

HOLLYSTOWN **T 01 8207444**
ELMGREEN **T 01 8200797**
HOWTH **T 01 8323055**
SUTTON **T 01 8322965**

ICE SKATING

DOLPHINS BARN SCR, Dublin 8 **T 01 4534153** Admission includes equipment hire. Pro shop.Café. Expert tuition on Sundays.

SAILING

IRISH SAILING ASSOCIATION, 3 Park Road, Dun Laoghaire, Co Dublin **T 01 2800239**

SWIMMING

Public pools in Dublin City, sea swimming at Sandycove.

WALKING

DAILY HISTORICAL WALKING TOURS: Meet at front gate of Trinity College for walking trails include Georgian, Old City, Cultural, Rock 'n Roll, and James Joyce.

GUIDED TOUR OF OLD DUBLIN Meet at main entrance of Christ Church

THE ROYAL CANAL WAY A 78 mile/125km walk from Spencer Dock in Dublin to the 40th lock at Mullawomia, with scenery ranging from fairly unsavoury urban to pleasantly rural,. Only part is sign-posted, so an Ordnance Survey map is essential .

Clontarf Golf Club

WHERE TO STAY

HOTELS

AA RECOMMENDED

SEE UNDER WHERE TO EAT FOR ALL HOTEL RESTAURANTS WITH AA ROSETTES

AA ★★★★★ RATING

BERKELEY COURT
Lansdowne Rd
T 01 6601711 F 01 6602365
The flagship hotel of the Doyle Group, on Dublin's famous Lansdowne Road, is the embodiment of elegance, warmth and comfort. Dine in the Berkeley Room Restaurant or the less formal Conservatory, or relax over a drink in the richly panelled Royal Court Bar.
188 bedrooms incl some no-smoking ££££ Off-peak rates Lift Night porter Parking Gardens Gym

AA ★★★★ RATING

Red Cow Morans Hotel

BURLINGTON
Upper Leeson St
T 01 6605222 F 01 6603172
Very comfortable hotel with good dining options and Buck Mulligans Dublin pub.
450 bedrooms incl some no-smoking Lift Night porter Parking Use of facilities at fitness club

CLARENCE
6-8 Wellington Quay
T 01 670 9000 F 01 6707800
The only Red Star rated hotel in Dublin. No further information as we went to press
50 bedrooms ££££ Conference facilities

CONRAD INTERNATIONAL
Earlsfort Terrace
T 01 6765555 F 01 6765424
Just off St Stephen's Green, opposite the National Concert Hall. Excellent cooking in the Alexandra Restaurant.
191 bedrooms incl some no-smoking ££££ Off-peak rates Lift Night porter Air conditioning 80 Covered parking spaces

GRESHAM
O'Connel St T 01 8746881 F 01 8787175
The Gresham upholds traditional hotel-keeping standards. Facilities include the Aberdeen Restaurant and 24-hr room service.
200 bedrooms including some non-smoking ££££ Off-peak rates Lift Leisure facilities Business Centre Night porter Parking

JURYS
Pembroke Rd, Ballsbridge
T 01 6605000 F 01 6605540
Conveniently located just south of the city centre, with several restaurants, including the excellent Alexandra Restaurant. A wide range of accommodation is offered.
292 bedrooms including 120 for no-smoking ££££ Off-peak rates Lift Night porter Parking Whirlpool Masseuse Indoor & outdoor swimming pools (heated)

RED COW MORANS HOTEL
Red Cow Complex, Naas Rd
(at junction of M50 &N7 Naas road on the city side of the motorway)
T 01 4593650 F 01 4591588
Named after the original Red Cow Inn, this smart hotel has spacious, well-equipped bedrooms and superb function facilities.
123 bedrooms ££££

SHELBOURNE
St Stephen's Green *(in city centre)*
T 01 6766471 F 01 6616006
A Georgian hotel, famous as the location for the drafting of the Irish constitution in 1922.
164 bedrooms incl some no-smoking ££££ Off-peak rates Lift Night porter Parking Beauty Salon

AA ★★★ RATING

ABBERLEY COURT,
Belgrad Rd, Tallaght
T 01 4596000 F 01 4621000
This smart hotel has a lounge bar serving food all day and the first-floor restaurant.
40 bedrooms £££ Off-peak rates Lift Night porter Parking

ADAMS TRINITY,
28 Dame Lane
(in city centre, from O'Connell St go over O'Connell Bridge, take right past Trinity College on to Dame St, hotel on the left)
T 01 6707100 F 01 6707101
Stylish hotel in heart of old Dublin. Comfortable bedrooms. All-day food
28 bedrooms £££ Lift Night porter

BEWLEY'S,
Newlands Cross, Naas Rd
(M50 take N7 Naas road, hotel close to junc of N7 with Belgard Rd at Newlands Cross)
T 01 464 0140 F 01 464 0900
Modern hotel on the outskirts of Dublin. All-day self-service food. Evening meals.
126 bedrooms (inc family rooms) some no-smoking ££ Lift Night porter Parking

OYLE MONTROSE,
tillorgan Rd T 01 2693311 F 01 2691164
ttractive bedrooms make this hotel a opular choice. Set in a quiet suburb
79 bedrooms incl some no-smoking ££££)ff-peak rates Lift Night porter Parking

OYLE GREEN ISLE,
aas Rd T 01 4593406 F 01 4592178
on N7, 6 miles SW of the city centre)
'ery modern hotel providing up-to-date ccommodation and facilities.
0 bedrooms Lift Night porter Parking

OYLE SKYLON,
rumcondra Rd
T 01 8379121 F 01 8372778
lear airport. Hotel has well appointed edrooms,good value restaurant.
2 bedrooms Lift Night porter Parking

OYLE TARA,
lerrion Rd T 01 2694666 F 01 2691027
modern hotel on the coast road south f Ballsbridge with comfortable rooms.
13 bedrooms ££££ Lift Night porter 'arking

IBERNIAN
astmoreland Place, Ballsbridge
T 01 6687666 F 01 6602655
'ne Victorian building,with luxurious ecor and an exquisite restaurant.
1 bedrooms IR£110-£180 Off-peak rates ift Night porter Parking

URYS CHRISTCHURCH INN,
hristchurch Place
T 01 4540000 F 01 4540012
ustling 'one-price' hotel. Less emphasis n traditional room service and porterage,
82 bedrooms incl some no-smoking ££ ift Night porter

Hibernian

JURYS CUSTOM HOUSE INN
Custom House Quay
T 01 6075000 F 01 8290400
Landmark location. with light, airy rooms..Family rooms are good value.
234 bedrooms, 140 no smoking £££ Parking is available closeby at special rates.

LONGFIELD'S
Fitzwilliam St T 01 6761367 F 01 6761542
Intimate town house near centre. Good food and service.Relaxed atmosphere.
26 bedrooms Lift Night porter Restricted service 23 Dec-27 Jan

MARINE
Sutton Cross T 01 8390000 F 01 8390442
(from City centre follow signs to Hawth)
On the north shore of Dublin Bay, close to the Howth rapid railway Superb cuisine.
26 bedrooms ££ Off-peak rates Night porter Parking No coaches Gardens Leisure facilities

PARLIAMENT HOTEL
Lord Edward St T 01 6708777
F 01 670787
Near the Castle. Modern hotel with pleasant rooms,popular bar and pleasant
63 bedrooms £££

STEPHEN'S HALL
The Earlsfort Centre, Lower Leeson St
(from N11 into Dublin, hotel is on left after Hatch St junction)
T 01 6610585 F 01 6610606
Every room has a well equipped kitchen with microwave. Superb food in bistro.
37 bedrooms ££££ Off-peak rates Lift Night porter Covered parking

TEMPLE BAR,
Fleet St, Temple Bar
T 01 6773333 F 01 6773088
In the heart of old Dublin.Some rooms suitable for the less able. All-day food
108 bedrooms incl some no-smoking ££££ Continental breakfast Off-peak rates Lift Night porter Conference facilities

AA ★★ RATING

ORTE POSTHOUSE,
ublin Cloghran
ocated on Dublin Airport complex)
T 01 8444211 F 01 8446002
arge modern hotel with a wide range of ervices and amenities.
88 bedrooms incl some no-smoking ££££ ff-peak rates Night porter Parking ardens Free use of nearby sports club

FORTE TRAVELODGE,
Swords By Pass
T 01 8409233 F 01 8409257
Good standard of family rooms for overnight stops. Little Chef nearby.
40 bedrooms (ome no-smoking) ££

HARDING,
Copper Alley, Fishamble St, Christchurch
T 01 6796500 F 01 679 6504
In the Temple Bar area, this hotel has a friendly atmosphere. Popular. bar
53 bedrooms ££ Lift

STOP PRESS

MERRION HOTEL
Upper Merrion Street, Dublin 2
T 01 6030600 F 01 6030700
Just opened as we went to press. Beautifully restored from Georgian houses.
146 bedrooms ££££ Gardens

Call the AA Hotel Booking Service on 0990 050505 to book at AA recognised hotels and B&Bs in the UK and Ireland, or through our internet site: http://www.theaa.co.uk/hotels

BED & BREAKFAST ACCOMMODATION

AA RECOMMENDED

AA QQQQQ RATING

Glenogra

ABERDEEN LODGE
53/55 Park Av
T 01 2838155 F 01 2837877
Fine Edwardian house in prestigious road. Some bedrooms have air spa baths.
16 bedrooms Licensed Parking

ARIEL HOUSE
52 Lansdowne Rd
(turn off at Irish Bank, Ballsbridge on left before Lansdowne Rugby Stadium)
T 01 6685512 F 01 6685845
Victorian mansion.Beautifully furnished rooms. Close to the city rapid rail service.
28 bedrooms £££ Smoking permitted in one lounge only Parking No children under 5yrs

BUTLERS TOWN HOUSE
44 Lansdowne Rd, Ballsbridge
T 01 6674022 F 01 6673960
Restored Victorian house with charming breakfast room. Good room service menu.
19 bedrooms ££££ No smoking in part of the dining room Parking Credit cards

CEDAR LODGE
T 01 6684410 F 01 6684533
98 Merrion Rd, Ballsbridge
(opposite the British Embassy)
Lovely old house with a modern extension.Accessible to disabled guests.
10 bedrooms ££ No smoking in dining room/lounges Licensed Parking

GLENOGRA
64 Merrion Rd, Ballsbridge
(opposite Royal Dublin Showground)
T 01 6683661 F 01 6683698
Fine gabled house offering comfort with more than a touch of elegance
9 bedrooms, inc 1 family ££ All no smoking No smoking in dining room Parking

THE GREY DOOR
22/23 Upper Pembroke St
(city centre, near St Stephens Green)
T 01 6763286 F 01 6763287
Charming house with two restaurants.Cooked breakfast extra.
7 bedrooms including 1 for non-smokers £££ No smoking in day rooms Licensed

MERRION HALL
54-56 Merrion Rd, Ballsbridge
T 01 6681426 F 01 6684280
Elegant town house. Friendly owners provide a warm welcome
15 bedrooms ££ Parking

Butlers Town House

AA QQQQ RATING

AARON HOUSE
152 Merrion Rd, Ballsbridge
(600yds on left past British Embassy)
T 01 2601644 & 2601650 F 01 2601651
Near city centre in a residential suburb. Friendly, comfortable house.
6 bedrooms inc 1 non-smoking No smoking in dining room/lounges ££ Parking

AARONMOR HOUSE
1c Sandymount Av, Ballsbridge
T 01 6687972 F 01 6682377
A comfortably furnished family-run house near the showground and rugby ground.
6 bedrooms incl some no-smoking No smoking in dining room/lounges ££ Parking

BEAUFORT HOUSE
25 Pembroke Park, Ballsbridge
T 01 6689080 F 01 6609963
Bedrooms have every comfort. Barbecues are sometimes organised in the summer.
7 bedrooms incl 3 family & 2 no smoking ££ Parking Credit cards

CHARLEVILLE
268/272 North Circular Rd
(300 yards from St Peters Church)
T 01 8386633 F 01 8385854
Close to Phoenix Park, this elegant terrace of Victorian houses offers high standards.
20 bedrooms, all no smoking ££ Parking

COPPER BEECH COURT
11 Hollybrook Park, Clontarf
T 01 8333390 F 01 8351808
Fine Victorian house stands in its own grounds.
Spacious bedrooms Parking

CUMBERLAND LODGE
54 York Rd **T 01 2809665 F 2843227**
(S from city centre, follow Dun Laoghaire ferry signs, on approaching Georges St, R at Cumberland Inn into York Rd)
Close to the ferry and DART, this charming Regency house has comfortable rooms.
4 bedrooms (1 family) No smoking in bedrooms, dining rooms or 1 lounge CTV all bedrooms No dogs (ex guide dogs

iarleville

ILINTON MANOR
Eglinton Rd, Donnybrook T 01 2693273
t in lovely gardens, this Victorian
wnhouse has charming bedrooms.
rking

.ENVEAGH TOWNHOUSE
Northumberland Rd, Ballsbridge
01 6684612 F 01 6684559
:ractive Georgian house with
mfortable, well equipped bedrooms.
bedrooms incl some no-smoking No
oking in dining room ££ Parking
osed 22-29 Dec

DIGAN'S GUEST HOUSE
lyallan House, 14 Hollybrook Park, Clontarf
01 8531663 & 8531665 F 01 8333337
edrooms (4 family) £ Children welcome
rking

NGSWOOD COUNTRY HOUSE
d Kingswood, Naas Rd, Clondalkin, Dublin
(turn left off M50 heading south, premises
on left past Green Isle Hotel)
01 4592428 & 4592207 F 01 4592428
endly proprietors provide comfortable
commodation and good home cooking
edrooms Licensed ££ Parking

NSDOWNE MANOR
'48 Lansdowne Rd, Ballsbridge
n left at Trinity College continue down
ussa St, Mount St and Northumberland
, turn left at traffic lights, premises on left)
01 6688848 F 01 6688873
o Victorian houses, converted into a
el, lavishly furnished in period style.
bedrooms No smoking in dining
m/lounges££ Parking

unt Herbert Ltd

MERRION LODGE
148 Merrion Rd, Ballsbridge
(2 miles S of Dublin City Centre on the main road between Dublin/Dun Laoghaire)
T 2691565 F 2839998
6 bedrooms No smoking in dining room ££ Parking

Park lodge

MOREHAMPTON LODGE
113 Morehampton Rd, Donnybrook
T 01 2837499 F 01 2837595
Restored Victorian house close to the city centre. Excellent bedrooms.
5 bedrooms No smoking in dining room/lounges ££ Parking

MOUNT HERBERT LTD
7 Herbert Rd, Lansdowne Rd
T 01 6684321 F 01 6607077
Victorian house in Dublin's embassy belt. Restaurant, gardens, children's playground
200 bedrooms ££ No smoking in dining room Lift Licensed Parking Leisure facilities Conference facilities Gift shop

NORTHUMBERLAND LODGE
68 Northumberland Rd, Ballsbridge
(beside US Embassy)
T 01 6605270 F 01 6688679
Georgian house with attractive gardens and large bedrooms have many comforts.
6 bedrooms ££ Covered Parking

NUMBER 66
66 Northumberland Rd, Ballsbridge
T 01 6600333 & 6600471 F 01 6601051
Imposing house with pleasant bedrooms. Lovely conservatory and attractive lounges
6 bedrooms No smoking in dining room No smoking in lounges££

NUMBER 88
88 Pembroke Rd, Ballsbridge
T 01 6600277 F 01 6600291
Three Georgian houses interlinked to produce this luxurious guest house.
50 bedrooms No smoking in area of dining room ££ Lift Parking

PARK LODGE
19 Deerpark Dr, Castleknock
T 01 8212887 F 01 8212887
A luxurious housewith gardens and a patio for those who like to eat outdoors.
3 bedrooms, all no smoking No smoking in dining room/lounges ££ Parking Open March-1 Nov

RAGLAN LODGE
10 Raglan Rd, Ballsbridge
T 01 6606697 F 01 6606781
Charming Victorian lodge with easy access to city centre. Pleasant rooms
7 bedrooms incl some no-smoking No smoking in dining room Parking

Call the AA Hotel Booking Service on 0990 050505 to book at AA recognised hotels and B&Bs in the UK and Ireland, or through our internet site: http://www.theaa.co.uk/hotels

AA QQQ RATING

AARONA
150 Clonkeen Rd, Deansgrange, Blackrock
(2 miles south-west of Dun Laoghaire ferry port on the road leading to the N11.)
T 01 289 3972 F 01 289 8622
A semi-detached house with a TV lounge and dining room overlooking a flower-filled back garden.
4 bedrooms No smoking Parking

AILEACH
3 Rossmore Grove, off Wellington Ln, Templeogue
(turn left off M50 South onto N81, at next rdbt left for Wellington Lane signposted Crumlin, first right Rossmore Rd first right again Rossmore Grove)
T 01 490 2939 F 01 492 9416
A comfortable house with a TV lounge and separate dining room.
4 bedrooms, all no smoking No smoking in dining room/lounges £ Parking

ARDAGH HOUSE
1 Highfield Rd, Rathgar
T 01 4977068 F 01 4973991
This Victorian residence offers spacious bedrooms with many comforts. Easy access to the RDS and city centre.
17 bedrooms inc some non-smoking £ No smoking in dining room Parking

BEDDINGTON
181 Rathgar Rd
T 01 4978047 F 01 4978275
Attractive house with comfortable bedrooms using crisp linen sheets. Relaxing lounge.
14 bedrooms No smoking in dining room/lounges Licensed Parking No children under 7yrs

BEECHWOOD
6 Butterfield Av, Rathfarnham
T 01 4943526
Spacious, comfortable bedrooms with pretty day rooms.
4 bedrooms No smoking in dining room/lounges ££ Parking No children under 4yrs

BELGRAVE
8-10 Belgrave Square, Rathmines
T 01 4963760 & 4962549 F 01 4979243

Belgrav

Interlinked period houses provide well equipped bedrooms and a dining room overlooking the gardens.
24 bedrooms No smoking in area of dining room ££ Parking

BUSHFIELD HOUSE
57 Philipsburgh Av, Fairview
T 01 8370237 F 01 8376475
Point Theatre and the Financial Services Centre nearby. Georgian house with pretty bedrooms in pleasant surroundings.
8 bedrooms No smoking in dining room £££ 6 parking spaces

CHARLSTON MANOR
15/16 Charleston Rd, Ranelagh
(on main road between Ranelagh & Rathmines) T 01 4910262 F 01 4966052
10 minutes from the city centre, two red-brick houses have been restored to give 5 bedrooms at ground floor level.
5 bedrooms No smoking in dining room ££ Parking

CLIFDEN
32 Gardiner Place
(city centre) T 01 8746364 F 01 8746122
10 bedrooms £ No smoking in dining room/lounges Parking

EGAN'S
7/9 Iona Park, Glasnevin
T 01 8303611 & 8305283 F 01 8303312
Comfortable accommodation is offered at this family-run Victorian house in a quiet suburb on the north side of the city.

25 bedrooms No smoking in dining room £ Licensed Parking

FERRYVIEW HOUSE
96 Clontarf Rd, Clontarf T 01 8335893
Right on the seafront, this comfortable modern house offers cheerful bedrooms and two lounges.
6 bedrooms(4 family), all non smoking No smoking in dining room £ Parking

THE FITZWILLIAM
41 Upper Fitzwilliam St
T 01 6600199 F 01 6767488
Situated near city centre. Well equipped bedrooms. Pleasant lounge. Restaurant.
12 bedrooms Licenced Parking Open 5 Jan-15 Dec

HERBERT LODGE
65 Morehampton Rd, Donnybrook
(1.25m from city centre on N11)
T 01 6603403 F 01 4730919
6 bedrooms incl some no-smoking Parking

IONA HOUSE
5 Iona Park T 01 8306217 & 8306855
Victorian house with large bedrooms, a comfortable lounge and a small garden.
2 bedrooms No smoking in area of dining room ££ No children under 3yrs Closed Dec-Jan

INISRADHARC
see under Howth, Co Dublin

MARELLE
92 Rathfarnham Rd, Terenure
T 01 4904690
An attractive house set back from the roa in its own gardens. .
6 bedrooms No dogs ££ Parking No children under 5yrs

ST AIDEN'S
32 Brighton Rd, Rathgar
T 01 4902011 & 4906178 F 01 4920234
Victorian house, near Rathgan village, wit well equipped bedrooms.
10 bedrooms including some non-smoking No smoking in dining room £ Licensed Parking

Ardagh House

VISTOCK HOUSE
Ranelagh Rd, Ranelagh
01 4967377 01 4967377
hough on the outskirts, this neat house very convenient for the city centre.
edrooms (1 family) inc 3 for non-smokers smoking in dining room £ Parking

EDEN HOUSE
123 Morehampton Road, Donnybrook
01 2696363 01 2600808
Pleasant terrace house. The bedrooms are modestly comfortable but with good beds.
4 bedrooms (4 family) £ No smoking in dining room No children under 4yrs Parking Closed Xmas

WHITE HOUSE
125 Clontarf Road 01 8333196
6 bedrooms £ No smoking in dining room No children under 8yrs Parking Closed 24–25 Dec

WHERE TO EAT

RESTAURANTS

AA RECOMMENDED

EXANDRA RESTAURANT
nrad International Hotel, Earlsfort Terrace
01 676555 01 6765424
imaginative range of continental and h dishes might include a salad of ster, hearts of palm and mangoes, with valnut vinaigrette and truffles, and a ssoulet of seafood in a velouté sauce h a Mediterranean risotto.
C £££

E BERKELEY ROOM
keley Court Hotel, Lansdowne Road, olin 01 6601711 01 6617238
rench carte with English translations ers an extensive choice. Typical dishes a rich prawn bisque laced with Pernod d Brandy, and half a roast duckling, with ausage and potato stuffing, served with cabbage and orange sauce.
ED L ££ D £££ ALC £££

E CLARENCE HOTEL
Wellington Quay
01 670 9000 01 6707800
erb restaurant.

E COMMONS
86 St Stephen's Green, Dublin 2
01 4752608 01 4780551
ng established, formal basement aurant. Magret of honey-roasted goose a bed of colcannon, with a broad bean am sauce, and light almond gâteau n compote of red berries are typical of polished repertoire.
ed L ££ ALC £££

ERNIAN HOTEL
moreland Place, Ballsbridge
01 6687666 01 6602655
taurant with the very highest standards uisine.

PRIOL
ower Camden Street, Dublin 2
01 4751235 or 4985496
opular Italian restaurant noted for a xed atmosphere. Order delicious ach tortellone, veal escalopes alla riciosa and zabaglione. Reservations .
£££

THE MERIDIAN
Marine Hotel, Sutton Cross
01 8390000 01 8390442
Seafood is a feature of this restaurant's carte, with dishes such as stuffed fillets of Dover sole with Dublin Bay prawns from 'Neptune's Lair', alongside Wicklow lamb and chicken choucoute from 'The Bountiful Earth'.
Fixed L ££ ALC £££

MORELS BISTRO
Stephen's Hall All-Suite Hotel, The Earlsfort Centre, Lower Leeson Street
01 6610585 01 6610606
A lively city-centre bistro whose menu features fresh Irish produce with a Mediterranean flavour, though Oriental influences are also apparent. Dishes might include mushroom risotto, with white butter and parmesan shavings, followed by roast monkfish with basil potatoes, balsamic dressing and crispy leeks.
Fixed L ££ ALC £££

NUMBER 10
Longfield's Hotel, Fitzwilliam Street, Dublin
01 6761367 01 6761542
A basement restaurant where the limitations of space do little to deter an enthusiastic clientele. A strong feature is the varied choice of dishes, with a balance of Irish and Mediterranean flavours.
Fixed L ££ ALC £££

NUMBER 27
The Shelbourne Hotel, 27 St Stephen's Green
01 6766471 01 6616006
An elegant hotel restaurant offering contemporary Irish cuisine using the best quality local produce. Dishes might include ravioli of king scallops with florettes of crunchy vegetables, and Kildare rack of lamb with a herb nut crust and roast vegetables.
FIXED £££ ALC £££

RAGLANS RESTAURANT
Jury's Hotel, Pembroke Road, Ballsbridge, Dublin 01 6605000 016605540
Excellent food.
FIXED L ££ ALC £££

RESTAURANT PATRICK GUILBAUD
Hotel Merrion, 21 Upper Merrion Street
01 6764192
One of the key pacesetters in changing the face of Irish cooking, Patrick Guilbaud's modern French Hibernian style is consistently successful. The wine list includes twenty house wines, and the sommelier's skill in decanting is a pleasure to watch.
Fixed L £££ ALC £££

ROLY'S BISTRO
7 Ballsbridge Terrace
T 01 6682611 F 01 6608535
High quality contemporary-style cooking, a lively atmosphere and moderate prices draw the crowds. The menu is set at lunchtime and carte in the evening. Extras, such as a wide choice of breads and freshly made coffee are all excellent.
Fixed L ££ ALC £££

LA STAMPA
35 Dawson Street
T 01 6778611 or 6772119 F 01 6773336
A popular, attractive restaurant with a strong Italian bias to the menu. Veal, bacon and spinach terrine; baked cod with oyster mushrooms, chorizo and mashed potato, have all been enjoyed.
Fixed L ££ ALC £££

THORNTON'S
1 Portobello Rd
T 01 4549067 F 01 4532947
A superb restaurant and something quite different, where the emphasis on game dishes with few concessions to 'non-exotic' dining. The upmarket, canal-side restaurant is favoured by a young, fashionable and sophisticated crowd.
Fixed L ££ ALC £££

PUBS, INNS & OTHER PLACES

Dublin pubs are renowned for their conviviality; the talking, laughing and music, summarised by the Irish as the crack (craic). Pubs are open 10.30am-11pm (11.30pm in summer) Monday to Saturday; 12.30pm-2pm and 4pm-11pm on Sunday. Though some city centre pubs may have licenses to stay open later during festivals.

AN BÉAL BOCHT
58 Charlemont Street, Dublin 2
Traditional music nights at this pub

AULD DUBLINER,
17 Anglesea Street, Dublin 2
A likely pub for traditional music.

BAILEY,
2 Duke Street, Dublin 2
Joycean associations keeps this pub eternally popular.

BESHOFF'S,
14 Westmoreland Street, Dublin 2
Great fish and chips; Edwardian bistro decor.

BEWLEY'S ORIENTAL CAFÉ IN FOUR CENTRAL LOCATIONS:
South Great George Street, Mary Street, Westmoreland Street, and the main one in Grafton Street **T 01 6776761**
Coffee shop with mahogany and stained glass. Food ranges from sticky buns to full meals. Museum in Grafton Street.

BLEEDING HORSE,
24-5 Upper Camden Street, Dublin 2
T 01 4752705
Bar food downstairs, à la carte dining upstairs in Wrenn's. Live music on Saturdays.

BOSS CROKER'S,
39 Arran Quay, Dublin 7
Worth trying this pub for traditional music, and sometimes jazz.

BRAZEN HEAD,
20 Lower Bridge Street, Dublin 8
Claims to be Ireland's oldest pub, dating back to 1198.

BURDOCK'S,
2 Werburgh St, Dublin 2 **T 01 45403606**
Omni Centre, Santry, Dublin 9 (200-seat restaurant) **T 01 8426266**
Legendary fish and chips.

CAFÉ EN SEINE,
40 Dawson Street, Dublin 2 **T 01 6774369**
Stylish café for morning coffee with free newspapers, all-day cake and coffee, and Sunday brunch with jazz.

CAFÉ ITALIANO,
7 D'Olier Street, Dublin 2 **T 01 6793859**
Lively, cosmopolitan atmosphere with music. Serving pasta dishes, soups, sandwiches, cake cappuccino and wine.

CAFÉ JAVA,
145 Upper Leeson St, Dublin 4
T 01 6600675
Daytime meals, excellent coffee. Weekend brunch plus newspapers.

CASTLE VAULTS BISTRO,
Dublin Castle, Dublin 2 **T 01 6770678**
Daytime only, with À la carte menu, salad bar, lunchtime specials and afternoon teas.

CHAPTER ONE,
18-19 Parnell Square, Dublin 1 **T 01 217766**
Dublin Writers' Museum restaurant serving Irish, continental and vegetarian food.

CITY ARTS CENTRE CAFÉ,
23-25 Moss Street, Dublin 2 **T 01 6770643**
Coffee, wine and food, including good sandwiches.

CONWAYS PUB & RESTAURANT ,
70 Parnell Street, Dublin 1 **T 01 8732687**
Providing food and drink to Dubliners since 1745. Sunday brunch with music.

CORA'S ITALIAN RESTAURANT,
1 St Mary's Rd, Dublin 4 **T 01 6600585**
Warm, down to earth, Italian family restaurant.

CORNUCOPIA,
19 Wicklow Street, Dublin 2
Vegetarian food.

DAVY BYRNE'S,
21 Duke Street, Dublin 2
Another pub with Joycean associations.

DOHENY & NESBITTS,
5 Lower Baggot Street, Dublin 2
Complete with 'snugs', this pub attracts barristers, journalists and loyal regulars.

DROPPING WELL,
Milltown, Dublin
Fashionable pub with relaxed atmosphere offering an excellent bar menu and separate, more formal restaurant

THE DUKE,
Duke Street, Dublin 2 **T 01 4540228**
Starting point for Literary Pub Crawls, 7.30pm every evening

EASTERN TANDOORI,
34-35 S. William St, Dublin 2 **T 01 671042**
An authentic Indian restaurant specialisin in tandoori dishes. Excellent service provided by staff in traditional dress.

FITZERS, NATIONAL GALLERY RESTAURANT,
Merrion Square, Dublin 2
Good self-service restaurant with reasonably priced wine. Day time only.

FXB'S,
Pembroke Street, Dublin 2
Owned by a Dublin butcher, meat is the speciality here. Children welcome. Sister restaurant in Monkstown, Co Dublin.

GALLAGHER'S BOXTY HOUSE,
20 Temple Bar, Dublin 2
Traditional Irish potato cakes with a varie of savoury fillings - bacon and cabbage, champ, smoked fish and other Irish fare.

GLENSIDE,
Churchtown, Dublin
Old-style pub, very popular with locals. B menu available.

GREY DOOR,
22/23 Upper Pembroke Street, Dublin
A popular restaurant located in an AA recommended hotel in the heart of Georgian Dublin.

HUGHE'S,
Chancery Street, Dublin 7
Pub venue for traditional music.

IRISH FILM CENTRE RESTAURANT,
6 Eustace Street, Temple Bar, Dublin 2
Lunch, dinner and bar food including a good vegetarian choice.

IRISH MUSEUM OF MODERN ART,
Royal Hospital Kilmainham, Dublin 8
Daytime coffee shop.

JOXER DALY'S,
103 Dorset Street, Dublin
Lovely pub noted for its lunches and snacks.

KEHOE'S,
South Anne Street, Dublin 2
Snugs is this pub were immortalised by Sean O'Casey.

:ENNY'S,
incoln Place, Dublin 2
\ pub and student haunt, close to Trinity :ollege, known for its traditional music.

:ILKENNY KITCHEN,
lassau Street, Dublin 2
)n the first floor of Kilkenny Design :entre. Self-service coffee shop and estaurant. Always busy at lunchtime.

:INGFISHER RESTAURANT,
66 Parnell Street, Dublin 1
'ish restaurant with great chips (home-nade from home-grown potatoes).

:INSELLA BAR,
1-32 Lower Mount Street, Dublin 2
Bar food, international cuisine.

:ITTY O'SHEA'S,
3-25 Upper Grand Canal St, Dublin 4
)elightful looking pub with traditional nusic nights. Good Sunday brunch.

ARRY O'ROURKE'S,
2 Upper Dorset Street, Dublin 1
'raditional music pub.

ONG HALL,
1 South Great George's Street, Dublin 2
'ub with luxuriant Victorian-style urnishings.

ORD EDWARD,
3 Christchurch Place, Dublin 8
'raditional fish restaurant.

ICDAID'S,
Harry Street, Dublin 2
)rinking spot for Dublin's bygone literati.

IAGIC CARPET,
:ornelscourt Village, Dublin 8
American-style with burgers and kebabs. 'amily barbeque Wed-Sun with live music. ully licensed; great for kids.

IARKS BROTHERS,
' South Great George's Street, Dublin 2
'opular café with good sandwiches, soup nd salads.

I B SLATTERY,
'2 Upper Grand Canal Street, Dublin 4
Good pub for Irish music.

IEAN FIDDLER,
Wexford Street, Dublin 2
:nown for music, from traditional to rock. :offee shop open bar hours.

HE MERCHANT,
2 Bridge St, Dublin 8 (off Merchant's Quay)
'ub known for its traditional Irish music.

IITCHELL'S CELLARS,
:1 Kildare Street, Dublin 2
Bistro-style wine bar and restaurant, erving patés, quiches and casseroles. unchtime only.

IOONEY'S,
Lower Abbey Street, Dublin 1
'ub frequented by James Joyce's Leopold Bloom.

MULLIGAN'S,
8 Poolbeg Street, Dublin 2
Looks its 200 years; ambience lends itself to an extraordinary sampling of Irish life. Featured in the film 'My Left Foot'.

NATIONAL MUSEUM CAFÉ,
Kildare Street, Dublin 2
Grand surroundings with good value light snacks to more substantial dishes served from the counter throughout the day.

NEARY'S,
1 Chatham Street, Dublin 1
Central pub serving excellent sandwiches. Popular with actors from the Gaeity.

O'DONOGHUE'S,
15 Merrion Row, Dublin 2
Doyen of traditional pubs with music of the 'bring your own' variety.

O'DWYERS,
8 Lower Mount Street, Dublin 2
Busy pub with a good buzz. The Howl at the Moon nightclub attracts a more youthful crowd later in the evening.

OLD STAND,
37 Exchequer Street, Dublin 2
Lovely old pub, attracting sporty types. Good pub food.

OLIVER ST JOHN GOGARTY,
junction of Fleet Street/Anglesea Street, Dublin 2 **01 4780191**
Starting point for Musical Pub Crawls, every night except Friday. Bar lunch and all-day menu. Restaurant on second floor serving Irish food.

O'NEILL'S,
Suffolk Street, Dublin 2
Near Trinity College, popular with students.

OVAL,
Middle Abbey Street, Dublin 1
Journalist's haunt.

PALACE BAR,
21 Fleet Street, Temple Bar, Dublin 2
Old pub with tiles and mirrors.

PASTA FRESCA,
3-4 Chatham Street, Dublin 2
Italian cuisine, good examples of favourite dishes as well as the more unusual.

PERIWINKLE SEAFOOD BAR,
Powerscourt Centre, S. William St, Dublin 2
Bar-counter seafood restaurant popular with shoppers.

PIER 32,
23 Upper Pembroke Street, Dublin 2
Seafood restaurant in a pub setting

PLANET HOLLYWOOD
St Stephen's Green
Movie memorabilia crowds the walls, including the fur coat worn by Daniel Day Lewis. The menu is impressive - but a bit steep for fast food.

PORTER HOUSE,
16-18 Parliament Street, Dublin 2
Restored with flair, Dublin's first microbrewery opened in 1996. Sample the beers and enjoy the popular bar meals.

RAJDOOT,
26-28 Clarendon St, Dublin 2
Enjoyable Moghul specialities in discreetly elegant setting.

ROYAL HOSPITAL,
Kilmainham Lane, Dublin
A good coffee shop restaurant serving simple home cooking.

SEAN O'CASEY'S,
105 Marlborough Street, Dublin 1
Pub known for both traditional and rock music.

SICHUAN,
4 Lower Kilmacud Rd, Stilorgan
01 2884817
State-owned Chinese restaurant (owned by the People's Republic of China, that is).

SLATTERY'S,
129 Capel Street, Dublin 2
A favourite pub for music enthusiasts; traditional, folk and blues.

STAG'S HEAD,
best approached from Exchequer Street.
A relaxed 200-year-old pub with a large cast of regulars.

TONER'S VICTORIAN BAR,
139 Lower Baggot Street, Dublin 2
Highly sociable mix of students and artists.

WHELAN'S,
25 Wexford Street, Dublin 2
Pub known for all types of music - traditional, rock and jazz.

WILLIAM RYAN'S,
28 Parkgate Street, Dublin 8
Pub interior unchanged since 1896.

YELLOW HOUSE,
Willbrook Road, Rathfarnham, Dublin 14
A local landmark due to its distinctive brickwork. Straightforward dishes are served.

COUNTY DUBLIN

The county of Dublin is dominated by the capital, and the other major town Dun Laoghaire, which is familiar to many visitors to the Republic arriving by ferry. However, the area around the city provides plenty of sporting and leisure opportunities for residents and visitors alike - notably an abundance of golf courses. The county is also rich in country homes, castles and beautiful gardens, and has some fine beaches, providing a welcome retreat from the rigours of urban life.

PRINCIPAL TOWNS

DUN LAOGHAIRE

As a major entry port, Dun Laoghaire (pronounced Dunleary) will be many a visitor's first sight of the Republic. The harbour was constructed in the early 19th century by a Scotsman, John Rennie, and at that time its huge granite piers were the largest in the world. Apart from its commercial traffic, Dun Laoghaire is also a major yachting centre, and home to the National Maritime Museum. The town's name refers to Laoghaire, the 5th-century High King of Tara, under whose auspices St Patrick set up his first mission in Ireland.

DALKEY

Indulge in some celebrity spotting here, as Dalkey has become the fashionable place to live. Sitting prettily at the southern end of Dublin bay, and just half an hour's drive from the city centre, this Heritage Town has an old world atmosphere with a charming medieval streetscape buildings. Visit the 8th-century church of St Begnets, the 16th-century Archbold's Castle and the Town Hall.

MUST SEE

MALAHIDE CASTLE
Malahide T 01 8462184 F 01 8462537
The contours of one of Ireland's oldest and most romantic castles have changed very little in 800 years. It was occupied by the Talbot family from 1185 until 1873, when the last Lord Talbot died, and the story of the family reflects Ireland's own turbulent history. The house is beautifully furnished with period pieces and there is an extensive collection of Irish portrait paintings, many from the Irish National Gallery. The castle is surrounded by 250 acres of parkland, and is set in the attractive seaside resort of Malahide.

JAMES JOYCE TOWER
Sandycove, Dun Laoghaire T 01 2089265
This Martello tower was a temporary home to James Joyce., and is the setting for the first chapter of Joyce's great novel, Ulysses, which is described pretty much as you will see it today. The gun platform has extraordinary views .You can see rare editions of Joyce's work, letters, photos and personal possesssions. The tower is a focus for the annual Bloomsday celebrations. (8 miles/13km from Dublin on the coast road)

NEWBRIDGE HOUSE & TRADITIONAL FARM
Donabate
T 01 8436534 & 8462184 F 01 8462537
Built in 1737 for Charles Cobbe, Archbishop of Dublin. Many splendidly refurbished rooms featuring fine plasterwork, furniture and paintings, including the Red Drawing Room with a beautiful white marble chimney piece and rococo ceiling, and sculpture gallery. Also of interest, downstairs, are the kitchen and laundry. The Museum of Curiosities features many artefacts collected by the Cobbe family on their travels throughout the world. Special events during the year include demonstrations of sheep shearing, weaving, dying, pottery and harness-making

BIG OUTDOORS

DALKEY ISLAND
Lying off the mainland at Dalkey, Dalkey Island was first inhabited by Stone Age settlers around 3,500BC.

KILLINEY PARK
This beautiful park, a short walk from Dalkey, was originally part of the Killiney Castle estate. Further on is the Vico Road, with magnificent views of Killiney Bay.

GREAT FOR KIDS

ANIMAL FARM
Reynoldstown Naul
(18 miles/29km north of Dublin; 3 miles/5km inland from the seaside town of Balbriggan in the vale of Fingal)
T 01 8412615/8411202
A family-run, working organic farm of 150 acres/60ha, sweeping down to the River Delvin. Tours are guided and include the chance to handle and feed the animals.

BEACHES
Blue Flag awards for maintaining high environmental standards have been awarded to: Rush, Loughshinny, Donabate, Seapoint and Killiney beaches.

FORT LUCAN
(signposted off Strawberry Beds near Lucan)
T 01 6280166
Outdoor adventure world for children 2-14 yrs, with assault course, arial runways, 40ft/12m slides, pedulum swings, kart track, suspension bridges, maze and tot's area. Restaurant and tea room.

FRY MODEL RAILWAY
Malahide Castle, Malahide
T 01 8463779 F 01 8462537
A rare collection of '0' gauge trains and trams begun in the 1920s, in a purpose-built setting adjacent to Malahide Castle. The scale models depict the history of Irish rail transport.

LAMBERT PUPPET THEATRE & MUSEUM
Clifton Lane, Monkstown
T 01 2800974 F 01 2804772
The Lambert family's puppets are much loved in Ireland for their TV and theatre appearances, and the museum houses an extensive collection. Performances every Saturday.

LEISUREPLEX
Village Green Centre, Tallaght
T 01 4599411
Open 24 hours, seven days a week, including Bowler Vision, Quasar, snooker/pool, children's play area, video games and restaurant.

HISTORIC & ANCIENT SITES

ST DOULAGH'S CHURCH
Portmarnock
A 13th-century church with an original stone roof, chapel and battlemented tower. In a nearby field, there is an octagonal well house with a stone roof.

DUNSOGHLY CASTLE
3 miles/5km N of Finglas (right of the N2)
A National Monument, dating from the 15th-century, with its original oak roof beams intact. It has a square tower with rectangular turrets - worth the climb for the view.

HOMES & GARDENS

ARDGILLAN CASTLE
Balbriggan *(on R127)*
T 01 8492212 F 01 8492786
An elegant manor house, built 1738, set amid extensive parkland overlooking the coast as far as the Mourne mountains. The kitchens and Victorian conservatory have recently been restored.

CASINO
Marino *(3 miles/5km north of Dublin off the Malahide Road)* T 01 8331618
A former summer house - not a casino in the gambling sense - built in 1758 from a plan by Sir William Chambers. It has been called one of the world's most perfect Palladian buildings.

DRIMNAGH CASTLE
Long Mile Road, Drimnagh T 01 4502530
The last surviving medieval castle in Ireland with a flooded moat. The Great Hall and Undercroft have been restored and are set off by 17th-century style formal gardens.

FERNHILL GARDENS
(7 miles/11km south of the city near Sandyford)
About 40 acres/16ha of gardens, with thousands of plants, in the southern suburbs of Dublin.

HOWTH CASTLE RHODODENDRON GARDENS
Howth *(9 miles/14km NE Dublin)*
T 01 8322626 F 01 8392405
The castle is justly famous for its attractive

gardens, rhododendron walk and panoramic views. The walk is open all year, but is at its floral best in May and June.

PRIMROSE HILL
Lucan **T 01 6280373**
A Regency villa, attributed to James Gandon, with a traditional Irish garden. It has a good showing of spring flowers in February, and a developing arboretum.

TALBOT BOTANIC GARDENS
Malahide **T 01 8727530**
The garden created by Lord Milo Talbot between 1948 and 1973, with an emphasis on plants from the Southern Hemisphere, many personally collected by Lord Talbot.

MUSEUMS & ART GALLERIES

HERITAGE CENTRE
Castle Street, Dalkey **T 01 2054745**
Situated close to an 8th-century church, the Centre holds a mine of information of the area and is a good place to start a tour of Dalkey.

NATIONAL MARITIME MUSEUM
Haigh Terrace, Dun Laoghaire
Formerly the Mariners' Church, the museum houses a French longboat captured at Bantry, Co Cork in 1796 and an old optic from the Baily Lighthouse on Howth Head.

NATIONAL TRANSPORT MUSEUM
Howth Castle Demesne, Howth
Museum of public utility, military and horse-drawn transport, including trams and buses.

ESSENTIAL INFORMATION

CRAFTS

DUBLIN CRYSTAL GLASS COMPANY
Brookfield Terrace, Carysfort Avenue, Blackrock, **T 01 2887932**
By appointment, visitors can watch crystal being blown and see the Visitor Showroom.

SHOPPING

WEEKEND MARKETS
Christchurch and Blackrock Easily accessible by DART

THE SQUARE TOWNCENTRE Tallaght
The largest shopping centre of its kind in Ireland with 145 shops under a great dome of natural light.

SPORTS & LEISURE

ANGLING

The River Liffey is a great source of game fishing, especially around Lucan and Islandbridge.

For information on coarse, game and sea angling:**EASTERN REGIONAL FISHERIES BOARD, MOBHI BOREEN,** Glasnevin, Dublin 9 **T 01 379209 F 01 360060**

GOLF COURSES

LUTTRELLSTOWN CASTLE
Clonsilla **T 01 8208210 F 01 8205218**
Just 4 miles/6km from Dublin, set within the castle estate, and is full of character.

PORTMARNOCK Portmarnock
T 01 8462968 F 01 8462601
Internationally renowned course, 12 miles/19km from Dublin. Nearly every top tournament has been held there, including the Walker Cup. Surrounded by sea on three sides. Widely acclaimed as the fairest of the championship courses.

PORTMARNOCK Strand Road, Portmarnock
T 01 846 1800 F 01 8461077
This excellent links course was designed by Bernard Langer.

ROYAL DUBLIN North Bull Island, Dollymount **T 01 8336346**
Considered to be less severe than Portmarnock. Popular with visitors for its design subtleties, the condition of its links.

ST MARGARET'S St Margaret's
T 01 8640400 F 01 8640289
Described by Sam Torrance as having 'the best finishing hole I have ever seen ... and possibly the strongest and most exciting in the world.'
Also
BALBRIGGAN T 01 8412229
BEAVERSTOWN T 01 8436439
CITYWEST T 01 4588566
CORBALLIS PUBLIC LINKS T 01 8436583
CORRSTOWN T 01 8640533/8640534
DEER PARK HOTEL Howth **T 01 8322624**
DUN LAOGHAIRE T 01 2803916
FINNSTOWN FAIRWAYS T 01 6280644
GLENCULLEN T 01 2940898
HOLLYWOOD LAKES T 01 8433407
THE ISLAND T 01 8436205
KILLINEY T 01 2852823/2851983
KILTERNAN T 01 2955559
MALAHIDE T 01 8461611/8461642
THE OPEN GOLF CENTRE T 8640324
SWORDS OPEN T 01 8409819/8901030
TURVEY GOLF & COUNTRY CLUB
T 01 8435169/8435179
TYRELLSTOWN T 01 8213206
WOODBROOK T 282 4799

EQUESTRIAN CENTRES

BROOKE LODGE RIDING CENTRE
Burrow Rd, Stepaside **T 2952153**

COOLMINE Coolmine House, Saggart
T 01 4588447 F 01 4573080

GORMANSTOWN FARM
Knocknagin Rd, Balbriggan **T 01 8412508**

KILRONAN Kilronan, Cloghran, Swords
T 01 8403499

PUDDEN HILL Moorepark, Garristown
T/F 01 8354313

SPRUCE LODGE Spruce Lodge, Kilternan
T 01 2952109 F 01 2950588

THE PADDOCKS RIDING CENTRE
Woodside Rd, Sandyford **T 01 2954278**

THORNTON PARK EQUESTRIAN CENTRE
Thornton, Kilsallaghan **T 01 8351164**

woodbrook Golf Club

HORSE RACING

LEOPARDSTOWN RACECOURSE,
Stillorgan, Dublin *(5 miles/8 km north of Dublin on N11 Wexford road.)*
T 01 2893607
Picturesque track,close to Dublin.Excellent viewing. Impressive number of flat and National Hunt races.

SAILING

There are plenty of opportunities for sailing in Co Dublin, in the Howth, Malahide and Dun Laoghaire areas. For further information contact the Irish Sailing Association, 3 Park Road, Dun Laoghaire
T 01 2800239

WHERE TO STAY

HOTELS

AA RECOMMENDED

SEE UNDER WHERE TO EAT FOR ALL HOTEL RESTAURANTS WITH ROSETTES

DALKEY

ALKEY ISLAND ★★
oliemore Harbour *(2 miles from Dun aoghaire & Ferry Port on the coast road)*
01 2850377 F 01 2850141
eorgian-style building not far from the ld Coliemore Harbour. Sea views from ıost rooms and the excellent restaurant.
0 bedrooms ££££ No smoking in dining oom Night porter Parking

DUN LAOGHAIRE

IERRE ★★
ictoria Terrace, Seafront
01 2800291 F 01 2843332
riendliness is the keynote at this rominent seaside hotel. Bedrooms are ell equipped and comfortable.
2 bedrooms including some for non-nokers No smoking in dining room Night orter Parking

OYAL MARINE ★★★
Iarine Rd *(follow signs for Car Ferry)*
01 2801911 F 01 2801089
his Victorian hotel is a well known local ndmark, which provides a range of cilities including a restaurant, bars, and e popular Bay Lounge.
04 bedrooms ££££ Off peak rates No noking in dining room Lift Night porter arking Gardens

KILLINEY

OURT HOTEL ★★★
llliney Bay **T 01 2851622 F 01 2852085**
rom Dublin - N11 via Donnybrook & tillorgan, turn left off dual carriageway at affic lights 1.6km after Cabinteely, right at ext traffic lights)
you don't want to stay in Dublin, this ttractive hotel is just 12 miles away and near the fast commuter train service.
86 bedrooms inc 29 family rooms ££££ Parking Gardens

Finnstown Country House Hotel & Golf Course

FITZPATRICK CASTLE ★★★
T 01 2840700 F 01 2850207
Set in attractive grounds, this converted and extended castle has wonderful views over Dublin Bay.
90 bedrooms including some for non-smokers No smoking in dining room Lift Night porter Parking Gardens Leisure facilities

LUCAN

FINNSTOWN COUNTRY HOUSE HOTEL & GOLF COURSE ★★★
Newcastle Rd (on B200)
T 01 6280644 F 01 6281088
Lovely 18th-century mansion, set in 45 acres of woodland. Wide range of leisure facilities. The newest bedrooms are the garden suites, but all are good.
45 bedrooms including some for non-smokers ££££ Off-peak rates No smoking in dining room Night porter Parking Gardens Leisure facilities

LUCAN SPA ★★★
(just off N4, 7miles from Dublin centre)
T 01 6280494 F 01 6280841
This long-established hotel has every modern comfort, and is very popular for business conferences and meetings.
65 bedrooms including some for non-smokers ££ Off-peak rates No smoking in dining room Night porter Air conditioning Parking Gardens

PORTMARNOCK

PORTMARNOCK HOTEL & GOLF LINKS ★★★★
Strand Rd **T 01 8460611 F 01 8462442**
(Dublin Airport - N1, rdbt 1st exit, 2nd rdbt 2nd exit, next rdbt 3rd exit, T-junction turn left, over crossrds and cont, hotel is left past the Strand)
Awarded our Courtesy and Care award, this 19th-century mansion is set right beside the sea and overlooks golf links.
103 bedrooms Lift Night porter Parking

BED & BREAKFAST ACCOMMODATION

AA RECOMMENDED

CASTLEKNOCK

HERRYTREE LODGE QQQ
) Parkview, Castleknock
rom N2 R at Halfway House pub, pass arden Centre, then R.)
01 8203356 F 01 8203356
wo interconnecting reception rooms verlook fine gardens. The en suite edrooms are well equipped and bright.
bedrooms £ Parking

DUN LAOGHAIRE

CHESTNUT LODGE QQQQQ
2 Vesey Place, Monkstown
T 01 2807860 F 2801466
Quietly tucked away in a terrace of listed houses, there is much to appreciate in the house including lovely decorated plaster work in the lounges.
7 bedrooms, all no smoking ££ No smoking in dining room

GLENVIEW HOUSE QQQ
5 Glenview, Rochestown Av
(opposite Killiney shopping centre)
T 353 2855043
A modern house with comfortable bedrooms and a friendly landlady who provides a selection of home baking.
6 bedrooms, all no smoking £ No smoking in area of dining room Parking

LISADELL QQQ
212 Glenageary Road Upper
T 01 2350609 F 01 2350454
(from Dun Laoghaire seafront, pass People's Park onto Lower Glenageary Rd, cont to rdbt, L at 1st exit)
Modern detached house, within easy reach of Dublin's centre. Bedrooms are en suite and one is on the ground floor.
5 bedrooms No smoking in bedrooms £ Parking

HOWTH

INISRADHARC QQQ
Balkill Rd, Howth T 01 8322306
A pleasant house with comfortable bedrooms and pretty gardens. Not far from Dublin city and the airport.
3 bedrooms inc 2 family ££ No smoking Parking

SKERRIES

THE RED BANK QQQ
12 Convent Lane
T 01 8491005 F 01 8491598
Pleasant guest house in a pretty fishing port. Sample the seafood and other dishes served in the AA-rosetted restaurant of the same name just round the corner.
5 bedrooms £

WOODVIEW QQ
Margaretstown
T 01 8491528
Farmhouse in a quiet location near Ardgillan Park. Bedrooms are comfortable and you are welcome to join the family in the main lounge.
6 bedrooms £ No smoking in dining room/ lounge Parking 5 acres market garden

CAMPING & CARAVANNING

AA RECOMMENDED

CLONDALKIN

CAMAC VALLEY TOURIST CARAVAN & CAMPING PARK,
Corkagh Park
T 01 4640644
Four pennants site of 15 acres, suitable for touring caravan, motor caravans and tents. Open all year, with 163 touring pitches, electric hook-up, shower, launderette, children's playground, public telephone, fast food/take-away, shop on site.

SHANKILL

SHANKHILL CARAVAN PARK
Sherrington Park
T 01 2820011
A 7-acre site with 82 touring pitches and 9 statics. Open all year, electric hook-up, shower, electric shaver point, cold storage, Calor Gas, Camping Gaz, battery charging, public telephone, shop on site.
Within three miles of site: stables, golf course, boats for hire, cinema, fishing, launderette. Last departure noon.

Shankhill Caravan Par

WHERE TO EAT

RESTAURANTS

AA RECOMMENDED

FITZPATRICK CASTLE RESTAURANT ❀
Fitzpatrick Castle, Killiney
T 01 2840700 F 01 2850207
Set in a castle setting, this pleasant restaurant has lovely views over the grounds and Dublin Bay. Excellent cuisine.
Fixed L ££ ALC £££

LIGHTHOUSE RESTAURANT ❀❀
Dalkey Island Hotel, Coliemore Harbour, Dalkey T 01 2850377 F 01 2850141
As you would expect, the fish is excellent here, but those who prefer other dishes will not be disappointed.
Fixed L ££ ALC £££

THE OSBORNE ❀
Portmarnock Hotel, Strand Road, Portmarnock
T 01 8469611 F 01 8462442
Skilful cooking soundly based on fresh local produce. Pithivier of marinaded chicken livers, set on a morel sauce, for example, could precede suprême of chicken with a ginger stuffing, sliced on a nest of braised chicory with baby vegetables and butter sauce.
Fixed L £££

THE RED BANK RESTAURANT ❀
7 Church Street, Skerries
T 01 8491005 F 8491598
Although specialising in imaginatively served seafood of every description, meat-eaters are well served with Drogheda smoked loin of pork glazed with honey and servedwith a bitter sweet orange sauce, or perhaps fillet of Golden Vale venison with a plum and port wine sauce.
Dinner only.
Fixed D £££ ALC£££

PUBS, INNS & OTHER PLACES

ABBEY TAVERN,
Abbey Street, Howth ☎ **01 390282**
Overlooking the harbour, the old tavern specialises in fish. Traditional Irish music.

AN POITIN STIL PUB,
off Naas Road, Rathcoole
Shrine to local hero, Arkle the steeplechaser. A good range of food in the bar orrestaurant. Irish music several nights.

AYUMI-YA,
Newpark Centre, Newtownpark Avenue, Blackrock ☎ **01 2831767**
Authentic Japanese food.

BO'SUN BAR,
Monkstown ☎ **021 842172**
Good bar food. Book if you want to dine in the restaurant. Close to the Cobh ferry

CASA PASTA,
12 Harbour Road, Howth ☎ **01 8393823**
Overlooking harbour serving pasta, and other Mediterranean dishes. Best to book.

THE CULTURLANN,
32 Belgrave Square, Monkstown
Known for traditional music nights.

DANIEL'S,
34A Glasthule Road, Sandycove, Dun Laoghaire ☎ **01 2841027**
European dishes.

EASTERN TANDOORI,
New Street, Malahide ☎ **01 8454154**
Sister to the Dublin restaurant of the same name. Overlooks the marina.

FXB'S,
3 The Crescent, Monkstown ☎ **01 2846187**
Owned by a Dublin butcher, steaks are the speciality here. A sister to one in Dublin.

GIOVANNI'S,
Townyard Lane, Malahide ☎ **01 845 1733**
Popular family restaurant serving pasta and other dishes.

GUINEA PIG,
17 Railway road, Dalkey ☎ **01 2859055**
Accomplished seafood specialities; good value Early Bird menu.

JOHNNY FOX'S FAMOUS SEAFOOD PUB,
Dublin Mountains, Glencullen ☎ **01 2955647**
Speciality seafood, including wild Irish smoked salmon. Famous for Irish music.

KING SITRIC,
East Pier, Howth ☎ **01 8325235**
Former harbour master's house overlooking bay. Fish and seafood.

LA CASA STEP IN,
Stepaside ☎ **01 2956202**
Italian restaurant with Early Bird prices between 5.30-7.30pm Monday-Friday.

LAVINS,
The Old Village, Stillorgan ☎ **01 2883026**
Game and fish specialities.

MILL HOUSE,
Lower Kilmacud Rd, Stillorgan
☎ **01 2888672**
Daily carvery and standard bar food.

NA MARA,
Railway Station, Harbour Road, Dun Laoghaire ☎ **01 2806767**
Meat and fresh seafood in one of Ireland's earliest railway stations.

O'BRIEN'S IRISH SANDWICH BAR,
Dun Laoghaire Centre ☎ **01 2846250**
Good coffee, doorstep sandwiches and gourmet platters.

OLD SCHOOLHOUSE,
Swords ☎ **01 8402846**
Friendly bistro with home-cooked food.

PURTY KITCHEN,
Old Dunleary Rd, Monkstown
Dates from 1728. Emphasis on music and comedy. Interesting menus.

QUEENS PUB & LA ROMANA RESTAURANT, Castle Street, Dalkey
Atmospheric and popular pub. Simple bar menu plus an Italian restaurant.

STILLORGAN ORCHARD,
The Hill, Stillorgan ☎ **01 2888470**
Country cottage atmosphere in this pub close to a large shopping centre.

COUNTY KILDARE

Kildare is at the centre of Ireland's bloodstock industry - a bulwark of the country's economy - and in Co Kildare's rolling grasslands you will see those elegant thoroughbreds grazing or exercising. Many visitors are drawn here by the legendary annual races, and you attend you will certainly experience the very essence of part of the Irish way of life. The Curragh hosts all of Ireland's classic events - the Oaks, the Derby, and the St Leger, and Naas holds its big race meeting in April at Punchestown. However, horses aren't the whole of Kildare, and there are plenty of other sites of interest worth a look.

PRINCIPAL TOWNS

ATHY

Designated as a Heritage Town of Ireland, Athy takes its name from Baile Ath I (the ford of Ae). Nowadays it is a milling town with an innovative Catholic church built in 1965, but its history stretches back to the 13th century The 16th-century White Castle, once the home of the Earls of Kildare, still guards the river Barrowx

KILDARE

An ancient cathedral town steeped in history, dating from the sixth century when St Brigid founded a nunnery here. The magnificent cathedral was built over the site in the 13th-century and part of the castle belonging to the Earls of Kildare still stands in the town centre.

NAAS

Naas, Kildare's county town, enjoys the prosperity associated with the horse - the breeding, the racing and the tourism, and is a thriving, fairly industrial town. Naas (Nas na Ri) means the 'assembly place of the kings', and in early times it was the seat of the kings of Leinster - you can still see the motte, the stronghold of the kings, to the north of the town. Naas was fortified by the Normans, but was sacked in the 14th century, and the remains of one their castles was incorporated into the Protestant church.

MUST SEE

PANESE GARDENS
lly *(1 mile/1.5km south of Kildare)*
Ⓣ 045 522963
ese superb gardens at the Irish National ud were laid out in 1906 by the panese gardener Eida and his son noru. Considered by many to be the est in Europe, their design symbolically rtrays the life of man from the cradle to e grave. A garden centre offers bonsai ees for sale, and tea rooms provide stenance.

GH CROSSES
uth Kildare has several well preserved gh Crosses. The best are at Moone and astledermot. The Moone example stands er 5m (16ft) and depicts biblical scenes ane signposted near post office). There e two crosses at Castledermot, again rved with scriptural themes. Both sites and in the ruins of ancient monasteries.

NATIONAL STUD & NATIONAL HORSE MUSEUM
Tully *(1 mile/1.5km south of Kildare)*
Ⓣ 045 522963
Home to the National Stud, set up in 1902 by a Scot, William Hall-Walker, whose breeding methods were somewhat eccentric. Stallions and mares were paired according to their signs of the zodiac, and a horoscope was drawn up for every foal. If the omens were not good, the foal was sold. You are welcome to look around the palatial quarters inhabited by the resident stallions and their offspring. The National Horse Museum is also here.

BIG OUTDOORS

NALS
Kildare is traversed by two great canal stems, the Royal and Grand Canals, hich connect Dublin with the interior kelands and the Rivers Shannon and arrow.

EATLAND WORLD
llymore, near Rathangan **Ⓣ 045 60133**
interpretative centre explaining the gnificance of bogland ecology.

OBERTSTOWN
is is where to find out more about the nals. Trips run from the Old Canal Hotel, ilt in 1803 to serve canal-borne ssengers; candlelit dinners with music e held in summer.

HOMES & GARDENS

CASTLETON HOUSE,
Celbridge **Ⓣ 01 6288252**
Ireland's first and foremost Palladian mansion, built in the 1720s by William Conolly. Its elegant interior features fine 18th-century furniture and plasterwork by the Francini brothers.

LARCHILL ARCADIAN GARDENS
Kilcock *(19 miles/30km west of Dublin)*
Ⓣ/Ⓕ 01 6287354/6284580
A rare example of a ferne ornée, in the mid-18th century style. Ten follies are situated around a half mile/1km circular walk, and the parkland is populated with exotic breeds of farm animals.

MUSEUMS & ART GALLERIES

HERITAGE CENTRE
Athy **Ⓣ 0907 31694 Ⓕ 0907 31085**
Full of information on the town and the surrounding area, such as the powerful St Michel family from the 13th century and the Earls of Kildare who built the 16th-century White Castle.

STEAM MUSEUM
Lodge Park, Straffan **Ⓣ 01 6273155**
The model railway collection here depicts the development of the Irish locomotive since the 18th century. Also on display are full-size stationary engines working under full steam.

ESSENTIAL INFORMATION

TOURIST INFORMATION

dare Town
Ⓣ 045 522696 (June-mid-September)

LEPHONES
e area code for Naas is 045.
ernational dialling code 00 353 then 45 Naas.
e area code for Carlow (Co Carlow) is 03.
ernational dialling code 00 353 503.

CRAFTS

ood quality leatherwork, saddlery and dle-making can be found in one of the ain horse-breeding areas in Ireland.

SPORTS & LEISURE

ANGLING

The Grand Canal in Co Kildare is well known for its coarse fishing.

GOLF COURSES

THE K CLUB Straffan **Ⓣ 01 6273111**
Designed by Arnold Palmer to provide 'a blend of pleasure, skill and challenge'.
KILKEA CASTLE Castledermot
Ⓣ 0503 45156
Rolling parkland course with a 12th-century castle and a river
KNOCKANALLY Donadea, North Kildare
Ⓣ 045 869322 Ⓕ 045 869322
Designed by Noel Lyons Set in the grounds of a Palladian mansion.
Also:
BODENSTOWN Ⓣ 045 897096
HIGHFIELD Ⓣ 0405 31021
KILLEEN Ⓣ 045 866003
NAAS Ⓣ 045 874644/879509

HORSE RACING

THE CURRAGH
27 miles/43km SWt of Dublin on N7, 1 mile/1.5km past Newbridge). **Ⓣ 045 441205**
Home of Irish Flat racing, playing host to all five Irish Classics.
PUNCHESTOWN Naas
(20 miles/32km south of Dublin on N7, 2 miles/3km outside Naas). **Ⓣ 045 897704**
Almost rivals Cheltenham and Aintree.
Also:
NAAS RACECOURSE
Kingsfurze, Tipper Road, Naas **Ⓣ 045 97391**

WALKING

The canal system in Co Kildare provides a variety of towpath walks, radiating from Robertstown.

WHERE TO STAY

HOTELS

AA RECOMMENDED

The Kildare Hotel & Country Club

KILL

AMBASSADOR ★★★
(20/25 mins from Dublin centre on the N7 to the South and South West)
T 045 877064 F 045 877515
Comfortable, well appointed bedrooms. Various dining options.
36 bedrooms ££ Off-peak rates No smoking in dining room Night porter Parking

LEIXSLIP

LEIXSLIP HOUSE HOTEL ★★★
18th-century stone-built country house with many original features. The bedrooms are delightful . Good restaurant .
15 bedrooms ££££ Off peak rates Parking

MAYNOOTH

MOYGLARE MANOR ★★★
Maynooth **T 01 6286351 F 01 6285405**
Elegant Georgian house with convivial bar lounge. The restaurant has earned a high reputation
17 bedrooms ££££ Gardens No children under 12yrs

NEWBRIDGE

KEADEEN ★★★
T 045 431666 F 045 434402
Set in 8 acres of gardens, and just a mile from the famous Curragh Racecourse. Bedrooms are comfortable and well equipped.
37 bedrooms £££ Off-peak rates Night porter Air conditioning Parking Leisure facilities

PROSPEROUS

CURRYHILLS HOUSE ★★
(5 miles from N7 and N4)
T 045 868150 F 045 868805
A 19th-century house with a modern bedroom extension standing in 100 acres of gardens and parklands.
10 bedrooms £££ Off peak rates No smoking in dining room Parking Gardens Closed 23-31 Dec

STRAFFAN

BARBERSTOWN CASTLE ★★★
T 01 6288157 & 6288206 F 01 6277027
The castle has been elegantly refurbished and provides high standards of comfort. Superb restaurants.
26 bedrooms ££££ No smoking in dining room Night porter Parking Gardens No children under 12yrs

THE KILDARE HOTEL & COUNTRY CLUB ★★★★★
(from Dublin take N4, take exit for R406 hotel entrance is on right in Straffan)
T 01 6273333 F 01 6273312
In 330 acres of parkland beside the River Liffey, this very grand and luxurious hotel is known for its country elegance and the quality of its decor and furnishings.
46 bedrooms (10 in annexe) No smoking in dining room Lift Night porter Parking Gardens Leisure facilities

BED & BREAKFAST ACCOMMODATION

AA RECOMMENDED

ATHY

COURSETOWN HOUSE
Stradbally Rd *(turn off N78 at Athy or N80 at Stradbally on to R428)*
T 0507 31101 F 0507 31101
Victorian country house with spacious rooms. Convalescent or disabled guests are especially welcome.
5 bedrooms No smoking Parking No children under 8yrs

SILVERSPRING HOUSE
Firmount **T 045 868481**
Modern farmhouse situated in its own 25 acres of grounds. Gardens surround the house, complete with free-range chickens to provide the eggs for breakfast.
4 bedrooms, all no smoking No smoking in dining room ££ Parking Open Mar-Nov

CLANE

ASHLEY
Richardstown, Clane **T 045 868533**
(about 0.5 miles from the main Celbridge/Clane road (A403))
Charmingly set in a quiet wooded area, a complimentary car service is provided for guests attending local functions.
4 rooms £ No smoking in bedrooms

KILCULLEN

CHAPEL VIEW COUNTRY HOME
Gormanstown **T 045 481325**
(take N7 to Naas then N9 to Kilcullen, turn left at traffic lights, at crossroads follow signs)
Set in a stud farm location, this modern house is run in friendly style. The hosts offer good company as well as good cooking, and en suite bedrooms.
6 bedrooms £ Parking Dogs welcome Open 1 Mar-1 Dec

NAAS

MRS J MCLOUGHLIN
Setanta, Castlekeely, Caragh, Mondello Rd
(at Town House in Naas take Mondello Rd, Setanta is signposted from this road)
T 045 876481
Lots of peace and quiet at this modern farm bungalow set amidst 25 acres in a tranquil setting.
5 bedrooms, all no smoking No smoking in dining room £ Open Mar-Oct

Chapel View Country Home

M & E NOLAN QQ
Westown, Johnstown
(Johnstown is 4km from Naas on the Dublin road N7. Turn off N7 at Johnstown Garden Centre & follow signs to Farmhouse).
T 045 97006
A pleasant and comfortable house half a mile off the N7, surrounded by gardens and farmland.
5 bedrooms £ Closed 16 Dec-Jan

NEWBRIDGE

THE GABLES RYSTON QQQQ
Kilcullen Rd *(from Dublin exit M7 at junc 8)*
T 045 435330 F 045 435355
The Liffey curves gently by this well appointed house. Lovely views from the dining room make for a very relaxing stay.
9 bedrooms ££ Parking Leisure facilities Fishing Closed 23 Dec-2 Jan

STRAFFAN

BARBERSTOWN HOUSE QQQQ
Barberstown Cross
T 01 6274007 & 6274018
Georgian dwelling just 15m from Dublin and near to Goff's Bloodstock Sales, equestrian centres and a golf course.
5 bedrooms No smoking in dining room Parking Tennis Closed 21 Dec-5 Jan

WHERE TO EAT

RESTAURANTS

AA RECOMMENDED

BARBERSTOWN CASTLE
Straffan
T 01 6288157 & 6288206 F 01 6277027
Typical dishes include salad of smoked duck with walnut and balsamic vinaigrette, followed perhaps by peppered monfish tail with cherry tomato fondue and grilled chorizo sausage. Try classic crème brûlée for a classy finale.
FIXED £££

DERBY RESTAURANT
Keadeen Hotel, Newbridge
T 045 431666 F 045 434402
The fixed-price menu offers a good choice of robust dishes, including venison terrine, poached suprême of salmon with rich prawn sauce and puff pastry fleurons, and rack of Curragh lamb with mustard and poppy seed crust carved on a warm redcurrant jelly.
Fixed £££

BYERLEY TURK RESTAURANT
Kildare Hotel & Country Club, Straffan
(from Dublin take N4, take exit for R406 hotel entrance is on right in Straffan)
T 01 6273333 F 01 6273312
Named after one of the three Arab progenitors, in the male line, of every thoroughbred in the world, as you might expect, the restaurant is pretty classy, offering a classical carte, menu du jour, and an exclusive fixed price 'dining experience'. The cuisine is French with a distinctive Irish flavour, notable in a dish of pan-fried Clonakilty black and white pudding with colcannon potato and parsley jus. Hot soufflés are a speciality of the house, with flavours such as Bailey's and chocolate chip, or pistachio and Amaretto.
Fixed £££ ALC £££

LEIXLIP HOUSE HOTEL
Captain's Hill, Leixlip
T 01 6242268 F 01624 4177
The fixed-price four-course menu might include terrine of wild wood pigeon studded with pistachio nuts and served with an apricot chutney, followed by a soup or sorbet. Typical main courses are roast fillet of turbot with scallops and chive sauce, or fillet of beef with glazed shallots and garlic with rich red wine sauce.
FIXED L ££ D £££

MOYGLARE MANOR
Maynooth
T 01 6286351 F 01 6285405
Enjoy the elegant surroundings of this lovely restaurnant with food to match.
Fixed L ££ ALC £££

PUBS, INNS & OTHER PLACES

BALLYMORE INN,
Ballymore Eustace T 045 864585
Interesting mix of a plain village pub and an aesthetic restaurant, which is also reflected in the menus.

FLETCHER'S,
Commercial House, Naas T 045 897328
Understated traditional pub that is interesting in a stark 1930s sort of way.

MANOR INN,
Main Street, Naas T 045 8974741
Welcoming pub, decorated with racing mementoes - both horse and motor.

MOONE HIGH CROSS INN,
Bolton Hill, Moone T 0507 24112
Welcoming old country inn. Good bar food serving some traditional dishes.

COUNTY LOUTH

Co Louth is the smallest of the 32 counties of Ireland, but includes two of the region's major towns, Drogheda and Dundalk. Inland it has a gentle landscape of hills and lakes, which grows more dramatic towards the east where the Mountains of Mourne loom across Carlingford Lough. All around Drogheda, stretching into Co Meath, is a rich cluster of pre-historic and Celtic sites, great abbeys and castles.

PRINCIPAL TOWNS

DROGHEDA

Drogheda began as two towns, one each side of the mouth of the River Boyne, made one by the Anglo-Norman Hugh de Lacy and was the largest English town in Ireland in 1412.

Millmount, a vast, circular, grassy mound topped by a Martello tower, was first raised by the Celts, used by the Vikings for ceremonial purposes, and then fortified by the Normans. The town was also the scene of one of the most brutal of Cromwell's Irish massacres, in 1649, when an estimated 3,000 people were killed.

A shrine in St Peter's Roman Catholic Church, West Street, displays the embalmed head of St Oliver Plunkett, Archbishop of Armargh, who was disembowelled, beheaded and burnt in London in 1681.

DUNDALK

Dundalk is a border town, close to the most sensitive section of the Northern Ireland frontier. The huge bird reserve at Dundalk Bay is a wonderful sight with thousands of wading birds searching for food and shelter among the mudflats.

MUST SEE

BATTLE OF THE BOYNE SITE
4 miles/7km west of Drogheda
At the county border between Louth and Meath, a large orange and green sign marks the site where the armies of William of Orange and James 11 met in battle in 1690. The places where each side camped and where the river was crossed are also marked. A trail leaflet is available at the site.

CARLINGFORD VILLAGE
Co Louth's loveliest village shelters on the Cooley peninsula side of Carlingford Lough, and has a wealth of castles and white-washed cottages, some of which are eccentrically decorated by a local primitive painter.

MONASTERBOICE
North of Drogheda, off the N1
Don't miss Monasterboice, one of Ireland's best known Christian sites. Founded in the 6th century by St Buite (also called St Boyce), the area contains a 10th-century round tower, three high crosses, the ruins of two churches, a pre-Gothic sundial and a decorated grave slab, all in a walled graveyard. Look out for the South Cross (or Cross of Muiredach) - this impressive cross is 1,000 years old, stands nearly 20ft/6m high and bears numerous biblical scenes in deep relief.

GREAT FOR KIDS

MOSNEY HOLIDAY CENTRE
South of Drogheda
A complete antidote to the historical saturation of the Boyne Valley, the county's first subtropical funpool, including the Black Hole, Swamp Experience and the Dragon ride.

HISTORIC & ANCIENT SITES

CATHEDRAL OF ST PATRICK
Dundalk
Dundalk's most noteworthy building, a pastiche of King's College Chapel, Cambridge, with rich mosaics inside.

MELLIFONT ABBEY
(6 miles/10km west of Drogheda, signposted on unclassified road)
Ireland's first Cistercian monastery, founded in 1142. Remains include a substantial square gatehouse, ruins of a cloister, a two-storey octagonal lavabo and a 13th-century chapter house.

PROLEEK DOLMEN
Ballymascanlon
(4 miles/7km north-east of Dundalk)
This massive 5,000-year-old mushroom-like stone structure has a capstone weighing over 46 tonnes. Don't miss the Bronze Age wedge-shaped gallery grave located nearby.

MUSEUMS & ART GALLERIES

LOUTH COUNTY MUSEUM
The Carroll Centre, Jocelyn Street, Dundalk
T 042 27056
A major industrial heritage exhibition, supported by temporary exhibitions, on four floors in a restored late 18th-century warehouse. Group activities for children.

MILLMOUNT MUSEUM
Drogheda **T 041 36391**
18th-century military barracks housing historic relics, including painted banners of the old trade guilds, household and factory artefacts, and a leather-covered circular coracle.

ESSENTIAL INFORMATION

TOURIST INFORMATION

Jocelyn Street, Dundalk
T 042 35484 F 042 38070

TELEPHONES

The area code for Drogheda is 041.
The area code for Dundalk is 042.
International dialling code 00 353 then 41 for Drogheda.
International dialling code 00 353 then 42 for Dundalk.

CRAFTS

MILLMOUNT MUSEUM & CRAFT CENTRE
Drogheda **T 041 24722 or 37664**
Visitors can experience crafts first-hand here: ceramics, knitting, weaving, jewellery and furniture restoration. Other crafts displayed are: appliqué design work, Irish glass, pottery, basket work, woodwork and ceramics.

SPORTS & LEISURE

GOLF COURSES

SEAPOINT GOLF CLUB
Termonfeckin **T 041 22333 F 41 22331**
A links course designed by Des Smith, with golden sands to the eastern perimeter where water comes into play on six of the first nine holes.

Also:
COUNTY LOUTH T 041 22329
GREENORE T 042 73212/73678
KILLIN PARK T 042 39303

HORSE RACING

DUNDALK RACECOURSE
Dowdaliehill, Dundalk **T 041 753870**

SCENIC DRIVE

An excursion to the Cooley Peninsula, and the delightful lakeside village of Carlingford, is recommended. This is the setting for one of Ireland's greatest epics, Táin Bo Cuaigne, the Cattle Raid of Cooley, in which Queen Maeve, who is jealous of her husband's prize white bull, attempts to take the brown bull of Cooley by force. Cuchulainn, the Hound of Ulster, becomes the hero of the hour, but is mortally wounded during the battle.

WALKING

The Cooley Mountains, rising to 1,935ft/590m in Slieve Foyle, the highest peak of Carlingford Mountain, are a walker's paradise - try the 19 mile/30km Tàin Trail.

WHERE TO STAY

HOTELS

AA RECOMMENDED

DROGHEDA

BOYNE VALLEY HOTEL & COUNTRY CLUB ★★★
T 041 37737 F 041 39188
A new and extensive leisure/fitness centre with a 20-metre pool adds to the appeal of this hotel. Emphasis is placed on good food and attentive service.
35 bedrooms £££ Off-peak rates No smoking in dining room Leisure facilitites Gardens

THE WESTCOURT ★★★
West St T 041 30965 F 041 30970
(located on Main St, 'West St' approx 200yds from St Peters Church)
A long established hotel, recently rebuilt to a high standard. Although the absence of a lift is a disadvantage, the three floors of bedrooms are comfortable and well equipped.
27 bedrooms including some for non-smokers ££ Off-peak rates No smoking in dining room Night porter Parking Nightclub

DUNDALK

BALLYMASCANLON HOUSE ★★★
(north of Dundalk take T62 to Carlingford. Hotel is approx 3/4 mile)
T 042 71124 F 042 71598
A major construction programme is due to have been completed here, including a range of bedrooms and a leisure centre.
55 bedrooms £££ Off-peak rates No smoking in dining room Lift Night porter Parking Gardens Leisure facilities (incl golf course)

FAIRWAYS HOTEL & LEISURE CENTRE ★★★
Dublin Road *(on N1 2m S of Dundalk)*
T 042 21500 F 042 21511
48 bedrooms £££ Off-peak rates No smoking in dining room Night porter Parking Leisure facilitlies

IMPERIAL ★★
Park St T 042 32241 F 042 37909
Busy town-centre hotel on the Dublin-Belfast road offers a comfortable bar, a restaurant and coffee shop.
47 bedrooms No smoking in dining room Lift Night porter No smoking

BED & BREAKFAST ACCOMMODATION

AA RECOMMENDED

CARLINGFORD

JORDANS TOWNHOUSE & RESTAURANT QQQQQ
Newry St, Carlingford
T 042 73223 F 042 73827
A Premier Selected guest house, this lovely house provides the very highest standards of accommodation.
5 bedrooms, inc 1 family room ££ Parking Licensed Closed Jan 5-26

DROGHEDA

BOYNE HAVEN QQQQ
Dublin Rd *(opposite Rossnaree Hotel)*
T 041 36700
Recently extended modern bungalow, well screened from the noise and view of the road outside.
4 bedrooms, all no smoking ££ No smoking in dining room Parking

TULLYESKER COUNTRY HOUSE QQQQ
Tullyesker, Monasterboice
(3 miles N on Drogheda/Belfast road N1 on right just past Papal Cross)
T 041 30430 & 32624 F 041 32624
Large family-run house overlooking the Boyne Valley and Drogheda.
5 bedrooms, all no smoking ££ Parking No children under 10yrs Open 1 Mar-31 Oct

DUNDALK

ROSEMOUNT QQQ
Dublin Rd, Dundalk
(on N1, 2 kms S of Dundalk)
T 042 35878
6 bedrooms, inc 4 family £ No smoking in bedrooms or dining room Parking

Tullyesker Country House

WHERE TO EAT

PUBS, INNS & OTHER PLACES

ANCHOR BAR, Carlingford T 042 73106
Popular with the local sailing fraternity.

BRAKE TAVERN, Main St, Blackrock, T 042 21393
Welcoming seafront pub

MAGEE'S BISTRO, T 042 73751
Darcy Magee Centre, Carlingford
Wholesome cooking & wonderful views

MONASTERBOICE INN,
Monasterboice, nr Drogheda
Lovely old stone building standing amidst wonderful scenery. Good range of meals.

COUNTY MEATH

Meath is a county rich in ancient burial sites, abbeys and castles, and includes the Hills of Slane and Tara - the stuff of legends. From Slane the River Boyne sweeps south then north again, and here, in the Boyne Valley, is one of the most important Stone-Age sites in Europe, the large pre-Christian burial ground with its three great tumuli at Knowth, Newgrange and Dowth. Oldbridge, marks the site of the Battle of Boyne, where in 1690 the Protestant William III defeated the Catholic James II.

PRINCIPAL TOWNS

NAVAN

Situated where the River Boyne meet the Blackwater, Navan makes a good base from which to explore places of interest in the area. In the town itself, over the bridge, is Athlumney Castle, a15th-century tower house. The story goes that its last owner, Sir Lancelot Dowdall, a devout catholic, set fire to it himself, rather than see it fall into William's hands after the Battle of the Boyne. It is said that he watched his home burn all night, from the opposite bank of the river.

KELLS (CEANNANAS)

Kells is steeped in antiquity and was the birthplace of the Book of Kells. in the 9th century when monks from Iona in Scotland took refuge here having being evicted by the Vikings. They devoted their time to writing the magnificently illuminated book, a latin text of the four gospels, which was removed to the safety of Trinity College, Dublin, during the Cromwellian wars and can be sen there today.

TRIM

Designated as a Heritage Town of Ireland, Trim and Newtown a mile downstream.on the Boyne, has perhaps the greatest and most underestimated treasury of medieval monuments in Ireland.

MUST SEE

BOYNE VALLEY ARCHAEOLOGICAL PARK (BRU NA BOINNE) ☎ **041 24488**
(7 miles/11km south-west of Drogheda)
Compasses over 40 monuments, ranging from the massive Megalithic tombs of Newgrange, Knowth and Dowth to a variety of standing stones and earthworks. Newgrange, one of Europe's most important Stone Age sites, is open to the public- often queues for guided tours - which are worth waiting for. The passage grave, over 4,000 years old and pre-dating the Pyramids of Egypt, is an extraordinary sight. The mound over the tomb, constructed of water-rolled pebbles, rises to a height of 36ft/11m, and is surrounded by an incomplete circle of stones, and mysterious 'artwork' can be seen inside. A roof box incorporated in the structure allows the rays of the rising sun to penetrate a narrow slit and engulf the chamber with light - just briefly, once a year at the winter solstice. This is reproduced artificially for the benefit of visitors. Interpretative centre. Shop.

OLDCASTLE *(3 miles/five km SE)*
At Loughcrew stands a remarkable group of 30 or more Neolithic chambered cairns

HILL OF TARA
(8 miles/13km south of Navan)
☎ **046 25903** *(for guided tour information)*
Commanding majestic views,it was the seat of the High Kings. A passage tomb was built in the Stone Age. and has been a major political and religious centre.

BIG OUTDOORS

SLANE HILL *(13km west of Drogheda)*
It was here in 433, tradition has it, that St Patrick proclaimed the arrival of Christianity. The hill provides a splendid view of the Boyne Valley in fine weather.

GREAT FOR KIDS

NEWGRANGE FARM
Newgrange, Slane ☎ **041 24119**
A working farm with opportunities to handle animals, or even bottle feed a lamb, rural life museum, forge, herb garden, teas and picnic area.

HISTORIC & ANCIENT SITES

BECTIVE ABBEY
Situated between Navan and Trim
One of the earliest examples of a Cistercian foundation in Ireland. Most of the ruins date from the 15th century, and stand in a gloriously peaceful setting in a field by the Knightsbrook River.

CASTLE Trim *(town centre)*
One of the most imposing and the largest Anglo-Norman fortress in Ireland. The ruins cover about a hectare and include a vast keep flanked by rectangular towers. If there are not many people around, try out the wonderful ehco from the Echo Gate towards the old cathedral across the river. Nearby are the ruins of the Royal Mint and a gaunt skeleton called the Yellow Steeple, dating from the 14th century, the last remnants of an Augustinian abbey destroyed in 1649.

HOMES & GARDENS

BUTTERSTREAM GARDENS
Kildalkey Road, Trim ☎ **046 36017**
A wonderful series of garden 'rooms' by inspirational plant collector and garden designer Jim Reynolds, with some fine roses, old and new, and 'tantalising herbaceous plants'.

GLEBE GARDENS
Ratoath ☎ **01 8256015/8256219**
Two contrasting houses and gardens, Glebelands, dating from 1813 with a mature, tree-filled garden, and Glebewood, built in 1990, with a 'sculptured' garden on a formerly flat site.

MUSEUMS & ART GALLERIES

TRIM HERITAGE CENTRE
☎ **046 31238/37227**
The Power & The Glory, a multi-media exhibition portraying medieval Trim, and the lives of the knights, Norman bishops and ordinary townsfolk. (Also in French, German and Italian.)

ESSENTIAL INFORMATION

TOURIST INFORMATION

Mill Street, Trim ☎ **046 37111**

TELEPHONES

Area code for Navan is 046
International dialling code 00 353 then 46 for Navan.
Area code for Drogheda (Co Louth) is 041.
International dialling code 00 353 then 41 for Drogheda.

COACH TOURS

ENFIELD COACHES Rathcore, Enfield
☎ **0405 55666 Mobile 088 2706160**
Boyne Valley Tours, day tours with guide, Tourist Board approved.

SPORTS & LEISURE

GOLF COURSES

COUNTY MEATH *(Trim)* ☎ **046 31463**
LAYTOWN & BETTYSTOWN ☎ **041 27170**
MOOR-PARK ☎ **046 27661/27181**
ROYAL TARA, ☎ **046 25508/25244**

HORSE RACING

FAIRYHOUSE RACECOURSE Ratoath
12 miles/19km north-west of Dublin
☎ **01 8 256167**
Highlight of this glorious country venue is the three-day Easter Festival, (Irish Grand National). All year racing.
Also:
LAYTOWN RACECOURSE ☎ **041 23425**
NAVAN RACECOURSE ☎ **046 21350**

SCENIC DRIVE

This part of the eastern coast of Ireland may lack the grandeur of the north and west, but there is pleasant gentle coastal scenery with sandy beaches and shingle

WALKING

BATTLE OF THE BOYNE SITE
Co Louth & Co Meath
At Townley Hall, the Forest and Wildlife Service has developed a way-marked trail that takes the walker close to the site of the Battle of the Boyne, and gives views over the valley. The walk up the wooded banks of the river is steep in places. A trail leaflet is available at the site.

WHERE TO STAY

HOTELS

AA RECOMMENDED

SEE UNDER WHERE TO EAT FOR ALL HOTEL RESTAURANTS WITH ROSETTES

KELLS (CEANANNUS)

HEADFORT ARMS ★★
Ceanannus
T 046 40063 & 40121 F 046 40587
18 bedrooms No smoking in dining room Night porter Parking Gardens

NAVAN (AN UAIMH)

ARDBOYNE HOTEL ★★★
T 046 23119
A modern hotel set in its own attractive gardens in a quiet situation off the Dublin Road.
27 bedrooms (25 family) No smoking area in restaurant ££ Parking

SLANE

CONYNGHAM ARMS ★★
(from N2 turn onto N51, hotel is 25 yards on the left) **T 041 24155 F 041 24205**
This hotel has recently had five new bedrooms with lovely bathrooms added. Public rooms include the Estate Agent's Restaurant.
16 bedrooms ££ No smoking in dining room Parking Gardens

BED & BREAKFAST ACCOMMODATION

AA RECOMMENDED

DULEEK

ANNESBROOK COUNTRY HOUSE QQQ
Annesbrook *(N2 from Dublin, 7kms from Ashbourne take R152, house signposted)*
T 041 23293 F 041 230
18th-century country house set in 10 acres of gardens, orchards and woodland. Bedrooms and lounges are spacious.
bedrooms £ No smoking in dining room Parking Open May-September Closed Xmas & Easter Restricted Service October-April (open for 6+ bookings)

DUNSHAUGHLIN

OLD WORKHOUSE QQQQ
Ballinlough **T 01 8259251**
(on N3 road 1mile E of Dunshaughlin village)
Converted workhouse with four attractive bedrooms and a pleasant lounge and drawing room. Welcoming atmosphere and excellent cooking
4 bedrooms, all no smoking £

NAVAN (AN UAIMH)

KILLYON QQQQ
Dublin Rd **T 046 71224 F 046 72766**
(on N3, River Boyne side, opposite Ardboyne Hotel)
Luxurious house with fine views of the River Boyne. Bedrooms are comfortable and the lounge is pretty. Wide range of home-cooking offered.
4 bedrooms incl 2 for non-smokers £ No smoking in dining room/ lounges Parking

OLDCASTLE

BEECHES QQQ
Lough Bane **T 044 66164** *(L142 from Kells to Lough Bane via Crossakiel)*
Magnificent house on the shores of Lough Bane. Built and furnished in the Italian style, with luxurious bedrooms.
3 bedrooms, all no smoking £ No smoking in dining room No smoking in 1 lounge Parking Fishing Closed 15 Sept -15 Oct Closed 6 Jan-15 Feb

WHERE TO EAT

PUBS, INNS & OTHER PLACES

LOFT,
6 Trimgate Street, Navan **T 046 71755**
Fully licensed restaurant with laid back atmosphere, jazz and soul music. Typical dishes include steaks and Cajun chicken.

O'CONNELLS,
Skyrne, nr Tara **T 046 25122**
Unspoilt country pub near the old castle at the top of the hill.

O'SHAUGHNESSY'S,
Market St, Ceanannas Mor (Kells)
T 046 41110
Just behind St Columba's Church (where the copy of The Book of Kells is housed). Traditional pub grub at good prices.

THE ROADHOUSE,
Rathdrinagh, Beauparc, Navan
T 046 24320
Welcoming pub with impromptu music and decent food.

SNAIL BOX,
Kilmoon, Ashbourne **T 01 8354277**
No food at this friendly local but there is live music on Fridays.

STATION HOUSE,
Kilmesson **T 046 25239**
Down to earth setting for fresh, local produce.

COUNTY WICKLOW

Co Wicklow is a favourite retreat for Dublin's citizens, among other visitors, and it is easy to see why. The Wicklow Mountains, reaching 3,281ft/1,000m in Lugnaquilla (Ireland's third highest peak) provide the most beautiful, wild and unpopulated scenery. A drive around the Sally Gap, taking in Glencree and Glenmacass is recommended, and there are some lovely stretches of sandy coastline southwards from Bray, and at Brittas Bay south of Wicklow Head. There's no shortage of tourist attractions, restaurants and hotels either.

PRINCIPAL TOWN

WICKLOW

The county town is small, pleasant and not far south of Dublin. The River Varty meets the sea here, opening into a lagoon divided from the sea by a grassy spit. The safe harbour attracted the Vikings, who took over what was St Mantan's 5th-century monastic settlement, giving the town the name Wykinglo. For hundreds of years the Irish clans fought it out with the Anglo-Normans here, and the remains of the Norman stronghold, Black Castle, can still be seen on a rocky promontory above the harbour. Other sights of interest are a ruined 13th-century friary, and the parish church with its Byzantine dome and fine Romanesque doorway.

MUST SEE

AVOCA VILLAGE
(2.5 miles/4km south of Avondale)
A little village in a picturesque valley, where the confluence of two rivers, the Avonberg and the Avonmore inspired Thomas Moore to write his poem The Meeting of the Waters in 1807. Avoca is now better known as the location of the BBC TV series Ballykissangel. The village set includes the Church of St Mary, and Fitzgeralds, the pub otherwise known as the Fountain Bar. (Also Avoca Handweavers - see page 00).

WICKLOW MOUNTAINS
These wild hills on Dublin's doorstep are a great boon to city dwellers. From the southern suburbs you can gaze at them on clear days; by public transport or by car they take just half an hour to reach. The rounded hills of ice-eroded schist and granite enfold a strange mixture of bleak, awesome glens and boggy plateaux, interspersed with welcoming Shangri-La valleys like Glendalough or the Vale of Avoca. The improbable cones of the Great and Little Sugar Loaf Mountains protrude suddenly from the surrounding contours, their granite caps more resilient than the rest.

GLENDALOUGH
(10miles/16km west of Wicklow)
☎ 0404 45351/2 (Interpretative Centre)
Glendalough is the setting of Ireland's most important early Christian settlement, founded by St Kevin in the 6th century. It grew into a centre of learning and its fame spread throughout Europe. Among the ruins are a near-perfect round tower, a church with fine Irish Romanesque decoration, an oratory (St Kevin's Kitchen) and a 10th-century cathedral. An excellent interpretative centre is run at the site by the Office of Public Works.

POWERSCOURT
Enniskerry, near Bray **☎ 01 2867676**
The main block of this Palladian-style house was gutted by fire in 1974, but has recently been restored, incorporating a restaurant, craft shops and an interpretative area. The gardens are among the finest in Europe, including English, Italian and Japanese sections, enhanced by sculptures, a fountain and terraces, formal flower beds and tall conifers. The grounds include play areas, a garden centre, trails and picnic sites. The Powerscourt Waterfall, at 390ft/120m, is the highest in Ireland.

BIG OUTDOORS

DEVIL'S GLEN
(in the Vartry)
A deep chasm with craggy, overgrown sides. On entering the glen the river plunges nearly 100ft/30m into the Devil's Punchbowl. There are good waterfall views from well-sited paths.

WICKLOW HEAD
(2 miles/3km south-east of the town)
Enjoy the fine views from this point, which has no fewer than three lighthouses. Further south the sandy beaches of the 'Silver Strand' extend down the coast to Brittas Bay and Mizen Head.

WICKLOW MOUNTAINS NATIONAL PARK
Includes two nature reserves, run by the Office of Public Works. One protects the Glenealo Valley including the Upper Lake, bog and heathland, which is an important habitat for moorland birds and other wildlife. The other conserves the oak woods of Glendalough Nature Reserve.

GREAT FOR KIDS

ANNAMOE LEISURE PARK
(between Roundwood & Laragh)
☎ 0404 45470
Trout fishing, canoeing, children's play areas, picnic and barbecue facilities.

BEACHES
Blue Flag awards for maintaining high environmental standards have been awarded to: Brittas Bay South & Brittas Bay North.

CLARA VILLAGE
The smallest village in Ireland, with two houses, a church and a school, set in a beautiful valley south-east of Glendalough.

CLARA LARA FUNPARK
(between Rathdrum & Laragh)
☎ 0404 46161
Adventure playground, junior play area, fishing, crazy golf, picnic and barbecue facilities on the banks of the Avonmore River.

GLENROE OPEN FARM
Kilcoole **☎ 01 2872288 Ⓕ 01 2872298**
Featured in the TV series Glenroe, with attractions from the programme alongside farm animals, which children can handle, and a collection of farm implements. Picnic area.

HOMES & GARDENS

AVONDALE HOUSE
Rathdrum **☎ 0404 46111**
Avondale is the restored home of the nationalist leader Charles Stewart Parnell (1846-91). Part of the house is devoted to a museum.

KILMACURRAGH
Rathdrum **☎ 01 6613111**
A beautiful 19th-century arboretum, planted by Thomas Acton along with David Moore and his son, Sir Frederick Moore.

KILLRUDDERY HOUSE & GARDENS
Bray **☎ 01 2863405/2862777**
A French-style garden dating from the 1680s with two canals running between the house and an avenue of lime trees. Later additions include a large rock garden and Victorian conservatory.

MOUNT USHER GARDENS
Asford *(on the main Dublin/Wicklow road)*
☎ 0404 40116
A fine 'wild garden', along the banks of the River Vartry. Laid out in 1868, it contains rare trees, shrubs and flowers from all over the world, including 70 species of eucalyptus.

NATIONAL GARDENS EXHIBITIONS CENTRE
Calumet Nurseries **☎ 01 2819890**
(7 miles/11km south of Bray - turn off the N11 at Kilpedder)
Keen gardeners will enjoy the 15 different gardens created by Ireland's leading landscapers and designers, with several water features and a pretty man-made mountain stream. There is a garden centre, lectures and guided tours.

RUSSBOROUGH HOUSE
Blessington **☎ 045 65239**
A mid 18th-century mansion with sumptuous plasterwork, home to the Beit Art Collection (works by Gainsborough, Murillo and Velasquez). Late spring visitors will be able to enjoy the lovely rhododendron gardens.

ESSENTIAL INFORMATION

TOURIST INFORMATION

WICKLOW COUNTY TOURISM
St Manntans House, Kilmantin Hill, Wicklow
T 0404 66058 F 0404 66057

MIDLANDS-EAST TOURISM
Rialto House, Fitzwilliam Square, Wicklow
T 404 69117 F 404 69118

TELEPHONES

Area code for Arklow is 0402.
International dialling code 00 353 then 402 for Arklow.
Area code for Wicklow is 0404.
International dialling code 00 353 then 404 for Wicklow.

CRAFTS

Look out for hand spinning and weaving, wall hangings, batik work, pottery, woodcraft, traditional furniture reproduction, gold and silver jewellery, basket-weaving and rushwork.

ARKLOW POTTERY
Arklow T 0402 32401
Factory shop with functional and decorative pottery. Open 7 days.

AVOCA HANDWEAVERS
Kilmacanogue & Avoca T 0402 35105
Handweaving and pottery. Good restaurant. Open 7 days.

CRAFTS COMPLEX
Glendalough T 0404 45156
Gallery with weaving and jewellery. Open 7 days. Tearooms.

GUIDED TOURS

VIEWS UNLIMITED
8 Prince of Wales Terrace, Bray
T 01 2856121/2860164 F 01 2861330.
Guided tours along the DART (Dublin Area Rapid Transit) electric trains, with an award-winning commentary.

SPORTS & LEISURE

ANGLING

Principal stretches for small brown trout are River Aughrim, Avonmore, Avonbeg, Dargle, Liffey (below Golden Falls Lake), Slaney (below Baltinglass), Vartry Reservoir at Roundwood and the Poulaphouca Lakes. The latter is also good for coarse fishing. For sea trout, try the lower reaches of the Dargle, the Potters River (night fishing) and the Ennereilly River. There is a new all-year trout angling lake at Aughrim (tel 0402 36552), suitable for disabled anglers.
The coast from Bray to Arklow has now been recognised by the Tourist Board as a major shore angling coast: whiting and codling in winter, and bass and flat fish in summer.

CYCLING

GLENDALOUGH MOUNTAIN BIKE TREKS
T 01 6611348 or 087 609362
From May until the endof October.

CYCLE HIRE

BLACK CYCLES
Upper Main Street, Arklow T 0402 31898

HILLCREST HIRE
Main Street, Blessington T 045 865066

E R HARRIS & SONS
87 Greenpark Road, Bray T 01 2863357

J KENNY
Laragh T 0404 45236

T MCGRATH
Main Street, Rathdrum T 0404 46172

JOHNNY PRICE'S GARAGE
Main Street Roundwood T 01 2818128

WICKLOW HIRE SERVICE
Wicklow T 0404 68149

GOLF COURSES

POWERSCOURT Powerscourt Estate, Enniskerry T 01 2760503 F 01 2761303
A lovely course set in ancient parkland with an elegant Georgian-style clubhouse.

RATHSALLAGH
Dunlavin T 45 403316 F 45 403295
The course was designed by Christy O'Connor and Captain Peter McEvoy to satisfy the most discriminating golfers and is set amid mature parkland.

Also:

ARKLOW T 0402 32492

BLAINROE T 0404 68168

DRUIDS GLEN T 01 2873600

OLD CONNA, Bray T 282 6055

ROUNDWOOD T 01 2818488

WICKLOW T 0404 63379

WOODENBRIDGE T/F 0402 35202

EQUESTRIAN CENTRES

BALLINTESKIN FARM
near Wicklow T 0404 69441

BEL AIR RIDING SCHOOL
Ashford T 0404 40109

BLESSINGTON ADVENTURE CENTRE
T 045 865092

BRENNANSTOWN RIDING SCHOOL LTD
Hollybrook, Bray T 01 2863778

BROOMFIELD RIDING SCHOOL
Tinahely T 0402 38117

BROOM LODGE STABLES
Nun's Cross, Ashford T 0404 40404

CASTLE HOWARD EQUESTRIAN CENTRE
Avoca T 0402 35164

CLARABEG RIDING HOLIDAYS
Roundwood T 0404 46461

COOLADOYLE RIDING SCHOOL
Newtownmountkennedy T 01 2819906

DEVILS GLEN EQUESTRIAN CENTRE
Ashford T 0404 40637

FOREST WAY RIDING HOLIDAY
Roundwood T 01 2818429

LARAGH TREKKING CENTRE LTD
T 0404 45282

OAKFIELD EQUESTRIAN CENTRE
Enniskerry T 01 2829296

THE WICKLOW TRAIL RIDE
Calliaghstown (near Blessington)
T 01 4589236

HORSE DRAWN CARAVANS

CLISSMAN HORSE DRAWN CARAVANS
T 0404 48188

POLO

POLO WICKLOW, *c/o Herbst Group,* Wicklow Town T 0404 67159

SCENIC DRIVES

The road from Sally Gap to Laragh rises and falls wonderfully, with views across the Cloghoge Valley to War Hill. The road goes south through rugged mountain land into forest plantations and passes Glenmacnass, a deep glen formed by glaciers, with a magnificent waterfall.

WALKING

Co Wicklow provides plenty of scope, all year round, for the active and occasional walker. Guide books and maps are available from the Tourist Board.

THE WICKLOW WAY extends from Marlay Park, south of Dublin, to Clonegal, Co Carlow, a distance of 132km/82 miles. The walk takes 8-10 days, and accommodation can be found in hostels and B&B establishments along the way, which should be booked in advance. The route is mainly way-marked through forests, along old bog roads and up steep mountain tracks, including views of Luggala, Glendalough and wild Glenmalure.
If you want to do the walk, get a copy of the Wicklow Way Map/Guide by East West Mapping T 054 77835.

WHERE TO STAY

HOTELS

AA RECOMMENDED

BLESSINGTON

OWNSHIRE HOUSE ★★★
n N81) **T 045 865199 F 045 865335**
et in lovely gardens, this small Georgian otel is being sensitively restored
5 bedrooms (11 in annexe) ££ No noking in dining room Night porter arking Gardens Leisure facilities Closed 22 ec-6 Jan

BRAY

OYAL ★★★
ain St **T 01 2862935 F 01 2867373**
oing south on N11. First exit for Bray, 2nd :it from rdbt, through 2 sets traffic lights across idge, Main Street, hotel on the left side)
n the main street near the seafront. ccellent leisure centre.
I bedrooms £££ Off-peak rates Lift ight porter Parking Leisure facilities reche

ENNISKERRY

NISCREE LODGE HOTEL & ESTAURANT ★★
encree Valley
ff N11) **T 01 2863542 F 01 2866037**
omfortable lodge in the Glencree Valley. ar has a blazing log fire when cold
) bedrooms ££ No smoking in dining om Parking Gardens

Tinakilly Country House & Restaurant

GLENDALOUGH

THE GLENDALOUGH ★★★
T 0404 45135 F 0404 45142
Many bedrooms and the charming restaurant have lovely views
44 bedrooms £££ Off-peak rates No smoking in dining room Lift Parking Fishing Closed 1 Dec-Jan

RATHNEW

HUNTER'S ★★★
(1mile from village off N11)
T 0404 40106 F 0404 40338
One of Ireland's oldest coaching inns, with plenty of character as well as modern amenities.Lovely gardens. Restaurant.
16 bedrooms No smoking in dining room Parking Gardens

TINAKILLY COUNTRY HOUSE & RESTAURANT ★★★
(500m from town on R750 Wicklow rd)
T 0404 69274 F 0404 67806
An elegant house set in seven acres of gardens. Some bedrooms have four-poster. Superb country house cuisine.
29 bedrooms ££££ Off-peak rates Parking Gardens Leisure facilities

WOODENBRIDGE

WOODENBRIDGE ★★
(between Avoca & Arklow)
T 0402 35146 F 0402 35573
Comfortable hotel, beautifully situated in the Vale of Avoca
23 bedrooms ££ Off-peak rates No smoking in the dining room Lift Night porter Parking Gardens Snooker Children's facilities Conference/banqueting suite

BED & BREAKFAST ACCOMMODATION

AA RECOMMENDED

ARKLOW

LLINSKYDUFF FARMHOUSE QQ
n N, off N11) **T 0402 32185**
omely modern farmhouse on the itskirts of Arklow near the sea.
bedrooms, all no smoking No smoking in ning room Parking No Children under 12 165 acres hens tillage Open Jun-Sep

AVOCA

SHDENE QQQ
ockanree Lower *(turn off R752 into lage. House 1 mile on right beyond Avoca ındweavers on Avoca/Redcross road)*
T 0402 35327 F 0402 35327
eal for touring Co Wicklow. Very good eakfasts here and comfortable rooms
bedrooms, all no smoking £ No smoking dining room Parking Tennis (grass) Open ır-Oct

SHEEPWALK HOUSE QQQQ
Beech Rd **T 0402 35189 F 0402 35189**
(W off N11, Beech Road to Avoca, 2 miles from Arklow, 2 miles from Avoca)
18th-century house overlooking Bay. Welcoming bedrooms and a sun lounge.
8 bedrooms £ Parking Open Feb-Nov

OLD COACH HOUSE QQQ
(take road from Rathdrum follow signs for Avoca, Meeting of the Waters 500yds beyond on right) **T 0402 35408 F 0402 35720**
Tastefully restored coaching inn with a warm atmosphere
6 bedrooms including some for non-smokers £ No smoking in area of dining room Licensed Children welcome

DUNLAVIN

TYNTE HOUSE QQQ
(from N81 at Hollywood Cross turn R at Dunlavin, follow signs for Tynte House, past market house in the centre of the town)
T 045 401561 F 045 401586
Farmhouse standing in a country village, with 200 acres of farmland behind
7 bedroms including some for non-smokers £ No smoking in dining room Children welcome Closed 23 Dec-2 Jan

GLENEALY

BALLYKNOCKEN HOUSE QQ
(turn right after Jet garage in Ashford (N11)
T 0404 44627 & 44614 F 0404 44627
Farmhouse in 270 acres of farmland.
7 bedrooms, all no smoking £ Licensed No smoking in dining room Parking Tennis court Closed 14 Nov-14 Mar

LARAGH

CARMEL'S ANNAMOE ◘◘◘
T 0404 45297
Pleasant bungalow.Personal touches create a warm feeling of care of attention.
4 bedrooms £ Open Easter-Oct

GLEANN ALIBHE ◘◘◘
(Glendelough main road beside post office)
T 0404 45236
Set in the village beside the Post Office. Good for those who want to walk.
3 bedrooms, all no smoking No smoking in area of dining room £ Parking

RATHDRUM

ABHAINN MOR HOUSE ◘◘◘
Corballis **T 0404 46330**
(at crossroads on R752, Rathdrum/Avoca road 2k S of Rathdrum)
Set in peaceful surroundings, there is a spacious sitting room and conservatory.
6 bedrooms include 2 family £ No smoking in bedrooms or dining room Childrens facilities Tennis court (grass) Parking

AVONBRAE HOUSE ◘◘◘
(200 yds on Laragh Road after leaving village) **T/F 0404 46198**
Rose gardens surround this rural retreat. Delightful bedrooms. Pre-book dinner
7 bedrooms include 2 family ££ Indoor swimming pool (heated) Parking

WICKLOW

LISSADELL HOUSE ◘◘◘
Ashtown Ln **T 0404 67458**
(exit N11 at Beehive pub onto R751, premises signposted)
Comfortable house standing in 285 acres. Pleasant bedrooms and lounges
4 bedrooms, all no smoking £ No smoking in dining room Open Mar-Nov

THE OLD RECTORY COUNTRY HOUSE & RESTAURANT ◘◘◘◘
(on R750, 1 mile S of Rathnew)
T 0404 67048 F 0404 69181 Mar-Dec
Recent winner of the AA Guesthouse of the Year Award. Cooking utilises organic vegetables and fresh local produce.
7 bedrooms ££££ No smoking in dining room and 1 lounge Licensed Parking Leisure facilities

CAMPING & CARAVANNING

AA RECOMMENDED

DONARD

MOAT FARM CARAVAN & CAMPING PARK
Signposted. Nearby town: Baltinglass
T 045 404727
Q award/3 pennants. Open all year. Booking advisable bank holidays and Jun-Aug. Last arrival 22.30hrs. Last departure noon. A 2.75-acre site with 40 touring pitches. Electric hook up, shower, electric shaver point, launderette, hairdrier, separate TV room, cold storage, children's playground, Calor Gas, Camping Gaz, battery charging, public telephone, baby care, picnic area, dog exercise area on site, shop on site, disabled facilities. *Facilities within three miles of site: stables, golf course, fishing*

ROUNDWOOD

ROUNDWOOD CARAVAN PARK
Signposted. Nearby town: Bray
T 01 2818163
4 pennants Open Apr-Sep. Booking advisable Jun-Aug. Last arrival 11.00hrs. Last departure noon. A 5-acre site with 45 touring pitches and 33 statics. Campers kitchen and dining room. Electric hook up, shower, electric shaver point, launderette, hairdrier, games room, separate TV room, cold storage, children's playground, Calor Gas, Camping Gaz, battery charging, public telephone, picnic area, shop on site. *Facilities within three miles of site: stables, golf course, fishing*

WHERE TO EAT

RESTAURANTS

AA RECOMMENDED

ENNISCREE LODGE HOTEL ❁
Enniskerry **T 01 2863542 F 01 2866037**
Wonderful views of Glencree from this hotel restaurant, where the menus offer a good range of dishes. Attention to detail adds to the experience, noticed in the quality of the bread, and the carefully cooked vegetables.
Fixed L ££ ALC £££

HUNTER'S HOTEL ❁
Newrath Bridge, Rathnew **T 0404 40106**
Local produce is a feature of the menus at this traditional-style hotel restaurant Look out for locally caught fish, Wicklow lamb and comforting puddings using home-grown produce.
Fixed L ££ ALC £££

THE RESTAURANT ❁❁
Tinakilly Country House, Rathnew
T 0404 69274 F 0404 67806
Local produce is used to good effect in a varied range of dishes, including wild Wicklow venison with cabbage, pancetta and Meaux mustard cream.Other highlights are the delicious home-made bread, irresistible puddings, and the excellent wine list.
Fixed L ££ D£££ ALC £££

WOODENBRIDGE HOTEL ❁
Woodenbridge *(between Avoca & Arklow)*
T 0402 35146 F 0402 35573
Dishes might include pan-fried medallion of pork Provençal, roast half Peking duck with peach and walnut stuffing, and poached darne of salmon on a red onion marmalade with cream of saffron sauce.
Fixed £££

PUBS, INNS & OTHER PLACES

AVOCA HANDWEAVERS RESTAURANT
Kilmacanogue . Informal restaurant.

BLAZERS, 36 Main St, Bray **T 01 2869798**

COOPERS,
The Harbour, Greystones **T 01 2873914**

LARAGH INN, Laragh **T 0402 12345**
Well-known dining pub

THE MEETING OF THE WATERS INN,
Avonmore **T 0402 35226**
Renowned for outdoor traditional music

OLD RECTORY, Wicklow **T 0404 67048**
Dinner is served in one sitting at 8pm.

ROUNDWOOD INN,
Roundwood **T 01 281 8107**

TREE OF IDLENESS,
Seafront, Wicklow **T 01 2863498**
Greek-Cypriot restaurant on the seafront

WICKLOW HEATHER RESTAURANT
Laragh, Glendalough **T 0404 45157**

THE SOUTHEASTERN COUNTIES

COUNTIES CARLOW, KILKENNY, TIPPERARY, WATERFORD AND WEXFORD

In contrast to some of the the wilder regions of Ireland, the Southeast is characterised by rich, fertile pastureland, encompassing Tipperary's prosperous Golden Vale.The comparatively gentle landscape is ideal for activity holidays, and cycling, riding, fishing and watersports are all popular here. Fine beaches and a kind climate attract plenty of holiday-makers from both Ireland and abroad, to what remain fairly low-key resorts, small and characterful, apart from Tramore, which offers more in the way of amusements. Naturalists will particularly appreciate a trip to the reclaimed Wexford Slobs, Hook Head Peninsula or the Saltee Islands.Walkers may be lured inland by the the hill ranges of the Comeragh, Blackstairs and Knockmealdown Mountains. Popular walking routes include the South Leinster Way, through Carlow and Kilkenny, including the lovely Nore and Barrow valleys, and the Munster Way, along theTipperary/Waterford border, over the spectacularVee Gap and through the valley of the Nire. If you're fascinated by ancient abbeys and castles, there is much to see. Chief among the area's attractions is the Rock of Cashel, an outcrop of limestone in the middle of the plain topped with a magnificent complex of ruins.

EVENTS & FESTIVALS

January

Wellington Race and Parade
Castlecomer, Co Kilkenny

March

St Patrick's Day (17th March)
Parades and festival of traditional song and dance

April

Hunter Trials
Kilmoganny, Co Kilkenny

Hunter Trials
North Kilkenny, Co Kilkenny

Festival of Motor Sport
Inistioge, Co Kilkenny

May

AIMS Choral Festival
New Ross, Co Wexford

Goresbridge Boat Rally
Goresbridge, Co Kilkenny

Kells Gymkhana
Kells, Co Kilkenny

Mini Jazz Festival
Kilkenny City, Co Kilkenny

Thomastown Horse Show,
Thomastown, Co Kilkenny

June

Ballyfoyle
Gymkhana, Co Kilkenny

"The Cat Laughs" International Comedy Festival
Kilkenny, Co Kilkenny

County Wexford Strawberry Fair,
Co Wexford

Eigse, Carlow Arts Festival
Co Carlow

Enniscorthy Strawberry Fair
Enniscorthy, Co Wexford

International Air Rally
Kilkenny, Co Kilkenny

Irish-style barbecues
Kells, Co Kilkenny

Slate Quarry Festival
Tullahought, Co Kilkenny

July

Freshford Heritage Festival
Freshford, Co Kilkenny

Johnstown Gymkhana
Johnstown, Co Kilkenny

Kells Celt Festival
Kells, Co Kilkenny

Kilkenny Agricultural Show
Kilkenny Co Kilkenny

Kilmore Quay Seafood Festival
Co Wexford

August

Castlegannon Horse Show
Co Kilkenny

Clogh Heritage Festival
Clogh, Co Kilkenny

Croppy Boy Festival
Co Wexford

Gorey Summer Festival
Gorey, Co Wexford

Graiguenamanagh Regatta
Graiguenamanagh, Co Kilkenny

Inistioge Vintage Festival
Inistioge, Co Kilkenny

Kilkenny Arts Festival
Kilkenny, Co Kilkenny

eptember

Ireland Ploughing ampionship
Carlow

resbridge International rse Sales
esbridge, Co Kilkenny

rk Agricultural Show
own, Co Kilkenny

terford International Festival of ht Opera
terford, Co Waterford

October

Waterford Festival of Light Music
Co Wexford

Wexford Festival (last 2 wks in October)
Wexford, Co Wexford

Wexford Opera Festival
Co Wexford

November

Duiske Concerts in Graiguenamanagh
Co Kilkenny

Wexford Opera Festival
Co Wexford

December

St Stephen's Day Festival
Tullaroan, Co Kilkenny

COUNTY CARLOW

The Celtic centre of Ireland, with links to the ancient past at every turn, Carlow is the second smallest county in Ireland, with friendly people, quiet villages and attractive scenery. The landscape ranges from the valleys of two great rivers, the Barrow and the Slaney, to the Blackstairs Mountains in the east and the Killeshin Hills in the west. There are significant stages of two major Waymarked Walks, the Barrow Way and the South Leinster Way, plus many local walks and scenic drives. It is good walking, cycling and horse-riding country, with plenty of opportunities for championship golf, course and game angling.

PRINCIPAL TOWN

CARLOW

The county town of Carlow lies on the east bank of the Barrow in the once tempestuous borderland at the edge of the Pale. Old warehouses line its former quays, there are a few nice old shop fronts, and the ruined castle stands in the grounds of a mineral water bottling plant. The 19th-century Gothic cathedral is easily spotted by its unusual lantern spire, looking like a crown of thorns. It contains an elaborate pulpit and a finely sculptured marble monument to Bishop Doyle, or JKL (James of Kildare and Leighlin). The story goes that the artist, John Hogan, forgot to include the bishop's ring and was so mortified by this omission that he committed suicide.

MUST SEE

HE ADELAIDE MEMORIAL CHURCH
lyshall
his miniature copy of Salisbury Cathedral vas built in 1913 by John Duguid, a ondon businessman, as a memorial to is wife Adelaide who died in 1903, and is daughter Constance. Constance was ngaged to a young gentleman in the area, the heir to the big house, and during a visit to make her wedding arrangements she was tragically killed in a riding accident. The church features stained glass windows by Evy Hone, and interesting carvings and mosaics.

BROWNE'S HILL DOLMEN
Carlow
(2 miles/3km east of Carlow)
This impressive dolmen, dating from around 2,000BC, has the largest capstone in Ireland, estimated to weigh more than 100 tons/101 tonnes. The front end is supported by three uprights, while the rear has collapsed and rests on the ground. It is situated on land belonging to Browne's Hill, a country house built in 1763.

HE CASTLES OF COUNTY CARLOW
arlow is renowned for its castles. The vading Normans began the castle-uilding trend, and by the mid 14th entury there were 150 in the county. By e early part of the 15th century all but vo of them were controlled by the ighty Kavanaghs. Several ruins remain nd some to look out for are:

BALLYLOUGHAN CASTLE, NEAR BAGENALSTOWN
A large castle, probably 13th-century, whose ruins include a twin-towered gatehouse, the hall and the foundations of one of the corner towers.

BALLYMOON CASTLE, NEAR BAGENALSTOWN
A ruined early 14th-century fortress.

CLONMORE CASTLE, CLONMORE
A 13th-century fortress with later additions.

LEIGHLINBRIDGE CASTLE, LEIGHLINBRIDGE
The Normans built a castle here to defend the river crossing. It was damaged in 1577 by Rory O'More and finished off by Cromwell. A 14th-century tower and part of the bawn remain.

RATHNAGEERAGH CASTLE, NEAR MYSHALL
A ruined castle with a square, two-storey gatehouse remaining.

ARLOW CASTLE,
arlow
13th-century castle which survived romwell's forces but was badly damaged y attempts to reduce the thickness of its alls with explosives. This foolhardy xploit was the work of a Dr Middleton, ho planned to turn the castle into a natic asylum.

BIG OUTDOORS

GHADE
renowned local beauty spot on the River aney.

ELLESHIN RESERVOIR *(accessible from arlow, Leighlinbridge & Milford)*
easant walking area and wildlife habitat.

OUNT LEINSTER
ount Leinster, at 2,611ft/796m is worth e climb for its views of three counties - arlow, Wexford and Wicklow. Follow the ount Leinster Scenic Drive signposts om Borris.

AK PARK *(2 miles/3km northeast of Carlow the N9 Dublin road)*
beautiful wooded park.

OSSMORE PARK
park in an elevated position offering od views of the county. It has a picnic ea, toilets and a car park. On summer ındays there is organised music and ancing boards.

GREAT FOR KIDS

BALLYKEENAN PET FARM & AVIARY
Myshall, Ballykeenan **☎ 0503 57665**
Farm animals and exotic birds set among the old stone outbuildings of this former farm.

CRACKER JACKS ACTIVITY CENTRE
14a Carlow Shopping Centre, Carlow
☎ 0503 33244
A new attraction for children aged 2-11 years, with soft play area, ball pool, slides, tunnels and bouncy castle.

HISTORIC & ANCIENT SITES

CLOCHE-A-FOIL *(S of Tullow in Ardristan)*
An ancient holed stone, probably from a Megalithic tomb. It has long been believed that sick babies passed through its 6-inch /15cm hole would be restored to health.

CLONMORE
A small village rich in antiquities: an unfigured High Cross, a 13th-century castle, St Mogue's well, and a huge triple bullaun - a hollowed out stone used as a Prehistoric pestle and mortar.

HAROLDSTOWN DOLMEN
Tobinstown, Tullow
A well preserved portal dolmen, with ten verticle stones supporting two slightly tilted capstones.

RATHGALL HILL FOTIFICATION
Rath, Shillelagh Road
An extensive hill fortification, dating from the 8th century BC, in a remarkable state of preservation.

ST PATRICK'S COLLEGE,
Carlow
The first Catholic seminary in Ireland to be sanctioned by the British, dating from 1793.

HOMES & GARDENS

ALTAMOUNT GARDENS
Tully **0503 59128** *(signposted off the N80 & N81 between Tully and Bunclody)*
Large, romantic gardens with a lily pool, arboretum, bog garden and ice-age glen. Teas, craft shop, garden centre,art gallery.

DUNLECKNEY MANOR, NEAR BAGENALSTOWN
The original 15th-century building, the family seat of the Bagenals, was incorporated in the present Tudor-Gothic mansion, which was built in the 1820s

HUNTINGTON CASTLE
Clonegal **054 77552**
Castellated building, developed from an original tower house, continuously occupied since 1625. Also the Temple of Isis and Ulrich Ruckriem Sculpture Shed.

LISNAVAGH GARDENS
Rathvilly **0503 61104**
Ten acres of pleasure gardens, designed by architect Daniel Robertson and planted in the 1850s. Spring flowers, mixed borders, a rock garden and many original trees.

SHANKILL CASTLE
Paulstown **0503 26145**
Set amid lovely gardens and parkland, this castellated house incorporates an earlier building from 1713.

MUSEUMS & ART GALLERIES

THE COTTAGE COLLECTION
Ardattin, Tullow
A unique collection of domestic appliances, representing years of collecting

COUNTY CARLOW MUSEUM
Town Hall, Centaur St, Carlow
0503 40730
Local history museum managed by the Old Carlow Society.

HILLVIEW MUSEUM
Corries, Bagenalstown **0503 21795**
Household artefacts and vintage farm machinery.

ST MULLINS HERITAGE CENTRE
Themed around St Moling, who founded the monastic settlement here in the 7th century. Also boating trips.

TULLOW MUSEUM
Bridge Street, Tullow
Local history museum, including vestments worn by Father John Murphy, a local leader of the 1798 Rising whose monument stands in the town square.

ESSENTIAL INFORMATION

TOURIST INFORMATION

KENNEDY AVENUE
Carlow **0503 31554**

CARLOW RURAL TOURISM
College Street, Carlow **0503 30411**

GENEALOGY

CARLOW GENEALOGY COMMITTEE
c/o Carlow County Council, Athy Road, Carlow **0503 51233**
A member of the Irish Family History Foundation.

CRAFTS

BLOOMS
Knockbeg, Carlow **0503 42477**
Traditionally preserved flowers made into a range of attractive gift items.

BORRIS LACE,
Babs Kelly, Rathanna, Borris/Mary Beck Woodlands Park, Borris **0503 73342**
A revival of a traditional Borris home industry. Lace can be made to order.

CARLOW CRAFT SHOP
College Street, Carlow **0503 40491**
Many different crafts here.

CLOYDAGH WOODCRAFT
Cloydagh **0503 32294**
(3 miles/5km from Carlow)
A joiner and wood-turner, making bowls, clocks, table lamps, four-poster beds and other items of furniture.

CLARE KEARNS
17 Greenhills Estate, Brownshill, Carlow
0503 42720
Individually cut & handpainted woodcraft.

DOLMEN POTTERY
113 Green Road, Carlow **0503 42693**
Award-winning pottery, experimenting with local clays, stone dusts and wood ash for glazes. Open by appointment.

PEMBROKE ART STUDIO
Pembroke **0503 41562**
(off Burin Street), Carlow
Exhibition of paintings and ceramics.

RATH WOOD
Rath, Tullow **0503 56285**
Solid pine furniture, garden furniture, pottery, toys and shrubs.

WILD IRISH CRAFTS
Kilquiggan, Tullow **0503 56228**
Specialising in pressed wild Irish flowers, the centre is involved in the propagation and conservation of wild flowers, and has a five-acre nature trail (wheelchair accessible).

SPORTS & LEISURE

ANGLING

The River Slaney offers the best trout and salmon fishing in the region. The River Barrow is good for coarse angling, around Carlow and Bagenalstown, where bream, tench, perch, rudd and pike are plentiful. There is also some game fishing on the Barrow in the tidal waters at St Mullins. Local gillies are available through Carlow Rural Tourism **0503 30411**

CYCLING

RENT-A-BIKE, A E COLEMAN
Dublin Street, Carlow **0503 31273**

EQUESTRIAN CENTRES

CARRIGBEG RIDING STABLES,
Bagenalstown **0503 21962**

THE FORGE STABLES RIDING SCHOOL
Tollerton, Killeshin **056 42570**

GOLF COURSES

MOUNT WOLSELEY COUNTRY CLUB,
Tullow **0503 51674**
A challenging parkland golf course designed by Christy O'Connor Junior, situated on the Wolsey family estate between the Wicklow and Blackstairs mountains.

Also:
BORRIS *(9-hole course)* **0503 73143**
CARLOW **0503 31695**
CARLOW DRIVING RANGE **0503 41683**

HANG-GLIDING

Mount Leinster is an internationally renowned, multi-directional site for hang-gliding, for further information
01 4556437.

SCENIC DRIVES

There are several clearly signposted touring routes in Co Carlow, including the Barrow Drive, Mount Leinster Drive, The Ridge (Killeshin Drive) and the Slaney Drive. For further information contact the local Tourist Office.

WALKING

There are significant stretches of two major waymarked walking routes in Co Carlow; the Barrow Way, a towpath walk with no steep bits and plenty of pubs, shops and villages, and the South Leinster Way, a varied trail from Kildavin to Graiguenamanagh. A number of local routes explore the slopes of Blackstairs, the Killeshin Hills, and the Barrow and Slaney valleys. Details: Carlow Rural Tourism, College St, Carlow **0503 304**

WATERSPORTS

For details of canoeing, sculling and cruising on the rivers Barrow and Slaney, contact Seamus Maher, Slaney Quarter, Tullow. **0503 63606**
BARROW CANOEING & KYAK CENTRE
0503 46157
Offering a day on the river in a two or three-person canoe. They will set you down and pick you up, returning you to your accommodation.

WHERE TO STAY

HOTELS

AA RECOMMENDED

CARLOW

OLMEN HOTEL ★★★
kenny Road
0503 42002 F 0503 42375

Set in 20 acres of landscaped grounds, this modern hotel is in a scenic riverside location, linked by footbridge to a private island; a great place to relax and enjoy the free coarse fishing. Enjoy the comfortable bedrooms, excellent restaurant, and the lounge with river views.
40 bedrooms (1 family) ££

3ED & BREAKFAST ACCOMMODATION

AA RECOMMENDED

CARLOW

.RROWVILLE TOWN HOUSE QQQQ
kenny Road *(on N9 southside of town,)0m south of N80 junction)*
0503 43324 F 0503 41953
steful Regency house with pretty drooms. Excellent breakfast menu. rman spoken.
bedrooms, all no smoking £ No smoking dining room Parking No children under yrs

Barrowville Town House

NAD HOUSE QQQQ
kenny Road T 0503 41562
m from Carlow on the Kilkenny Road)
stinctive house with large lounge and easant bedrooms. Baking a speciality.
edrooms, all no smoking £ No smoking area of dining room and 1 lounge Parking uzzi Open Apr-Oct

OONLARA QQQ
kenny Road T 0503 41863
n N9 3km from Carlow on Kilkenny side, banks of River Barrow beside Dolmen Hotel)
Modern house by the river with pleasant bedrooms. Salmon and trout fishing.
3 bedrooms (all family) £ No smoking in bedrooms/dining room Parking

GREENLANE HOUSE QQQ
Dublin Road T 0503 42670
Purpose built, family-run and very comfortable. Smart house with good bedrooms and sitting room.
7 bedrooms No smoking Parking

RATHVILLY

BAILE RICEAD QQQ
T 0503 61120
4 bedrooms (2 family) No smoking establishment £ Parking Open 17 Mar-Nov

WHERE TO EAT

PUBS, INNS & OTHER PLACES

LD BLACK KETTLE
l St, Tullow T 0503 51788
'aditional setting for home-cooked food.

AMS RESTAURANT
Dublin Street, Carlow T 0503 31824
l coaching inn.Seafood and game

ZZ'S BAR
ow Street, Carlow T 0503 43307
althy lunchtime fare.

NTRAL CAFÉ
Square, Tullow T 0503 52022
acks and grills all day till late night.

NETTE'S FEAST
lin Glebe, Bennekerry T 0503 40817
aginative four-course dinner menu.

YLE'S SCHOOL HOUSE RESTAURANT
n Street, Castledermot T 0503 44282
ality food in a former schoolroom setting.

EWING'S LOUNGE
Town Hall Square, Carlow T 0503 31600
All-day home-cooked food

THE GREEN DRAKE INN
Main Street, Borris T 0503 73116
A charming village inn

KENNEDY'S LOUNGE
Tullow Street, Carlow T 0503 31518
Good quality home cooking.

LANE COURT HOTEL
Kilkenny Road, Carlow T 0503 42002
Pleasant setting in parkland on river bank

LAWLOR'S INN, Rathvilly T 0503 61112
Good food in traditional surroundings.

LORD BAGENAL INN
Leighlinbridge T 0503 21679
Famous 18th-century inn

MANOR HOUSE
Market Square, Bagenalstown T 0503 21085
All-day bar menu, and candlelit dinners.

THE OWL Dublin St, Carlow T 0503 43156
Popular steak house.

REDDYS Tullow St, Carlow T 0503 42224
Lounge bar and restaurant

ROYAL HOTEL
Dublin St, Carlow T 0503 31621
Convenient town centre location

TARA ARMS
Church Street, Tullow T 0503 51305
Good dining pub

TEACH DOLMAIN
76 Tullow Street, Carlow T 0503 31236
Open daily for good food.

TAYLOR'S LOUNGE
Shillelagh T 055 29120

COUNTY KILKENNY

Kilkenny is a county of productive farmland, medieval remains and attractive scenery, particularly along the rivers Nore and Barrow, with picturesque villages such as Graiguenamanagh and Inistioge. It is a hospitable county, with good quality hotels, pubs and restaurants, attracting visitors in growing numbers to its various festivals, including the international festival of comedy, The Cat Laughs. Renowned as a centre for art, music and design, it has a thriving community of artists and Craftspeople. Kilkenny is also closely associated with the traditional game of hurling.

PRINCIPAL TOWN

KILKENNY

Kilkenny is a lovely medieval town, situated on the banks of the River Nore, with narrow winding streets, which can often be clogged with tourist traffic. The town is particularly popular during Arts Week Festival, the last two weeks in August. There is plenty from the town's rich historical heritage to be seen, and the surrounding countryside is very beautiful. Kilkenny is divided into three districts, Irishtown, around the cathedral; Hightown, where you'll find Kilkenny Castle, and the eastern district over the river, in the area of St John's Priory.

MUST SEE

JNMORE CAVE
miles/11km north of Kilkenny, on N78)
056 67726
series of chambers formed over millions years, with well-lit walkways leading st enormous stalagmites and stalactites. visitor centre explains the history and ology of the cave system.

RPOINT ABBEY
mile/1.5km south of Thomastown on the 9)
ne of Ireland's finest monastic ruins, the mains of this 12th-century Cistercian bey are awe-inspiring. The main atures are the restored cloisters with eir superb carving, and the beautiful East se Window.

KILKENNY CASTLE
Kilkenny **T 056 21450 F 056 63488**
The castle dates from 1172 and was the key stronghold of the Butler family, Earls and Dukes of Ormonde from 1391 to the present day. It saw conflict as recently as 1922, during the Civil War, when it was occupied briefly by anti-Treatyites. The castle has recently been restored to its 1830s splendour, illustrating the life of the most powerful family in Ireland over the centuries, and housing the National Furniture Collection. The Butler Art Gallery, in the former servants' rooms, mounts frequently changing exhibitions of contemporary art.

BIG OUTDOORS

NKINSTOWN PARK
nmore
woodland park with farm birds and me birds of prey in evidence.

WPARK MARSH AND FEN
25 miles/2km from Kilkenny, off stlecomer road)
haven for birdwatchers, with many ecies to be seen.

GREAT FOR KIDS

TYSCOPE EXHIBITION
se Inn Street, Kilkenny **T 056 51500**
hree-dimensional scale model of 17th-ntury Kilkenny City, with other small ale exhibits, housed in the 16th-century ee Alms House, along with the Tourist ice.

KENNY CASTLE PARK
ods, an artificial lake and a children's y area.

RE VALLEY PARK
namult, Bennettsbridge, Kilkenny
056 27229
open farm where you can cuddle a bit, bottle-feed a lamb and learn where ur food comes from. Crazy golf, play a, shop and tea room.

HISTORIC & ANCIENT SITES

LLYLARKIN ABBEY
shford
mall abbey with wonderful carvings ing from 1350.

LLAN
o sites of interest: the Augustinian Friary 62) by the King's River and St Mary's Church on Main Street, a parish church since 1250.

CLARA CASTLE
A 15th-century castle retaining several original features, including its timber floors.

COLLEGIATE CHURCH
Gowran
A richly ornamented church dating from 1275. Key available locally.

DUISKE ABBEY
Graiguenamanagh **T 0503 24238**
A restored early Cistercian abbey of massive grandeur. Interesting features include early medieval tiles and and effigy of a Crusader knight.

GRANAGH OR GRANNY CASTLE
(By the River Suir close to Waterford)
A picturesque ruin overlooking the river, with examples of architecture from several centuries.

KELLS PRIORY,
Kells
A large Augustinian Priory dating from 1193 with a complex of medieval church buildings and a fortified outer wall with seven towers. Direct access from car park.

ST CANICE'S CATHEDRAL
Dean Street, Kilkenny **T 056 64971**
One of the finest 13th-century buildings in Ireland, renowned for its grandeur, used by Cromwell as a stable. The neighbouring round tower dates from the 6th century.

MEDIEVAL KILKENNY CITY
The city has a large concentration of medieval buildings, as well as the castle, many of them ecclesiastical. These include Black Abbey (1225), which is still in use today by the Dominican order. Nearby is the last remaining city gateway, the Black Freran Gate (14th century). St Francis Abbey is also in this area, in the grounds of the brewery that shares its name. Behind the Town Hall is St Mary's Old Parish Church (13th century), and in St John's Street there is St John's Priory (also early 13th-century), once known as the Lantern of Ireland, because of its numerous windows.

HOMES & GARDENS

KILFANE GLEN & WATERFALL
(north of Thomastown)
A garden from the Romantic era (1790), beautifully restored, featuring a waterfall and thatched cottage orné, which is reached by winding paths providing lovely vistas.

MOUNT JULIET
Thomastown **T 056 24455 F 056 24522**
Beautiful 18th-century parkland by the River Nore, with mature oak, lime and chestnut trees, walled gardens, lawns and shrubs. The great house is now a hotel (see Where To Eat and Where To Stay).

THE RICE HOUSE
Callan t **056 25141**
Birthplace of Edmund Ignatius Rice (1762-1844), and typical of a late 18th-century farmer's house. Admission on request to the adjoining monastery.

THOMASTOWN WATERGARDEN
T 056 24690
Watergarden and café, open all year.

WOODSTOCK ESTATE FOREST PARK
Inistioge
Extensive parkland gardens dating from the 19th century surrounding the ruins of Woodstock House. The gardens include some rare Far Eastern species.

MUSEUMS & ART GALLERIES

NORE VALLEY FOLK MUSEUM
A privately run museum of local artefacts.

ROTHE HOUSE MUSEUM,
Parliament Street T 056 22893
A stone-built Tudor mansion rambling around cobbled courtyards, now a museum featuring a fine display of period costume and frequent temporary exhibitions.

SHEE ALMS HOUSE
Rose Inn Street T 056 51500
Built in 1582 to house the poor and now home to the Tourist Office. Various exhibitions and presentations are staged here, including Cityscope (see GREAT FOR KIDS).

MUSEUM
Tullaherin, Bennettsbridge T 056 27211
Local museum opening Sunday afternoons June to September.

LORY MEAGHER HERITAGE CENTRE
Tullaroan T 056 69107
A fully restored 17th-century thatched mansion house, incorporating the County Hurling Museum, among other attractions

ESSENTIAL INFORMATION

TOURIST INFORMATION

ROSE INN STREET
Kilkenny T 056 51500 F 056 63955

GENEALOGY

KILKENNY ARCHAEOLOGICAL SOCIETY
Rothe House, Kilkenny T 056 22893
The Society provides assistance in tracing ancestors, particularly those from the locality.

CRAFTS

A & S HERALDICS
T 056 63053
Heraldic souvenirs and hand-painted coats of arms.

ABBEY CENTRE GALLERY,
Graiguenamanagh T 0503 24238
Contemporary Christian art.

CHESNEAU LEATHER GOODS
Bennettsbridge
T 056 27456 F 056 27329
Leather goods made of stablehide leather with solid brass fittings,sold in leading stores around the world.

CRESCENT WORKSHOPS
Castle Yard, Kilkenny T 056 61804
Crafts Council of Ireland training centre for young designers. Crafts include ceramics, jewellery, leather and textiles.

CUSHENDALE MILLS
Graiguenamanagh T 0503 24118
Tweed, mohair and lambswool products.

DUISKE GLASS
Graiguenamanagh T 0503 24174
Hand cut glass, engraved by intaglio.

JERPOINT GLASS STUDIO
Stoneyford T 056 24350 F 056 24778
A chance to see glassmakers make and finish glassware by hand.

JENKINSTOWN HOUSE,
Jenkinstown T 056 67804
Hand-made pottery, craftwork and Staurday Bluebell Market.

KILKENNY CRYSTAL WORKSHOP
Callan T 056 25132
Crystal showroom,shop and café.

NICHOLAS MOSSE POTTERY,
Bennettsbridge T 056 27126
Brightly coloured earthenware in Irish clay

MARY O'GORMAN
The Old Creamery Yard, Bennettsbridge
T 056 29156
Pottery and shop.

O'CARROLL WOOD ART
Gowran T 056 26468
Furniture, sculpture, carvings.

PADMORE & BARNES
Wolfe Tone Street, Kilkenny T 056 21037
'Wallabees' shoes, leather and craft items.

RUDOLF HELTZEL, GOLD & SILVERSMITH,
10 Patrick Street, Kilkenny T 056 21497
Contemporary jewellery

STONEWARE JACKSON POTTERY
Bennettsbridge T 056 27175
F 056 27493
Pottery and showroom

TONER LEATHERS,
Thomastown T 056 24055
High quality hand-made leather goods.

SPORTS & LEISURE

ACTIVITY CENTRES

COUNTRYSIDE LEISURE ACTIVITY CENTRE
Bonnettsrath, Kilkenny
T 056 61791 & 087 448491
KILKORAN HOUSE
Cuffesgrange T 056 28253 or 088 545618
Clay pigeon shooting.
NORESIDE ADVENTURE CENTRE
Woollengrange, Bennettsbridge
T 056 27273 F 056 27692
REGGIE BOOTH GO-KARTING,
New Rd, Mooneeroe, Castlecomer
T 056 41177

ANGLING

The River Barrow, is good for coarse fishing,.The River Nore is known for its trout and salmon. Permits are available from angling suppliers.

BOATING

VALLEY BOATS Barrow Lane, Graiguenamanagh T 0503 24945

CYCLING

RENT-A-BIKE Walls of Maudlin Street, Kilkenny T 056 21236

EQUESTRIAN CENTRES

FANNINGSTOWN HOUSE,
Piltown T 051 643535
GRAIGUENAMANAGH RIDING CENTRE,
Graiguenamanagh T 0503 24357
MOUNT JULIET EQUESTRIAN CENTRE,
Thomastown T 056 24455
NUENNA FARM RIDING SCHOOL,
Kilkenny Road, Freshford T 056 32193
VOCATIONAL SCHOOL EQUESTRIAN CENTRE,
Newtown, Thomastown T 056 24511
WARRINGTON TOP FLIGHT EQUESTRIAN CENTRE,off Bennettsbridge Road, Kilkenny
T 056 22682

GOLF COURSES

MOUNT JULIET
Thomastown T 056 24455 F 056 2452
A Jack Nicklaus signature golf course.
Also:
CALLAN T 056 25136
CASTLECOMER T 056 41139
KILKENNY DRIVING RANGE,T 056 221

GREYHOUND RACING

JAMES PARK
Freshford Road, Kilkenny T 056 21214

HORSE RACING

GOWRAN PARK
Kilkenny T 056 26126

WALKING

BARROW BANK WALK
From St Mullins to Gorebridge via Graiguemamagh.
BRANDON HILL
Graiguenamanagh
A signposted walk to the summit of Brandon Hill (1703ft/520m). Follow the South Leinster Way signs from Graiguenamanagh.
THE SOUTH LEINSTER WAY
Join this waymarked walk for its Kilkenny stretch at Graiguenamanagh. It goes on Inistioge, Piltown and Carrick-on-Suir, where it links with the North Munster W
TYNAN TOURS
T 056 65929
The city's official walking tour guides of medieval Kilkenny.

WHERE TO STAY

HOTELS

AA RECOMMENDED

KILKENNY

LUB HOUSE ★★
atrick Street T 056 21994 F 056 21994
ity centre)
/elcoming 200-year-old hotel with
:tractive bedrooms.
2 bedrooms ££ Off-peak rates Night orter Parking Leisure facilities No smoking dining room

OTEL KILKENNY ★★★
ollege Road T 056 62000 F 056 65984
ollow ring road to Callan/Clonmel rdbt, otel located 150yds off last exit)
leasant hotel.set in extensive grounds, which some bedrooms overlook..
0 bedrooms ££ Off-peak ratesNight porter arking Gardens Leisure facilities No noking in dining room

Club House

NEWPARK ★★★
Castlecomer Road
T 056 22122 F 056 61111
Set in parkland, this friendly hotel has a an interestingly designed restaurant & lounge.
84 bedrooms, including some for non-smokers ££ Off-peak rates Night porter Parking Gardens Leisure facilities No smoking in dining room Conference/banqueting facilities

THOMASTOWN

MOUNT JULIET ★★★★❀❀
T 056 24455 F 056 24522
A beautiful Palladian mansion combining elegance and luxury. A haven for golfers, there are many leisure activitiesavailable.
43 bedrooms (21 in annexe) ££££ Off-peak rates Night porter Parking Gardens Leisure facilities No smoking in dining room Closed 1st 2wks Jan

Jewpark

Hotel Kilkenny

BED & BREAKFAST ACCOMMODATION

AA RECOMMENDED

GRAIGUENAMANAGH

/ATERSIDE QQQQ
he Quay
T 0503 24246 & 24737 F 0503 24733
onverted granary on riverbank, simply ut comfortably furnished. Restaurant.
4 bedrooms £ No smoking in area of ning room Licensed Fishing Snooker Iountain bikes Canoes Closed early Jan-arly Feb

INNISTIOGE

GARRANAVABBY HOUSE QQ
(turn off N79 to R700, proceed for 2 miles and turn on to R705 for 330m, farmhouse on the right) T 051 423613
Idyllically set between the two rivers, this farmhouse iis perfect for relaxing.
3 bedrooms, all no smoking £ No smoking in dining room Parking No children under 10yrs 96 acres mixed Open Apr-Sep

KILKENNY

BUTLER HOUSE QQQQ
Patrick Street
T 056 65707 & 22828 F 056 65626
Once the dower house of the Castle, many original features remain .
14 bedrooms ££ No smoking in area of dining room Parking

Newlands Country House

ALCANTRA QQQ
Maidenhill, Kells Road T 056 61058
(on R697, 400m from jct with R910)
4 bedrooms (1 family) No smoking establishment £ Parking Closed 23-30 Dec

CILL PHAOIN QQQ
off Castlecomer Rd, Greenshill
T 056 22857
Welcoming house with gardens, to which some bedrooms have access. .Parking
4 bedrooms £ No smoking in dining room

MOUNT DANVILLE QQQ
Bennetsbridge Road T 056 21521
Just past the Castle, set in secluded gardens with a lovely sun lounge.
4 bedrooms, all no smoking £ No smoking in dining room Parking Open Apr-Sep

NEWLANDS COUNTRY HOUSE QQQQQ
Sevenhouses
T 056 29111 & 29171 F 056 29171
High standards of comfort and hospitality. Some bedrooms have whirlpool baths.
4 bedrooms (3 family) No smoking establishment £ Parking Closed Xmas

SHILLOGHER HOUSE QQQQ
Callan Road T 056 63249
Tastefully furnished new house, where you will be made to feel at home
5 bedrooms, all no smoking ££ No smoking in dining room Parking

KNOCKTOPHER

KNOCKTOPHER HALL QQQQ
T/F 056 68626
Prettily furnished with some fine period furniture.Lovely Georgian country house
4 bedrooms (1 family) No smoking establishment £ Table license Parking Closed 15 Dec-2 Jan

THOMASTOWN

ABBEY HOUSE QQQQ
Jerpoint Abbey
(on the N9 from Dublin directly opposite Jerpoint Abbey)
T 056 24166 F 056 24192
Historic house on a riverbank. Excellent comfort and standards.Pre-book dinner
7 bedrooms ££ No smoking in dining room & 1 lounge Parking Children's facilities Fishing

BURLEY QQ
Maudlin Street T 056 24297
(on N9)
Secluded with lovely gardens, this smart bungalow offers pleasant rooms
3 bedrooms (2 family) £ Parking

CAMPING & CARAVANNING

AA RECOMMENDED SITES

BENNETTSBRIDGE

ORE VALLEY PARK
earby town: Kilkenny
056 27229
pennants Caravans, motor caravans fand nts. Open Mar-Oct. Booking advisable bank hols & July. Last arrival 22.00hrs. Last departure 16.00hrs.
A 4-acre site with 70 touring pitches. Bread & farm produce, river walks, crazy golf. Electric hook up, shower, electric shaver point, games room, separate TV room, cold storage, children's playground, Calor Gas, Camping Gaz, public telephone, barbeque area, picnic area, shop, disabled facilities.
Facilities within three miles of site: golf course, fishing

WHERE TO EAT

RESTAURANTS

AA RECOMMENDED

ADY HELEN DINING ROOM ❁❁
ount Juliet Hotel, Thomastown
056 24455 F **056 24522**
assic Irish cooking served from a fixed-price four-course dinner menu, amid the 18th-century splendour of a fine country house. Expect the likes of mille-feuille of artichokes and sweetbread; grilled medallion of monkfish and salmon with a fondue of spinach and prawn velouté.
FIXED D £££

PUBS, INNS & OTHER PLACES

KILKENNY CITY

OLLARDS
eran Street **056 21353**
estaurant and bar.

AFÉ SOL
lliam Street **056 64987**
ce bistro-style establishment.

AISLEAN UN CHUAIN
gh Street
ar, food and music.

EERE'S
rliament Street
r, food and music

IE DEANERY
an Street **056 52822**
stro-style food.

WARD LANGTON'S,
hn Street **056 21728**
cellent old-style pub with bar food and nservatory restaurant. Good for music.

IE EMIGRANT
hn Street
staurant, bar and music.

NNELLY'S
rliament Street
r, food and music.

AGSTONE
liament Street
ne bar, food and music.

ALIAN CONNECTION
rliament Street **056 64225**
ry nice Italian food.

KILFORD ARMS
John Street
Restaurant and bar.

KILKENNY DESIGN CENTRE, THE PARADE
056 22118
Sparkling self-service restaurant in upper floors of the castle stable block.

KYTLER'S INN
Kieran Street **056 21064**
Restaurant and music.

LACKEN HOUSE
Dublin Road **056 61085**
Traditionally furnished cellar dining rooms serving international cuisine.

LAUTRECS WINE BAR
Kieran Street **056 62720**
Bistro-style menu.

MATTHEW DUGGAN'S,
Parliament Street
Bar food.

MATT THE MILLERS
John Street
Restaurant, bar and music.

M DORE
High Street **056 63374**
A family restaurant serving fresh food with quick service.

O'RIADAS
Parliament Street
Bar, food and music.

PARIS TEXAS
High Street **056 61822**
Bistro-style menu, bar and music.

PARLIAMENT HOUSE
Parliament Street **056 63666**
Upmarket place, with fish as a speciality.

RAFTER DEMPSEY'S,
Friary Street
Bar, food and music.

RISTORANT RINNUCCINI
The Parade **056 61575**
Irish and Italian cooking.

TROYSGATE HOUSE
Greensbridge
Restaurant and bar.

CO KILKENNY

THE LONG MAN
Kilfane, Thomastown **056 24786**
Irish cooking.

MOSSE'S MILL CAFÉ
Bennetsbridge **056 27644**
Bistro-style cooking in stylish surroundings.

THE MOTTE
Plas Newydd Lodge, Instioge **056 58655**
A candlelit restaurant in a lovely village setting, serving good seasonal fare.

SHELL RESTAURANT
Urlingford
Traditional Irish cooking.

URLINGFORD ARMS,
Urlingford **056 31626**
Fish is the house speciality.

COUNTY TIPPERARY

The county of the Golden Vale, Tipperary has some of the country's lushest pasturelands, and this is reflected in the prosperity of the farming community and in the region's towns and shopping centres. The main natural features are the Galtee and Knockmealdown Mountains, and the River Suir that cuts through the heart of the county. Tipperary is rich in archaelogical remains, including the famous Rock of Cashel, dating back to a thousand years before St Patrick was born. There are also plenty of castles and ancient ecclesiastical buildings to explore.

PRINCIPAL TOWNS

BALLINA

Designated a Heritage town with its partner Killaloe, sitting on the other side of the beautiful river Shannon in County Clare. They share a Heritage Centre and a majestically arched bridge. They are close to Kincora where Ireland's most famous king Brian Boru, held court over a millenium ago.

CLONMEL

Tipperary's county town, attractively set on the north bank of the River Suir, is a thriving place full of activity. It has lots of good shops and restaurants, and is a hospitable base for touring the surrounding countryside, which extends south to the Comeragh Mountains. The town is associated with field sports (fox-hunting and hare-coursing); horse and dog-breeding (notably greyhounds); and cider-making. Laurence Sterne, born 1713, author of Tristram Shandy, is perhaps Clonmel's most famous son.

CASHEL

Cashel's cluster of medieval buildings stand out dramatically against the backdrop of the Tipperary's Golden Vale, and other buildings date from much earlier. Once the seat of the Kings of Munster, there is a huge amount to see and discover here. The Heritage Trams are a useful way to find your way around the town at leisure.

TIPPERARY

Tipperary is an old and successful market town, retaining much of the charm and character of earlier times, and good examples of domestic and commercial architecture. One claim to fame is the Bridewell Jail which held the famous Ned Kelly before his deportation to Australia. Another was during the Land War in the 19th century when local people established New Tipperary outside the town, temporarily abandoning the houses they occupied as tenants of the Smith Barry Estate.

CAHIR

Cahir Castle was once the state-of-the-art defensive castle of 15th-century Ireland, and has now been extensively restored. Cahir is a place of contrasts: John Nash the well-known Regency architect who designed Brighton Pavilion and Regent Street in London, was reponsible for St Paul's Church and the Swiss Cottage just outside the town.

MUST SEE

BRÚ BORÚ HERITAGE CENTRE
Cashel T 062 61122 F 062 62700
BrúBorú- the Palace of Ború- is a national heritage centre at the foot of the Rock of Cashel, a 4th-century stone fort. It is a cultural and interpretative village designed around a village green, and is home to the study and celebration of Irish music, song, dance, storytelling, theatre and Celtic studies. There is a Folk Theatre where three performances a day are held in the summer, and in the evening banquets evoke the Court of Brian Ború, the 11th-century High King of Ireland, with songs, poems and sagas. The Teach Ceoil - music house - celebrates Irish music, song and dance in a less formal atmosphere.

CAHIR CASTLE (NATIONAL MONUMENT)
Cahir T 052 641011
One of the largest fortresses in Ireland, with many films to its credit, Cahir Castle was constructed in the 12th century, though much of what you see today is 15th century with many later alterations. It was formerly a stronghold of the powerful Anglo-Norman Butler family, Dukes and Earls of Ormonde. Queen Elizabeth I's favourite, the Earl of Essex, rammed a few cannon balls into its masonry in 1599, but it survived Cromwellian times virtually unscratched, and recent restoration has left it in fine condition. The huge walls enclose three separate 'wards', outer, middle and inner, the inner one guarded with a portcullis. Rooms in the keep are whitewashed and contain armour displays and period furniture from the 16th and 17th centuries. Don't miss the splendid audio-visual presentation. Limited access for those with disabilities.

LAR NA PAIRCE - THE STORY OF THE GAELIC GAMES
Slievenamon Road, Thurles, Co Tipperary
T/F 0504 23579
The history of the Gaelic Games up to the present day, including exhibits on hurling, football, camogie and handball. Includes the Sam Melbourne Collection of Gaelic Athletic Association memorabilia and a database of information on the great players from every country.

ROCK OF CASHEL
Cashel
T 062 61437
The Rock of Cashel soars 197ft/60m above the Golden Vale. Legend has it that the Devil took a bite out of the nearby Slieve Bloom Mountains, then spit it out in disgust on the plains when he saw St Patrick preparing to build a great church.

Crowning the rock is a wealth of medieval architecture. The oldest building, the Round Tower, is thought to date from the 10th century, but it is certain that the site was hallowed in pre-Christian times. The High Kings of Munster are said to have been crowned on the summit.

Cormac's Chapel, completed in 1134, is the best-preserved of the Rock's buildings and is also the earliest of Ireland's surviving Romanesque churches. It was built by Cormac Macarthy, King of Desmond and Bishop of Cashel, and its twisted columns, steeply pitched roof and fantastic carvings contribute to its unique beauty.

St Patrick's Cathedral, the largest building, came a century later. It was burned down in 1495 and restored in the 16th century. The Apostles and scenes from the Apocalypse are represented in sculptures in the north transept, and there is a splendid view of the surrounding vale from the top of the central tower.

The Hall of Vicars is the first building to be reached by those approaching the Rock from Cashel town. It was built in the 15th century for eight vicars who assisted in the cathedral services. On the ground floor is the original St Patrick's Cross (the one outside is a replica), a high cross, less ornately carved than usual.

BIG OUTDOORS

THE CELTIC PLANTARUM
Dundrum T 062 71303 F 062 71526
Featuring 60,000 plants, a waterfall and lakes with ornamental fish. Crannog, dolmen, a fairy fort and a reconstructed cairn pursue the Celtic theme. Wheelchair accessible. Café

BANSHA WOOD
(on the N24 Cahir/Tipperary road)
Marked forest walks and a viewing point. Facilities include a car park and picnic site.

GLENGARRA WOOD
(On the N8 south of Cahir)
Rare trees and shrubs, forest and riverside walks, a car park and picnic tables.

GLEN OF AHERLOW
Northwest of Cahir, between the Galtee Mountains and a parallel wooded ridge of hills to the north, extends the wide Glen of Aherlow; attractive, fertile and good walking country.

KILLBALLYBOY WOOD
(R668 Clogheen to Lismore road)
Facilities including seating by the fast flowing river, picnic sites and a car park.

MARLE BOG DEVELOPMENT
An extensive forest area with a number of lakes. Facilities include a car park, signposted walks and display boards.

MITCHELSTOWN CAVE, BURNCOURT
(midway between Cahir and Michelstown)
T 052 67246
Visitors can take escorted tours through the spectacular rock formations of these massive, high-ceilinged chambers, only discovered in recent times.

SLATE QUARRIES
Ahenny
A collection of large outdoor sculptures, created as a result of the 1992 festival.

GREAT FOR KIDS

PARSONS GREEN PARK & PET FARM
Clogheen T 052 65290
Featuring a farm museum, Viking sweat house, a pet field, pony and trap rides, boating trips and a picnic area.

HISTORIC & ANCIENT SITES

HENNY
ıere are two splendid High Crosses at 'ıenny, dating from the 8th/9th century.

THASSEL PRIORY
ear Golden
ıe ruins of Ireland's largest medieval onastery, now a National Monument, ɔvering 4acres/1.6ha, including the ıurch and impressive tower.

STERCIAN ABBEY
lcooley
little known abbey with a superb east se window, situated in the grounds of a rge estate.

IANT'S GRAVE
onmel *(Signposted off the N24)*
nine-foot/2.75m pillar stone with osses on two faces.

OLY CROSS ABBEY
ɔlycross
miles/7km south of Thurles, on R660)
ɔunded in 1169, left derelict and restored the 15th century, and again in 1971. ıere is 12th and 15th-century chitecture, with excellent stone carvings.

OUREEN PEAKAUN
ı ancient monastic site, including a ıurch with some fine carving.

IOMES & GARDENS

LENLEIGH GARDENS
ogheen 052 62251
eautiful informal gardens set against the ıockmealdown Mountains.

ORMONDE CASTLE
Carrick-on-Suir **051 640787**
A finemanor house, unfortified despite its name, built by the 10th Earl of Ormonde in anticipation of a visit by his cousin Queen Elizabeth 1 (who never turned up).

SWISS COTTAGE, KILCOMMON
Cahir **052 41144**
(1 mile/1.5km from town on Ardfinnan road)
Delightful thatched 'cottage orné' built in the early 1800s to a design by the famous Regency architect John Nash.

MUSEUMS & ART GALLERIES

BALLINA/KILLALOE HERITAGE CENTRE
061 376866
Unusually this is a shared Centre between the towns of Ballina, Co Tipperary and Killaloe, Co Clare. The River Shannon flows between them and are joined by a magnificent bridge.

BRIDEWELL JAIL AND HERITAGE UNIT
Tipperary **062 33466**
The famous criminal Ned Kelly was held here before his deportation to Australia. The Heritage Unit is now housed here

CARRICK-ON-SUIR HERITAGE CENTRE
(in former Church of Ireland off Main Street)
051 640200
Local artefacts, photographs and documents.

CASHEL FOLK VILLAGE
Main Street, Cashel **062 62525**
A collection of reconstructed houses and shops displaying furniture, artefacts and tools portraying local life from the 18th to the 20th century.

CASHEL OF THE KINGS HERITAGE CENTRE
Main Street, Cashel **062 61846**
The story of the Kings of Cashel from AD300. Model of the 17th-century town.

FOLK, FARM & TRANSPORT MUSEUM
Cashel Road, Fethard **052 31516**
Over 2,500 items arranged in 'real life' reconstructions, in the freight depot of an old railway station, including a forge, country kitchen, jaunting car, baker's van and horse-drawn hearse.

GPA BOLTON LIBRARY, GROUNDS OF ST JOHN THE BAPTIST CATHEDRAL,
John Street, Cashel **062 61232**
A fine collection of illuminated manuscripts, books and maps. Occasional Exhibitions of antique books and silver.

NENARGH HERITAGE CENTRE
Nenargh **067 32633**
(opposite the Castle Keep)
The former county gaol housing the town's Heritage Centre, featuring an excellent Lifestyles exhibition. Also exhibitions of paintings and photographs.

SLIEVEARDAGH HERITAGE CENTRE
Killenaule **052 56165**
The chequered history of the local area portrayed in a 19th-century former church.

TIPPERARY COUNTY MUSEUM
Municipal Library, Parnell Street, Clonmel
052 25399
A permanent display of 19th- and early 20th-century items of political, civic and industrial interest. Also frequent exhibitions staged in association with the National Museum and Library.

ESSENTIAL INFORMATION

TOURIST INFORMATION

CAHIR
Castle Street T 052 41453

CLONMEL
Community Office, Nelson Street
T 052 22960

TIPPERARY
James Street T 062 51457

GENEALOGY

BRÚ BORÚ HERITAGE CENTRE,
Cashel T 062 61122 F 062 62700

TIPPERARY HERITAGE UNIT,
Bridewell, St Michael Street, Tipperary
T/F 062 52725

CRAFTS

CRAFT SHOP
Davis Street, Tipperary T 062 51113

PADRAIG O'MATHUNA,
Main Street, Cashel T 062 61741
Silver and other precious metals.

ROSSA POTTERY,
Cashel/Cahir Road, Carrick-on-Suir
T 062 61388
Pottery open all year Mon-Sat.

SARAH RYAN CERAMICS
Palmers Hill, Carrick-on-Suir tel 062 61994
Sculpture and decorative pieces.

TIPPERARY CYSTAL,
Ballynoran *(on the N24 near Carrick-on-Suir)*
T 051 641118 F 051 641190
Tipperary Crystal is an obvious choice for souvenirs. The factory was founded by workers who learnt their skills at the more prestigious Waterford Crystal, but were made redundant during hard times. Using their redundancy money in this rival company, employing similar techniques, though their products are slightly cheaper. Factory tours during the season, and permanent display of glass housed in two adjoining thatched cottages. There is also a pleasant restaurant.

ENTERTAINMENT

TIPPERARY EXCEL CENTRE,
Dan Breen House, Tipperary
T 062 33466 F 062 52670
A new complex including an interpretative centre, theatre, cinemas, art galleries, and a multi-purpose art and craft facility.

SPORTS & LEISURE

ACTIVITY CENTRES

TIPPERARY RACEWAY
T 052 26658 or 088 689498
Hot rod car racing at the Oval track.

CYCLING

CYCLE HIRE : OK SPORTS
New Street, Carrick-on-Suir T 051 641642

EQUESTRIAN CENTRES

BANSHA HOUSE STABLES,
Glen of Aherlow, Bansha T 062 54194

CAHIR EQUESTRIAN CENTRE,
Ardfinnan Road, Cahir T 052 41426

HILLCREST RIDING CENTRE,
Galbally, Glen of Aherlow T 062 37915

DAREAG DAIR ICELANDIC HORSE STUD,
Upper Burncourt, Cahir T 052 67448

DAVERN EQUESTRIAN CENTRE
Clonmel T 052 27327

LISSAVA HOUSE STABLES
Cahir T 052 41117

MOANGARIFF RIDING SCHOOL
Clonmel T 052 23720

WHITECHURCH RIDING SCHOOL
Carrick-on-Suir T 052 640289

GOLF COURSES

CO TIPPERARY GOLF & COUNTRY CLUB
Dundrum House Hotel, Dundrum
T 062 71116 F 062 71366
The course was designed by Philip Walton and built into a mature Georgian estate using the features of woodland and parkland adorned by the Multeen River.
Also:
BALLYKISTEEN T 062 33333
CAHIR PARK T 052 41474
CARRICK-ON-SUIR T 051 640047
CASHEL DRIVING RANGE T 062 62111
CLONMEL T 052 24050
NENAGH T 067 31476
ROCKWELL T 062 61444
ROSCREA T 0505 21130
TEMPLEMORE T 0504 31400
THURLES T 0504 21983
TIPPERARY T 062 51119

GREYHOUND RACING

CLONMEL T 052 21118

THURLES T 0504 21003

HORSE RACING

CLONMEL RACECOURSE
Powerstown Park, Clonmel
T 052 22611 F 052 26446

THURLES RACECOURSE
Tipperary T/F 0504 22253

TIPPERARY RACECOURSE,
Limerick Junction T 062 51357
F 062 51303

SCENIC DRIVES

From Clonmel, the circular drive to the south, along the Nire and Suir valleys is well worthwhile on a fine day. So are trips to the unspoilt Comeragh mountains. Also look out for the signposted touring routes, including the Glen of Aherlow Drive, Knockmealdown Mountains Drive, the Premier Drive, the Suir Drive, and the Vee, Ballyporeen, Clogheen & Cahir Drive (details from local Tourist Office).

WALKING

There are many established walks in the county, including the North Munster Way, linking Carrick-on-Suir with the Vee, and the Pilgrim Way, an ancient trackway from Ardmore to Cashel.

GUIDED WALKING TOURS INFORMATION

Cashel T 062 62511
Clonmel T 052 2210
Suir Valley and Knockmealdown Mountains T 052 36359.

WHERE TO STAY

HOTELS

AA RECOMMENDED

AHERLOW

HERLOW HOUSE ★★★
miles from Tipperary, turn left at traffic ghts coming from Limerick)
062 56153 F 062 56212
ovely forest views at this Tudor-style ouse with comfortable lounges and staurant. Sporting activities nearby.
bedrooms ££ Off-peak rates Parking ardens No smoking in dining room Closed n-mid Mar

CAHIR

AHIR HOUSE HOTEL ★★★
e Square **T/F 52 42727**
avelling S on N8 turn off at Cahir by-pass, llow N24 to town)
xpect traditional standards of hospitality nd cuisine and tastefully furnished edrooms at this welocming hotel.
bedrooms (3 family, 2 for non-smokers) £ Parking Licensed Garden Closed 25 ec

CASHEL

ASHEL PALACE HOTEL ★★★
ain Street *(On N8)*
062 61411 F 062 61521
nce a bishop's palace , this luxury hotel as elegant rooms and excellent service.

Minella

Private walk to the famous Rock of Cashel.
13 bedrooms (6 family) ££££ Lift Parking Garden Private fishing Sauna Gymnasium

CLONMEL

MINELLA ★★★
T 052 22388 F 052 24381
Attractive mansion standing in large grounds. Elegant lounges and bedrooms, some with jacuzzis. Excellent restaurant
70 bedrooms, including some for non-smokers ££ Off-peak rates Night porter Parking Gardens Fishing No smoking in dining room

ROSCREA

GRANT'S ★★★
Castle Street
T 0505 23300 F 0505 23209
This attractive hotel is as inviting inside as out. Bedrooms are pleasantly furnished. The Lemon Tree is the award-winning restaurant but there are good options.
25 bedrooms ££ Night porter Parking

TIPPERARY

ROYAL ★
Bridge Street
T 062 33244 F 062 33596
16 bedrooms £ Off-peak rates Parking No smoking in dining room

BED & BREAKFAST ACCOMMODATION

AA RECOMMENDED

BANSHA

ANSHA HOUSE
rn off N24 in village of Bansha opposite so filling station)
062 54194 F 062 54215
vely Georgian house, comfortable and etty bedrooms. Excellent home-baking.
bedrooms £ No smoking Licensed Parking shing Riding Registered Equestrian centre 0 acres mixed Closed end Dec

BORRISOKANE

LLYCORMAC HOUSE
lish **T 067 21129 F 21200**
omplete peace at this old farmhouse run an American couple. Organic fruit & veg
bedrooms £ No smoking Licensed rking

CASHEL

ARDMAYLE HOUSE
(northwest on road to Gooldscross)
T 0504 42399 F 0504 42420
Tranquil Georgian house with a fFriendly, relaxed atmosphere.Excellent breakfasts.
5 bedrooms, all no smoking £ No smoking in dining room Parking Fishing 300 acres dairy Open Apr-Oct

Ardmayle House

KNOCK-SAINT-LOUR HOUSE QQQ
T 062 61172
7 bedrooms Parking 30 acres mixed Open Apr–Oct

LEGEND'S QQQQ
The Kiln T 062 61292
Dramatic location with mystical floodlit views, especially from restaurant.. Very comfortable bedrooms .
5 bedrooms £ No smoking in area of dining room & 1 lounge Licensed No children under 10yrs

CLONMEL

BRIGHTON HOUSE QQ
1 Brighton Place T 052 23665
Listed building near town centre. Spacious bedrooms have antique furniture.

FARRENWICK QQQ
Poulmucka, Curranstown
(from N24, Clonmel-Cahir road turn right onto R687, signed to guest house)
T 353 52 35130 F 353 52 35377
Modern house where comfortable bedrooms have orthopoedic beds.
4 bedrooms £ No smoking Parking (one covered parking space)

WOODROOFFE HOUSE QQQ
Cahir Road T 052 35243
(0.5 mile off N24 between Cahir/Clonmel)
Spacious farmhouse in a peaceful location. Attractive bedrooms and lounges.
3 bedrooms, all no smoking £ Parking 270 acres mixed Open mid Mar–mid Oct

NENAGH

ST DAVID'S COUNTRY HOUSE & RESTAURANT QQQQQ
Puckane T 067 24145 F 067 24388
(8 miles northwest of Nenagh on R493, from Puckaune, turn left at Grotto)
Country house with lake views, good bedrooms and interesting cuisine.
10 bedrooms, all no smoking ££££ Licensed Parking Fishing Open mid Mar–mid Jan

NINE MILE HOUSE

GRAND INN QQ
(situated on the main Clomnel/Kilkenny road, N76)
T 051 647035
Set in the scenic Valley of Slievenamon, this welcoming 17th-century inn has comfortable accommodation..
5 bedrooms £ Parking

ROSCREA

CREGGANBELL BIRR ROAD QQQ
(on N62 0.5 miles from centre of Roscrea town) T 0505 21421
A comfortable bungalow with a spacious sitting room and sun lounge. Gardens.
4 bedrooms No smoking £ Parking

Riverrun Hous

TOWER GUEST HOUSE & RESTAURANT QQQ
Church Street
(on N7 Dublin to Limerick road alongside Round Tower)
T 0505 21774 & 21189 F 0505 22425
Comfortable guest house, restaurant and bar featuring locally crafted furniture.
10 bedrooms No smoking in area of dining room £ Licensed Parking

TERRYGLASS

RIVERRUN HOUSE QQQ
(turn off N7 at Nenagh drive through Borrisokane for Portumna, turn left at Carrigahorrig for Terryglass)
T 067 22125 F 067 22187
Charming pink house with big bedrooms, some have access to pretty gardens.
6 bedrooms £ Parking Tennis (hard)

THURLES

INCH HOUSE QQQQ
(turn off N8 for Thurles, straight through town, R at top of square for Nenagh Rd ther drive 4 miles)
T/F 0504 51348
Well restored Georgian house with an elegant drawing room. Very comfortable.
5 bedrooms (3 family) £ Table licence Parking Closed Xmas

TIPPERARY

ACH-NA-SHEEN QQ
Clonmel Road T 062 51298
Close to the main street, this large mode bungalow has comfortable bedrooms.
10 bedrooms, including some for non-smokers No smoking in dining room &1 lounge £ Parking

Woodrooffe House

CAMPING & CARAVANNING

AA RECOMMENDED SITES

ATHERLOW

BALLINACOURTY HOUSE CAMPING & CARAVAN PARK
T 062 56230
Signposted Nearby town: Tipperary
4 pennants Caravans, motor caravans & tents. Open Easter-end Sep. Booking advisable high season and bank hols. Last arrival 22.00. Last departure noon.
A 5-acre site with 58 touring pitches. Electric hook up, shower, electric shaver point, hairdrier, tennis court, mini golf, games room, separate TV room, cold storage, licensed bar, children's playground, Camping Gaz, battery charging, café/restaurant, public phone, fast food/takeaway, barbeque area, picnic area, dog exercise area, shop.
Facilities within three miles of site: stables, golf, mini golf, fishing

WHERE TO EAT

RESTAURANTS

AA RECOMMENDED

THE BUTLER'S PANTRY RESTAURANT ❀
Cahir House Hotel, The Square, Cahir
T 052 42727
Promising Irish cuisine and hospitality at its best, the emphasis at this restaurant is on quality local produce. There's plenty of seafood, a good vegetarian choice, and a variety of dishes including pine kernel and tagliatelle salad, wild Irish salmon marguery, and medallions of Golden Vale venison.
FIXED ££ ALC £££

GRANT'S HOTEL ❀❀
Castle St, Rocrea
T 0505 23300 F 0505 23209
An attractive hotel, situated opposite the 13th-century castle and Heritage Centre, offering a good food choice. There's the main restaurant, the Lemon Tree, the Bistro for less formal dining, and Kitty's Tavern, a pub and café-bar.
FIXED ££

MINELLA HOTEL ❀
Clonmel
T 052 22388 F 052 24381
This imposing mansion peacefully standing in nine acres of lovely grounds, provides and impressive setting for this excellent restaurant.

PUBS, INNS & OTHER PLACES

BEES KNEES BISTRO
Clonmel **T 052 21457**
Good wholefood café for daytime snacks.

CASHEL PLACE,
Cashel **T 062 61411**
Cosy place for a snack,meal or drink.

CHEZ HANS, ROCKSIDE
Cashel **T 062 61177**
Converted chapel with good food range.

INCH HOUSE
Bouladuff **T 0504 51348** *(near Thurles)*
Lovely restauarant with five-course dinner.

J & C DONOVAN
58-59 O'Brien Street, Tipperary
T 062 51384
Lounge bar, serving lunches and dinner.

KICKHAM HOUSE
50 Main Street, Tipperary **T 062 51716**
Carvery lunches and evening meals, plus traditional music on Tuesday nights.

KIELY'S BAR
22 Main Street, Tipperary **T 062 51239**
Serving lunches and evening meals.

KNOCKLOFTY HOUSE
Clonmel **T 052 38353 F 052 38300**
Elegant dining room with wonderful views

MULCAHYS
47 Gladstone Street, Clonmel
T 052 22825 F 052 24544
Irish and international specialities.

THE SPEARMAN
97 Main Street, Cashel **T 062 61143**
A family-run restaurant serving robust fare

TOWER GUEST HOUSE & RESTAURANT
Church Street, Roscrea
T 0505 21774 & 21189 F 0505 22425
Open for breakfast, lunch and dinner.

COUNTY WATERFORD

County Waterford is a maritime county with a spectacular coastline and miles of safe, sandy beaches. Coastal attractions range from picturesque fishing villages to brash resorts such as Tramore, and the bustling port city of Waterford. To the west of the county, is some of Ireland's most beautiful scenery including some fine mountain passes.

PRINCIPAL TOWNS

WATERFORD

Waterford is by far the largest town in the Southeast, with its busy seaport and thriving industry. It is best known for Waterford Crystal, hand blown cut glass, which is exported all over the world. Visitors flock to its factory, just out of town, to join the free guided tours and maybe pick up an exclusive souvenir. While Waterford is a major commercial centre, it also has a proud history, with Viking remains to explore and fine Georgian houses to admire.

LISMORE

A most beautiful town to visit on the banks of the river Blackwater. Lismore's history is inextricably linked with the Church, from St Carthage's monastery built in the 6th century to the Cathedral named in his honour nearly a thousand years later.

MUST SEE

ARDMORE MONASTIC SITE, ARDMORE
(signposted off the N25 between Dungarvan and Youghal)
According to legend, 30 years before St Patrick arrived in Ireland in the 5th century, St Declan crossed from Wales and established a monastic settlement at Ardmore. He chose a magnificent location, with stunning views over the bay. To this day the site is known as Old Parish - believed to be the oldest parish in Ireland.

The site of the original monastic foundation is marked by the well-preserved 11th-century round tower of the ruined Cathedral of St Declan. The graveyard, pitching steeply towards the coast, contains St Declan's Oratory, where the saint is believed to be buried.

Roofless though it is, the old cathedral is an evocative place, with strikingly carved murals depicting the Adoration of the

Magi, the Judgement of Solomon and the Weighing of Souls.

CELTWORLD, RAILWAY SQUARE,
Tramore T 051 386166
The mystery and mythology of Celtic life in early Ireland is told in a high-tech presentation which employs three-dimensional images and larger-than-life moving figures, including the work of renowned Irish Celtic artist Jim Fitzpatrick.

WATERFORD CRYSTAL VISITOR CENTRE
Waterford *(on N25, 1 mile/1.5km from city centre)* T 051 73311 F 051 78539
The largest manufacturers of mouth-blown and hand-cut crystal open their doors to visitors for fascinating factory tours. Visitors can see masterCraftspeople at work, blowing glass, sculpturing and engraving crystal. In the gallery there is a fine display of Waterford Crystal and an audio visual presentation every 20 minutes.

BIG OUTDOORS

BALLYSAGGARTMORE TOWERS
Gothic-style buildings near Lismore, not open to the public, but surrounded by woodland walks, and picnic sites.

PEOPLE'S PARK, WATERFORD
Established over 100 years ago, People's Park provides 16 acres of recreational land close to the city centre. There are public performances from the bandstand in the summer months.

WEST WATERFORD VINEYARDS
Cappoquin T 058 54283
Wine is produced here from 2,000 vines in a stunning setting. Tasting and wine sales.

GREAT FOR KIDS

BEACHES
Beaches with the Blue Flag award are Bunmahon, Clonea, and Dunmore East's Councillors Strand. Tramore is a more commercial-style resort, with lots of fast food outlets and a fun park with a big dipper, bumper cars, and a boating lake.

LASERWORLD
Tramore T 051 386565
Computer-monitored electronic laser game with a Celtic maze and special effects.

LEMYBRIEN DOLL EXHIBITION
Lemybrien *(6 miles/10km northeast of Dungarvan on N25*
A private collector's display of antique dolls and toys dating from 1820.

SPLASH WORLD
Tramore T 051 390176 F 051 390214
Indoor water park including wave machine, indoor and outdoor flumes, rapids, splash slides, whirlpools, water cannons, fountains, geysers and a baby pool.

TOURANEEMA HERITAGE CENTRE,
Touraneema, Ballinamult
(off R672, 12 miles/19km from Dungarvan)
T 058 47353 F 058 47353
A 300-year-old thatched farmhouse, with a working dairy, blacksmith's, old machinery, gypsy wagon, baking and buttermaking, staff in period costume, pet farm and children's play area.

HISTORIC & ANCIENT SITES

CHRIST CHURCH CATHEDRAL
Cathedral Square, Waterford
An ornate Renaissance-style structure, designed by Waterford architect John Roberts and built in the 1770s to replace an 11th-century church on the same site.

CITY WALLS,
Waterford
Considerable stretches of the ancient city walls remain, dating from the 9th century. Walking tours run from the Granville Hotel - telephone Waterford Tourist Services on 051 873711 or 051 851043

LISMORE CASTLE
One of Ireland's most evocative fortresses, looming above the Blackwater valley, built in 1185 and extensively remodelled in the 19th-century. Only the gardens are open to the public.

FRENCH CHURCH
Cathedral Square, Waterford
Across the square from Christ Church Cathedral is the roofless French Church, founded as a Franciscan friary in 1240 and later used by Huguenot refugees.

HOLY TRINITY CATHEDRAL
Barronstrand Street, Waterford
The simple exterior of the Roman Catholic Cathedral, also designed by John Roberts, conceals an extravagantly decorated interior hung with chandeliers of Waterford Crystal.

REGINALD'S TOWER
The Mall, Waterford T 051 873501
Built by the Vikings in 1003 as part of Waterford's defences, this massive tower has served as a royal residence, mint and gaol. Now a civic museum.

HOMES & GARDENS

LISMORE CASTLE GARDENS
T 058 544 F 058 54896
A walled and woodland garden with a fine collection of camellias and magnolias and a remarkable Yew Walk. Spencer is believed to have written Faerie Queene here.

CURRAGHMORE HOUSE GARDENS
Portlaw T 051 387101 F 051 387481
An intriguing feature of these landscaped gardens is the Countess of Tyrone's shell house, dating from 1754.

MUSEUMS

LISMORE EXPERIENCE
Lismore Heritage Centre, Lismore
T 058 54975 F 058 53009
An audio-visual presentation of Lismore's rich history where the story of the naming of the cathedral is rather beguilingly told.

MARKET HOUSE
Lower Main Street, Dungarvan
T 058 41231
Local history museum with a maritime display and photographic collection displayed in the 17th-century Market House.

WATERFORD HERITAGE CENTRE
Greyfriars Street, Waterford T 051 871227
Viking and Norman artefacts unearthed during extensive excavations in the city in the 1980s, displayed in a 19th-century church, including leatherware, pottery and jewellery.

WATERFORD ROOM
Municipal Library, Lady Lane, Waterford
A special reference room of local material, including records and newspapers.

ESSENTIAL INFORMATION

ACCESS

AIR ACCESS

Waterford Regional Airport, Co Waterford
T 051 75589 F 051 77809

TOURIST INFORMATION

DUNGARVAN
Priory Street T 058 41741

TRAMORE
Railway Square T 051 381572

WATERFORD
41 The Quay
T 051 875788 F 051 877388

Waterford Crystal, Cork Road, Waterford
T 051 358397

GENEALOGY

WATERFORD HERITAGE GENEALOGICAL CENTRE,
St Patrick's Church, Jenkins Lane, Waterford
The place to trace your ancestry.

CRAFTS

ALISON TRIGG
Toutane House, Lismore T 058 54110
Hand-painted plasterwork.

ANNE O'LEARY
Kilgabriel, Clashmore T 024 96277
Hand-painted silk.

ARDMORE POTTERY
Ardmore T 024 94152
Hand-thrown earthenware pots.

CRIOSTAL NA RINNE
An Rinn T 058 46174
Individually designed and handcrafted cystal giftware.

ELEANOR HOWARD POTTERY
Main Street, Lismore 058 53033
Decorative earthenware.

FANTASY FOLK
Monatarriv, Lismore T 058 53144
Handcrafted wooden and ceramic dolls, puppets and marionettes.

IRISH WILDLIFE MOBILES
An Sean Phobal T 058 46281
Hand cut and painted timber mobiles.

WATERFORD WOODCRAFT
Dunabrattin, Annestown T 051 396110
Fine woodturning in Irish hardwoods.

SPORTS & LEISURE

ACTIVITY CENTRES

DUNMORE EAST ADVENTURE CENTRE
The Harbour, Dunmore East
T 051 383783 F 051 383786
Archery, hill-walking, Canadian canoeing, kayaking, orienteering, sailing, snorkeling and windsurfing.

ANGLING

Angling opportunities in Co Waterford abound, on rivers and lakes, on the coast and out at sea.

BLACKWATER LODGE FISHERIES
Upper Ballyduff T 058 60235
Fishing on the Blackwater River.
BRIAN BARTON
Ballincourty, Dungarvan T 058 44962
Sea-going angling.
CLONANAV ANGLING CENTRE
Ballymacarbry T/F 052 36141
Offering a complete service to anglers on the rivers Suir, Nire and Tar, and mountain lake fishing.
DUNGARVAN SEA ANGLING CLUB
T 058 41298
DUNMORE EAST ANGLING CHARTERS
Fairy Bush, Dunmore East T 051 383397
GONE FISHING,
42 Lower Main Street, Dungarvan
T 058 43514 F 058 43424
Sea-going angling.
MURWOOD FISHERIES,
Lismore T 058 60414

CYCLING

RENT-A-BIKE
Wrights Cycle Depot, 19-20 Henrietta Street, Waterford T 051 874411 F 051 873440

CYCLING ROUTES

Four themed cycle routes in the Barony of Gaultier T **051 382677.**

EQUESTRIAN CENTRES

CALLAGHANE RIDING & TREKKING
Dunmore Road, Waterford
T 051 382154 or 088 525922
COLLIGAN EQUESTRIAN CENTRE,
Dungarvan T 058 68261
FINISK VALLEY RIDING CENTRE,
Kilmolash Bridge, Cappoquin T 024 96257
KILOTTERAN EQUESTRIAN CENTRE,
Waterford T 051 384158
LAKE TOUR STABLES,
Carrigavantry, Tramore T 051 381958
MELODY'S TRAIL RIDING CENTRE,
Ballymacarbry T 052 36147
PALLAS EQUESTRIAN CENTRE,
Woodstown T 051 382112

GOLF COURSES

WATERFORD CASTLE COUNTRY CLUB
The Island, Ballinakill, Waterford
T 051 871633 F 051 871634
A lovely island course, a short ferry trip across a channel of the River Suir, in estate parklands adjoining the Castle.

WEST WATERFORD GOLF CLUB,
Dungarvan T 058 43216 F 058 44343
Designed by Eddie Hackett, the course is on 150 acres of rolling parkland by the Brickey River with a backdrop of hills.
Also:
DUNGARVAN T 058 43310/41605
DUNMORE EAST T 051 383151
FAITHLEGG T 051 382241
GOLD COAST T 058 42249
GOLD COAST RANGE T 058 44318
LISMORE T 058 54026
NEWTOWN RANGE T 051 381322
OLD COURT RANGE, T 051 54939
TRAMORE T 051 386170
WATERFORD T 051 876748

HORSE RACING

TRAMORE RACECOURSE
T 051 381574 or 088 599478

Dungarvan Golf Club

WHERE TO STAY

HOTELS

AA RECOMMENDED

Ballyrafter House

DUNGARVAN

LAWLORS★★★
T 058 41122 & 41056 F 058 41000
An ideal touring centre, this pleasant family-run hotel is most popular.
89 bedrooms Lift Night porter Parking

LISMORE

BALLYRAFTER HOUSE★★
(0.75 mile from Lismore opposite Lismore Castle)
T 058 54002 F 058 53050
Spectacular views and a haven for anglers. A tranquil atmosphere with home cooking
.10 bedrooms ££ No smoking in dining room Off-peak rates Parking Gardens Fishing Closed Nov-Feb 040>

BEECHCROFT★★★
Deerpark T 058 54273
(Opposite Presentation Convent School)
Warm hospitality and very comfortable bedrooms and lounge.Lovely gardens.
3 bedrooms No smoking in bedrooms £ Parking Closed 15 Dec-1 Jan

TRAMORE

MAJESTIC HOTEL★★★
(turn off N25 through Waterford onto R675 to Tramore)
T 051 381761 F 051 381766
Good sea views and friendly atmosphere.Entertainment in summer.
57 bedrooms (4 family, 5 for non-smokers) ££ Parking Swimming pool Lift

WATERFORD

BRIDGE★★★
The Quay T 051 77222 F 051 77229
Comfortable bedrooms, country-style bistro, restaurant, and traditional Irish pub.
96 bedrooms ££ Off-peak rates Lift Night porter Air conditioning

DOOLEY'S★★★
30 The Quay T 051 73531 F 051 70262
Friendly place with comfortable bedrooms, and i popular with local diners.
35 bedrooms, including some for non-smokers ££ Off-peak rates Night porter No smoking in dining room

GRANVILLE★★★
The Quay T 051 855111 F 051 870307
Quayside hotel with bright, airy bedrooms and spacious public rooms.
74 bedrooms including some for non-smokers £££ Off-peak rates Lift Night porter Parking (IR£1 per night) No smoking in dining room

IVORY LODGE INN
Tramore Rd T 051 358888 F 051 358899
Modern hotel where restaurant specialises in seafood. Golf packages arranged.
40 bedrooms (20 family) £ Parking Garden Closed 24-30 Dec

JURYS★★★
Ferrybank
(on N25 0.5 mile from city centre)
T 051 832111 F 051 832863
Large hotel in parkland with spacious lounges and comfortable bedrooms.
98 bedrooms including some for non-smokers Lift Night porter Parking Gardens Leisure facilities

ROUND TOWER HOTEL
T 024 94494 & 94382 F 024 94254
Friendly country house with a relaxed ambience and pleasant restaurant.
10 bedrooms (2 family) Family room £ Licenced Parking Garden Open Mar-Nov

TOWER HOTEL★★★
The Mall T 051 875801 F 051 870129
(opposite Reginald's Tower in the centre of town)
Excellent leisure facilities, pleasant restaurant and a bar overlooking the river.
141 bedrooms ££££ Off-peak rates Lift Night porter Parking Leisure facilities No smoking in dining room Banqueting/conference facilities

Bridge

WALKING

There are many established walks in the county, including the Ann Valley Walk along the Waterford coastline, the Brickey River and Kilnafarna Hill Walk, and the Barony of Gaultier Walking Circuits in East Waterford (tel 051 382677). There is a stretch of the Munster Way in the county and, another long distance walk, St Declan's Way, an old pilgrimage route from Ardmore to the Rock of Cashel

BED & BREAKFAST ACCOMMODATION

AA RECOMMENDED

Newtown View

ANNESTOWN

ANNESTOWN HOUSE QQQQ
(6 miles west of Tramore on R675 coast Road)
T 051 396160 F 051 396474
This period house has lovely bedrooms and public areas. Dinner by arrangement..
5 bedrooms, all no smoking £ Licensed Parking Tennis (grass) Snooker Croquet lawn Private beach

ARDMORE

NEWTOWN VIEW QQQ
Grange *(on N25 Dungarvan to Youghal road, turn left at Flemings public house)*
T 024 94143 & 088 600799 F 024 94143
The lounge and bedrooms are particularly pleasant. Secure children's play area.
6 annexe bedrooms No smoking in dining room £ Parking Tennis (hard) Snooker 110 acres dairy beef Open Apr-mid Oct

BALLINAMULT

SLIABH GLUA FARMHOUSE QQQ
10miles N of Dungarvan, signposted off the R672)
This comfortable farmhouse has lovely gardens and a well equipped play room.

BALLYMACARBRY

GLASHA FARMHOUSE QQQQ
Four Mile Water, Glasha **T 052 36108**
(8 miles from Clonmel on T27, turn right at Glasha Accommodation sign and drive for 0.5 mile)
Home baking is a speciality at this comfortable country house. Trout fishing in the river which runs through the grounds.
4 bedrooms Parking

CAPPOQUIN

RICHMOND HOUSE QQQQ
(on N72, 0.5 mile from Cappoquin on Dungarvan road)
T 058 54278 F 058 54988
Georgian house in wooded parkland with pretty bedrooms and restaurant .
9 bedrooms £ No smoking in area of dining room Licensed Parking Closed 23 Dec-1 Feb

CHEEKPOINT

THREE RIVERS QQQQ
(from Waterford follow R684 towards Dunmore East then follow signs for Cheekpoint)
T 051 382520 F 051 382542
River views,comfortable bedrooms, attractive gardens and a sunny balcony.
14 bedrooms, all no smoking £ No smoking in dining room Parking

DUNGARVAN

CASTLE FARM QQQQ
Millstreet, Cappash
(from N72 take R671 for 3.5 miles, turn right at Millstreet, farm 200yds on the right)
T 058 68049 F 058 68049
Intriguing west wing of a castle where the owner loves to cook. Pre-book dinner.
5 bedrooms £ Licensed Parking Tennis (hard) Fishing 120 acres dairy Open Mar-Oct.

KILLINEEN HOUSE QQ
Waterford Road **T 051 291294**
(off N25, 4.5 miles east
Surrounded by grassland, this house has lovely gardens with wonderful views.
5 bedrooms, all no smoking 50 acres grass

DUNMORE EAST

FOXMOUNT QQQQ
Passage East Road, off Dunmore Road
(from Waterford take Dunmore East road, after 3.5 miles take left fork at Maxol garage towards Passage East for 0.5 mile. Right at next Y junct)
T 051 874308 F 051 854906
Tastefully modernised farmhouse with comfortable rooms. Produce from farm.
6 bedrooms, all no smoking ££ Parking Tennis 200 acres dairy Open Mar-Nov

KILMACTHOMAS

COUMSHINGAUN LODGE ★★★
Kilclooney **T 051 646238**
(turn N from N25 onto R676 at Leamybrien, house is 6 miles on right)
Bedrooms have spectacular views. Relaxed atmosphere prevails. Pre-book dinner.
5 bedrooms (3 family, 3 for non-smokers) No smoking in dining room or lounges £ Parking Open 13 Mar-27 Oct

STRADBALLY

CARRIGAHILLA HOUSE & GARDENS QQQQ
Carrighilla **T 051 293127 F 051 293127**
(exit N25 at Stradbally turn off by Griffins Garage, house behind church)
Lovely old convent with many original features. Secret garden. Pre-book dinner.
4 bedrooms all no smoking, dining room or lounge £ Licensed Parking Over 3 acres of ornamental gardens Closed Jan

TRAMORE

GLENORNEY QQQQ
Newtown *(on R675 opposite the Golf Club)*
Spectacular views and great attention paid to detail. Extensive breakfast menu .
6 bedrooms No smoking £ Lift Parking Open Mar-Nov

Glasha Farmhouse

ƗUSHMERE HOUSE
Ɓranch Road T 051 381041
'on Waterford Road beside Majestic Hotel)
Ɔverlooking the sea this 100-year-old ɿouse stands in lovingly tended gardens.
ƽ bedrooms £ No smoking in dining room

ƽEA VIEW LODGE
ƽeaview Park T 051 381122
Ɐttractive bungalow with comfortable ɔedrooms, views and sun trap.
ƽ bedrooms No smoking in bedrooms, dining ʳoom or lounge No children under 5yrs Ƥarking Closed Nov–Mar

Coach House

Diamond Hill

WATERFORD

ASHBOURNE HOUSE
Ƨlieverue T 051 832037
'on the main N25 Waterford/Wexford road. Turn off at the Slieverue sign 2m from Waterford.)
Good hospitality and friendliness prevails at this comfortable ivy-clad house.
7 bedrooms £ Parking 25 acres beef Open Mar–Nov

BROWN'S TOWN HOUSE
29 South Parade
T 051 870594 F 051 871923
Freindly town centre Victorian house. Home made breads and jams are part of the big breakfasts served here.
4 bedrooms £ No smoking in dining room

COACH HOUSE
Butlerstown Castle, Butlerstown
(2 miles from Waterford off N25 towards Cork, signposted on left)
T 051 384656 F 051 384751
Contemporary facilities incorporated with subltety to provide excellent bedrooms.
7 bedrooms £ Licensed Parking Sauna

DIAMOND HILL
Diamond Hill, Slieverue
(situated a mile from Waterford City off Rosslare/Waterford Road N25)
T 051 832855 & 832254 F 051 832254
Set in superb gardens, inside is just as pleasant.. Good breakfasts and dinners.
10 bedrooms including some for non-smokers £ No smoking in dining room Parking

MARSUCI COUNTRY HOME
Oliver's Hill, Butlerstown
(take N25 towards Cork for 2 miles to Holy Cross public house and turn right, signposted. At T junction turn right and house 0.5 mile on right hand side)
T 051 370429 & 350982 F 051 350983
Peaceful rural house with comfortable bedrooms and lounge. Pre-book dinner.
6 bedrooms including some for non-smokers £ No smoking in dining room Licensed Parking

VILLA EILDON
Belmont Road, Ferrybank T 051 832174
(situated on N25 Waterford to Rosslare Road)
Beautifully decorated house with a pleasant outlook from the bedrooms.
6 bedrooms Double room £ No smoking Parking No children under 7yrs Open Jun–Oct

Brown's Town House

ART GALLERIES

DYEHOUSE GALLERY
Dyehouse Lane, Waterford
T 051 878166 F 051 850399
Paintings and pottery.

GARTER LANE ART GALLERY
O'Connell Street, Waterford
T 051 855038
Temporary exhibitions.

RIVER GALLERY
Patrick Street T 051 873328
Local artists' gallery.

CAMPING & CARAVANNING

AA RECOMMENDED SITES

CLONEA

CASEY'S CARAVAN PARK
T 058 41919
Signposted Nearby town: Dungarvan
3 pennants Caravans, motor caravans & tents
Open 15 May-10 Sep. Booking advisable May-Jun. Last arrival 22.00hrs. Last departure noon.
A 4.5-acre site with 40 touring pitches & 90 statics. Electric hook up, shower, electric shaver point, hairdrier, games room, separate TV room, cold storage, children's playground, Calor Gas, Camping Gaz, public telephone, shop.
Facilities within three miles of site: golf, boats for hire, cinema, fishing

WHERE TO EAT

RESTAURANTS

AA RECOMMENDED

BELLS RESTAURANT
Granville Hotel, The Quay
T 051 855111 F 051 870307
An elegant restaurant in a historic quayside hotel. The carte offers a range of dishes tagged with local place-names, as in Lobster and Crab Dunmore East (cooked with brandy and tomatoes) and Chicken Cappoquin (fillet of chicken filled with chorizo sausage in a cream and sherry sauce).

PUBS, INNS & OTHER PLACES

WATERFORD CITY

DWYERS
Mary Street T 051 77478
Intimate restaurant near the waterside.

GALLEY CRUISING RESTAURANT
Waterford Quay T 051 42123
Go up river while you eat.,not as touristy as it sounds. Afternoon tea at 3pm.

HARICOTS,
11 O'Connell Street
Wholefood restaurant.

HARVEST RESTAURANT
George's Street
Tourist menu.

JACK MEADES PUB
Cheekpoint Road T 051 873187 or 850950
Situated under the old stone bridge by the millrace. Some musical evenings plus an animal farm and agricultural museum.

JADE PALACE,
3-4 The Mall T 051 55611 F 051 54632
International menu plus exotic seafood.

LA PALMA RESTAURANT
4 Parnell House T 051 879823
Italian cooking.

LOUGHMANS
George's Court
Restaurant and coffee shop.

THE OLD STAND,
45 Michael Street
T 051 879488 F 051 857646
Waterford's oldest tavern.All-day bar food, lunchtime carvery, sandwich and salad bar.

THE REGINALD
The Mall, Waterford T 051 55087
F 051 71026
This bar and restaurant enjoys an historical setting by the old city wall.

T & H DOOLANS,
31-32 George's Street
T 051 841504 F 051 857646
One of Ireland's oldest pubs, serving Irish food and seafood. Traditional Irish music

BALLYRAFTER HOUSE HOTEL
Lismore T 058 54002 F 058 53050
Local produce features prominently. House honey is used to good effect.

BARRONS BAKERY & COFFEE HOUSE
Cappoquin T 058 54045 F 058 52012
Quality baking from an olf brick oven in a 50's-style coffee shop.Try Waterford Blas - a kind of crusty bap.

BRIDE VIEW BAR & RIVER ROOM RESTAURANT,
Tallow, Waterford
T 058 56522 F 058 56729
Home-cooked meals in a riverside setting.

BUGGY'S GLENCAIRN INN,
Glencairn, near Lismore T 058 56232
Traditional inn offering freshly prepared food. in bar or dining room.

CANDLELIGHT INN
Dunmore East T 051 383239
F 051 383289
Traditional Irish home cooking;.

CARRIGAHILLA HOUSE & GARDEN
Stradbally T 051 293127
Four-course dinners are served at this former convent.

HANORA'S COTTAGE, NIRE VALLEY
Ballymacarbry T 052 36134 F 052 3654[illegible]
Local produce is used to create interesting dishes. Delicious bread, home-baked daily

MELODY'S NIRE VIEW BAR
Ballymacarbry T 052 36147
A traditional pub serving freshly prepared food.. Music some nights. Pony trekking .

MERRY'S RESTAURANT
Lower Main Street, Dungarvan T 058 4197[illegible]
Dine in an old shop full of bric-a-brac

RICHMOND HOUSE,
Cappoquin T 058 54278
A Georgian country house featuring local produce and some vegetarian dishes.

ROUND TOWER HOTEL
Ardmore
T 024 94494 or 94382 F 024 94254
Former convent serving bar food, lunch, dinner and afternoon tea.

SEANACHI BAR & RESTAURANT
Dungarvan West T 058 46285
F 058 46305
A pretty thatched pub with simple food iincluding seafood and children's dishes

SHIP INN
Dunmore East T 051 83141
Nautically decorated pub with fishy dishes

STRAND SEAFOOD RESTAURANT
Dumore East T 051 383174 F 051 38375[illegible]
Right on the beach with terrific views. Seafood, of course, is the house speciality.

COUNTY WEXFORD

This pleasant and fairly unremarkable county has an extraordinarily rich and bloody history. The many harbours and estuaries of the region gave entry to marauding Vikings, who held power for many years, only to be followed by the Anglo-Normans. The disaffected locals, led by the MacMurrough Kavanaghs, maintained their resistance against the English until they were crushed by Cromwell, who slaughtered hundreds of unarmed civilians at Wexford. The 18th century saw a period of relative peace, until confrontation with the yeomanry brought simmering resentment to the surface in 1798 and the people of Carlow and Wexford took up their pikes in a heroic, but ultimately doomed, stand against English canons at the battle of Vinnegar Hill, Enniscorthy. Today, the county is better known for its pleasant beaches, heritage parks, Opera Festival and the Stawberry Fairs of Wexford and Enniscorthy.

PRINCIPAL TOWN

WEXFORD

Despite its violent history, Wexford is a pretty, peaceful place with few traces of its ancient past. It enjoys its share of the limelight, however, each October during the Opera Festival. It's not difficult to see how the town got its Viking name, Waesfjord - harbour of the mudflats. The slow moving River Slaney and several of its tributaries empty their silt-laden waters into the estuary here, providing a valuable habitat for thousands of wading birds.

MUST SEE

IRISH NATIONAL HERITAGE PARK, FERRYCARRIG
(2 miles/3km miles from Wexford on N11)
T 053 20733 F 053 20911
Fourteen historic sites set in a magnificent 35-acre mature forest explaining Ireland's history from the Stone and Bronze Ages, through the mighty Celtic period and concluding with the Vikings and Normans. Among the exhibits are a reconstructed Mesolithic camp, a Viking boatyard with two full size ships and a Norman motte and bailey. Other attractions include ancient breed animals, an audio-visual presentation Ireland Through the Ages, coffee shop, craft shop and guided tours. Ring for details of special events.

BIG OUTDOORS

JOHN F KENNEDY PARK & ARBORETUM
Dunganstown T 051 388171 F 051 388172
(7 miles/12km south of New Ross), off R733
Situated above the Kennedy ancestral home, this collection of 4,500 types of trees and shrubs is set in 623 acres/252 hectares. In summer, you can go round it by pony and trap or miniature railway, depending on your fancy.

SLIEVE COILLTE HILL
Access to the hill (886ft/270m) is opposite the entrance to the John F Kennedy Arboretum. The views are quite spectacular, including those over Waterford Harbour. There is a car park and picnic site here.

WEXFORD WILDFOWL RESERVE,
North Sloblands, Wexford T 053 23129
(take coast road over bridge for 1.5 miles/3km, signs show turning at right)
Internationally important reserve on the Slaney Estuary for Greenland white-fronted geese, Brent geese, Bewick's swans and wigeon. Do make use of the hides, observation tower and visitor centre.

GREAT FOR KIDS

BEACHES
Blue Flag beaches are Courtown, Curracloe, Duncannon and Rosslare.

CURRACLOE NATURE TRAIL
An 875yd/800m nature trail through sand dunes by the sea. Information booklet available for a small charge from The Winning Post at Curracloe or the County Council Office in Wexford (tel 053 42211).

FUN HOUSE, REDMOND PLACE
Wexford T 053 46696
Indoor children's adventure play.

KIA ORA INDOOR MINI FARM
T 055 21166
Animals from home and abroad.

YOLA FARMHOUSE,
Tagoat T 053 31177
Reconstructed farm buildings, nature walks, craft studio and children's play area.

YOUNG MCDONALD'S ANIMAL PARK
Askamore T 05526312
Animals, play area, river walks and café.

HISTORIC & ANCIENT SITES

BALLYHACK CASTLE
T 051 89468
A 16th-century castle with two renovated floors housing a number of exhibits.

DUNBRODY ABBEY VISITORS CENTRE
Dunbrody Abbey, Campile, New Ross
T 051 88603
Based around the abbey and Dunbrody Castle, including an intriguing yew hedge maze, a museum, pitch and putt course, shop and garden centre.

DUNCANNON FORT
T 051 389454
Built on the site of an Iron Age fortification, in response to fears of attack from the Spanish Armada, this imposing fort dates from 1588.

ENNISCORTHY CASTLE
T 054 35926
A 13th-century Norman castle, now home to Wexford County Museum.

FERNS CASTLE
A ruined 13th-century Norman castle, held by the MacMurrough Kavanaghs for 200 years and retaken by Lord Grey in 1536 - now owned by the state.

HOOK LIGHTHOUSE
Built in 1172, this 100ft/30.5m structure was about 600 years ahead of its time - lighthouses were first built in the 18th century.

LADY'S ISLAND
A place of pilgrimage since the beginning of recorded time, believed to pre-date the pre-Christian period, including a ruined Augustinian priory and a leaning Norman castle tower.

RATHMACKNEE CASTLE (NATIONAL MONUMENT)
A five-storey tower castle with 15th-century battlements. The rare five-sided bawn has walls four feet /1.2m thick and 25ft/7.5m high.

SLADE CASTLE
A late 15th-century castle overlooking the harbour at Slade. The adjoining fortified house was built much later.

TINTERN ABBEY
T 01 6613111 or 051 562321
A Cistercian Abbey built in 1200 by William, Earl Marshall, in fulfilment of a promise he made to God during a perilous sea voyage, should his life be spared. Recently restored.

HOMES & GARDENS

BERKELEY FOREST HOUSE,
New Ross T 051 21361
An extensive collection of 18th- and 19th-century toys, dolls and costumes.

Irish Agricultural Museum

UNMAIN HOUSE
ew Ross T 051 62122
n imposing slate-covered,17th-century ouse with a history of intriguing stories, ne subject of many a novel, including Guy Mannering by Sir Walter Scott.

OHNSTOWN CASTLE GARDENS,
Wexford T 053 42888
4 miles/6.5km southwest)
ifty acres/20ha of grounds, with lakes, vildfowl, walled gardens and hot houses, lus the ruins of the medieval Rathlannon astle. (The 19th-century mansion is osed to the public.)

AM HOUSE GARDENS
oolgreany
T 0402 37238 or 32006 F 0402 31205
Mature gardens, surrounding an old ouse, divided into 'rooms', each with its wn treatment. The gardens include a ttle stream, pond and a woodland glade.

MUSEUMS & ART GALLERIES

BALLYMORE HISTORIC FEATURES
Camolin T 054 83189
A traditional farm with a period farmyard, small museum, church and holy well .

CRAANFORD MILL
Craanford T 055 28124 or 055 28392
17th-century water mill in working order, with interpretative display and restaurant.

IRISH AGRICULTURAL MUSEUM
Johnstown Castle Old Farmyard, Wexford
(4 miles southwest of N25)
T 053 42888 F 053 42213
A museum set in old farm buildings with extensive displays on rural transport, farming and the farmhouse, and replicas of workshops, including a blacksmith, cooper and basket-maker.

GUILLEMOT LIGHTSHIP MARITIME MUSEUM
Kilmore Quay Harbour T 053 29655
The last remaining light ship in Kilmore Quay Harbour, with a display of artefacts.

NATIONAL MUSEUM OF AGRICULTURE & RURAL LIFE
Johnstown Castle, Johnstown
T 053 42888 F 053 42213
Established on the former estate farm, within the grounds of Johnstown Castle.

WEXFORD COUNTY MUSEUM
Enniscorthy T 054 35926
Local history museum housed in a medieval castle.

WEXFORD MEDIEVAL EXPERIENCE,
Westgate Heritage Centre, Wexford
T 053 46506 F 053 45947
An audio-visual presentation of the town's history, set in a 13th-century gate tower, part of the town's Viking/Norman walls.

ESSENTIAL INFORMATION

ACCESS

SEA ACCESS

Pembroke or Fishguard to Rosslare Ferry erminal, Rosslare

TOURIST INFORMATION

NNISCORTHY
he Castle T 054 34699

OREY
Main Street T 055 21248

EW ROSS
ennedy Centre, North Quay T 051 21857

OSSLARE
erry Terminal T 053 33622 F 053 3421

VEXFORD
rescent Quay T 053 23111 F 053 41743

GENEAOLOGY

YOLA FARMSTEAD, TAGOAT
T 053 31177
research service for Wexford

CRAFTS

ocal craft pottery is a good choice for ouvenirs of the region.
BADGER HILL POTTERY
Enniscorthy T 054 35060
Oven to table stoneware.
BUTLERSLAND CRAFT CENTRE
Butlersland, New Ross T 051 422612
Extensive range of hand-woven crafts
CARLEY'S BRIDGE POTTERY
Enniscorthy T 054 33512
Makers of fine terracotta pots since 1640
CASTLE HILL CRAFTS
Enniscorthy T 054 36800
Established more than 400 years ago.
KILTREA BRIDGE POTTERY
Kiltrea T 054 35107
Planters and kitchenware.
KYLE GALLERY & CRAFT CENTRE
Crossabeg T 053 28433
Fine art plus a range of craft products.
LAVERY POTTERY
Near New Ross T 051 428478
Hand-thrown pottery.
THE LOFT GALLERY
The Quay, New Ross T 051 425389

SPORTS & LEISURE

ACTIVITY CENTRES

PIRATES COVE
Courtown T 055 25555
Golf, ten pin bowling and other attractions for both adults and children.
HOUSE OF STORYTELLING
T 054 44148
A monthly evening of storytelling, drama, art and prayer - bring your own refreshments

ANGLING

The Slaney River is good for salmon. Contact local Tourist Office for details. Shore fishing on the coast is free. For deep sea angling, contact the following:
DICK HAYES T 053 29704
SALTEES PRINCESS,
Kilmore Quay T 053 29900
SHARK HUNTER T 053 42966/087 429517
WEXFORD BOAT CHARTERS T 053 45888

CYCLING

RENT-A-BIKE, Paddy Meyler, 6 Bridge Street, Wexford T 051 25348

EQUESTRIAN CENTRES

BALLINGALE FARM RIDING SCHOOL,
Taghmon T 053 34387
BLACKSTONE TREKKING CENTRE,
Blackstone, Duncormick T 053 63126
BORO HILL EQUESTRIAN CENTRE,
Clonroche, Enniscorthy T 053 44117
HOOK TREKKING CENTRE,
Duncannon T 051 89166
HORETOWN EQUESTRIAN,
Horetown House, Foulksmills T 051 63786
LARAHEEN PONY TREKKING,
Laheen House, Gorey T 055 28289
SEAVIEW FARM PONY TREKKING,
St Kearns, Saltmills, New Ross T 051 562239

GOLF COURSES

ST HELEN'S BAY COUNTRY CLUB
T 053 33234 F 053 33803
Challenging championship course
Also:
BALLYMONEY T 055 21976
COURTOWN T 055 25166 F 055 25553
ENNISCORTHY T 054 33191
NEW ROSS T 051 21433
ROSSLARE T 053 32203
TARA GLEN COUNTRY CLUB T 055 45413 **WEXFORD** T 053 42238

GREYHOUND RACING

ENNISCORTHY TRACK T 054 33172
WEXFORD RACECOURSE,
Newtown Rd, Wexford T 051 21681

WALKING

GUIDED WALKING TOURS OF:
ENNISCORTHY T 054 36800
NEW ROSS T 051 25028
WEXFORD (DAYTIME) T 053 46506
WEXFORD (EVENING) T 053 41081
WEXFORD COASTAL PATH T 053 42211
A well signposted route from Kilmichael Point to Ballyhack.

WATERSPORTS

ROSSLARE SAILBOARD & WATERSPORTS CENTRE T 053 32114
Minimum age 10 years.

WHERE TO STAY

HOTELS

AA RECOMMENDED

Ferrycarri

ARTHURSTOWN

DUNBRODY COUNTRY HOUSE HOTEL & RESTAURANT ★★★
Arthurstown, New Ross
(12 miles S of New Ross. From N11 follow signs from Duneannor/Ballyhack)
Elegant and comfortable house, set in parkland. Beaches, golf, horse riding and walking nearby.

COURTOWN HARBOUR

COURTOWN ★★
(5 miles off N11)
T 055 25210 & 25108 F 055 25304
Noted for good food and a friendly atmosphere. Dinner theatre shows in summer.
21 bedrooms ££ Off-peak rates Night porter Parking Gardens Leisure facilities Children's facilities No smoking in dining room Closed Nov-mid Mar

BAY VIEW ★★
T 055 25307 F 055 25576
Family-run hotel complex offers a range of leisure facilities.; many bedrooms have sea views
17 bedrooms Parking Leisure facilities No smoking Closed Nov-mid Mar

ENNISCORTHY

MURPHY-FLOOD'S ★
Market Square
(follow signs to hotel in the town centre)
T 054 33413 F 054 33413
A central family-run hotel. Carvery lunches, grills and snacks are served throughout the day.
21 bedrooms including some for non-smokers £ Off-peak rates No smoking in dining room Night porter

GOREY

MARLFIELD HOUSE ★★★
T 055 21124 F 055 21572
Elegance and luxury pervades throughout, lovely views of grounds and wildlife reserve. Excellent restaurant.
19 bedrooms ££££ Off-peak rates Parking Gardens Leisure facilities Closed mid Dec-Jan

NEW ROSS

THE OLD RECTORY ★★
Rosbercon **T 051 421719 F 051 422974**
(cross the bridge, turn off to the right and follow road for 200yds up hill, hotel on right)
12 bedrooms ££ Off-peak rates Parking Gardens No smoking in dining room Closed Jan

ROSSLARE

CEDARS ★★★
(off N25)
T 053 32124 F 053 32243
Pleasant lounges, restaurants and bedrooms. Nightly enterntainment in summer.
34 bedrooms (some fmly) ££ Off-peak rates No smoking in dining room Night porter Air conditioning Parking Gardens Children's facilities Closed Jan-mid Apr

KELLY'S RESORT ★★★★
T 053 32114 F 053 32222
Wonderful food and high levels of comfort in this special hotel. Emphasis on family holidays.
99 bedrooms Lift Night porter Parking Gardens Leisure facilities Children's facilities Closed mid Dec-late Feb

ROSSLARE HARBOUR

HOTEL ROSSLARE ★★★
T 053 33110 F 053 33386
Friendly atmosphere and good food are priorities, plus an interesting old bar.
25 bedrooms ££ Off-peak rates No smoking in dining room Night porter Parking Fishing Leisure Facilities

WEXFORD

FERRYCARRIG ★★★
Ferrycarrig **T 053 20999 F 053 20982**
(on N11 by estuary, beside Ferrycraig Castle)
Superb food and location to match on a sea inlet. Very smart bedrooms, some with balconies.
39 bedrooms ££ Off-peak rates No smoking in dining room Lift Night porter Parking Gardens Leisure facilities (inc indoor pool, gym, jacuzzi & sauna)

TALBOT ★★★
Trinity Street **T 053 22566 F 053 23377**
(on waterfront on Rosslare side of town)
Pretty bedrooms, comfortable lounge. Country-kitchen style food.*100 bedrooms, including some for non-smokers No smokin in dining room Lift Night porter Parking Leisure facilities*

WEXFORD LODGE ★★
(beside Wexford Bridge on R741)
T 053 23611 F 053 23342
Overlooking the harbour with pleasant lounges and super bedrooms .
19 bedrooms Parking

WHITE'S ★★★
George Street
T 053 22311 F 053 45000
Charming old coaching inn, part of which is a converted saddlery and forge.
82 bedrooms (6 in annexe) ££ Off-peak rates No smoking in dining room Lift Night porter Parking Leisure facilities

WHITFORD HOUSE ★★★
New Line Road
T 053 43444 & 43845 F 053 46399
Smart modern hotel, in a rural setting with large bedrooms, charming lounges and a popular restaurant..
23 bedrooms £ Off-peak rates Night porter Parking Gardens Indoor Swimming pool Tennis Children's playground Restricted service 24 Dec-31 Jan

Call the AA Hotel Booking Service on 0990 050505 to book at AA recognised hotels and B&Bs in the UK and Ireland, or through our internet site: http://www.theaa.co.uk/hotels

BED & BREAKFAST ACCOMMODATION

AA RECOMMENDED

Harbour House

ARTHURSTOWN

GLENDINE COUNTRY HOUSE QQQ
T 051 389258
Overlooking the estuary.Spacious sitting room and comfortable bedrooms.
4 bedrooms (inc 2 no-smoking) £ No smoking in dining room & 1 lounge Garden Childrens facilities Parking Open Mar-Nov

BALLYHACK

MARSH MERE LODGE QQQQ
T 051 389186
A pretty pink house with many personal touches and delightful bedrooms. Parking
5 bedrooms No smoking Open Mar-Nov

COURTOWN HARBOUR

HARBOUR HOUSE QQQ
Near Gorey **T 055 25117**
Imposing house close to a sandy beach. Manybedrooms have sea views. Also self-catering mobile home park.

ENNISCORTHY

BALLINKEELE HOUSE QQQQ
Ballymurn **T 053 38105 F 053 38468**
(from Wexford take N11 N to Oilgate village then turn right and follow signs)
Classical house with original features Warm atmosphere.Well prepared dinners.
5 bedrooms, all no-smoking ££ Licensed Parking Leisure facilities 350 acres Open Mar-mid Nov Res mid Nov-Feb

Ballinkeele House

LEMONGROVE HOUSE QQQ
Blackstoops **T 054 36115**
(0.5 mile north of Enniscorthy at roundabout on Dublin to Rosslare road - N11)
Large house in grounds with comfortable bedrooms. Rosslare Ferry nearby
5 bedrooms, all no smoking ££ No smoking in dining room Parking

FERNS

CLONE HOUSE QQQQ
(2 miles southeast off N11)
T 054 66113 F 054 66113
Hospitable house. Fine furniture from past generations enhance modern comforts.
5 bedrooms, all no smoking or in dining room Parking Leisure facilities Fishing 280 acres mixed Open Mar-Oct

FOULKESMILL

HORETOWN HOUSE QQQ
Lovely 18th-century manor house standing in parkland.Country house-style cuisine .
12 bedrooms (10 fmly) No smoking in dining room Licensed Parking Riding Centre 214 acres mixed

GOREY

GLENBOWER HOUSE QQQQ
The Avenue **T 055 20514 F 055 22333**
Restored spacious ivy-clad town house,. Beach, golf and sea angling nearby.
5 bedrooms, all no smoking £ No smoking in dining room Parking (2 covered spaces) Riding Closed mid Dec-mid Jan

HILLSIDE HOUSE QQQQ
Tubberduff **T 055 21726 22036**
(turn off N11, 1 mile after passing Tom Byrnes pub, signposted Hillside House)
Lovely rural location with mountain and sea views, near beach.Evening meals.
6 bedrooms, all no smoking £ No smoking in dining room Licensed Parking Children's facilities

WOODLANDS QQQQ
Killinierin *(signposted from N11)*
T 0402 37125 & 37133 F 0402 37133
Pleasant Georgian-style residence. Some bedrooms have balconies. Set dinner
6 bedrooms, all no smoking £ No smoking in dining room Licensed Parking Leisure facilities Tennis Pony rides 8 acres beef (non-working) Closed Nov-Feb

KILMORE

QUAY HOUSE QQQ
Kilmore Quay *(turn off N25 onto R739 following sign to Kilmore Quay, house on left after Hotel Saltees)*
T 053 29988 F 053 29808
6 bedrooms (all family) No smoking in bedrooms £ Parking

NEWBAWN

WOODLANDS HOUSE QQQ
Carrickbyrne *(on N25 Rosslare/New Ross Road, close to Cedar Lodge Hotel)*
T 051 428287 F 051 428287
Run with loving care by bee-keeping .Backs onto a forest with signed trails.
4 bedrooms, all no smoking £ No smoking in dining room Parking No children under 6yrs Games room Honey making demonstration Open Mar-Nov

NEW ROSS

CARBERY QQQ
Montgarrett **T 051 422742**
Pleasant residential area. Attractive bedrooms overlooking the gardens.
3 bedrooms (1 family) £ Open May-Sep

CASTLEFIELD FARM QQQ
Listerlin, Tullogher **T 051 427346**
Find generous hospitality and humour at this comfortable house. Dinner available.
4 bedrooms (2 family, 1 for non-smokers) £ 200 acre mixed farm

ROSSLARE HARBOUR

CHURCHTOWN HOUSE QQQQQ
Tagoat **T 053 32555 F 053 32555**
(take R736 from N25 at Tagoat, turn between Cushens pub and church)

Charming period house near ferry. Spacious and elegant. rooms.
12 bedrooms £ Licensed Parking No children Open mid Feb-mid Nov

KILRANE HOUSE
(on N25 opposite Cullens Pub)
T 053 33135 F 053 33739
Near harbour. Many original features plus open fires and a superb guest lounge.
6 bedrooms No smoking in dining room Parking

THE LIGHT HOUSE
Main Road **T 053 33214**
Replica lighthouse in front garden. Bright, clean contemporary bungalow
4 bedrooms No smoking £ Parking

Killiane Castle

O'LEARY'S
(exit N25 in Kilrane between the two pubs, left at crossroads, right at junction for 1 mile)
T 053 33134
This farmhouse is located in a peaceful setting overlooking St George's Channel.
10 bedrooms, all no smoking £ No smoking in dining room Parking 100 acres arable

ORCHARD PARK
Rosslare Rd **T 053 32182 F 053 32182**
(turn off N25 at Cushen spub in Tagoat onto the R736, premises 0.75 mile on the left)
Extended farm bungalow in a quiet location. Spacious lounge and play area.
6 bedrooms, all no smoking £ No smoking in dining room & 1 lounge Parking Tennis (hard) Trampoline 80 acres arable

Hillside House

WEXFORD

ARD RUADH MANOR
Spawell Rd **T 053 23194 F 053 23194**
(opposite County Hall on N25)
Magnificent former vicarage, with large bedrooms and luxurious lounge.
5 bedrooms £ No smoking in dining room Parking No children under 3yrs

THE BLUE DOOR
18 Lower George Street **T 053 21047**
Restored town house Inear Theatre Royal. Pretty bedrooms and inviting sitting room.
4 bedrooms (1 family) No smoking in dining room & lounge £ Closed 22-30 Dec

CLONARD HOUSE
Clonard Great *(signposted on R733/N25 roundabout. Take R733 south for 500m, first road on left and first entrance on left)*
T 053 43141 & 47337 F 053 43141
Lovely Georgian farmhouse with good views. Some bedrooms have four posters.
9 bedrooms, all no smoking £ Licensed Parking 120 acres dairy

DARRAL HOUSE
Spallwell Road **T 053 24264**
Excellent rooms and choice at breakfast.
4 bedrooms No smoking in bedrooms & dining room £ Parking

KILLIANE CASTLE
Drinagh **T/F 053 58885** *(turn off N25 at Farmers Kitchen Hotel. 3m from Wexford.)*
Near13th-century castle. Pleasant property, furnished in keeping with the era.
8 bedrooms (2 family) £ No smoking Tennis Licensed 230 acre dairy farm Closed Mar-Nov

MCMENAMIN'S
3 Auburn Terrace, Redmond Road
(situated to W of town opp railway/bus)
T 053 46442 F 053 46442
Fine Victorian house with some fine antique beds and lovely lounge.
6 bedrooms £ No smoking in dining room & 1 lounge Parking

MOUNT AUBURN
1 Auburn Terrace, Redmond Road
(from direction of Dublin on N11, turn left Ferrycraig Bridge. House 2 miles on right)
T 053 24609 & 21470
Inviting house with pretty bedrooms, some with four-posters. Pre-book dinner
6 bedrooms (2 family, 2 non-smokers) No smoking in dining room or lounge £ Parking

O'BRIENS AUBURN HOUSE
2 Auburn Terrace, Redmond Rd
(opposite railway station)
T 053 23605
Do not be confused with the similarly named house next-door. Attractive bedrooms and comfortable lounge.
5 bedrooms £ No smoking in dining room

RATHASPECK MANOR
Rathaspeck
(signposted on N25, near Johnstone castle)
T 053 42661 & 45148
Old country house with large bedrooms and pleasant lounge. Pre-book dinner.
6 bedrooms £ Licensed Parking No children under 10yrs Golf Tennis (hard) Open May-early Nov

SHANORA LODGE
Newtown Rd **T 053 41414**
(1 mile on N11/N25, 100m from services)
Lovely views and pretty gardens. Spacious lounge, two bedrooms on ground floor.
5 bedrooms (1 family) No smoking in dining room £ Parking

SLANEY MANOR
Ferrycarrig *(on N11 400m W National Heritage Park)*
T 053 20051 & 20144 F 053 20510
Period manor house where richly decorated bedrooms have four-posters
8 bedrooms £ No smoking Licensed Lift 60 acres Parking Closed Dec-Jan

Kilrane House

CAMPING & CARAVANNING

AA RECOMMENDED SITES

KILMUCKRIDGE

IORRISCASTLE STRAND CARAVAN & 'AMPING PARK
Iorriscastle **T 053 30124 & 01 4535355 off season)** *Signposted Nearby town: Gorey*
pennants, caravans, motor caravans and ents. Open Jul-Aug (restricted service Iay-Jun & Sep, shop, reception, games oom, take-away food). Booking advisable Vhitsun weekend & mid Jul-mid Aug. Last rrival 22.00hrs. Last departure 16.00hrs. o dogs.A 16-acre site with 100 touring itches and 150 statics. Dish-washing oom, indoor cooking facilities. Electric ook up, shower, electric shaver point, aunderette, tennis, games room, cold torage, children's playground, Calor Gas, amping Gaz, public telephone, fast food/take away, shop, disabled facilities. *Facilities within three miles of site: stables, golf, mini golf, cinema, fishing*

LADY'S ISLAND

ST MARGARET'S BEACH CARAVAN & CAMPING PARK,
St Margaret's **T 053 31169** *Signposted*
2 pennants, caravans, motor caravans and tents. Open Mar-Oct.
A 2-acre site with 20 touring pitches and 20 static. Electric hook up, hairdrier

WEXFORD

FERRYBANK CARAVAN PARK
Ferrybank **T 053 44378 or 43274**
Signposted
Q award, 3 pennants, attractive environment, first class washing and sanitary facilities, caravans, motor caravans and tents. Open Whit weekend-Aug (restricted service Easter and Sep, no shop). Booking advisable Whit weekend and Aug bank holiday. Last arrival 22.00hrs. Last departure 16.00hrs.
A 10-acre site with 130 touring pitches. Electric hook up, shower, electric shaver point, launderette, indoor swimming pool, games room, separate TV room, cold storage, children's playground, café/restaurant, public telephone, fast food/takeaway, picnic area, shop, disabled facilities. *Facilities within three miles of site: stable, golf course, mini golf, boats for hire, cinema, fishing*

WHERE TO EAT

RESTAURANTS

AA RECOMMENDED

:OURTOWN HOTEL ❀
ourtown Harbour, Courtown
5 miles off N11)
T 055 25210 & 25108 F 055 25304
friendly seaside hotel noted for its xcellent food. Summer entertainment akes the form of dinner theatre shows.

HE CONSERVATORY ❀❀
errycarrig Hotel, Ferrycarrig, Wexford
n N11 by Slaney Estuary, beside Ferrycraig Castle)
T 053 20999 F 053 20982
waterside conservatory restaurant with a arte menu, which makes good use of ocal produce, particularly seafood.
LC £££

UNBRODY COUNTRY HOUSE ❀❀
unbrody Country House Hotel & estaurant, Arthurstown, New Ross
12 miles S of New Ross. From N11 follow gns from Duneannor/Ballyhack)
T 051 389600 F 051 389601
The priorities of Catherine and Chef/patron Kevin Dundon are generous hospitality, a tranquil ambience and outstanding food in luxurious surroundings, although at first glance the menu may seem understated. Char-grilled monkfish and mussels come superbly presented as a colonnade of mussels forming a guard of honour and taste every bit as good as it looks.

KELLY'S RESORT HOTEL
Rosslare **T 053 32114 F 053 32222**
Menus are varied and generous at this large, elegant hotel restaurant, and local produce, particularly seafood, figures prominently. Typical dishes are bruschetta topped with Kilmore prawns and basil dressing, roast Rosslare lamb with potato dauphinoise and mint, and Clonroche strawberries and cream.
FIXED L ££ D £££

MARFIELD HOUSE HOTEL ❀❀
Gorey **T 055 21124 F 055 21572**
A stunningly presented restaurant and conservatory in a country house setting. Much of the produce offered from the seasonal menus comes from the hotel's own kitchen garden. The four-course dinner menu might include risotto of smoked duckling with parmesan and pear; baked Kinsale lobster with escargot butter, served with herb salad and new season potatoes, and to finish, glazed lemon tart with blackberry sorbet.
FIXED L ££ D £££

WHITFORD HOUSE HOTEL ❀
New Line Road, Wexford
T 053 43444 & 43845 F 053 46399
A popular restaurant, in a smart modern hotel, with a country setting on the edge of Wexford. There's a big choice of fish from 'rivers, lakes and seas', steaks and Wexford lamb from an extensive carte.
ALC £££

PUBS, INNS & OTHER PLACES

'ELLAR RESTAURANT,
loretown House, Foulksmills **T 051 63771**
ountry cooking in the splendid setting of 300-year-old manor house.

HE GALLEY
lew Ross **T 051 21723**
Iobile, cruising restaurants operating etween Waterford and New Ross during ne summer, offering fresh local produce.

MARLFIELD HOUSE
Gorey **T 055 21124**
The style of the food matches the rest of the house - rich, opulent and complicated.

NEPTUNE
Ballyhack **T 051 89284**
Near castle and car ferry ,this agreeable little seafood restaurant is worth crossing the water for. Perhaps a harp recital.

OYSTER RESTAURANT
Rosslare Strand **T 053 32439**
Wine bar and seafood restaurant in the heart of the resort.

The South Western Counties

COUNTIES CORK, KERRY AND LIMERICK

This southwestern corner of Ireland has just about everything you might want from a tourist destination - a pleasant climate, interesting towns, beautiful scenery and plenty of things to do and places to see. Visitors are very well catered for in terms of quality accommodation and restaurants, and the area is renowned for its good local produce and fine food. This has not always been the case - the region suffered terribly during the Great Irish Famine of the 1840s, and the consequent mass emigration to the New World brings many visitors from overseas, paying their respects to the ancestral home. Features of the Southwest are the two big towns of Cork and Limerick, and the beautiful coastline, including the Dingle peninsula, one of the largest Gaeltacht (Irish speaking) regions in the country.

EVENTS & FESTIVALS

February

Biddy Festival,
Waterville, Co Kerry

March

Adare Jazz Festival,
Adare, Co Limerick

Kerry Arts Festival (Samhlaiocht Chiarrai),
Tralee, Co Kerry

Roaring 20s Festival,
Killarney, Co Kerry

April

Annual Horse Race Road Trotting,
Ballydehob, Co Cork

Irish Film Festival,
Limerick, Co Limerick

May

Bantry Mussel Fair,
Bantry, Co Cork

Cork International Choral Festival,
Cork, Co Cork

Listowel Writers' Week,
Listowel, Co Kerry

June

Ballybunion Batchelor Festival,
Ballybunion, Co Kerry

Blarney International Three-Day Horse Trials,
Blarney, Co Cork

Clonakilty Agricultural Show,
Clonakilty, Co Cork

Cork Youth Arts Festival,
Cork, Co Cork

July

Buttevant Horse Fair,
Buttevant, Co Cork

International Folk Dance Festival,
Cobh, Co Cork

Killarney Racing Festival,
Killarney, Co Kerry

August

Beara Arts Festival & Festival of the Sea,
Co Cork

Castletownbere Regatta,
Castletownbere, Co Cork

Cobh People's Regatta,
Cobh, Co Cork

Festival of the Carberries Leap & Glandore,
Co Cork

International Busking Festival,
Youghal, Co Cork

International Storytelling Festival,
Co Cork

Kinsale Annual Regatta,
Kinsale, Co Cork

Limerick Food Festival,
Limerick

Millstreet International Horse Show,
Millstreet, Co Cork

Puck Fair,
Killorglin, Co Kerry

Rose of Tralee Festival,
Tralee, Co Kerry

Rose of Tralee Racing Festival,
Balbeggan Park, Tralee, Co Kerry

September

Listowel Racing Festival,
Listowel, Co Kerry

October

Cork Jazz Festival,

International Gourmet Festival,
Kinsale, Co Cork

International Sea Angling Festival,
Cobh, Co Cork

Kinsale Gourmet Festival,
Kinsale, Co Cork

November

Millstreet International Indoor Horse Show,
Millstreet, Co Cork

Youghal International Festival,
Youghal, Co Cork

December

Christmas Racing Festival,
Limerick, Co Limerick

COUNTY CORK

Everything that makes Ireland attractive to the tourist is available in abundance in Co Cork. The cultural attractions of Cork City, fine food at Kinsale, the country's gourmet capital, and historical sights, particularly at Clonakilty and Skibbereen. Birdwatchers should head for Clear Island, where the first migrants land in the spring and autumn, or the muddy estuaries around Timoleague. Cork has excellent walking and cycling country, including the Beara Way and Hungry Hill on the Beara Peninsula. There is good fishing to the north and great golf across the county.

PRINCIPAL TOWNS

COBH

The colourful seaside town of Cobh was the last bit of Irish soil emigrants trod before sailing across the oceans in the 19th century and it was from here that the liners Lusitania and the Titanic left for their ill-fated voyages.

CORK

The inhabitants of Cork, the second largest city in the Republic, are never slow in declaring their rivalry with Dublin. Indeed, the city is generally held to be the cultural centre of southern Ireland, with several august institutions to its credit. Cork has always been at the forefront of Ireland's struggle for independence, and was the base for the Nationalist Fenian movement in the 19th-century. The centre, the oldest part of the city, is more or less an island, surrounded by two arms of the River Lee. Cork is designated a Heritage Town.

KINSALE

For centuries, the picturesque town has been a haven for travellers and traders, whose cosmopolitan influence has ensured that Kinsale is now considered to be the Gourmet Capital of Ireland. The charming narrow streets, the fishing harbour, historic buildings and delightful coastal walks all beg to be explored.

MUST SEE

LARNEY CASTLE & ROCK CLOSE,
arney *(5 miles/8km from Cork on main ad towards Limerick)*
T 021 385252 or 385669 F 021 381518
veryone has heard of the Blarney Stone, nd when coach parties clog the village it eems as if everyone has come to see it, o. The stone, said to impart eloquence those who kiss it, is located in the pper tower of the castle. The visitor, held y the feet, must lean backwards down e inside of the battlements in order to ceive the gift of the gab.

CREAGH GARDENS,
Skibbereen
T 028 22121 F 028 22121
Gardeners will enjoy a visit to the life work of Gwendoline and Peter Harold-Barry who bought Creagh in 1945. Inspired by the background of a Rousseau painting, they inspirationally transformed 20 acres/eight hectares of informal gardens sloping down to the picturesque estuary. Enjoy the beauty of the serpentine mill-pond and do not miss the large walled garden dating from the Regency period, which has been restored as a traditional and organic kitchen garden.

FOTA WILDLIFE PARK,
Fota Estate, Carrigtwohill *(Turn for Corby from N25, Cork-Waterford road)*
T 021 812678
More than just for kids, this conservation park has more than 70 species of exotic wildlife in open and natural surroundings. Giraffes, zebras, ostrich, antelope and other animals enjoy the 40 acres/16 ha of grassland. Monkeys swing through trees on lake islands, while kangaroos, macaws and lemurs have complete freedom of the park. Only the cheetahs have a conventional fence. Facilities include a children's corner, tour train, lakeside coffee shop and picnic benches. Make time to visit the internationally renowned arboretum.

MESON HERITAGE CENTRE,
dleton *(20 miles/32km east of Cork wards Waterford)*
T 021 613594 or 613596 F 021 613642
ven if whiskey is not your drink, the eritage Centre for Jameson Irish Whiskey a memorable place to visit. Tours consist a 20-minute audio/visual presentation, en a 35-minute guided tour of the scinating Old Distillery, then back to the meson Bar to sample the product (soft ink savailable). Tour and audio-visual ds are available in five languages.

UEENSTOWN STORY,
bh Railway Station, Cobh
T 021 813591 F 021 813595
nce the port of Cork, Cobh has strong sociations with Atlantic crossings and it as from here that many Irish emigrants eparted for America. The Titanic made its last stop here before its fateful Atlantic crossing, and it was off Cobh that the Lusitania was sunk in 1914 (see the Lusitania Monument on the waterfront). The Queenstown Story is a visitor attraction at Cobh Railway Station, with displays on the theme of emigration, sail and steam, with lifelike tableaux. If you are feeling peckish, there is a café and the Blarney Woollen Mills Gift Shop may tempt you.

BIG OUTDOORS

ORK HERITAGE PARK
essboro, Skehard Road, Blackrock
.5 miles/4km from centre of Cork)
T/F 021 358854
x acres/2.5ha of the former Bessboro state, with an Environmental Centre and xhibits of the area's natural, maritime and cheological heritage, plus a restored 9th-century farmyard.

ONERAILE FOREST PARK
alk, play or relax in this lovely 18th-entury park, home to herds of deer.

ROMBEG STONE CIRCLE
miles/3km west of Ross Carbery, on the 597, which loops back on the N71 just fore Leap)
e best of many stone circles in West ork, dating from 100BC and 30ft/9m in ameter. Look out for the nearby cooking ace, where hot stones can bring water to e boil in 15 minutes.

GARINASH ISLAND
(10 minutes by boat from Glengarriff)
T 027 63040
Take delight in the rare sub-tropical plants on a colourful island in Bantry Bay. The beautiful Italianate gardens, with colonnades, pools and terraces, were laid out between 1810 and 1913.

GEARAGH NATIONAL RESERVE,
Macroom
Full of rare plants and wildfowl, this nature reserve is not far from the town of Macroom.

LOUGH HYNE,
Skibbereen
A land-locked sea lake, linked to the sea by a narrow passage down which the receding tide cascades. The area is now a nature reserve.

MILL STREET COUNTRY PARK
T 029 70810
Nature and ecology park.

MIZEN VISION,
Mizen Head Fog Signal Station
A fascinating place to go, The visitor centre explains all and there is the keeper's house, engine room, suspension bridge and 99 steps to explore.

GREAT FOR KIDS

BEACHES
Beautiful beaches at Barley Cove, Youghal, and around the Clonakilty area.

SCHULL PLANETARIUM
T 028 28552
The only planetarium in the Republic of Ireland, attached to the Community College at Schull. Regular star shows in the summer season to whet the appetite.

WEST CORK MODEL VILLAGE RAILWAY,
Inchydoney Road, Clonakilty
(signposted at road junction. Village is at bay side of Clonakilty)
T 023 33224 F 023 33224
Depicting the prominent buildings, landmarks and way of life of six towns and villages in West Cork - Clonakilty, Bandon, Skibbereen, Dunmanway, Kinsale and Bantry.

WOODLAND FARM,
Waterloo, Blarney T 021 385733
Children will enjoy the animals on this farm open to the public.

HISTORIC & ANCIENT SITES

BARRYSCOURT CASTLE,
Carrigtwohill
Dating from 1206, the castle has a colourful history and was home for a time to Sir Walter Raleigh. The audio-visual presentation is not to be missed, and there is a shop and café.

CHARLES FORT,
Summer Cove T 021 772684
(2 miles/3km east of Kinsale)
Built in the late 17th century after the defeat of the Spanish and Irish at the Battle of Kinsale. One of Europe's most complete star-shaped forts covering some 12 acres/5ha of clifftop.

ST FINN BARRE'S CATHEDRAL,
Bishop Street, Cork
The 19th-century French Gothic cathedral, with its three spires, stands on the site of a 6th-century monastery, founded by St Finbarr, who also founded Cork in the 7th century.

TIMOLEAGUE ABBEY & CASTLE GARDENS,
Timoleague *(signposted in the village)*
One of Ireland's best preserved early Franciscan friaries, founded in 1240. Overlooking the abbey, palm trees and exotic flora flourish in walled gardens.

HOMES & GARDENS

ANNES GROVE,
Castletownroche T/F 022 26145
A romantic early 20th-century garden, incorporating an earlier ornamental glen, overlooking the River Awbeg. Join one of the winding paths to the limestone cliffs from the 18th-century house.

BALLYMALOE COOKERY SCHOOL GARDENS,
Shanagarry, Midleton
T 021 646785 F 021 646909
A series of new gardens by renowned cook Darina Allen, several with a culinary theme. Mature features include an old orchard and shell house. A Celtic maze is being developed.

BANTRY HOUSE,
Bantry T 027 50047 F 027 50795
(main gate at harbour wall)
A Georgian mansion to be enjoyed, surrounded by gardens, and displaying the Second Earl of Bantry's impressive collection of furniture and tapestries. Tea room, craft shop, and exhibition in the stables.

FITZGERALD'S PARK,
Cork
Just the place to stroll to in Cork, this park is just a short walk from the city centre and offers 18 acres/7.25ha of lovely gardens, plus Fitzgerald's museum in a Georgian house.

ILNACULLIN,
Garinish Island, Glengarriff T 027 63040
Bathed in the warm waters of the Gulf Stream, this lovely Italianate garden, designed by Harold Peto, has a fascinating collection of tender plant, plus a Martello tower and Grecian temple.

LISSELAN ESTATE,
Ballinascarthy, Clonakilty
Farm and garden tours, including the site of the ancestral homestead of Henry Ford, founder of the Ford Motor Company.

MUSEUMS & ART GALLERIES

BANDON HERITAGE CENTRE,
Bandon
A display of artefacts from the locality housed in Christ Church Heritage Building.

CORK CITY GAOL,
Convent Avenue, Sundays Well
(1 mile/2km from Patrick Street, Cork)
T 021 305022 F 021 307230
This superbly restored prison housed 19th-century prisoners in wretched conditions. These can be appreciated thanks to the authentically furnished cells, lifelike characters and sound effects. Sound tours in several languages.

Cork City Gaol,

CORK PUBLIC MUSEUM,
Fitzgerald Park, Mardyke, Cork
(north of University College)
T 021 270679 F 021 270931
Collections covering the economic, social and municipal history of Cork covering every era from the Mesolithic period. Fine displays of silver, glass and needlepoint lace. Shop

CRAWFORD ART GALLERY,
Emmet Place
A free art gallery, worth a visit.

FITZGERALD'S MUSEUM,
Cork
Set amid Fitzgerald's park, not far from th centre of the city, the museum is located in a Georgian house and displays a number of interesting artefacts.

KINSALE COURT HOUSE
Kinsale
The history and crafts of Kinsale, set in th historic surroundings of the Court House

MICHAEL COLLINS MEMORIAL CENTRE,
(signposted) 5 miles/8km west of Clonakilty
Michael Collins was a leader in the arme struggle for Irish independence. The hous where he was born still stands, but the family's later house was burnt down by the Black & Tans in 1921.

ROYAL GUNPOWDER MILLS,
(on Cork/Killarney road)
T 021 874430 F 021 874836
An amazing industrial complex on the banks of the River Lee. The mills supplie vast quantities of explosives for British military forces throughout the world fron 1794 to 1903.

YOUGHAL HERITAGE CENTRE
(Located in the Market House, next to the Tourist Information Office).
T 050 31444 F 050 31083
The Centre is a good starting point to explore the history of the town. Guided tours follow in the footsteps of the likes Sir Walter Raleigh through the main stree past an 18th-century clock tower and building dating from the 13th century.

ESSENTIAL INFORMATION

ACCESS

AIR ACCESS

ork Aiport T **021 313131**

er Lingus, Academy Street, Cork
T **021 274331**

SEA ACCESS

wansea Cork Ferry, 1a South Mall, Cork
T **021 276000**

erry Terminal T **021 378036**

RISH FERRIES
Bridge Street, Cork T **021 504333**

TOURIST INFORMATION

ANTRY
he Square T **027 50229**

ORK
rand Parade
T **021 273251** F **021 273504**

INSALE
ier Road T **021 772234** F **021 774438**

IDLETON
ameson Heritage Centre T **021 613702**

KIBBEREEN
orth Street T **028 21766**

OUGHAL
oughal Heritage Centre T **024 92390**

CRAFTS

ANDON POTTERY SHOP
t Finbarrs Place, Bandon T **023 43525**

LARNEY WOOLLEN MILLS
arney T **021 385280**

ASTNET CANDLES
kibbereen T **028 21885**

INSALE CRYSTAL
larket Street, Kinsale T **021 774493**

OUND TOWER CRAFT GALLERY
ain Street, Bantry T **027 51678**

HE RYNHART COLLECTION LTD
he Mill, Drimoleague T **028 31666**

HE SPINNING WHEEL
lengarriff T **027 63347**

TEPHEN PEARCE POTTERY
mporium & Café, Shanagarry
T **021 646807**

EDAGH CANDLES
ealkil, Bantry T **027 66177**

ENTERTAINMENT

ORK OPERA HOUSE
mmet Place, Cork T **021 270022**

VERYMAN PALACE
lacCurtain Street T **021 501673**

RISKEL ARTS CENTRE
ff South Main Street T **021 272022**

Bandon Pottery Shop

SPORTS & LEISURE

ACTIVITY CENTRES

THE YOUGHAL CHALLENGE CENTRE,
Market Square, Youghal T **024 92793**
A variety of sport and leisure activities.

ANGLING

CORK HARBOUR BOATS LTD
Glenbrook, Passage West T **021 841348**

GERALD O'NEILL
Leap T **028 33510**

MIZEN CHARTERS
Rossbrin, Schull T **028 37370**

BOAT TRIPS & CRUISES

ATLANTIC BOATING SERVICES
Letter, Skibbereen T **028 22145**

CAPE CLEAR & SHERKIN ISLAND TRIPS
Pier Road, Schull T **028 28138 or 28278**

CORK HARBOUR CRUISES
T **021 277085**

GLENGARRIFF & GARNISH BOATS
The Pier, Glengarriff T **027 63116**

MURPHY'S FERRY SERVICE
Lawrence Cove, Bere Island
T **088 517452 (mobile)**

CAR FERRY

CROSS RIVER FERRIES LTD
Atlantic Quay, Cobh T **021 811223**

CAR HIRE

AVIS RENT-A-CAR
Emmet Place, Cork T **021 281111**

CAR RENTALS IRELAND
Monahan Road, Cork T **021 962277**

COACH TOURS

BUS EIREANN Capwell, Cork
T **021 506066**

CRONIN'S COACHES
Shannon Buildings, Mallow Roa, Cork
T **021 309090**

CYCLE HIRE

KRAMER'S BICYCLES
Glengarriff Road, Newtown, Bantry
T **027 50278**

RENT-A-BIKE
Cycle Scene, 396 Blarney Street, Cork
T **021 301183**

ROYCROFT CYCLES
Ilen Street, Skibbereen T **028 21235**

EQUESTRIAN CENTRES

BALLINADEE RIDING CENTRE
Ballinadee T **021 778152**

BANTRY HORSE RIDING CENTRE
Coomanore South, Bantry T **027 51412**

HITCHMOUNT RIDING SCHOOL
Highland Lodge, Monkstown T **021 371267**

THE LIMBO RIDING CENTRE
Skibbereen T **028 21683**

ROSSCARBERY RIDING CENTRE
Burgatia, Rosscarbery T **023 48232**

GOLF

FOTA ISLAND,
Carrigtwohill T **021 883700 or 883713**
A testing parkland course with traditional features, linked with Irish Amateur Open.

LEE VALLEY GOLF & COUNTRY CLUB,
Clashanure, Ovens T **021 331721**
Superstitions abound about the ancient ruins at this parkland course; some golfers have been inclined to blame mischievous spirits for less than exemplary play. Designed by Christy O'Connor Junior.

ALSO:

BANDON T **023 41111**

BANTRY PARK T **027 50579**

BEREHAVEN T **027 70700**

CASTLETOWNBERE T **027 70299**

CHARLEVILLE T **063 81257**

COBH T **021 812399**

COOSHEEN T **028 28182**

CORK, Little Island T **021 353451**

DONERAILE T **022 24137**

DOUGLAS T **021 891086**

DUNMORE T **023 33352**

EAST CORK, Midleton T **021 631687**

Mallow Golf Club

FERMOY Ⓣ 025 32694

FERNHILL Ⓣ 021 373103

FITZPATRICK SILVER SPRINGS Ⓣ 021 507533

FRANKFIELD Ⓣ 021 363124

GLENGARIFF Ⓣ 027 63150

HARBOUR POINT Ⓣ 021 353094

KANTURK Ⓣ 022 47238

KINSALE Ⓣ 021 774722

MACROOM Ⓣ 026 41072

MAHON Ⓣ 021 318313

MALLOW Ⓣ 022 21145

MITCHELTOWN Ⓣ 025 24072

MONKSTOWN Ⓣ 021 841376

MUSKERRY Ⓣ 021 385297

OLD HEAD LINKS Ⓣ 021 778444

RAFFEEN CREEK Ⓣ 021 378430

SKIBBEREEN Ⓣ 028 613499

WATER ROCK Ⓣ 021 613499

YOUGHAL Ⓣ 024 92787

GREYHOUND RACING

CORK CITY GREYHOUND TRACK,
Western Road, Cork Ⓣ 021 543013

HORSE RACING

CORK RACECOURSE,
Mallow Ⓣ 022 21592 Ⓕ 022 42750

SCENIC DRIVES

To West Cork from Kinsale through Clonakilty and Skibbereen to the Mizen Head. Details of a number of tours are available from Cork Kerry Tourism at Grand Parade, Cork Ⓣ 021 273251

SAILING

BANTRY BAY SAILING CLUB
The Abbey, Bantry Ⓣ 027 51724

GLENANS IRELAND
Baltimore Ⓣ 028 20154

GLENANS IRELAND
Bere Island Ⓣ 027 75012

MARITIME TOURISM LTD
Castlepark Marina, Kinsale Ⓣ 021 774959

ROYAL CORK YACHT CLUB
Crosshaven Ⓣ 021 831023

WALKING

Walking tours of Kinsale, from outside the Tourist Office, available in various languages, check with Tourist Office for details. The Beara Way is a newly established walk circling the Beara Peninsula.

WHERE TO STAY

HOTELS

AA RECOMMENDED

SEE UNDER WHERE TO EAT FOR ALL HOTEL RESTAURANTS WITH ROSETTES

CORK CITY

RBUTUS LODGE ★★★✿✿
liddle Glanmire Road, Montenotte
Ⓣ 021 501237 Ⓕ 021 502893
harming period house with welcoming
tmosphere. Stylish bedrooms. Superb
od. Suites with kitchens available.
6 bedrooms £££ Parking Sports facilities

TZPATRICK SILVER SPRINGS ★★★★
voli *(from N8 southbound take Silver prings exit. Turn right across overpass - hotel on right)*
Ⓣ 021 507533 Ⓕ 021 507641
ttractive hotel in impressive setting.
hoice of Executive or Standard rooms,
vo restaurants and spacious lounges.
09 bedrooms incl some no-smoking ££££ ift Parking Leisure & sports facilities

AYFIELD MANOR ★★★★✿
errott Avenue, College Road
Ⓣ 021 315600 Ⓕ 012 316839
uxurious hotel nearcity centre. Fine
rawing room and excellent restaurant.
arble bathrooms in lovely bedrooms.
6 bedrooms incl some no-smoking ££££ eisure & sports facilities Parking

IMPERIAL HOTEL ★★★
South Mall
Ⓣ 021 274040 Ⓕ 021 275375
Noted for a most welcoming atmosphere, with impressive public rooms. Bedrooms are most comfortable. Pleasant restaurant.
98 bedrooms £££ Lift Parking

JURYS ★★★★✿
Western Road *(close to city centre, on main Killarney road from Cork) (Jurys)*
Ⓣ 021 276622 Ⓕ 021 274477
Rverside setting near the University , close to city centre. Good dining options.,two restaurants, bars and Cork's pub.
185 bedrooms ££££ Lift Parking Leisure & sports facilities Parking Conference &banqueting facilities

JURYS INN ★★★
Anderson's Quay
(on east side of city, on the river Lee)
Ⓣ 021 276444 Ⓕ 021 276144
133 bedrooms ££ Lift Parking

METROPOLE ★★★
MacCurtain Street
Ⓣ 021 508122Ⓕ 021 506450
Pleasant hotel and bedrooms with choice of restaurants; one overlooking the swimming pool makes interesting use of natural light.
108 bedrooms incl some no-smoking ££££ Lift Parking Leisure & sports facilities Conference facilities

TRAVELODGE
Blackash **Ⓣ 01 21310722 Ⓕ 01 21310707**
Spacious and well equipped bedrooms, all can be used for family use. Nearby budget restaurant.
40 bedrooms incl some no-smoking £

VIENNA WOODS ★★
Glanmire **Ⓣ 021 821146 Ⓕ 021 821120**
(off R639)
Beautifully located in large gardens and an ideal place to stay for peace and quiet. Interesting views over Cork Harbour.
20 bedrooms £ Parking

BED & BREAKFAST ACCOMMODATION

AA RECOMMENDED

NTOINE HOUSE QQQ
Vestern Road *(1 mile from city centre on the Cork-Macroom-Killarney road)*
Ⓣ 021 273494 Ⓕ 021 273092
lose to the University, this tall
haracterful house is popular with both
isure and business guests.
bedrooms £ Parking

ARNISH HOUSE QQQ
dergrove, Western Road
Ⓣ 021 275111 Ⓕ 021 273872
pleasant three-storey house opposite
ne University on the main Cork/Killarney
oad.
3 bedrooms £ Parking

KILLARNEY HOUSE QQQ
Western Road *(from Cork city to Killarney road N22, premises just opposite University College)*
Ⓣ 21 270290 & 270179 Ⓕ 21 271010
A welcoming and attractive guest house, which stands near Cork University. The pleasant bedrooms have many comforts and guests may use the sitting room.
19 bedrooms incl some no-smoking £ Parking

REDCLYFFE QQ
Western Road *(take N22 from city centre, through traffic lights at University gates, premises situated on right before next traffic lights, at Gaol Cross)*
Ⓣ 021 273220 Ⓕ 021 278382
Not far from the town centre, this period house has pleasant bedrooms. You are welcome to use the family sitting room.
13 bedrooms £ Parking

ROSERIE VILLA QQQ
Mardyke Walk, off Western Road
(take N22 from city centre, pass Jury's Hotel on left, turn right at University College gates, right again for guest house on right)
Ⓣ 021 272958 Ⓕ 021 274087
Just 10 minutes' walk from the city centre, this family-run guest house provides many thoughtful extras in its bedrooms.
16 bedrooms £ No smoking in dining room Parking No children under 5yrs

Call the AA Hotel Booking Service on 0990 050505 to book at AA recognised hotels and B&Bs in the UK and Ireland, or through our internet site: http://www.theaa.co.uk/hotels

WHERE TO EAT

RESTAURANTS

AA RECOMMENDED

CORK CITY

ARBUTUS LODGE HOTEL ❀❀
Montenotte, Cork T 021 501237
Quality local produce, including herbs from the garden, are used to good effect. Enjoyable dishes include a confit chicken terrine with herb vinaigrette, moist escalope of salmon with a parsley crust, and roast loin of venison with foie gras and wild mushroom essence. The selection of the wine list is a particular passion of owner Declan Ryan.
FIXED L ££ D £££ ALC£££

BENEDICKS RESTAURANT ❀
Blackrock Castle, Blackrock
T 021 357414 F021 358109
The turret restaurant is atmospherically set right on the water's edge of Cork Harbour. You could try 'rock cuisine' - fish, seafood or steaks cooked on a sizzling rock. Other options could include deep fried Clonakity black and white pudding with apple coulis, king scallops in a lobster sauce or medallions of pork fillet cooked in a rum or banana sauce.
ALC £-££

GLANDORE RESTAURANT ❀
Jurys Hotel, Western Road
T 021 276622 F 021 274477
The split-level restaurant at this modern hotel has its own waterfall feature. There is an extensive carte with a good selection of appetisers, soups, fish, steaks and a range of popular international dishes, including lasagne and beef stroganoff, omelettes and vegetarian options.
ALC £££

THE MANOR ROOM
Hayfield Manor Hotel, Perrot Avenue, College Road
T 021 315600 F 021 316839
A country manor house in the town, with a grand restaurant offering a choice of menus. Typical dishes are Kinsale seafood and shellfish lasagne with fresh herbs and Champagne, fillet of lamb topped with a courgette and tomato mousse on a Madeira jus, and warm pineapple tarte tatin with ginger cream and mango sorbe
FIXED £££ ALC £££

Call the AA Hotel Booking Service on 0990 050505 to book at AA recognised hotels and B&Bs in the UK and Ireland, or through our internet site: http://www.theaa.co.uk/hotels

PUBS, INNS & OTHER PLACES

Isaacs Restaurant,

BULLY'S,
at Looney's Cross, Bishoptown Road
T 021 546838
40 Paul Street T 021 273555
Busy Italian-style restaurants specialising in pizza from a wood oven, pasta & seafood.

CAFÉ KYLEMORE,
Merchants Quay T 021 275026
Self-service restaurant offering good quality, freshly prepared food.

CAFÉ MEXICANA,
Carey's Lane T 021 276433
Mexican cooking with other international influences.

CHINA GOLD RESTAURANT,
Over Saxone, 43-44 Patrick Street
T 021 273535
A friendly and relaxed Chinese restaurant.

CRAWFORD GALLERY RESTAURANT,
Emmet Place T 021 274415
Daytime snacks and light meals on the ground floor of the Gallery.

EASTERN TANDOORI,
1-2 Emmet Place T 021 272020
Attractively presented Indian restaurant.

FLEMINGS, SILVER GRANGE HOUSE,
Tivoli T 021 821621
Georgian house in gardens overlooking the harbour. French carte with English translations.

HAROLD'S RESTAURANT,
Douglas T 021 361613
Modern food in stylish contemporary surroundings.

ISAACS RESTAURANT,
48 MacCurtain Street T 021 505511
Converted 18th-century warehouse servin aninternational menu including pasta, kebabs and seafood. Tempting vegetarian dishes.

IVORY TOWER,
35 Princes Street T 021 274665
Imaginative menu, unusual combinations and vegetarian options. Cheaper at lunchtime.

JACQUES,
9 Phoenix Street T 021 277387
Popular bistro with good salads, appetising vegetarian dishes and local seafood.

LOVETTS,
off Well Road, Douglas T 021 294909
Fixed-price menus at lunch and dinner. The evening brasserie features char-grills.

PROBY'S BISTRO,
Proby's Quay, Crosses Green T 021 31653
Modern Mediterranean decor and flavours are favoured at this relaxed bistro..

TOSCANI,
34 Patrick Street T 021 272895
Relaxed Italian restaurant.

WHERE TO STAY

HOTELS

AA RECOMMENDED

SEE UNDER WHERE TO EAT FOR ALL HOTEL RESTAURANTS WITH ROSETTES

COUNTY CORK

BALLYCOTTON

AY VIEW ★★★
T 021 646746 F 021 646075
etaining the character of the original
ilding, this lovely hotel has very high
andards. Superb views. Excellent food.
bedrooms ££££ Lift Cruiser for hire illwalking Horse riding Fishing Golf osed Nov–Apr

BALLYLICKEY

A VIEW ★★★
miles from Bantry on the Glengarriff side of 71)
T 027 50073 & 50462 F 027 51555
arming country house with delightful
rdens and bedrooms. Turf firesin winter.
perb food.Fishing or golfing nearby.
bedrooms £££ Closed mid Nov–mid ar

BALTIMORE

LTIMORE HARBOUR ★★★
T 028 20361 F 028 20466
nart, restful hotel overlooking the
rbour. Enthusiastic staff. Local
gredients are used to good effect.
bedrooms incl some no-smoking £££ isure and sporting facilities Closed Jan–ar

SEY'S HOTEL ★★
ltimore T 028 20197 F 028 20509
mous for its Irish music and excellent
afood, this well-established pub and
staurant also has comfortable bedrooms.

BANTRY

WESTLODGE ★★★
T 027 50360 F 027 50438
With attractive views over Bantry Bay, this busy modern hotel is set in its own grounds on the outskirts of town.
90 bedrooms ££ Sport & leisure facilities Closed 23–27 Dec

BLARNEY

BLARNEY PARK ★★★
(off village green)
T 021 385281 F 021 381506
Friencly hotel in large gardens. Good bedrooms. Plenty of play space in the grounds for children to let off steam.
76 bedrooms £££ Parking Leisure facilities

CHRISTY'S ★★★
(N20, exit at the Blarney sign, at the R617 3 miles from Cork city)
T 021 385011 F 021 38350
Part of Woollen Mills complex. Behind the 19th-century façade of the former mill building lies a modern, comfortable hotel.
49 bedrooms incl some no-smoking ££ Lift Parking Leisure & sports facilities

COURTMACSHERRY

COURTMACSHERRY ★★
T 023 46198 F 023 46137
Georgian house in lovely grounds near the beach.Excellent cooking. Horse riding, fishing and tennis available.
13 bedrooms ££ Parking Leisure & sports facilities Closed Oct–Mar

Casey's Hotel

CROSSHAVEN

WHISPERING PINES HOTEL ★★
T 021 831843 & 831448 F 021 831679
Hospitable, comfortable hotel with sun lounge and bar overlooking the river. Collection from airport. Great for anglers.
15 bedrooms ££ Parking Own angling boats fish daily

GARRYVOE

GARRYVOE ★★
(turn off N25 onto L72 at Castlemartyr between Midleton and Youghal and continue for 4 miles)
T 021 646718 F 021 646824
Comfortable family-run hotel with caring staff, in a delightful position facing a sandy beach.Bar popular with locals Super food.
19 bedrooms ££ Parking Sports facilities

GOUGANE BARRA

GOUGANE BARRA ★★
(off N22)
T 026 47069 F 026 47226
Pleasant hotel right on lake shore. Lovely views from the restaurant and bedrooms. Collection from train, boat or plane by prior arrangement.
28 bedrooms ££ Parking No children under 6yrs Closed early Oct–mid Apr

Acton's

INISHANNON

INISHANNON HOUSE ★★★❀❀
(off N71 at eastern end of village)
T 021 775121 F 021 775609
Charming country housewith a river flowing by. Lovely walks and gardens. Attractive bedrooms. Superb food.
12 bedrooms incl some no-smoking ££££ Parking

KINSALE

ACTON'S ★★★
Pier Road
T 021 772135 F 021 772231
Wonderful views of the harbour from many of the comfortable bedrooms and public areas. Imaginative food.
56 bedrooms Lift Parking Leisure facilities

TRIDENT ★★★❀
Worlds End
(take R600 from Cork city to Kinsale, drive along the waterfront, the hotel is located just beyond the pier)
T 021 772301 F 021 774173
On the harbour's edge, with its own marina and boats for hire. Superb views. Pleasant staff provide hospitable service.
58 bedrooms £££ Lift Parking Leisure facilities Games room

MACROOM

CASTLE ★★❀
Main Street
(on N22)
T 026 41074 F 026 41505
Everything about this hotel is comfortable, while leisure facilities will help you unwind. Excellent restaurant.Golf nearby.
42 bedrooms ££ Parking Leisure facilities

VICTORIA ★★
(in the centre of Macroom opposite the Town Hall, on the N22) (Logis)
T 026 41082 & 42143 F 026 42148
Town-centre hotel. Stylish lounge bar with scomfortable seatin. Bar food. Anglers tackle room and walk-in cold room.
16 bedrooms £ Parking

MALLOW

LONGUEVILLE HOUSE ★★★❀❀❀
(3 miles west on N72 to Killarney)
T 022 47156 & 47306 F 022 47459
Elegant Georgian mansion in a wooded estate. Comfortable bedrooms overlook the river valley or courtyard maze.
20 bedrooms £££ Parking Games Closed mid Dec-mid Feb

MIDLETON

MIDLETON PARK ★★★❀❀
(just off the N25 Cork/Rosslare road)
T 021 631767 F 021 631605
Comfortable modern hotel with a pleasar restaurant serving exceptionally good food.. Only 10 miles from Cork.
40 bedrooms ££ Parking Conference/banqueting facilities

ROSSCARBERY

CELTIC ROSS ★★★
(on N71)
T 023 48722 F 023 48723
Striking landmark overlooking lagoon. Comfortable hotel. Restaurant has a daily supply of fresh seafood. Popular Irish pub
67 bedrooms incl some no-smoking ££ Li Parking Leisure & sports facilities Conference/banqueting facilities

YOUGHAL

DEVONSHIRE ARMS ★★❀
Pearse Square
T 024 92827 & 92018 F 024 92900
Charming 19th-century hotel restored wit much care and attention to detail.. Super food in restaurant. Good bar food.
10 bedrooms ££ Parking

BED & BREAKFAST ACCOMMODATION

The Mills Inn

BALLINCOLLIG

THE MILESTONE QQQ
(2 miles west on N22)
T 021 872562 F 021 872562
Bedrooms are all pleasant and the house is attractively decorated. Golf, pitch and putt, horse riding, and lake fishing nearby
5 bedrooms, incl 2 for non-smokers £ No smoking in dining room or lounges Secure car parking

BALLINHASSIG

BLANCHFIELD HOUSE QQ
Rigsdale **T 021 885167 F 021 885305**
(main Cork/Bandon road N71)
Quiet but convenient location. Good home cooking, and if you enjoy fishing, private salmon and trout fishing are available.
6 bedrooms £

BALLYVOURNEY

THE MILLS INN QQQQ
(on main Cork/Killarney road N22)
T 026 45237 F 026 45454
More than just a charming mid-18th century inn: comfortable bedrooms, hot bar food all day, welcoming restaurant. and vintage car & folk museums. Shop
9 bedrooms £ No smoking in dining room Licensed Parking

BANDON

GLEBE COUNTRY HOUSE QQQQ
Ballinadee **T 021 778294 F 021 778456**
(exit N71 at Innishannon Bridge signposted Ballinadee, travel 5 miles along river bank, le after sign for village)
Period house with lovely gardens, run wit great attention to detail. Antiques throughout. Unusual breakfast menu. Country house-style dinner by reservation
4 bedrooms £ No smoking in bedrooms or dining room Parking Games facilities

BANTEER

CLONMEEN LODGE QQQQ
Near Mallow *(follow N72 to Killarney from roundabout in Mallows for 7 miles, at petrol station take next left, premises signposted at junction)*
T 029 56238 & 56277 F 029 56294
Neatly furnished and hospitable house beside a river. Comfortable bedrooms. Fishing, pony trekking, and golf nearby.
6 bedrooms £ Licensed Parking Cycle hire

BANTRY

DONEMARK RISE QQQ
Droumacoppil **T 027 51099**
(1 mile on N71 from Bantry/Gengarriff)
Pleasant, welcoming bu ngalow. Versatile

Duvane Farm

bedrooms. Pretty gardens. Pre-book dinner. French and some German spoken.
bedrooms £ No smoking in bedrooms or dining room Parking Open Apr-Sep

EDEN CREST QQQ
Newtown T 027 51110 F 027 51036
bedrooms, inc 1 for non-smokers £ Parking Open Mar-Nov

SHANGRI-LA QQQ
Glengarriff Road T 027 50244
F 027 50244
Bungalow set in lovely gardens on the outskirts of the town. Conservatory overlooks the Bay. Comfortable lounge.
bedrooms £ No smoking in area of dining room or in 1 lounge Parking Golf nearby Open mid Mar-mid Nov

BLARNEY

BLARNEY VALE HOUSE QQQ
Cork Road T 021 381511
(on R617 adjacent to golf driving range on approach to town)
bedrooms £ No smoking Parking Open Apr-Oct

BUENA VISTA QQQ
Station Road T 021 385035
(from village, take 3rd left into Station rd, house on right)
Pleasant modern bungalow in quet setting near town centre. Attractive rooms, simply furnished but fully equipped.
bedrooms £ No smoking in dining room Parking

SYLVAN MANOR QQQ
Tower T 021 381977
(off Blarney to Killarney Road)
Set on a hilltop, this modern house is very comfortable throughout. The owner pays great attention to detail.
4 bedrooms £ No smoking in dining room Parking

WHITE HOUSE QQQ
Shean Lower T 021 385338
(on R617, Cork/Blarney road)
Close to town, with views of Blarney Castle, this attractive house has a relaxing lounge. Power showers in some bedrooms
6 bedrooms £ Parking

CARRIGALINE

BEAVER LODGE QQ
T 021 372595 F 021 372245
Located in the village centre, this quaint old ivy-clad house stands in its own grounds.
6 bedrooms £ No smoking in bedrooms or dining room Parking

GLENWOOD HOUSE QQQQ
Ballinrea Road T 021 373878 F 021 373878 *(signed to Ringaskiddy Ferry Port, at rdbt follow signs for Carrigaline, on approaching village turn right posted to Glenwood)*
8 bedrooms £ No smoking in area of dining room & 1 lounge Parking

CLONAKILTY

DESERT HOUSE Q
Ring Road
(on N71, 0.5 mile east of Clonakilty)
T 023 33331 or 34490 F 023 33048
This fine Georgian farmhouse, overlooking Clonakilty Bay, is an ideal centre for touring West Cork and Kerry.
5 bedrooms £ Parking 100 acres dairy mixed

DUVANE FARM QQQ
Ballyduvane T 023 33129
(a mile from Clonakilty on the N71)
Comfortable throughout, this cheerful house has a pleasant sitting room. Super breakfasts. Dinner by arrangement.
4 bedrooms £ No smoking in bedrooms or dining room 100 acres Closed Nov-Mar

Clonmeen Lodge

Glebe Country House

COBH

ELMVILLE QQQ
Lower Road, Rushbrook T 021 813206
Overlooking the harbour, this attractive period house has pretty bedrooms leading onto the gardens. Generous breakfasts.
5 bedrooms £ No smoking in bedrooms or dining room Baby sitting Parking

FERMOY

BALLYVOLANE HOUSE QQQQQ
Castlelyons T 025 36349 F 025 36781
(from N8, turn off onto L188, follow signs)
Fine Italianate house in magnificent gardens, open to public in May. Bedrooms

Heron's Cove

and public rooms are filled with antiques.
6 bedrooms ££ No smoking in dining room or lounges Croquet Fishing Licensed Parking

GHILLIE COTTAGE
Kilbarry Stud T 025 32720 F 025 33000
(take N72 east towards Tallow/Lismore, take first left out of Fermoy signed to Clondulane, located 4 miles on right)
Modernised farmhouseset on a stud with lovely views. Comfortable bedrooms. Pre-book dinner .Munster Way nearby.
3 bedrooms £ Parking Fly Fishing Country Sports 26 acres

GOLEEN

HERON'S COVE
The Harbour T 028 35225 F 028 35422
In a sheltered cove, this friendly house has a pretty restaurant, some bedrooms have balconies overlooking the harbour.
5 bedrooms £ Licensed Parking No children under 10 Closed Xmas

KANTURK

ASSOLAS COUNTRY HOUSE
(3.5 miles northeast, off N72)
T 029 50015 F 029 50795
Old manor house set in prize-winning gardens. Magnificent lounges with log fires, local produce served in restaurant..
9 bedrooms £££ Licensed Parking Croquet Boating Open Mar-Nov

Ballyvolane House

KILLEAGH

BALLYMAKEIGH HOUSE
(6 miles west of Youghal on N25 signposted Killeagh Village at 'Old Thatch')
T 024 95184 F 024 95370
Delightful 250-year-old farmhouse. Lovely bedrooms. Elegant dining room provides the setting for a five-course dinner.
5 bedrooms £ No smoking in dining room Licensed Parking Sports & games facilities 180 acres dairy Open Feb-Nov

Cortigan House

TATTANS
(on N25, between Midleton & Youghal)
T 024 95173 F 024 95173
Town house with comfortable bedrooms, pleasant sitting room, large gardens. All day bar snacks and evening meals.
5 bedrooms £ Licensed Parking Tennis Open Mar-Oct

KINSALE

KIERAN'S FOLKHOUSE INN
Guardwell T 021 772382 F 021 774085
There is a night club at this town centre house. Smart, attractive bedrooms. The bar is popular, as you might imagine.
19 bedrooms No smoking in dining room Licensed Parking

THE MOORINGS
Scilly T 021 772376 F 021 772675
Lovely guest house overlooking harbour and marina. The very comfortable bedrooms all have their own character.
8 bedrooms Parking No children u 16yrs

OLD BANK HOUSE
11 Pearse Street *(next to Post Office)*
T 021 774075 F 021 774296
Elegant Georgian house. Pretty bedrooms combine charm with modern comforts. Dinner is offered in the owners' restaurant
9 bedrooms £££ No smoking in dining room or lounges Licensed No children under 11yrs

OLD PRESBYTERY
43 Cork Street *(opposite Parish Church)*
T 021 772027 F 021 772027
Charming period house in quiet street. Elegant lounge, delightful breakfast room and traditional bedrooms with brass beds.
6 bedrooms £ No smoking Parking No children

OLD RECTORY
Rampart Lane T 021 772678
F 021 772678
Quietly set in large gardens. Lovingly restored house provides luxury accommodation to tempt relaxation.
3 bedrooms ££££ No smoking in dining room Licenced Parking No children under 10yrs

ORCHARD COTTAGE
Farrangalway T 021 772693 *(off R607)*
4 bedrooms £ Parking

RIVERMOUNT HOUSE
Knocknabinny, Barrells Cross
(2 miles from Kinsale take R600 west towards Old Head, turn right at Barrelscross)
T 021 778033 or 778225 F 021 778225

3allymakeigh House

mmaculately kept house in lovely gardens vith children's play area. Pretty bedrooms, itting room, sun lounge. Evening meals.
bedrooms £ No smoking in bedrooms or ining room Parking Open Mar- Nov

VATERLANDS
'ork Road *(follow R600 to Kinsale. Turn off t 'Welcome to Kinsale' sign, Waterlands sign t this junction, turn right)*
T 021 772318 & 088 276 7917
F 021 774873
retty house in picturesque gardens. onservatory breakfast room, comfortable ounge and attractive bedrooms.
bedrooms £ No smoking in bedrooms, ining room & 1 lounge Parking Open 1ar-Oct

MALLOW

ORTIGAN HOUSE
rom centre pass tourist office, straight through affic lights, turn left, house signposted on left)
022 22770 F 022 22770
eriod house set in gardens, close to town entre, with friendly welcome. Pretty edrooms. Pool room overlooks gardens.
bedrooms £ No smoking in dining room r 1 lounge Parking

REENFIELD HOUSE
avigation Road **T 022 50231**
ight, airy modern house, designed and urnished to very high standards. Luxurious ooms overlook open country.
bedrooms Parking

AKLANDS HOUSE
pringwood **T 022 21127 F 022 21127**
urn off Killarney Rd N72 at railway bridge)
n quiet residential area.Inviting and ttractive bedrooms. Dining room verlooks the lovely gardens.
bedrooms, all no smoking £ Parking Open Mar-Oct

PRINGFORT HALL
Cork/Limerick N20, 4 miles from Mallow, urn R onto R581, premises 0.5m on right)
T 022 21278 F 022 21557
ountry house n woodlands and gardens. xcellent bedrooms. Restaurant features ocal produce. .Elegant sitting room.
4 bedrooms ££ No smoking in area of ining room Licensed Parking

MITCHELSTOWN

CLONGIBBON HOUSE
New Square
T 025 24116 24288 F 025 84065 7
7 bedrooms Licensed

SCHULL

OLD BANK HOUSE
(down main street, first left after AIB bank, house first on left)
T 028 28306 F 028 28306
A turn of the century house set in its own grounds.. Bedrooms, lounge and breakfast room are most comfortable.
4 bedrooms £ Parking Open Easter-Sep

STANLEY HOUSE
Colla Road **T 028 28425 F 028 28649**
Popular, friendly guest house. Comfort, tranquillity and spectacular sea views from the sun lounge contribute to its success.
4 bedrooms £ No smoking in bedrooms, dining room, lounge Parking Mar-Oct

SHANAGARRY

BALLYMALOE HOUSE
(Ballymaloe is on the L35 from Midleton, 2 miles beyond Cloyne on the Ballycotton Road)
T 021 652531 F 021 652021
Charming country house on a 400-acre farm. Some bedrooms in old gatehouse. Pleasant restaurant uses farm produce.
22 bedrooms, 10 in annexe ££££ No smoking in area of dining room Licensed Parking Heated outdoor swimming pool Golf Tennis Craft & kitchen shop

SKIBBEREEN

FERN LODGE
Baltimore Road **T 028 22327**
(2 miles, main Skibbereen to Baltimore Road)
Comfortable modern house in large grounds. Attractive bedrooms and a pleasant lounge. Dinner by arrangement..
6 bedrooms £ Parking Open Feb-Nov

ILENROY HOUSE
10 North Street *(100yds from the main street on the N71 Clonakilty Road)*
T 028 22751 & 21711 F 028 22552
Tall streetside house with attractive bedrooms, equipped to a high standard.
7 bedrooms £

WHISPERING TREES
Baltimore Road **T 028 21376**
(take N71 from Cork and continue on R595 in direction of Baltimore. House on left)
Quiet location. Attractive conservatory, lounge, breakfast room plus pretty bedrooms with thoughtful extras.
6 bedrooms £ Parking Feb-Nov

TOORMORE

FORTVIEW HOUSE
Gurtyowen **T 028 35324**
(6 miles east of Goleen on R591)
Popula and charming house. Traditional bedrooms, superb breakfasts. Evening meals served by arrangement.
5 annexe bedrooms £ No smoking in bedrooms or dining room Parking Open Mar-Nov

YOUGHAL

AHERNES
163 North Main Street
T 024 92424 F 024 93633
Pleasant house, spacious bedrooms, furnished with antiques. Pleasant restaurant, well known for seafood.
10 bedrooms ££££ No smoking in area of dining room Licensed Parking

CHERRYMOUNT FARMHOUSE
(turn north off N25 at the Blackwater Bridge, follow signs to farmhouse) **T 024 97110**
500-year-old farmhouse on high ground. Friendly welcome and traditional style accomodation in peaceful surroundings.
3 bedrooms £ Parking 70 acres dairy

Old Presbytery

CAMPING & CARAVAN SITES

AA RECOMMENDED

BALLINSPITTLE

GARRETSTOWN HOUSE HOLIDAY PARK
T **021 778156** *Signposted*
4 pennants, touring caravans, motor caravans & tents. Open mid May-mid September (restricted service Easter-mid May) Last arrival 22.00hrs Last departure noon. 7-acre site with 60 touring pitches and 80 statics. Disco, ceilidh, campers' kitchen. Electric hook up, electric shaving point, hairdrier, tennis court, games room, cold storage, children's playground, Calor Gas, Camping Gaz, battery charging, toilet fluid, café/restaurant, public telephone, shop. *Facilities within three miles of site: fishing, launderette*

BALLYLICKEY

EAGLE POINT CARAVAN & CAMPING PARK
T **027 50630** *Nearby town: Bantry*
Q award, 5 pennants, attractive environment, first class washing & sanitary facilities, outstanding range of sports & recreational facilities, touring caravans, motor caravans & tents. Open May-September. Last arrival 23.00hrs. Last departure noon. No dogs.
20-acre site with 125 touring pitches. Electric hook up, showers, electric shaver point, launderette, tennis, separate TV room, cold storage, children's playground, battery charging, public telephone, shop, disabled facilities. *Facilities within three miles of site: stable, golf course, fishing*

BLARNEY

BLARNEY CARAVAN & CAMPING PARK,
Stone View T **021 385167** *Signposted*
3 pennants, touring caravans, motor caravans & tents. Open all year. Booking advisable anytime. Last arrival midnight. Last departure noon.
3-acre site with 40 touring pitches. Mini golf. Electric hook up, shower, electric shaver point, hairdrier, separate TV room, cold storage, Camping Gaz, public telephone, picnic area, dog exercise area, shop.*Facilities within three miles of site: stable, golf course, mini golf, fishing, launderette*

CROOKHAVEN

BARLEY COVE CARAVAN PARK
T **028 35302 or 021 542444**
Signposted Nearby town: Schull
Q award, 5 pennants, touring caravans, motor caravans & tents. Open Easter & June-August (restricted service May & September). Booking advisable July-Agust. Last arrival 21.00hrs. Last departure noon. 9-acre site with 100 touring pitches and 50 statics. Pitch & putt, children's playhouse. Electric hook up, bath, shower, electric shaver point, launderette, hairdrier, tennis, games room, separate TV room, cold storage, children's playground, Calor Gas, Camping Gaz, battery charging, toilet fluid, café/restaurant, public telephone, fast food/takeaway, barbeque area, shop, disabled facilities. No dogs.*Facilities within three miles of site: stable, golf, fishing*

GLANDORE

MEADOW CAMPING PARK,
Kilfinnan T **028 33280**
Signposted Nearby town: Skibbereen
2 pennants, attractive environment, motor caravans & tents. Open mid March-mid September. Booking advisable July-August. Last arrival 22.30hrs. Last departure noon. No dogs. No cars by tents.
1.5-acre site with 19 touring pitches. Dining room. Electric hook up, shower, electric shaver point, launderette, cold storage, public telephone. *Facilities within three miles of site: stable, mini golf, water sports, boats for hire, fishing, shop*

Call the AA Hotel Booking Service on 0990 050505 to book at AA recognised hotels and B&Bs in the UK and Ireland, or through our internet site: http://www.theaa.co.uk/hotels

WHERE TO EAT

RESTAURANTS

AA RECOMMENDED

BALTIMORE HARBOUR HOTEL ❀
Baltimore T **028 20361** F **028 20466**
Fresh local ingredients form the basis of the menu. A varied choice from the fixed-price menu might include pan-fried fillet of home-smoked pork with glazed apples and Calvados sauce or baked salmon suprême with steamed mussels and beurre blanc..
FIXED ££

CASEY'S SEAFOOD RESTAURANT ❀
Baltimore T **028 20197** F**028 20509**
If you enjoy seafood and Irish music, this is definitely to place to go. Justly famous for its excellent seafood, the fixed-price menu offers options for both vegetarians and meat-eaters. Freshly-caught lobster, wild Atlantic salmon,and Roaring Water Bay Mussels are main features.
FIXED & ALC ££

BAY VIEW HOTEL ❀❀
Ballycotton T **021 646746** F **021 646075**
This elegant restaurant commands splendid views of the harbour. Freshly landed seafood is a feature of the menus, which are complemented by an interesting wine list.
FIXED & ALC £££

CASTLE HOTEL ❀
Macroom T **026 41074** F **026 41505**
A smart, family-run hotel with a welcoming restaurant serving good food.
FIXED ££

COURTMACSHERRY HOTEL ❀
Courtmacsherry T **023 46198 023 46137**
There is a good range of dishes at this family-run hotel near the beach. Main courses could include fillet of sea trout meunière, or Kinsale lamb cutlets with Provençal sauce.
FIXED ££ ALC ££

DEVONSHIRE ARMS HOTEL & RESTAURANT ❀
Pearse Square, Youghal
T **024 92827 or 92018** F **024 92900**
Good food is served in both the bar and the restaurant of this restored 9th-century hotel.

GARRYVOE HOTEL ❀
Garryvoe T **021 646718** F **021 646824**
A good-value four-course dinner menu is offered here.Typical dishes are warm salad with crispy bacon croûtons and blue cheese, sautéed monkfish with red pepper sauce, and squidgy chocolate log.
FIXED ££

INNISHANNON HOUSE HOTEL ❀❀
Inishannon T **021 775121** F **021 775609**
A charming country house situated by the River Bandon in its own lovely gardens. Good food is prepared from the freshest ingredients, with seafood a speciality.
FIXED L ££ D £££

MIDLETON PARK HOTEL
Midleton
T 021 631767 F 021 631605
Just ten miles from Cork, this lovely restaurant serves excellent food, beautifully presented. Very attentive service.
FIXED L ££ D ££ & ALC

PRESIDENTS RESTAURANT
Longueville House Hotel, Mallow
T 022 47156 or 47306 F 022 47459
A fine Georgian mansion, where the elegant restaurant is graced by an Adams fireplace. Chef William O'Callaghan shows flair, courage and sureness of touch in the preparation of an exciting range of dishes based on excellent fresh produce.
ALC £££

SAVANNAH RESTAURANT
Trident Hotel, Worlds End, Kinsale
T 021 772301 F 021 774173
Located at the harbour's edge, the Trident Hotel has its own marina, and the restaurant enjoys wonderful harbour views.

SEA VIEW HOTEL
Ballylickey **T 027 50073 & 50462** A lovely country house overlooking Bantry Bay, where the restaurant is made up of several smaller rooms, connected by archways, making for plenty of welcoming corners. There is a set-price five-course menu providing a good choice of dishes using fresh local produce.
FIXED £££

PUBS, INNS & OTHER PLACES

AHERNE'S SEAFOOD RESTAURANT
163 North Main Street, Youghal
T 024 92424 F 024 93633
A family-run bar and restaurant..

ALTAR RESTAURANT
Toormore, Schull **T 028 35254**
Cottage restaurant .

ANNIE'S BOOKSHOP & CAFÉ
Main Street, Ballydehob
Home-made soup, scones and cakes.

ANNIE'S
Main Street, Ballydehob **T 028 37292**
A tiny restaurant serving good quality food

AN SÚGÁN
41 Strand Road, Clonakilty **T 023 33498**
A lovely pub, full of character.

ASSOLAS COUNTRY HOUSE
Kanturk **T 029 50015 F 029 50795**
Much of the produce from kitchen garden.

BALLYMALOE HOUSE
Shanagarry, Midleton **T 021 652531**
Historic venue. Interesting food.

THE BARN RESTAURANT
Glanmire **T/F 021 866211**
Traditional set-price four-course menu.

BLAIRS COVE RESTAURANT
Durrus, Bantry **T 027 61127**
Lovely setting with stunning buffet.

BLUE HAVEN HOTEL RESTAURANT
3 Pearse St, Kinsale **T 021 772209**
Nautical theme

THE BOSUN
Monkstown **T 021 842172 F 021 842008**
Pub with bar and restaurant. food

BULLYS
Douglas Village, Douglas **T 021 892415**
Italian-style restaurant

BUSHE'S BAR
The Square, Baltimore **T 028 20125**
Old bar overlooking the harbour.

CASINO HOUSE RESTAURANT
Coolmain Bay, Kilbrittain **T 023 49944**
Interesting and adventurous food

CHEZ JEAN-MARC
Lower O'Connell St, Kinsale **T 021 774680**
Classic French cooking

CHEZ YOUEN
Baltimore **T 028 20136**
Wonderful seafood restaurant overlooking Baltimore Harbour. Lobster a speciality.

COTTAGE LOFT RESTAURANT
6 Main Street, Kinsale **T 021 772803**
Continental influences are apparent

DUNWORLEY COTTAGE
Butlerstown, nr Clonakilty **T 023 40314**
Dramatic coastland restaurant.

THE EARL OF ORRERY
140 North Main St, Youghal **T 024 93208**
Stylish restaurant with a modern menu.

FINDERS INN
Nohoval, Oysterhaven **T/F 021 770737**
Best fresh produce. Dinner only.

FIONNUALA'S
30 Ashe Street, Clonakilty **T 023 343555**
Italian-style food.with veggie options

GREGORY'S
Main Street, Carrigaline **T 021 371512**
A lively restaurant. Imaginative dishes.

HERON'S COVE RESTAURANT
Goleen **T 028 35225**
Seafood is prepared fresh from the tank.

JIM EDWARDS RESTAURANT
Market Quay, Kinsale **T 021 772541**
Nautical themed restaurant on three levels.

JOURNEY'S END
Crookhaven **T 028 35183**
A cottage restaurant by the sea

KALBO'S BISTRO
48 North Street, Skibbereen **T 028 21515**
Try lamb on courgette and carrot pancake.

KICKI'S CABIN
53 Pearse Street, Clonakilty **T 023 33384**
Fresh fish is the speciality.

LA COQUILLE
Schull **T 028 28642**
French traditional favourites.

LA JOLIE BRISE
The Square, Baltimore **T 028 20441**
Café serving a range from breakfast or smoked salmon to evening meals.

LARCHWOOD HOUSE RESTAURANT
Pearsons Bridge, Bantry **T 027 66181**
A small restaurant, overlooking the river

LAWRENCE COVE HOUSE
Lawrence Cove, Bere Island **T 027 75063**
Owner ferries diners in his fishing boat.

LETTERCOLLUM HOUSE
Timoleague **T 023 46251**
Former convent. Country-style cooking.

LISS ARD LAKE LODGE
Skibbereen **T 028 22365**
Five-course menu with non-dairy dishes.

MAN FRIDAY
Scilly, Kinsale **T 021 772260**
High above the harbour, with an emphasis on seafood.

MARY ANN'S BAR & RESTAURANT
Castletownsend **T 028 36146**
Good bar food. Little restaurant upstairs.

MAX'S WINE BAR
Main Street, Kinsale **T 021 772443**
Fresh fish and seafood.

O'CONNOR'S SEAFOOD RESTAURANT
The Square, Bantry **T 027 50221**
A long established seafood restaurant, with steak and game alternatives.

La Jolie Brise

COUNTY KERRY

The wild splendour of Kerry's scenery attracts many visitors to the county. The Ring of Kerry is the tourist honey pot, a scenic route circling the Iveragh Peninsula, providing a dramatic mix of rugged moorland and mountains, lakes, rivers and streams, cliffs, beaches and weatherbeaten islands. Tourist activity centres on Killarney, where jaunting cars and coaches compete in the busy streets. Just as lovely, but rather less busy, is the Dingle Peninsula, with its wealth of ring forts, high crosses and other ancient monuments. Flower lovers will appreciate the superb subtropical gardens, and rare bog plants and waterlilies of the quieter peninsulas. Among a number of annual festivals, the best known the Tralee Festival, with its famous beauty pageant open to all young women of Irish birth or ancestry, to compete for the title 'Rose of Tralee'.

PRINCIPAL TOWNS

KILLARNEY

Killarney is a dreadful tourist trap, packed to bursting in summer, and with little of great interest to engage the visitor (apart from the splendid Catholic cathedral designed by Pugin). However, it cannot really be avoided, because the area around it - the Killarney National Park - has to be seen.

KENMARE

Although the origins of Kenmare date back to the ancient stone circle (2200-500BC) next to the town, the town itself became a model estate town back in the 18th century and you can still follow the distinctive cross-pattern street plan. Kenmare was once famous for its distinctive lace-making and this art is kept alive at the Heritage Centre.

LISTOWEL

Listowel is a picturesque place which takes its name from Lios Tuathail (the fort of Tuathail), the remains of which look down on the market square, the many attractive shop fronts and the Gothic-style St John's Church.

MUST SEE

THE BLASKET CENTRE
Dunquin *(10 miles west of Dingle town, on Slea Head Drive)*
T 066 56444 or 56371 F 066 56446
In the early part of this century a small group of writers from the remote Blasket Island, just off the coast of Co Kerry, achieved world renown. They told their own story in their own language. Literary masterpieces from the 20s and 30s include The Islandman and Twenty Years A-Growing, which have been translated from the Gaelic into English, French and German, among other languages. The centre describes the lives of the hardy Blasket people before the sad abandonment of the island in 1953. Audio-visual documentary, restaurant and bookshop.

BLENNERVILLE WINDMILL VISITOR & CRAFT CENTRE
Blennerville, Tralee
(1 mile west on N86/R559)
T 066 21064 F 066 27444
The largest working windmill in Britain or Ireland is the focal point of a major visitor and craft complex. Facilities include an audio-visual theatre, guided tours, exhibitions on flour milling and 19th-century emigration, craft workshops, a craft shop and restaurant. Blennerville was a major port of emigration during the mid 19th century, with vessels such as the Jeanie Johnson (1847-58), reconstructed here to commemorate the 150th anniversary of the Great Irish Famine (1845-48).

KERRY THE KINGDOM MUSEUM
Ashe Memorial Hall, Denny Street, Tralee
T 066 27777 F 066 27444
One of Ireland's most visited attractions, combining three separate elements:
Geraldine Tralee, where you can travel by time car through the reconstructed streets and houses of the medieval town. Synchronised sound, smell and lighting effects make this an almost life-like experience!
Kerry In Colour, an audio-visual presentation of Kerry's spectacular scenery and historic monuments.
Kerry County Museum, featuring the priceless archaelogical treasures of Kerry, interactive media and life-size models.

MUCKROSS HOUSE & GARDENS
(on the N71 Kenmare road, 2.5 miles/4km outside Killarney)
T 064 31440
A furnished 19th-century neo-Tudor mansion designed by William Burn. Attached to it is a folk museum, where craftspeople demonstrate their trades, and several reconstructed farmhouses. No cars are allowed within the estate, but you can park by the house. To explore the extensive grounds, you can take a pony and trap ride (negotiate the fare carefully before you set off), or hire a bike. The lakeside gardens have wonderful rhododendrons and azaleas, best in early summer. The Meeting of the Waters is a popular spot between the Upper Lake and Lough Leane, where arbutus (Killarney strawberry) trees flourish in the mild climate. Lake boats 'shoot the rapids' here, and close by is the Torc Waterfall plunging 66ft/20m down the mountainside.

CRAG CAVE
Castleisland
(1 mile/1.5km north, signposted off N21)
T 066 41244 F 066 42352
One of the longest cave systems in Ireland, with a total length of 12,510ft/3.81km, where pale forests of stalagmites and stalagtites, thousands of years old, throw eerie shadows around vast echoing caverns, enhanced by dramatic sound and lighting effects. An all weather attraction; guided tours lasting about 30 minutes.

THE SKELLIG EXPERIENCE HERITAGE CENTRE,
Valentia Island, Ring of Kerry
T 066 76306
The Skellig Rocks are renowned for their scenery, sea bird colonies, lighthouses, early Christian monastic architecture and rich underwater life. The two Skellig islands - Skellig Michael and Small Skellig - stand like fairytale castles in the Atlantic Ocean, rising to 218 metres/715ft and their steep cliffs plunging 50 metres/164ft below the sea. The Heritage Centre (on Valentina Island, which is reached by bridge from the mainland) is themed around the early Christian monks, the Skellig lighthouses, sea birds and underwater sealife of Skelligs. There is a 16-minute audio-visual presentation, and personal sound tour in three languages. An optional part of the Experience is a boat trip around the Skellig Islands, and refreshments are available in a café overlooking the estuary.

BIG OUTDOORS

BEACHES
Ballybunion and Ballyheigue are favourite North Kerry seaside resorts offering golden sands, beautiful surf and cliff walks with delightful scenery.

GLENINCHAQUIN WATERFALL AMENITY AREA Tuosist, Kenmare
(12 miles/19km from Kenmare on the road to Lauragh) **T 064 84235**
A beautiful valley on the Beara Peninsula, with waterfalls, woodlands and lakes. Ample parking is provided and picnic areas close to the waterfall.

TRALEE-BLENNERVILLE STEAM RAILWAY
Ballyard Station, Dingle Road
(follow signs for Dingle on N86/R559)
T 066 28888 F 066 27444
Part of the famous Tralee & Dingle Light Railway (1891-1953) restored in 1993. Steam trains operate on the 3km stretch between the stations, and on-board commentary is provided.

GREAT FOR KIDS

THE AQUA DOME Tralee **T 066 28899**
Featuring sky-high water slides, rapids, wave pool, lazy river, geysers, whirl pools, toddler pool and slides, water cannons, medieval castle and adults-only sauna. Restaurant and refreshments.

DINGLE OCEANWORLD
Dingle Aquarium, near Dingle Harbour
T 066 52111 F 066 52155
A submarine view of the creatures of the deep, plus relics of the Spanish Armada.

THE ENCHANTED FOREST
Ventry **T 066 56234**
A fairytale museum.

FARM WORLD
Camp, Tralee **T 066 58200**

Rare breeds of sheep, cattle, pigs, goats, horses, deer and waterfowl, plus indoor playground with toy tractors, pets corner, lakeside walk, picnic area and facilities for the disabled.

FENIT SEAWORLD
The Pier, Fenit T 066 36544
The opportunity to experience, face to face, the creatures that inhabit the underwater world, where Tralee Bay meets the Atlantic.

JUNGLE JIM'S ADVENTURE WORLD
20 Pembroke Street, Tralee T 066 28187
Indoor adventure playground with ball pool, monster maze, various slides (including the giant tube) and the haunted house. Also big screen interactive video games.

THE SCIENCE WORKS
Godfrey Place, Tralee T 066 29855
Ireland's first interactive science centre, an entertaining approach to unravelling the mysteries of science and technology, with over 70 continually changing hand-on experiments.

HISTORIC & ANCIENT SITES

DUNBEG FORT
(on the R559 near Fahan, about 4 miles/6km west of Ventry)
Perched on a promontory high above Dingle Bay, this circular Iron Age fort is protected on its landward side by trenches and a 23ft/7m-thick wall.

GALLARUS ORATORY
(off the R559, between Ballyferriter and Ballynana)
The oratory is a perfect example of early Irish building, dating from the 8th or possibly the 7th century. Completely unmortared, it has remained watertight for over 1,200 years.

KERRY BOG VILLAGE
Glenbeigh
A glimpse into the past of a bog village, where turf was cut and stacked by hand to be used as domestic or industrial fuel. Complete with 19th-century-style peasant dwellings.

KILMALKEDAR CHURCH
(off the R559, near the Gallarus Oratory)
This ruined 12th-century church is a fine example of Romanesque architecture. The narrow east window is known locally as 'the eye of the needle', with reference to the biblical text.

MUCKROSS ABBEY
(on the N71 Kenmare road, 2.5 miles/4km outside Killarney)
Despite vandalism by Cromwell's troops in 1652, which left it roofless, the 15th-century Franciscan abbey remains in a surprisingly good state of preservation.

STONE CIRCLES
The area is rich in stone circles, one of the most impressive is just a short walk from the centre of Kenmare, signposted from the park end of Main Street.

HOMES & GARDENS

DERRYNANE HOUSE & NATIONAL HISTORIC PARK
Glanleam Subtropical Gardens, Valentia Island T 066 76176 F 066 76108
A 150-year-old garden, overlooking Valentia Harbour, with a unique collection of rare Southern Hemisphere plants, including palms, tree ferns, bananas and bamboo groves.

HOTEL DUNLOE CASTLE GARDEN
Beufort, Killarney
T 064 44111 F 064 44583
The garden surrounding the shell of MacThomas' medieval keep, with plants from around the world catalogued in a booklet by Roy Lancaster, who supervises all new planting.

MUSEUMS & ART GALLERIES

KENMARE HERITAGE CENTRE
The Square, Kenmare
T 064 31633 F 064 34506
The history of Kenmare, including famous visitors, the effects of the Famine, the landlords, historical sites, the Nun of Kenmare and the art of lace making is demonstrated as well as an exhibition of the very distinctive Kenmare lace.

KILLARNEY TRANSPORT MUSEUM
Scotts Hotel Gardens, Killarney
(centre of town, opposite railway station)
T 064 34677 F 064 32638
The glorious years of motoring relived in this fascinating collection of Irish veteran, vintage and classic cars, motorbikes, bikes, carriages and fire engines, including a 1930s garage.

TARBERT JAIL
Tarbert *(route N69)* T 066 36500
The Tarbert 'Bridewell', dating from 1831, displayed in all its unpleasantness recreating a scene from the early 19th-century. Coffee shop, gift shop and tourist information point.

THE WELLSPRING GALLERY
16 Denny Street, Tralee T 066 21218
Contempory fine art.

ESSENTIAL INFORMATION

ACCESS

AIR ACCESS
Kerry Airport T 066 64644

TOURIST INFORMATION

KENMARE
Heritage Centre T 064 41233

KILLARNEY
Town Hall T 064 31633 F 064 34506

TRALEE
Ashe Hall T 066 21288

CRAFTS

AVOCA HANDWEAVERS
Molls Gap T 064 34720

BLARNEY WOOLLEN MILLS
Main Street, Killarney T 064 33222

BRICIN
26 High Street, Killarney T 064 34902

FISHERY CRAFT SHOP
The Bridge, Killorglin

HOLDEN LEATHERGOODS
Baile an Ghoilin, Dingle T 066 51796

JOHN J MURPHY WEAVERS LTD
Currow Road, Farranfore
T 066 64659 F 066 64993
Manufacturers of scarves and throws in natural fibres. Shop on site open to visitors.

KENMARE LACE
Heritage Centre, Kenmare T 064 41491

KERRY WOOLLEN MILLS
Ballymalis, Beaufort T 064 44122

PAT'S CRAFT SHOP
Kells Post Office, Kells T 066 77601

ENTERTAINMENT

SIAMSA TIRE THEATRE
Tralee T 066 23055 F 066 27276
The National Folk Theatre of Ireland

SPORTS & LEISURE

ACTIVITY CENTRES

CELTIC NATURE EXPEDITIONS
The Old Stone House, Cliddaun
T 066 59882

KINGDOM KARTING
rear of Rock Business Centre, Upper Rock Street, Tralee T 066 29511
Indoor karting centre.

ANGLING

The Kerry Blackwater is good for grilse, salmon and brown trout, and Lough Brin for brown trout. The River Laun has salmon throughout the year, and Lough

Leane is famous for its brown trout. Information is available from South Western Regional Fisheries Board, 1 Neville's Terrace, Masseytown, Macroom T **026 41221.**

A ghilly service is also available. Permits can be obtained from the Board, local fishery officers and local angling suppliers.

ANGLING BOAT OPERATORS

AN TIARACHT ANGLING TRIPS
Ballydavid, Dingle T **066 55429**
DINGLE BAY ANGLING CENTRE
Gallarus, Ballydavid, Dingle T **066 55300**
M V ANCHORSIVEEN
The Anchor, Cahirciveen T **066 72049**
WEST KERRY ANGLING & FENIT SEA CRUISE CENTRE T/F **066 36049**

BOATING & CRUISING

BLASKET ISLAND BOATMEN
Dunquin T **066 56455**
DINGLE BOATMEN
The Pier, Dingle T **066 51136**
KILLARNEY WATERCOACH CRUISES LTD
3 High Street, Killarney T **064 31068**
LAIRD OF STAFFA
Blasket Passenger Ferry, Dingle
T **066 56188**
SEAFARI SCENIC & WILDLIFE CRUISES & ACTIVITY CENTRE
The Pier, Kenmare T **064 83171**
SKELLIG BOAT TRIPS
Portmagee T **066 72437**
VALENTIA ISLAND CAR & PASSENGER FERRY
Reenard Point T **066 76141** F **066 76377**

CAR HIRE

BUDGET RENT-A-CAR
c/o International Hotel, Killarney
T **064 34341**
HERTZ HENT-A-CAR
28 Plunkett Street, Killarney T **064 34126**
RANDLES CAR HIRE LTD
Kerry Airport/Muckross Road, Killarney
T **064 31237**

JAUNTING CAR TOURS

COUNIHANS TOURS
'Arbutus', 20 Park Road, Killarney
T **064 31493**
AUL TANGNEY
Muckross Road, Killarney T **064 33358**

COACH TOURS

CASTLELOUGH TOURS
High Street, Killarney T **064 31115**
CORCORAN'S TOURS
Kilcummin, Killarney T **064 43151**
CRONIN'S TOURS
College Street, Killarney T **064 31521**
DERO'S TOURS
Main Street, Killarney T **064 31251**
KILLARNEY BUS TOURS T **088 2757086**
KILLARNEY & KERRY TOURS
Innisfallen Mall, Main Street, Killarney
T **064 54041**
O'CONNOR AUTOTOURS LTD
Ardross, Ross Road, Killarney T **064 31052**

Ballinskelligs Watersports

CYCLE HIRE

THE BIKE SHOP
Pawn Office Lane, High Street T **064 31282**
FINNEGAN'S BIKE HIRE
Souvenir Shop, 37 Henry Street, Kenmare
T **064 41083**
FIOS FEASA RENT-A-BIKE
Holy Ground, Dingle T **066 51606**
FOXY JOHN MORIARTY
Main Street, Dingle T **066 51316**
KILLARNEY RENT-A-BIKE
Market Cross, Killarney T **064 32578**
O'CALLAGHAN CYCLES
College Street, Killarney T **064 31175**
O'NEILLS
Plunkett Street, Killarney T **064 31970**
PADDY'S RENT-A-BIKE
Dykegate Street, Dingle

EQUESTRIAN CENTRES

BALLINATAGGART HOUSE EQUESTRIAN CENTRE Racecourse Road, Dingle
T **066 51454** F **066 52207**
COIS LINNE RIDING STABLES
Deelis Bridge, Cahersiveen
T **066 72124 or 087 2364533**
DINGLE PENINSULA TRAIL RIDES
El Rancho, Ballard, Tralee T/F **066 21840**
EAGLE LODGE Tralee T **066 37266**
EL RANCHO RIDING CENTRE
Tralee T **066 21840**
KENNEDY EQUINE CENTRE
Tralee T **066 26453**
IVER VALLEY RIDING STABLES
Lounihan, Kilgarvan T **064 85360**
KENNEDY'S EQUINE CENTRE
Cahirwisheen, Tralee T **066 26453**
KILLARNEY RIDING STABLES
Ballydowney, Killarney T **064 31686**
ROCKLANDS STABLES
Rockfield, Tralee Road, Killarney
T **064 32592**
WOODLANDS
Faha, Killarney T **064 44142**

GOLF

KENMARE Killowen, Kenmare
T **064 41291** F **064 42061**
A mature parkland golf course overlooking Kenmare Bay and Kerry countryside.
Also :
ARDFERT, Tralee T **066 34744**
BALLYBUNION T **068 27146**
BALLYHEIGUE CASTLE T **066 33195**
BEAUFORT T **064 44440**
CASTLEGREGORY T **066 39444**
CEANN SIBEAL T **066 56255**
DOOKS T **066 68205**
DUNLOE T **064 44578**
KERRIES T **066 22112**
KILLARNEY T **064 31034**
KILLORGLIN T **066 61979**
LISTOWEL T **068 21592**
PARKNASILLA T **064 45122**
ROSS T **064 31125**
TRALEE T **066 36379**
WATERVILLE T **066 74102**

GREYHOUND RACING

KINGDOM GREYHOUND STADIUM
Oakview, Tralee
T **066 80008**

HORSE RACING

KILLARNEY RACECOURSE
T **064 31125**

WATER SPORTS

BALLINSKELLIGS WATERSPORTS
Dungegan, Ballinskelligs T **066 79182**
Day trips landing on the Skelligs; diving and angling trips

DERRYNANE DIVING SCHOOL
Derrynane Harbour, Caherdaniel
T **066 75119 or 087 2322275**

DINGLE BAT SAILING CLUB
Harbour Master, Dingle
T **066 51984 or 51341**

FOCUS WINDSURFING
Maharees, Castlegregory & Ventry Beach, West Kerry T **066 39411** F **066 39011**
Windsurfing, surfing, dinghy sailing, boogie boarding, canoeing, snorkelling and paddle boats, plus adventure club for kids and teens. RYA, ISA and BSA approved.

MERLIN DIVING
Ventry, Dingle T **066 59876**

SKELLIG AQUATICS LTD (DIVING)
Caherdaniel T **066 75277**

VALENTIA ISLAND SEA SPORTS & DIVE CENTRE Knightstown, Velentia Island
T **066 76204 or 087 420714**

VALENTIA ISLAND SEA SPORTS
Knightstown, Valentia Island
T **066 76204 or 087 420714**
F **066 76367**
Diving in the Skelligs, the Puffin Islands and the waters around Valentia Island. Also Canoeing, Sailing and windsurfing. Supervised hourly rental or classes.

WHERE TO STAY

HOTELS

AA RECOMMENDED

SEE UNDER WHERE TO EAT FOR ALL HOTEL RESTAURANTS WITH ROSETTES

BALLYHEIGE

THE WHITE SANDS ★★★❀
(11 miles from Tralee town on coast road, the hotel is situated on left on main street)
T 066 33102 F 066 33357
This seaside hotel, in a village near Tralee, has a good restaurant, two welcoming bars and pleasant staff.
81 bedrooms ££ Lift Parking Closed Nov-Feb

CAHERDANIEL

DERRYNANE ★★★
T 066 75136 F 066 75160
Half-way around the famous Ring of Kerry, overlooking the sea, this modern hotel offers a relaxed and friendly atmosphere.
75 bedrooms Parking Outdoor swimming pool Tennis (hard) Fishing Snooker Closed Oct-Apr

CAVAN

KILMORE ★★★
Dublin Road
(approx 2 miles from Cavan on N3)
T 049 32288 F 049 32458
A very comfortable hotel set on a hillside on the outskirts of Cavan. Food at the Annalee Restaurant is excellent.
39 bedrooms ££ Parking

DINGLE

SKELLIG ★★★❀❀
T 066 51144 F 066 51501
On the outskirts of town overlooking the bay, this modern hotel has bright airy bedrooms and pleasant lounges.
115 bedrooms £££ Indoor swimming pool (heated) Tennis (hard) Snooker Sauna Solarium Closed mid Nov-mid Mar

KENMARE

DROMQUINNA MANOR ★★★
Blackwater Bridge
T 064 41657 F 064 41791
Hotel situated in 42 acres of woodland and lawns. Bedrooms vary in size, including a treehouse suite.
30 bedrooms Parking Tennis (hard) Pool table Croquet lawn

RIVERSDALE HOUSE ★★★
T 064 41299 F 064 41075
Hotel in an idyllic location with wonderful views. The top floor has four mini-suites with balconies.
64 bedrooms ££ Lift Parking Closed Nov-Mar

Aghadoe Heights

PARK HOTEL ★★★★❀❀❀
(on R569 beside golf course)
T 064 41200 F 064 41402
A luxurious country house hotel above terraced gardens. Warm hospitality, sheer professionalism, and very good food.
49 bedrooms ££££ Lift Parking Tennis (hard) Snooker Gymnasium Croquet lawn Putting green Closed Jan-March & Nov-end Dec

SHEEN FALLS LODGE ★★★★❀❀
(from Kenmare take N71 to Glengarriff over suspension bridge, take the first turn left)
T 064 41600 F 064 41386
Situated beside the Sheen Falls in 300 acres of coutryside. The bedrooms are comfortable, and grounds magnificent.
60 bedrooms ££££ Lift Parking Leisure & sporting facilities Closed Dec-Jan

KILLARNEY

AGHADOE HEIGHTS ★★★★❀❀❀
(10 miles south of Kerry Airport and 3 miles north of Killarney. Signposted off the N22 Tralee road) **T 064 31766 F 064 31345**
The restaurant serves superb food and standards of service have earnt our own Courtesy and Care Award.
60 bedrooms ££££ Parking Leisure & sports facilities

ARBUTUS ★★
College Street
T 064 31037 F 064 34033
39 bedrooms ££

CAHERNANE ★★★❀❀
Muckross Road
T 064 31895 F 064 34340
Fine old country mansion which was awarded our Courtesy and Care Award for 1996/7. Award-winning restaurant.
47 bedrooms (33 of them in annexe) ££££ Parking Fishing Tennis Croquet Shop Closed Nov-Mar

CASTLEROSSE ★★★
(from Killarney town take R562 for Killorglin & The Ring of Kerry, hotel is 1.5m from town on the left hand side)
T 064 31144 F 064 31031
Set in 6,000 acres of lakeland , this beautifully situated hotel offers warm hospitality and good food.
110 bedrooms incl some no-smoking ££ Lift Parking Leisure & sporting facilities Closed Dec-Feb

GLENEAGLE ★★★❀
T 064 31870 F 064 32646
The restaurant offers a range of imaginatively presented food. Bedrooms vary from comfortable to compact.
200 bedrooms Lift Parking Leisure & sports facilities Conference and banqueting facilities

INTERNATIONAL ★★★
Kenmare Place
(town centre) **T 064 31816 F 064 31837**
A golfer's paradise, with two courses almost on the doorstep and several others within easy driving distance.
75 bedrooms £ Lift

KILLARNEY PARK ★★★★❀❀
Kenmare Place
T 064 35555 F 064 35266
Charming purpose-built hotel that won The AA's Hotel of the Year for Ireland for 1997/8 Award.
44 bedrooms incl some no-smoking £££ Lift Parking Leisure& sports facilities

KILLARNEY RYAN ★★★
Cork Road *(on N22 route)*
T 064 31555 F 064 32438
Hotel with a spacious lounge, smart restaurant and comfortable lounge bar. Many rooms can accommodate families.
168 bedrooms incl some no-smoking ££ Lift Parking Leisure & sports facilities

AKE HOTEL ★★★
uckross Road *(Kenmare rd out of Killarney)*
064 31035 F 064 31902
ormer mansion with five new bedrooms hich have balconies, jacuzzis and four-oster beds.
bedrooms ££ Lift Parking Leisure & orting facilities Closed Dec- mid Feb

UCKROSS PARK HOTEL ★★★★
uckross Village
om Killarney take road to Kenmare, hotel 5 miles on left)
064 31938 F 064 31965
8th-century hotel in Killarney National ark. Features a thatched pub, Molly arcys, or the more formal Bluepool.
bedrooms incl some no-smoking ££££ rking Closed Dec-Feb

OTTS ★★
ollege Street T 064 31060 F 064 31582
his town centre hotel has undergone a cent facelift to give 18 excellent new edrooms. The bar, restaurant and unges are all most pleasant.

HITE GATES ★★★
uckross Road
.5 mile from Killarney town on Muckross ad on left) T 064 31164 F 064 34850
stinctively painted with a blue and ochre lour scheme. Bedrooms are particularly tractive.
bedrooms ££ Parking

PARKNASILLA

GREAT SOUTHERN ★★★★
(on Kenmare road 2 miles from Sneem village)
T 064 45122 F 064 45323
Located on Kenmare Bay, many bedrooms have fine sea views. Enjoy the spacious lounges, and the Pygmalion Restaurant.
85 bedrooms ££££ Lift Parking Leisure & sporting facilities Closed Jan-Feb

TRALEE

ABBEY GATE ★★★
Maine Street T 066 29888 F 066 29821
New town centre hotel. Comfortable bedrooms, a cocktail bar, a traditional pub, and the Vineyard Restaurant.
100 bedrooms ££ Lift Parking Banqueting & conference suites.

THE BRANDON ★★★
T 066 23333 F 066 25019
Modern hotel situated in the town centre with leisure facilities, and within 30 minutes of six superb golf courses.
160 bedrooms Lift Parking Leisure & sport facilities

WATERVILLE

BUTLER ARMS ★★★
(N70 Ring of Kerry)
T 066 74144 F 066 74520
This hotel has been owned by the same family for over three generations and offers high traditional standards of service.
30 bedrooms ££££ Parking Fishing Tennis (hard) Snooker

Butler Arms

BED & BREAKFAST ACCOMMODATION

AA RECOMMENDED

CAHIRCIVEEN

A BREEZE QQ
nard Road *(turn off N70 at first junction uth of Cahirciveen)* T 066 72609
ttractively decorated house with most edrooms on the ground floor, and pretty ardens.
bedroom £ No smoking in bedrooms or ning room No children under 5yrs Open ar-Oct

ALENTIA VIEW FARMHOUSE QQQ
n N70 2m on the Waterville side of ahirciveen) T 066 72227 F 066 73122
d country farmhouse with a warm and ospitable atmosphere. Some wonderful ews of Valentia island and bay.
bedrooms £ Parking No children Under 2 onths 38 acres beef Open Mar-Oct

CAMP

ARNAGH BRIDGE OUNTRY HOUSE QQQQ
ave N86 Tralee/Dingle road at Camp and llow Conor Pass road for 0.5 mile)
066 30145 F 066 30299
eam coloured house where each edroom is named after a local flower and eir colour reflected in the decor.
bedrooms £ No smoking in dining room rking Open Mar-Oct

CASTLEGREGORY

GRIFFIN'S COUNTRY FARMHOUSE QQ
Goulane *(1m from Stradbally village)*
T 066 39147
Near one of Dingle's many unspoilt beaches. The owner believes in a warm welcome, good beds and home baking.
7 bedrooms £ Parking 150 acres dairy sheep Open Mar-Sep

STRAND VIEW HOUSE QQQQ
Kilcummin, Conor Pass Road
(20 miles from Tralee on the Dingle, Conor Pass Road 2 miles west of Stradbally)
T 066 38131
Brick house with a terraced rock garden to the rear. The luxury bedrooms enjoy panoramic views over Kilcummin beach.
10 bedrooms (5 of which are in an annexe) inc some for non-smokers £ No smoking in dining room or lounges Parking Open Feb-Oct

CAVAN

HALCYON DRUMALEE QQ
(turn right off N3 immediately after the cathedral, signed Cootehill. Turn right at X-roads, Halcyon 100yds on left) T 049 31809
This modern bungalow offers peaceful accommodation, and a sun lounge and sitting room which overlook the gardens.
5 bedrooms No smoking in dining room Parking No children under 2yrs

DINGLE

ALPINE QQQQ
Mail Road T 066 51250 F 066 51966
On the edge of Dingle, this large guest house is run by the welcoming O'Shea family, who maintain excellent standards.
10 bedrooms £ No smoking in dining room Parking No children under 5yrs

AN TOWERIN TRA QQQ
Baile Moir West, Ventry T 066 59820
A lovely modern bungalow overlooking the beautiful Ventry Harbour and the Kerry mountains beyond.
4 bedrooms £ Parking Open Mar-Oct

ARD-NA-GREINE HOUSE QQQQ
Spa Road
T 066 51113 & 51898 F 066 51898
This modern bungalow is situated on the edge of town towards Connor Pass. All the rooms offer wide range of facilities.
4 bedrooms ££ Parking No children under 7yrs

ARD-NA-MARA QQQ
Ballymore, Ventry T 066 59072
This country house overlooks Ventry harbour and offers comfortable bedrooms, good breakfasts, and warm hospitality.
4 bedrooms £ No smoking in bedrooms or dining room Open Apr–Oct

BALLYEGAN HOUSE QQ
Upper John Street T 066 51702
This large house is a short walk from the town centre, and has spectacular views over Dingle Bay.
6 bedrooms £ Parking

BAMBURY'S QQQQ
Mail Road T 066 51244 F 066 51786
An eye-catching pink house on the edge of Dingle. The lounge and dining room are very airy, and the bedrooms are excellent.
12 bedrooms

BOLANDS QQQ
Goat Street T 066 51426
Bolands has a distinctive lilac extension. Inside are a lounge, a conservatory, and bright cheerful bedrooms.
6 bedrooms No smoking in dining room

CLEEVAUN QQQQ
Lady's Cross, Milltown
(R559 from Tralee to Dingle follow sign for Slea Head scenic route)
T 066 51108 F 066 51108
Enjoy superb views of Dingle Bay from this luxury bungalow, set on a one-acre site. Bedrooms and facilities are excellent.
9 bedrooms Parking No children under 3yrs Open mid Jan–mid Dec

CLOOSMORE HOUSE QQQ
(2km from rdbt on Dingle/Sleahead road, on water's edge) T 066 51117
Modern bungalow two miles west of Dingle. The bedrooms are well appointed with a good range of equipment
3 annexe bedrooms including 2 for non-smokers No smoking in area of dining room or 1 lounge No children under 14yrs Parking

DINGLE HEIGHTS QQ
Ballinaboola T 066 51543
Overlooking Dingle Bay, this house features comfortable and nicely furnished accommodation.
4 bedrooms £ Parking

Bambury

DOYLES TOWN HOUSE QQQ
4 John Street *(in the heart of Dingle town)*
T 066 51174 F 066 51816
Charming town house with spacious bedrooms. Next door is their award-winning seafood restaurant.
8 bedrooms ££ No smoking in area of dining room Licensed Open mid Mar–mid Nov

GREENMOUNT HOUSE QQQQ
(on entering town turn right at rdbt & next right at T-junct)
T 066 51414 F 066 51974
Greenmount offers six new mini-suites with spacious bedrooms, a conservatory-style dining room and two sitting rooms.
12 bedrooms £ No smoking in bedrooms or dining room Parking No children under 8yrs

HURLEYS FARM QQQ
An Dooneen, Kilcooley T 066 55112
Hurleys farm is a welcoming and comfortable house featuring relaxing bedrooms, some with shower rooms.
4 bedrooms £ No smoking in 1 lounge Parking 32 acres mixed Open Easter–Oct

MILLTOWN HOUSE QQQQ
Milltown
(1 mile west of Dingle on Slea Head road, cross Milltown Bridge and turn left)
T 066 51372 F 066 51095
Situated on a sea channel, Milltown House offers attractive bedrooms, a welcoming sitting room, and a conservatory.
10 bedrooms £ No smoking in dining room or 1 lounge Parking No children

MOUNT EAGLE LODGE QQQ
Ventry
(3.5 miles west of Dingle on Slea Head Drive) T 066 59754
A lovely new house in a commanding position overlooking Ventry Bay, which provides an excellent breakfast buffet.
4 bedrooms £ No smoking in dining room or 1 lounge Parking Open Easter–Sep

PAX HOUSE QQQQ
Upper John Street
(turn right off N86 at finger post sign, then 0.75 miles on left) T 066 51518 & 51650
Bedrooms here are very comfortable and guests are treated to wonderful hospitalit and generosity from the owners.
7 bedrooms (2 family) £ No smoking in dining room or 1 lounge Children's faciliti Parking

GLENCAR

CLIMBERS INN QQ
T 066 60101 F 066 60101
(10m s of Killorglin)
Near to Ireland's highest mountain range this inn offers new en suite bedrooms an a wide range of local knowledge.
8 bedrooms (7 of which are in annexe) No smoking in bedrooms, in area of dining room, or in 1 lounge £ Licensed Parking No children under 7yrs

KENMARE

HARBOUR VIEW QQQ
Castletownbere Road, Dauros T 064 4175
Standing on the sea shore, this pristine house has a cheerful and caring landlady, whose home-baking is excellent.
4 bedrooms £ No smoking in dining room Parking Open Mar–Oct

SALLYPORT HOUSE QQQQQ
Glengarriff Road *(0.25m south on N71)*
T 064 42066 F 064 42067
Superbly refurbished house set in its own grounds, offering relaxing bedrooms with good-sized bathrooms.
5 bedrooms £££ Parking No children under 10yrs Open Apr–Oct

Climbers Inn

Call the AA Hotel Booking Service on 0990 050505 to book at AA recognise hotels and B&Bs in the UK and Ireland or through our internet site: http://www.theaa.co.uk/hotels

A SHORE FARM
›rid
uated off N71 Killarney Road, signposted t out of town by O'Sullivans Antiques)
T 064 41270
erlooking Kenmanre Bay, this pleasant odern bungalow stands in its own ›unds on the edge of town.
bedrooms £ Parking Sauna Private shore acres Open mid Mar- mid Nov

KILGARVAN

RCHWOOD
urch Ground
00m east of Kilgarvon village on R569)
T 064 85473 F 064 85570
uated on an elevated site facing a tural forest with bedrooms are mfortable and attractively decorated.
bedrooms £ Parking

KILLARNEY

ONDALE HOUSE
alee Road
.5 miles from roundabout on N22)
T 064 35579
distinctive pink house surrounded by tractive gardens, with a comfortable unge and relaxing bedrooms.
bedrooms £ No smoking in dining room rking No children under 8yrs Open Feb- ov

FFEY'S LOCH LEIN GUEST HOUSE
lf Course Road, Fossa
n R562, 3 miles west of Killarney)
T 064 31260 F 064 36151
mfortable bungalow in its own grounds. e owner enjoys interior decorating and s used this skill to good effect.
bedrooms incl some no-smoking £ No oking in dining room Parking Open mid ar-early Nov

UNTESS HOUSE
untess Road T 064 34247
uated in a residential area this cream d red brick house has cheerful drooms and a comfortable lounge.
bedrooms £ No smoking in the dining om & 1 lounge Parking Closed Jan

Cleevaun

COURTMURPH HOUSE
Muckross Road
(1.5 miles from Killarney town on the Muckross Road N71)
T 064 34586 F 064 36630
A modern house near the entrance to Killarney National Park. The bedrooms are comfortable and there are two lounges.
5 bedrooms £ No smoking in dining room or 1 lounge Parking Open mid Apr-Oct

CRAB TREE COTTAGE
Mangerton Road, Muckross T 064 33169
Set in Killarney National Park, encircled by gardens which can be enjoyed while having breakfast in the conservatory.
4 bedrooms £ No smoking in dining room Parking Open Apr-Oct

CRYSTAL SPRINGS
Ballycasheen
T 064 33272 & 35518 F 064 31188
A luxurious house surrounded by Killarney's National Park. Bedrooms are attractively decorated and well equipped.
6 bedrooms £ No smoking in bedrooms or dining room Parking

EARLS COURT HOUSE
Woodlawn Junction, Muckross Road
(on Muckross road turn off after Shell petrol station)
T 064 34009 F 064 34366
Contemporary in design and purpose-built with the added facility of balconies adjoining most bedrooms.
11 bedrooms ££ No smoking in dining room Parking Open Mar- Nov restricted service mid Nov- Feb

ELYOD HOUSE
Ross Road *(from Muckross road take road to Ross Castle, 0.5 mile on left just before Ross Golf Course)* T 064 36544 & 31510
A family-run modern house in its own grounds with a lounge, dining room, and two bedrooms with balconies
4 annexe bedrooms £ Parking

FOLEYS TOWN HOUSE
22/23 High Street
T 064 31217 F 064 34683
A delightful town house with charming bedrooms, welcoming lounge, bar, private car park, and adjoining seafood restaurant.
12 bedrooms incl some no-smoking ££ No smoking in area of dining room Licensed Parking Open Apr-Oct

FRIARS GLEN
Mangerton Road, Muckross
(from Killarney take N71 towards Kenmare and turn left immediately after Muckross Park Hotel. Entrance 300m on right next to garden centre) T 064 34044 F 064 34044
Modern house in the heart of Killarney National Park. Bedrooms are large, and public rooms are attractive.
4 bedrooms £ No smoking in bedrooms or dining room Parking Open Mar-Oct

GLENA HOUSE
Muckross Road
(0.5 miles from town centre on N71)
T 064 32705 & 34284 F 064 35611
A large, comfortable house close to town offering en suite accomodation and on-site parking
26 bedrooms incl some no-smoking ££ No smoking in area of dining room Licensed Library

GORMAN'S
Tralee Road *(on N22 Tralee Rd)*
T 064 33149 F 064 33149
Large and attractive bungalow, set in well cultivated gardens, with magnificent views from comfortable en suite bedrooms.
5 bedrooms incl some no-smoking £ No smoking in dining room Parking

GREEN ACRES
Fossa *(on T67 Killorglin road)* T 064 31454
This modern house is situated on the Ring of Kerry a mile and a half outside town.
8 bedrooms No smoking in dining room Parking

lena House

hussey's bar & townhouse

HUSSEY'S BAR & TOWNHOUSE
43 High St *(On High St towards Tralee Rd)*
T/F 064 33144
Smart town house with its own pub next door. Restful TV lounge, cheerful breakfast room, and comfortable bedrooms.
5 bedrooms No smoking in 3 bedrooms or dining room No dogs No children under 10 years

KATHLEEN'S COUNTRY HOUSE
Tralee Road *(on N22)*
T 064 32810 F 064 32340 7
Family-run, luxury accommodation in scenic countryside makes this an ideal touring centre.
17 bedrooms ££ Licensed Parking No children under 5yrs Croquet Reflexology Open Mar-mid Nov

KILLARNEY VILLA
Cork-Waterford Road
(N22 out of town, at roundabout continue on N22, at junction bear left on N72)
T 064 31878 F 064 31878
A luxurious country home with rooftop conservatory offering complimentary tea/coffee/biscuits in the morning.
6 bedrooms £ Parking No children under 6yrs Open Easter-Oct

LIME COURT
Muckross Road
T 064 34547 F 064 34121
A well maintained modern house with spacious sitting room, sun lounge, and well equipped bedrooms.
12 bedrooms incl some no-smoking £ No smoking in dining room & 1 lounge Licenced Parking

LOHAN'S LODGE
Tralee Road
(3 minutes drive from Killarney town on N22) **T 064 33871 F 064 33871**
This luxurious modern bungalow is set in its own landscaped gardens in scenic countryside.
5 bedrooms £ Parking No children under 7 Open Mar-early Nov

MCCARTHY'S TOWN HOUSE
19 High Street **T 064 35655 F 064 35745**
Town centre location next door to the Crock of Gold bar and restaurant, and run by the same owners.
8 bedrooms ££ Licensed Parking

NASHVILLE
Tralee Rd *(on the N22, 2m from Killarney)*
T 064 32924
This white house is easy to find. The bedrooms are bright and cheerful, and the owner and his family are very welcoming.

6 bedrooms incl some no-smoking £ Parking Golf Fishing Horse riding availal nearby Open Mar-Nov

OLD WEIR LODGE
Muckross Road **T 064 35593**
Fine Tudor-style house in landscaped gardens, with en suite bedrooms and modern facilities. Very welcoming hosts.
15 bedrooms, inc 10 for non-smokers £ No smoking in lounges Parking

PARK LODGE
Cork Road *(on N22)*
T 064 31539 F 064 34892
A large, double-fronted guest house on the Cork road beside the Killarney Ryan Hotel.
20 bedrooms incl some no-smoking No smoking in dining room £ Parking

THE PURPLE HEATHER
Glencar Road, Gap of Dunloe **T 064 4426**
This modern bungalow stands by the roadside among spectacular mountain scenery and is an ideal touring centre.
6 bedrooms £ No smoking in bedrooms, dining room or 1 lounge Parking Tennis (hard) Pool room Open Mar-Oct

SHRAHEEN HOUSE
Ballycasheen
(situated on the Ballycasheen/Woodlawn Ro 1 mile off N71, turn off at shell sign)
T 064 31286
A comfortable modern house set in two acres. Various leisure pursuits can be arranged and there is a large car park.
6 bedrooms £ Parking

Kathleen's Country Ho

Nashville

SLIABH LUACHRA HOUSE
Loretto Road **T 064 32012**
Modern house in gardens on a residentia road. Rooms vary in size, but all are furnished to the same degree of comfor
6 bedrooms £ No children under 12yrs Open Apr-Sep

SLIEVE BLOOM MANOR
Muckross Road
T 064 34237 F 064 35055
A substantial modern house standing on the edge of the town towards Kenmare. Bedrooms and lounges are comfortable.
14 bedrooms £ No smoking in dining roo Parking

KILLORGLIN

OMIN FARMHOUSE QQQ
N70 between Killorglin and Miltown)
066 61867
: on a sheep and cattle farm, this vated bungalow has a private TV nge, and babysitting can be arranged.
edrooms £ No smoking in dining room lounges Parking 42 acres dairy sheep en mid Mar-Oct

OVE LODGE QQQQ
arney Road *(0.5 mile from Killorglin dge on Killarney road - N72)*
066 61157 F 066 62330
ovely riverside house recently extended d developed to a high standard, with y comfortable rooms.
bedrooms £ No smoking in the bedrooms lining room Parking

TAHILLA

HILLA COVE QQQQ
the northern side of the Ring of Kerry - 0) **T 064 45204 F 064 45104**
nily-run, split-level bungalow on a 13-e estate with lawns and terraces eeping down to a sandy cove.
edrooms (6 of which in annexe) ££ No oking in dining room Licensed Parking en Easter-Oct

Old Weir Lodge

HEATHERVILLE FARM QQQ
Blennerville
(exit main Dingle Road N86 at Blennerville village, premises 0.5 mile on left)
T 066 21054 F 066 21054
Modern farmhouse just off the Tralee-Dingle road, close to the restored Blennerville Windmill and steam railway.
6 bedrooms £ No smoking Parking 40 acres dairy Open Mar-Oct

Call the AA Hotel Booking Service on 0990 050505 to book at AA recognised hotels and B&Bs in the UK and Ireland, or through our internet site: http://www.theaa.co.uk/hotels

Slieve Bloom Manor

ıan's Lodge

KLONDYKE HOUSE QQQ
New Line Road
(on N70, beside Waterville craft market)
T 066 74119 F 066 74666
An attractive house with a pretty sun lounge. Bedrooms are comfortable with semi-orthopaedic beds.
6 bedrooms Parking Tennis (hard)

O'GRADYS QQQ
Spunkane
(parallel to N70 on northern approach)
T 066 74350 F 066 74730
6 bedrooms £ No smoking in dining room Parking No children under 4yrs Open Mar-early Oct

TRALEE

LLINGOWAN HOUSE QQQ
eheight, Killarney Road
proach Tralee on N21/N22, premises on before McDonalds)
066 27150 F 066 20325
edrooms £ No smoking Parking children under 6yrs Open Mar-early v

WATERVILLE

GOLF LINKS VIEW QQQ
Murreigh *(on N70 north of village)*
T 066 74623 F 066 74623
A new house standing in developing gardens outside the town. Bedrooms are well appointed and have good views.
4 bedrooms £ Open Apr-Oct

SCENIC DRIVES

THE RING OF KERRY
In suitable weather, the Ring of Kerry is a road of extraordinary scenic beauty, encircling the Iveragh Peninsula. The total distance is 100 miles/158km, to which a detour to Valentia Island adds at least another 25 miles/40km. It is not really possible to do it justice in a day, and it should be remembered that at the height of the season traffic can be very heavy.

WALKING

Established walks in the county nclude the Dingle Way and the Kerry Way. The latter begins and ends in Killarney, and is a great way of seeing the Iveragh Peninsula. For further nformation contact the local Tourist nformation Office.

GUIDED WALKING TOURS

COUNTRYSIDE TOURS LTD
Glencar House, Glencar
T 066 60211 F 066 60217

CAMPING & CARAVANNING

AA RECOMMENDED SITES

CAHERDANIEL

WAVE CREST CARAVAN & CAMPING PARK
066 75188 *Signposted*
4 pennants, touring caravans, motor caravans and tents. Open April-September. Last arrival 22.00hrs. Last departure noon.
4.5-acre site with 45 touring pitches and two statics. Boat anchorage, fishing and pool room. Electric hook up, shower, electric shaver point, launderette, hairdrier, games room, separate TV room, cold storage, children's playground, Calor Gas, Camping Gaz, battery charging, toilet fluid, café/restaurant, public telephone, barbeque area, picnic area, dog exercising area, shop, disabled facilities.
Facilities within three miles of site: stable, golf, water sports, boats for hire, fishing

CASTLEGREGORY

ANCHOR CARAVAN PARK
066 39157 *Signposted Nearby town: Tralee*
4 pennants, first class sanitary facilities, touring caravans, motor caravans and tents. Open Easter-September. Last arrival 22.00hrs. Last departure noon.
5-acre site with 24 touring pitches and 6 statics. Electric hook up, shower, electric shaver point, launderette, games room, separate TV room, cold storage, children's adventure playground, battery charging, public telephone, picnic area, dog exercising area, shop, disabled facilities.
Facilities within three miles of site: stable golf, mini golf, watersports, boats for hire, fishing

KILLARNEY

FLESK MUCKROSS CARAVAN & CAMPING PARK,
Muckross Road **064 31704**
(1 mile south) Signposted
4 pennants, first class sanitary facilities, touring caravans, motor caravans and tents. Open mid March-mid October. Booking advisable. Last arrival 21.00hrs. Last departure noon.
7-acre site with 72 touring pitches. Bike hire, bar/club, tennis, pool all nearby. Electric hook up, shower, electric shaver point, launderette, hairdryer, games room, separate TV room, cold storage, Calor Gas, Camping Gaz, toilet fluid, public telephone, baby care, barbeque area, picnic area, dog exercise area, shop, disabled facilities.
Facilities within three miles of site: stable, golf course, mini golf, water sports, boat hire, cinema, fishing

FOSSA CARAVAN PARK,
Fossa **064 31497 or 31496**
(2.5 miles southwest on R562)
5 pennants, holiday centre, touring caravans, motor caravans and tents. Open Easter-September. Booking advisable July-August. Last arrival 23.00hrs. Last departure noon.
6-acre site with 100 touring pitches and 20 statics. Campers' kitchens and bikes for hire. Electric hook up, shower, electric shaver point, launderette, hairdrier, tennis court, games room, separate TV room, cold storage, children's playground, Camping Gaz, toilet fluid, café/restaurant, public telephone, baby care, fast food/take away, shop, disabled facilities.
Facilities within three miles of site: stable, golf course, mini golf, boats for hire, cinema, fishing

KILLORGLIN

WEST'S HOLIDAY PARK,
Killarney Road **066 61240** *Signposted*
3 pennants, touring caravans, motor caravans and tents. Open April-October. Booking advisable.
1-acre site with 17 touring pitches and 48 statics. River fishing, volleyball. Electric hook up, shower, electric shaving point, launderette, hairdrier, indoor swimming pool, tennis court, games room, separate TV room, children's playground, public telephone, shop.
Facilities within three miles of site: golf course, boats for hire, cinema, fishing

LAURARGH

CREVEEN PARK,
Healy Pass Road **064 83131**
(1 mile southeast on R574) Signposted
2 pennants, touring caravans, motor caravans and tents. Open Easter-October. Booking advisable August bank holiday. Last arrival midnight. Last departure noon.
2-acre site with 20 touring pitches. Electric hook up, shower, electric shaver point, launderette, separate TV room, cold storage, children's playground, Camping Gaz, battery charging, café/restaurant, picnic area, dog exercising area, shop.
Facilities within three miles of site: boats for hire, cinema, fishing

WATERVILLE

WATERVILLE CARAVAN & CAMPING,
Spunkane **066 74191**
Signposted
4 pennants, touring caravans, motor caravans and tents. Open Easter-September. Booking advisable July-August. Last departure noon.
4.5-acre site with 59 touring pitches and 22 statics. Playroom, cycle hire, campers' kitchen. Electric hook up, shower, electric shaver point, launderette, hairdrier, outdoor swimming pool, games room, separate TV room, cold storage, children's playground, Camping Gaz, battery charging, toilet fluid, public telephone, baby care, fast food/takeaway, shop, disabled facilities.
Facilities within three miles of site: stable, golf course, water sports, boats for hire, fishing

COUNTY LIMERICK

Limerick is the least favoured of the Southwestern counties in terms of scenic splendour, and tends to be passed through by visitors on their way to and from its more attractive neighbours. However, the county has its own gentle charm, with rolling countryside from the Golden Vale to the tidal estuary of the River Shannon. It also has its share of interesting places to visit, including historical and prehistoric sites, some appealing market towns, such as Castleconnell, Kilfinane, Kilmallock and Newcastle West, and Adare, one of Ireland's prettiest villages.

PRINCIPAL TOWNS

LIMERICK

Limerick is a significant city in terms of industry and population, currently vying with Galway for third place in the Republic. It has a rich historical background and plenty of interesting sights, but despite energetic attempts to revitalise the centre with new development of its wharves and warehouses, and careful conservation of its Norman and Georgian heritage, much of the city seems run down and unemployment is rife. It also has a higher crime rate than most Irish provincial cities, and there are places not to leave your car for too long.

ADARE

Adare has been called Ireland's answer to the welcoming English village, with thatched cottages and well-trimmed hedges linining the street to the gates of a Victorian manor, formerly owned by the Earls of Dunraven. History has further endowed an ivied Norman castle beside the River Maigue and a collection of medieval friaries, one of which is in the middle of a golf course. Adare came from Ath Dara (the ford of the oak tree).

MUST SEE

CELTIC PARK & GARDENS
(N69 Limerick to Tralee road)
Located on an original Celtic settlement within one of the most important Cromwellian plantations in the southwest of Ireland. The park, its two loughs and its environment are completely unspoilt by modern man. Visitors walking through the park are able to see a church built in 1250, a Mass Rock, dolmens, a 6/7th-century wooden church, a stone circle, lake dwellings, cooking area and other fascinating sights including one of the finest examples of an early surviving historic ring fort. The surrounding landscape offers meadow, scrubland, cragland and bog with many species of wild flower. The classic-style gardens afford a panoramic view of the surrounding countryside. Facilities include refreshments and a shop.

FLYING BOAT MUSEUM,
Foynes *(on N69, 23 miles/37km from Limerick City)*
T 069 65416 F 069 65416
The museum recalls the era of the flying boats during the 1930s and early 1940s, when Foynes was an important airport for air traffic between the United States and Europe. The flying boats brought in a diverse range of people from celebrities to refugees. Located in the original terminal building, it is the only museum of its kind in the world. There is a comprehensive range of exhibits, graphic illustrations and a 1940s-style cinema featuring a 17-minute film - all original footage from the 30s and 40s - and a tea room of the same era. Another point of interest is that Irish Coffee was invented here in 1943 by chef Joe Sheriden.

KING JOHN'S CASTLE,
Castle Street, Limerick
T 061 411201/2
A national monument, the 13th-century castle is an impressive Anglo-Norman fortress with an imposing twin-towered gatehouse and battle-scarred walls. Within the castle, imaginative models and three-dimensional displays demonstrate 800 years of Limerick's and Ireland's history. An audio-visual show depicts the wars, sieges and treaties of its past, and in the courtyard there are copies of ancient war machines. The castle is wheelchair accessible and other facilities include refreshments and a visitors' shop.

LOUGH GUR STONE AGE CENTRE,
Bruff Road, Holycross
T 061 385186 or 361511 F 061 363260
Lough Gur introduces visitors to the habitat of Neolithic Man on one of Ireland's most important archaeological sites. Near the lake is an interpretative centre, which tells the story of 5,000 years of man's presence at Lough Gur, with an audio-visual presentation, models of stone circles and burial chambers, and facsimiles of weapons, tools and pottery found in the area. Walking tours covering the archaeological features are conducted at regular intervals. Facilities include a café and shop.

BIG OUTDOORS

CURRAGHCHASE FOREST PARK
(16miles/26km southwest of Limerick City)
A 600-acre/243ha plantation with forest walkways, a lake, arboretum and nature trail, surrounding the ruins of the 18th-century Curraghchase House, home of the poet Aubrey de Vere.

SPRINGFIELD CASTLE DEER CENTRE
T 063 83162 or 088 503905
Guided tractor tours through herds of red, fallow and sika deer, plus woodland walks, picnic area, coffee shop and gift shop. Facilities for disabled visitors.

GREAT FOR KIDS

PETER PAN FUNWORLD,
Crescent Shopping Centre, Dooradoyle, Limerick **T 061 301033**
Indoor adventure playground with 16ft/5m free fall slide, ball pool, bouncy castle, tunnel slide, haunted cave, log climbs, boulder canyon, aerial glides, rope bridges and scrambling nets.

HISTORIC & ANCIENT SITES

ST MARY'S CATHEDRAL,
Bridge Street, Limerick
Built as a palace in the 12th century, the Protestant cathedral retains some original features. Grotesque carvings on the misericords in the choir stalls date from the 15th century.

HOMES & GARDENS

ADARE MANOR,
Adare **T 061 396566 F 061 396124**
A 19th-century manor house surrounded by 988 acres/400ha of parklands on the banks of the River Maigue. Formal gardens in geometric patterns date from the 1850s.

BALLYNACOURTY,
Ballysteen **T 061 396409 F 061 396733**
A relatively new series of small gardens, including a vegetable garden, soft fruit garden and laburnum walk underplanted with lavender. Garden open by appointment only.

GLIN CASTLE PLEASURE GROUNDS & WALLED GARDEN,
Glin **T 068 34112 F 068 34364**
Pleasure grounds with gothic follies from the 18th-century plus later ornamental and grey stone walled gardens lined with pears, fig trees and clematis. A fuschia hedge surrounds the orchard.

MUSEUMS & ART GALLERIES

ADARE HERITAGE CENTRE,
Adare **T 061 396666 F 061 396932**
The story of Adare, told through model enactments and an audio-visual presentation in six languages. Irish ceili nights, with music, dance and song, are a feature in summer.

DE VALERA MUSEUM,
Bruree **T 063 91300**
A small museum dedicated to the memory of former President Eamon de Valera, housed in his former school, with memorabilia from his school days to his presidency.

UNT MUSEUM,
niversity of Limerick, Limerick
T 061 202661 F 061 330056
n internationally important collection of ecorative art and antiquities, ranging om the Neolithic to the 20th century. The ersonal collection of John and Gertrude unt.

IRISH PALATINE EXPERIENCE,
Rathkeale *(on the N21 at Rathkeale)*
T 069 64397
In 1709 several hundred families from the German Palatinate settled in Ireland. The Centre features an exhibition, library and gift selection associated with their story

ESSENTIAL INFORMATION

TOURIST INFORMATION

RTHUR'S QUAY, LIMERICK
4-hour Information Point T 061 317522

DARE T 061 396255

CRAFTS

DARE COTTAGE SHOP,
dare T 061 396422
range of quality hand-crafted Irish gifts.

ISH DRESDEN,
omcollier T 063 83236
usiness founded by Oskar Saar in the 960s, using Irish craftsmen to produce esden figurines. Sale room and orkshop tours

SHOPPING

e traditional main shopping streets are Connell Street and William Street, and eets off. There are pedestrianised areas d some newer shopping malls, such as thurs Quay, plus two city-centre multi-orey car parks. For those who prefer not venture into the centre, there are the escent or Parkway suburban shopping ntres.

SPORT & LEISURE

ANGLING

ere are ample opportunities for sea, me and course fishing in the county. e River Maigure, running by the village Adare, is good for trout and salmon. etails from Tourist Information Offices.

CAR HIRE

ALAMO CAR & VAN RENTALS FREEPHONE
T 1 800 343536

THRIFTY IRISH CAR RENTALS
Shannon Airport T 061 472649

Limerick City
T 061 453049 F 061 326766

COACH TOURS

THE GREAT LIMERICK TOUR BUS EIREANN T 061 313333
An open-top bus tour of the city lasting about an hour and a half.

CYCLE HIRE

BIKE SHOP Quinlan Street T 061 315900

EMERALD CYCLES 1 Patrick Street, Limerick
T 061 416983

MCMATTONS 25 Roches Street
T 061 415202

EQUESTRIAN CENTRES

ASHROE RIDING CENTRE
Murroe T 061 378271

CLARINA RIDING CENTRE
Clarina T 061 353087

CLONSHIRE EQUESTRIAN CENTRE
Adare T 061 396770 F 061 396726

CRECORA RIDING CENTRE
Crecora T 061 355139

HILLCREST RIDING CENTRE
Galbally T 062 37915

RATHCANNON EQUESTRIAN CENTRE
Kilmallock T 063 90557 or 303841

WOODVIEW RIDING CENTRE
Newcastle West T 069 61554

YERVILLE STABLES
Pallasgreen T 061 351547

GOLF COURSES

LIMERICK COUNTY GOLF & COUNTRY CLUB
Ballyneety T 061 351881 F 061 351384
A lovely parkland course designed by Des Smith & Associates, including a driving range and refreshment area.

ALSO

ABBEYFEALE T 068 32033

ADARE Adare Manor Hotel
T 061 395044 F 061 396987

ADARE MANOR T 061 396204

CASTLETROY
T 061 335753 F 061 335373

KILLELINE Newcastle West
T 069 61600 F 069 62853

LIMERICK T 061 415146

NEWCASTLE WEST Adagh
T 069 76500 F 069 76511

GREYHOUND RACING

LIMERICK GREYHOUND TRACK
T 061 415170

HORSE RACING

LIMERICK RACECOURSE
Limerick T/F 061 229377

SCENIC DRIVES

It is a pleasant drive from the city of Limerick along the shores of the Shannon estuary, taking in Foynes and Glin and returning by Abbeyfeale, Newcastle West and Adare.

WALKING

An established walking route in the county is the Lough Dergh Way, from Limerick City to the village of Dromineer in Co Tipperary.

WHERE TO STAY

HOTELS

AA RECOMMENDED

SEE UNDER WHERE TO EAT FOR ALL HOTELS WITH ROSETTES

ADARE

ADARE MANOR ★★★★✿
(on the N21 in Adare village)
T 061 396566 F 061 396124
Magnificent gothic mansion, in 840 acres of woodland and formal gardens beside the River Maigue. Amenities, service, and standards are excellent.
64 bedrooms ££££ Lift Parking Leisure & sporting facilities

DUNRAVEN ARMS ★★★✿✿✿
T 061 396633 F 061 396541
18th-century country inn situated in one of Ireland's prettiest villages. Many bedrooms have their own dressing rooms.
75 bedrooms ££££ Lift Parking Leisure & sporting facilities

CASTLECONNELL

CASTLE OAKS HOUSE ★★★✿
T 061 377666 F 061 377717
Fine Georgian house with grounds reaching down to the River Shannon. Includes well-equipped modern bedrooms.
20 bedrooms ££ Parking Leisure & sporting facilities Angling centre

LIMERICK

CASTLETROY PARK ★★★★✿✿
Dublin Road *(on N7 3 miles from Limerick)*
T 061 335566 F 061 331117
Creatively designed hotel with fax and computer points in the bedrooms. McLaughlin's Restaurant serves good food.
107 bedrooms ££££ Lift Parking Leisure & sporting facilities

GREENHILLS ★★★
Caherdavin **T 061 453033 F 061 453307**
Set in landscaped gardens, and recently extended, adding some comfortable and well appointed bedrooms.
59 bedrooms £££ Parking Leisure facilities Conference facilities

Castletroy Pa

JURYS ★★★✿✿
Ennis Road **T 061 327777 F 061 326400**
Standing in 4 acres of grounds, includes The Copper Room restaurant and a separate bar and coffee shop.
95 bedrooms incl some no-smoking some with fax/modem ££££ Parking Leisure & sporting facilities

JURY'S INN ★★★
Lower Mallow Street
T 061 207000 F 061 400966
The spacious foyer, bar and restaurant are popular meeting places. Bedrooms are well equipped and offer good value.
151 bedrooms incl some no-smoking ££ Lift

LIMERICK RYAN ★★★✿
Ennis Road *(N22)*
T 061 453922 F 061 326333
In its own grounds, with lounges, restaurants, and a cocktail bar. Well equipped bedrooms are located in the modern extension.
181 bedrooms incl some no-smoking ££££ Lift Parking Gym nearby available free to guests

ROYAL GEORGE ★★
O'Connell Street
T 061 414566 F 061 317171
Many of the bedrooms have been refurbished and are well-equipped. A new addition is a traditional Irish bar.
54 bedrooms £ Lift Parking Free access to fitness club

TWO MILE INN ★★★
Ennis Road
(on N22, near Bunratty Castle & airport)
T 061 326255 F 061 453783
This hotel has bedrooms built to a high standard with attractive furnishings. The restaurant is very good value.
123 bedrooms incl some no-smoking £ Parking

WOODFIELD HOUSE ★★
Ennis Road **T 061 453022 F 061 326755**
An intimate hotel close to the city centre, offering well equipped en suite bedrooms, a restaurant, and a lounge bar.
22 bedrooms ££ Parking Tennis

TEMPLEGLANTINE

THE DEVON INN ★★★
T 069 84122 F 069 84255
Major building and refurbishment work has resulted in a new look for this hotel, including twenty new bedrooms.
59 bedrooms ££ Parking

BED & BREAKFAST ACCOMMODATION

AA RECOMMENDED

ADARE

ADARE LODGE QQQQ
Kildimo Road *(in village turn right at bank)*
T 061 396629 F 061 395060
Charming modern house, recently extended. En suite bedrooms are equipped with TV, tea/coffee trays and hairdriers.
6 bedrooms No smoking in dining room or 1 lounge

AVONA QQQ
Kildimo Road
T 061 396323 F 061 396323
Well appointed modern house with attractive en suite bedrooms, all with colour TV. There is also a separate breakfast room.
4 bedrooms £ No smoking in bedrooms or dining room

COATESLAND HOUSE QQQQ
Tralee/Killarney Road, Graigue
T 061 396372 F 061 396833
Coatesland House is very well appointed, offering attractive bedrooms, all with en suite facilities.
6 bedrooms No smoking in dining room £ Parking

OXHOLLOW HOUSE QQQQ
:room Road
T 061 396776 F 061 396776
edrooms are charming and well quipped. There is also a suite with its wn sitting room, bathroom and kitchen.
bedrooms No smoking in bedrooms, dining oom or lounges Parking

BRUREE

ALLYTEIGUE HOUSE QQQ
ockhill
ravelling south on N20 pass O'Roukes and ake next right, pass Rockhill Church, 1 mile om turn off premises are signposted)
T 063 90575 F 063 90575
leasant country house, with a pleasant tmosphere, comfortable accommodation nd a relaxing sitting room.
No smoking in dining room or lounges

KILMALLOCK

LEMINGSTOWN HOUSE QQQQ
n R512 2m from Kilmallock)
T 063 98093 F 063 98546
8th-century farmhouse, which has been odernised to provide stylish facilities roughout.
bedrooms £ (incl dinner) Parking 102 cres dairy Open Mar–Oct

Coatesland House

LIMERICK

CLIFTON HOUSE QQQ
Ennis Road T 061 451166 F 061 451224
This guest house has been refurbished to provide attractive and very comfortable bedrooms.
16l bedrooms £ Parking Closed 18 Dec–4

CLONEEN HOUSE QQQ
Ennis Road T 061 454461 F 061 455545
An attractive three-storey terrace house only ten minutes from the city centre.
6 bedrooms £ No smoking in dining room Parking

CLONMACKEN HOUSE QQQ
Clonmacken, off Ennis Road
T 061 327007 F 061 327785
This white-painted corner house has comfortable accommodation, a sitting room, and breakfast room.
10 bedrooms incl some no-smoking £ No smoking in dining room Parking

WHERE TO EAT

RESTAURANTS

AA RECOMMENDED

CORN RESTAURANT
astle Oaks House Hotel, Castleconnell
T 061 377666 F 061 377717
ishes might include fried Oakwell black udding with a warm olive croûton and ustard mousseline sauce, followed by an-fried supreme of wild salmon with lediterranean cous cous and red pepper oulis.

DARE MANOR HOTEL
dare T 061 396566 F 061 396124
ew restaurants can have more imposing ettings than this stately mansion hotel, et in 840 acres of woodland and formal ardens beside the River Maigue. The ooking is modern and international with n Irish influence, using produce from the otel gardens.
IXED £££ ALC £££

THE ARDHU RESTAURANT
Limerick Ryan Hotel, Ennis Road, Limerick
T 061 453922 F 061 326333
Dishes sampled include confit of duck with pink peppercorn sauce and star anise cream, and baked salmon with a cous-cous topping and brunoise of vegetables.
FIXED L ££ D £££

THE COPPER ROOM RESTAURANT
Jury's Hotel Ennis Road, Limerick
T 061 327777 F 061 326400
Options include hot oysters, glazed with a Guinness sabayon, duck Andalucia with olives and grapes in demerara sauce, and flambé dishes cooked at your table, such as monkfish Noilly Prat - or crêpe Suzette for a finish with a flourish.
FIXED D £££ ALC £££

MCLAUGHLIN'S RESTAURANT
Castletroy Park Hotel, Dublin Road, Limerick
T 061 335566 F 061 331117
McLaughlin's Restaurant offers a range of modern dishes. A starter of pan-fried chicken livers in Bourginnone sauce was followed by black sole with a soufflé of prawns and chervil sauce. The meal concluded with an excellent apricot and nut parfait.
FIXED L ££ D £££ ALC £££

THE MAIGUE ROOM
Dunraven Arms Hotel, Adare
T 061 396633 F 061 396541
The Maigue Room includes duck, salmon and trout on the menu. Dishes are prepared with imagination and executed with flair. Nearby, under the same ownership, is the Inn Between, which offers good food at somewhat lower prices.
FIXED £££

PUBS, INNS & OTHER PLACES

LIMERICK CITY

BEWLEY'S RESTAURANT,
Cruises Street T 061 414739
Efficient, friendly service and home-made Irish foods.

THE BRAZENHEAD,
102 O'Connell Street, Limerick
T 061 417412 F 061 417922
Popular bar, restaurant and nightclub in the city centre.

CAMPBELL CATERING PRIVATE DINING,
University of Limerick, Plassey
T 061 333644
Offers customers a classic culinary experience of creative fine food.

CHASERS RESTAURANT,
Pallasgreen T 061 384203
Good food and service, for parties big and small.

FREDDY'S BISTRO,
Theatre Lane, Lower Glentworth Street
T 061 418749 F 061 316141
19th-century family-run restaurant providing a blend of Mediterranean and Irish cuisine.

GREEN ONION CAFÉ,
Ellen Street T 061 400710
Trendy café serving finest Italian coffee, New World wines and quality meals.

HI-WAY RESTAURANT,
Dooradoyle T 061 227449
A long-established restaurant serving quality local produce.

JASMINE PALACE CHINESE RESTAURANT,
O'Connell Mall, O'Connell Street
T 061 412484
Oriental cuisine and fine wines in a relaxed atmosphere.

LA BELLA ITALIA,
43A Thomas Street T 061 418872
Fresh new ideas in Italian pasta.

LA PICCOLA ITALIA,
O'Connell Street T 061 315844
Family-style Italian cooking in a Neapolitan atmosphere.

LAVAZZA BISTRO,
Steamboat Quay T 061 319800
Fun, dynamic, cosmopolitan restaurant on the river front.

LIMERICK INN HOTEL,
Ennis Road T 061 326666
Enjoy the flavours of Irish cooking in the luxury of the Burgundy Room.

MING CHINESE RESTAURANT,
1-2 Lower Glentworth Street
T 061 316269 F 061 314492
Cantonese-style cooking.

MOLL DARBY'S,
8 George's Quay T 061 417270
One of Limerick's best loved restaurants; old world style, with international cuisine.

MORTELLS DELICATESSEN & SEAFOOD RESTAURANT,
49 Roches Street T/F 061 415457
Fresh seafood and meat dishes cooked in the Irish way. Open day time only.

MUSTANG SALLY'S,
103 O'Connell Street T 061 400417
A bit different - not many Tex-Mex restaurants yet in Ireland.

O'FLAHERTY'S BASEMENT RESTAURANT,
O'Connell Street T 061 316311
Old world presentation of fine food.

PLAYER'S CLUB,
P Punch's, Punch's Cross T 061 229588
Casual dining with a special touch.

QUENELLE'S RESTAURANT,
Lower Mallow/ Henry Street
T 061 411111 F 061 400111
A small gourmet restaurant, open for dinner only.

ROYAL GEORGE HOTEL,
O'Connell Street T 061 414566
Great home cooking at affordable prices in one of Limerick's best known hotels.

TEXAS STEAKOUT,
O'Connell Street T 061 410350
Western-style restaurant serving steaks and international fare.

TWO MILE INN,
Ennis Road T 061 326255
Fine dining in comfort and style.

WOODFIELD HOUSE HOTEL,
Ennis Road T 061 453022
An informal restaurant with a welcoming, friendly atmosphere.

CO LIMERICK

ABBOTS REST RESTAURANT,
The Heritage Centre, Adare T 061 396118
Traditional Irish and contemporary cooking offered in an informal setting.

ACORN RESTAURANT,
Castle Oaks House Hotel, Castleconnell
T 061 377666
Specialising in home cooking.

CROKERS BISTRO,
Limerick County Golf and Country Club, Ballyneety T 061 351881 F 061 351384
A striking glass-enclosed dining room.

GREAT SOUTHERN HOTEL,
Shannon T 061 471122
Elegant bistro-style Estuary Restaurant, overlooking the River Shannon.

THE INN BETWEEN RESTAURANT,
Adare T 061 396633 F 061 396541
Thatched cottage restaurant in a lovely village setting serving bistro-style food.

MILL RACE,
Croom Mills, Croom
T 061 397130 F 061 397199
Enjoy home-cooked food and baking to the sound of the slowly turning mill wheel. Modestly priced lunches and afternoon meals. Open Thu-Sat evenings for more formal dinners.

M J FINNEGAN BAR & RESTAURANT,
Dublin Road, Annacotty
T 061 337338 F 061 337171
A 17th-century tavern provides delightful surroundings for Irish fare, including seafood.

MUSTARD SEED,
Echo Lodge, Ballingarry
T 069 68508 F 069 68511
A renowned restaurant, where every detail counts, offering modern international cuisine, with French, Oriental and Irish influences, prepared and served with panache.

POACHERS RESTAURANT,
Bulgaden, Kilmallock
T 063 98209 F 063 98842
Quality home cooking based on local produce.

WILD GEESE RESTAURANT,
Rose Cottage Adare T/F 061 396451
A cottage restaurant specialising in French cooking with verve and style.

WOODLANDS HOUSE HOTEL,
Adare T 061 396118
Traditional Irish cooking, prepared from the best of Golden Vale produce.

THE WORRALL'S INN,
Main Street, Castleconell
T 061 377148 F 061 377148
Bar and restaurant food, including steaks, fresh fish and shellfish

THE WESTERN COUNTIES

COUNTIES CLARE, GALWAY, MAYO AND ARAN ISLANDS

A strongly Gaelic region, which evaded English influence until the 18th century, the people of the western counties are renowned for their very Irishness, which runs deep through their culture, their language and their music. The untamed landscape of bog and barren limestone makes for a tough living, and the Great Famine of the 1840s hit these counties very hard, and large numbers of local people emigrated. The area remains essentially rural, with few towns of any size. The scenic attractions are unparalled: the weird fascination of the Burren, the spectacular cliffs of Moher, the wild beauty of Connemara and the delights of Achill Island.

EVENTS & FESTIVALS

February

All-Ireland Dancing Championships,
Ennis, Co Clare

March

World Dancing Championships,
Oireachtas Rince na Cruinne, Salthill, Co Galway

April

Pan Celtic Festival,
Ennis, Co Clare

May

Fleadh Nua,
Ennis, Co Clare
Rythmn 'n Roots Festival,
Galway, Co Galway

June

Salthill Festival,
Galway, Co Galway

July

Darling Girl from Clare Festival,
Milltown Malbay, Co Clare

Galway Arts Festival,
Galway, Co Galway

Galway Races Summer Meeting,
Galway, Co Galway

Galway Summer Racing Festival,
Galway, Co Galway

Street Festival,
Westport, Co Mayo

Willie Clancy Summer School,
Milltown Malbay, Co Clare

August

Connemara Pony Show,
Clifden, Co Galway

Feakle Traditional Music Weekend,
Feakle, Co Clare

Fleadh Ceoil na hEireann,
Ballina, Co Mayo

September

Clifden Country Blues Festival,
Co Galway

European Pike Angling Challenge,
Co Galway

Galway Autumn Racing Festival,
Galway, Co Galway

Galway International Oyster Festival,
Co Galway

October

Ballinasloe Horse Fair,
Ballinasloe, Co Galway

Ballinasloe International October Fair & Festival,
Ballinasloe, Co Galway

COUNTY CLARE

The west coast of Clare has some of Ireland's most spectacular scenery, and the cliffs at Moher are undoubtedly the most impressive. Another scenic highlight is the Burren, a unique place well worth taking time off to explore. A landscape of rounded hills of porous grey rock and barren limestone pavements, little streams that seep away into the scarred surface of the land, underground rivers, caves and swallow holes, loughs that are full one day and dry the next, and an extraordinary mixture of arctic, alpine and Mediterranean plants clinging to life in any available nook or cranny

PRINCIPAL TOWNS

ENNIS

A market town and commercial centre set on the River Fergus, Ennis dates from 1240 when Donnchadh Cairbreach O'Brien facilitated the establishment of a Franciscan order through his hospitality to some itinerate friars. The old Abbey, built shortly after, is a fine National Monument.

KILLALOE

Designated a Heritage Town of Ireland, Killaloe shares a Heritage Centre with Ballina across the Shannon River in County Tipperary. Brian Borù, Ireland's most famous ancient king held court nearby at Kincora just one millenium ago

KILRUSH

It has been said that the 'rush' part of the name is erroneous, as the town is a relaxed resort overlooking the Shannon estuary. From the renovated square, streets lead down to the new marina, where once fishing smacks and pleasure steamers from Limerick were moored. Kilrush takes its name from Cill Rois (Peninsular Church)

MUST SEE

LWEE CAVE
/vaughan
065 77036 or 77067 F 065 77107
underground network of caves beneath world famous Burren. Guided tours you through large caverns, over ged chasms and alongside thunderous erfalls. There is a craft shop, a dairy ere cheese is made, a speciality food o and a tea room.

THE BURREN PERFUMERY & FLORAL CENTRE
Carron **T 065 89102 F 065 89200**
Ireland's longest established working perfumery. You can see the traditional still, capable of distilling 551lb/250kg of flowers and plants, and watch the extraction and blending of essential oils. Don't miss the audio-visual presentation and photographic exhibition.

THE BURREN SMOKEHOUSE VISITOR CENTRE
T 065 74432
Everything you ever wanted to know about the cold smoking of salmon, including live demonstrations and audio-visual presentations in four languages. You can also arrange to have the product posted to any part of the world.

IRATTY CASTLE & FOLK PARK
ratty
061 361511 or 360788 F 061 363260
tored in 1960, this is Ireland's most nplete medieval castle. It houses the d Gort collection of furniture, objet t, and paintings and tapestries dating n before 1650. One-day tours operate eason from Limerick and include a dieval banquet at the castle. Irish ge life at the turn of the century is ngly re-created in the folk park in the unds, with its typical 19th-century rural urban dwellings. There are eight nhouses, a watermill, a blacksmith's e, and a village street complete with ps and pub.

CRAGGAUNOWEN BRONZE-AGE JECT
n **T 061 367178 or 360788**
ll-scale reconstruction of a crannog, a nze-Age lake dwelling, with a onstructed ring fort and replicas of iture, tools and utensils. Another resting display is The Brendan, a ica of the leather boat used by St ndan the Navigator in the 6th century, ch sailed across the Atlantic Ocean in 1970s.

O'BRIEN'S TOWER & CLIFFS OF MOHER
Liscannor *(4 miles/6.5km north)*
T 065 81565 or 061 360788
F 061 363260
Just north of Liscannor on the coast of West Clare are the famous cliffs of Moher, standing defiantly as giant natural ramparts against the aggressive might of the Atlantic Ocean. They rise in places to 700ft/213m and stretch for almost five miles/eight km. O'Brien's Tower was built in the early 19th century as a viewing point for Victorian tourists on the highest point. From here you can see the Clare coastline, the Aran Islands and mountains as far apart as Kerry and Connemara. There is a visitor centre with tourist information.

Call the AA Hotel Booking Service on 0990 050505 to book at AA recognised hotels and B&Bs in the UK and Ireland, or through our internet site: http://www.theaa.co.uk/hotels

BIG OUTDOORS

PHINWATCH
igaholt **T/F 065 58156**
ort trip from the pier to see the nnon bottlenose dolphins, one of only groups of resident dolphins in Europe, information from the skipper about arine marine life.

DROMORE WOOD
(6 miles/10km north of Ennis)
Semi-natural woodland with guided walks and self-guided trails.

GREAT FOR KIDS

BEACHES
Main seaside resorts are Kilkee and Lahinch. Kilkee is known for its sheltered beach and Pollock Holes - natural swimming pools in the Duggerna Rocks.

LAHINCH SEAWORLD & LEISURE CENTRE
Lahinch **T 065 81900 F 065 81901**
Explore the undersea world of the Atlantic Ocean, and come face to face with conger eels, sharks and rays. The centre includes a 82ft/25m swimming pool and other leisure facilities.

HISTORIC & ANCIENT SITES

ENNIS FRIARY
Ennis **T 065 29100**
13th-century friary, in use by a Franciscan order until 17th century, with wonderful carving on the McMahon tomb.

DYSART O'DEA CASTLE & ARCHAEOLOGY CENTRE
Corofin **T 065 37401**
Archaeological centre housed in a 15th-century castle. Archaeology trail nearby.

hinwatch

QUIN ABBEY
Quinn
Built in the 14th century using some recycled curtain wall from the 13th-century Anglo-Norman castle. There is a great view from the top of the tower.

MUSEUMS & ART GALLERIES

THE BURREN CENTRE
Kilfenora ☎ 065 88030
An awarding-winning display explaining the archaeology and geology, flora and fauna of this unique area. Tea room, craft and bookshop. Wheelchair accessible.

CLARE HERITAGE & GENEALOGICAL CENTRE
Corofin *(8 miles/12.5km north of Ennis)*
Award-winning heritage museum in the former St Catherine's Church (1718). The main theme is Ireland's West 1800-1860 - a traumatic period in Irish history.

CORCOMROE ABBEY
(National Monument) (off the N67)
A ruined Cistercian abbey, founded in 1180. The church is well preserved.

DE VALERA MUSEUM & LIBRARY
Harmony Row, Ennis *(near the Abbey)*
Material on Ennis and the surrounding area, and the history of Ireland.

KILRUSH HERITAGE CENTRE
Kilrush ☎ 065 51577/51047
Tells the story of Kilrush's maritime hist

NEWTOWN CASTLE
Ballyvaughan ☎ 065 77200
A 16th-century tower house showing a variety of exhibitions, including early Iris law and writers of Co Clare.

POULNABRONE DOLMEN
(on the R480, south of Ballyvaughan)
Huge Megalithic tomb dated 3,000 BC.

SCATTERY ISLAND CENTRE
Merchants Quay, Kilrush ☎ 065 52139/52
An exhibition on the history and wildlife Scattery Island, based on the mainland.

ESSENTIAL INFORMATION

TOURIST INFORMATION

CLIFFS OF MOHER ☎ 065 81171

ENNIS Clare Road ☎ 065 28366

KILKEE ☎ 065 56112

KILRUSH Town Hall ☎ 065 51577

GENEALOGY

CLARE HERITAGE & GENEALOGICAL CENTRE
Corofin *(8 miles/12.5km north of Ennis)*
A professional service for people tracing their Irish ancestry in the Clare area.

CRAFTS

CLARE CRAFT & DESIGN CENTRE
20 Parnell Street, Ennis
Outlet for high quality work produced within the county - paintings, pottery, patchwork, woodturning, baskets, jewellery and stained glass.

CRAFT SHOWCASE
O'Connell Street, Kilkee ☎ 065 56880

DOOLIN CRAFTS GALLERY
Ballyvoe, Doolin ☎ 065 74309
Pictures, glassware, clothing, batik, leathergoods, ceramics, rugs, throws and jewellery. Beautiful gardens. Restaurant.

THE POTTERY SHOP
Church Street, Corofin ☎ 065 37020
Potter at work and the finished products on display.

ENTERTAINMENT

MEDIEVAL BANQUETS

SHANNON MEDIEVAL CASTLE BANQUETS & TRADITIONAL IRISH NIGHTS
☎ 061 360788
Fun and feasting with story-tellers, singers, musicians. Bunratty & Knappogue castles.

SPORT & LEISURE

ACTIVITY CENTRES

BURREN OUTDOOR EDUCATION CENTRE
Bellharbour ☎ 065 78066

KILKEE DIVING CENTRE
Kilkee ☎ 065 56707

O'BRIEN'S BRIDGE WATERSKIING CENTRE
O'Brien's Bridge ☎ 061 87278

SHANNONSIDE SAILING & ACTIVITY CENTRE
Killahoe ☎ 061 376622

ANGLING

The Lower Shannon and the lakelands of Co Clare offer some excellent sport to the angler. The coastline of Clare and the shoreline of the Shannon estuary are good for shore angling, and deep-sea charter boats operate out of Ballyvaughan, Liscannor and Kilrush ports. The East Clare lakes (there are more than 20 of them), along with the the River Shannon, the River Fergus and Lough Derg are among the best big-eel waters in Ireland. The Shannon is also known for salmon and grilse. Lakes have some of the best bream, tench and rudd fishing in the country.

BOATING & CRUISING

DERG PRINCESS RIVERBUS
Killaloe ☎ 061 376364 or 375011

CAR HIRE

TOM MANNION TOURS & RENTAL
71 O'Connell Street, Ennis ☎ 065 24212

COACH TOURS

BUS ÈIREANN
Ennis ☎ 065 24177

EQUESTRIAN CENTRES

BALLYHANNON RIDING CENTRE
Quin ☎ 065 25645

THE BURREN RIDING CENTRE
Lisdoonvarna ☎ 065 76140

CARROWBAWN FARM TREKKING CENTRE
Killaloe ☎ 061 376754

CASTLEFERGUS FARM RIDING STABLES
Quin ☎ 065 25914

CLARE EQUESTRIAN CENTRE
Doora, Ennis ☎ 065 40136

CLIFFS OF MOHER EQUESTRIAN CENTR
☎ 065 81283

SMITHSTOWN RIDING CENTRE
Newmarket-on-Fergus ☎ 061 361494

WILLIE DALY RIDING CENTRE
Ennistymon ☎ 065 71385

GOLF COURSES

KILKEE GOLF CLUB
Kilkee ☎ 065 56048 Ⓕ 065 56041
An Atlantic links course providing a real challenge, and spectacular views from th point of Georges Head.
Also:
CLONARA ☎ 061 354141
DROMOLAND ☎ 061 368144
EAST CLARE ☎ 061 921322/921388
ENNIS DRIVING RANGE ☎ 065 41515
ENNIS ☎ 065 24074
KILRUSH ☎ 065 51138
LAHINCH ☎ 065 81003
SHANNON ☎ 061 471849
SPANISH POINT ☎ 065 84198
WOODSTOCK ☎ 065 29463

WALKING

Established walks include the Burren W a 26 mile/42km waymarked trail from Licannor to Ballyvaughan in North Clare, and the 1,422yd/300m Newtown Trail running through an area of the Burren known for its historical and natural features.

WALKING GUIDES

BURREN EDUCATIONAL CENTRE
☎ 065 78066

BURREN HILL WALKS ☎ 065 77168

CARRIGANN HOTEL
Lisdoonvarna ☎ 065 74300

CHRISTY BROWN TOURS
Lahinch ☎ 065 8168

WALK IRELAND
Clarecastle, Ennis ☎ 065 20885

WHERE TO STAY

HOTELS

AA RECOMMENDED

SEE UNDER WHERE TO EAT FOR ALL HOTEL RESTAURANTS WITH ROSETTES

BALLYVAUGHAN

REGANS CASTLE ★★★❀❀
3.5 miles south on N67)
T 065 77005 F 065 77111
ramatic sea views. Expect a high level of ersonal service and hospitality at this very omfortable hotel .Superb food.
23 bedrooms £££ Parking Croquet lawn Closed mid Oct-early Apr

BUNRATTY

ITZPATRICK BUNRATTY SHAMROCK IOTEL ★★★
ake Bunratty by-pass, exit off imerick/Shannon dual carriageway)
T 061 361177 F 061 471252
Modern ranch-style building is by lawns nd flower beds. Bedrooms and rooms re timbered. Helipad in the grounds.
15 bedrooms inc some for non-smokers £££ Parking Leisure facilities

DOOLIN

RAN VIEW HOUSE ★★★
oast Rd T 065 74061 74420 F 065 74540
anoramic views of the Aran Islands. ttractive, comfortable hotel with convivial tmosphere. Traditional music on 3 nights
9 bedrooms (6 of which in annexe) ££ ool table Closed Nov-Mar

ENNIS

UBURN LODGE ★★★
alway Road *(N18)*
T 065 21247 F 065 21202
mart modern hotel with traditional-style ub with carvery and two restaurants. oomy and comfortable bedrooms.
00 bedrooms inc some for non-smokers £ arking Tennis

MAGOWNA HOUSE ★★
Inch, Kilmaley T 065 39009 F 065 39258
(from R474 pass golf course, and after approx 3 miles, hotel is signposted off to right)
Small family-run hotel, with good standards of comfort and enjoyable meals, standing in 14 acres of grounds .
10 bedrooms inc some for non-smokers ££ Parking

QUEEN'S ★★
Abbey St T 065 28963 F 065 28628
(town centre next to Franciscan Friary ruins)
Pleasant hotel with traditional Irish-style candlelit restaurant. Good bedrooms. Convenient for Shannon Airport.
52 bedrooms inc some for non-smokers £ Lift

TEMPLE GATE ★★★❀
The Square
(from Ennis follow signs for Temple Gate)
T 065 23300/23322 F 065 23322
Smart hotel where a 19th-century gothic building adds interest to the decor. Interesting bedrooms. Dining options.
34 bedrooms inc some for non-smokers ££ Lift Parking

WEST COUNTY CONFERENCE & LEISURE HOTEL ★★★
Clare Road T 065 23000 F 065 23759
(10 mins walk from Ennis town centre, next to St Flannans CollegeL
Emhasis here is on relaxation with comfortable day rooms, pleasant bedrooms and a superb leisure centre.
152 bedrooms inc 56 family £££ Night Porter Parking Snooker Leisure facilites Live entertainment Conference centre

KILKEE

HALPIN'S ★★
Erin Street T 065 56032 F 065 56317
Tradition of personal service at this charming family-run hotel with a commanding view over the old town.
12 bedrooms inc some for non-smokers Tennis (hard) Closed Jan-mid Mar

LAHINCH

ABERDEEN ARMS ★★★
T 065 81100 F 065 81228
Popular modernised hotel with comfortable day rooms where you will mingle with the golfing fraternity.
55 bedrooms ££ Parking Leisure facilities Snooker

LISDOONVARNA

SHEEDY'S SPA VIEW HOTEL ★★❀❀
T 065 74026 F 065 74555
Well-run family hotel providing warm hospitality and comfort.Pretty gardens. Excellent food. Close to the spa complex.
11 bedrooms ££ Parking Tennis (hard) Closed Oct-Mar

NEWMARKET-ON-FERGUS

CLARE INN GOLF & LEISURE HOTEL ★★★
(on N18, 9 miles from Shannon Airport)
T 065 230000 F 065 23759
Comfortable hotel set in countryside with excellent leisure facilities and friendly staff to ensure an enjoyable stay.
161 bedroom (some no-smoking) £££ (inc dinner) Parking Leisure & sporting facilities Horse riding Programme for children

BED & BREAKFAST ACCOMMODATION

AA RECOMMENDED

BALLYVAUGHAN

USHEEN LODGE QQQQ
n N67 0.75 mile from Ballyvaughan village)
T 065 77092 F 065 77152
harming house nestling in a valley. The osts are a mine of information about ocal folklore. Excellent bedrooms.
bedrooms £ No smoking in bedrooms or ining room Parking Closed mid Dec-Jan

BUNRATTY

CLOVER HILL LODGE QQQ
T 061 369039 F 061 360520
Modern bungalow on small road between Bunratty Castle and nearby Durty Nelly's pub. High standards of comfort here.
4 bedrooms £ Parking Open Apr-Oct

COROFIN

FERGUS VIEW QQ
Kilnaboy T 065 37606 F 065 37192
(2m N of Corofin towards Kilfenora past ruins of Kilnaboy Church)
Sensitively renovated and comfortable farmhouse. Wherever possible home-grown vegetables are used in meals.
6 bedrooms No smoking in bedrooms or dining room Licensed Parking 17 acres non-working

CRUSHEEN

LAHARDAN HOUSE ◘◘◘
Lahardan Ⓣ 065 27128 Ⓕ 065 27319
(take N18, at railway bridge beside Crusheen village follow signs for Lahardan, hotel 1.5 miles in the middle of the Clare Lakelands)
Charming old farmhous in peaceful surroundings. Spacious, relaxing rooms. Most welcoming owners. Pre-book dinner.
8 bedrooms, all no smoking £ Licensed 230 acres beef Res Nov-Apr

DOOLIN

CULLINAN'S ◘◘◘
(centre of Doolin at crossroads between McGann's Pub & O'Connors Pub)
Ⓣ 065 74183 Ⓕ 065 74239
Charminghouse with pine-furnished bedrooms. Local produce features on menus.. Lovely gardens by river.
6 bedrooms, all no-smoking £ Parking

DOONMACFELIM HOUSE ◘◘◘
Ⓣ 065 74503 Ⓕ 065 74129
Spacious modern house with comfortable accommodation, a pleasant lounge, a tennis court and friendly hospitality.
6 bedrooms £ Tennis Parking

ENNIS

AILING GHEAL ◘◘◘◘
St Flannans Cross, Limerick Rd
Ⓣ/Ⓕ 065 23810
(turn off N8 at St Flannan's Cross roundbt)
Spacious bedrooms, nicely furnished. Delicious breakfasts served, where pride of place goes to the fresh baking.
6 bedrooms, inc 3 family rooms £ No smoking Parking

CARRAIG MHUIRE ◘◘◘
Barefield Ⓣ 065 27106 Ⓕ 065 27375
(Located on N18 Ennis to Galway road)
Attractive bungalow with pretty gardens. Comfortable bedrooms. Nothing seems too much trouble for the charming hosts.
5 bedrooms No smoking in bedrooms or dining room £ Parking

CILL EOIN HOUSE ◘◘◘◘
Killadysert Cross, Clare Road *(on N18)*
Ⓣ 065 41668 Ⓕ 065 20224
A smart purpose-built house not far from town centre with excellent bedrooms. The atmosphere is friendly and hospitable.
14 bedrooms Parking Tennis

IRISH BREAKFASTS

Always a good-value meal, the traditional Irish breakfast usually comprising a plate full of bacon, eggs and sausages and soda or potato breads can really set you up for the day

Cill Eoin House

ENNISTYMON

GROVEMOUNT HOUSE ◘◘◘◘
Lahinch Road
Ⓣ 065 71431/71038 Ⓕ 065 71823
Smart purpose-built house near The Burren. Excellent bedrooms. Hospitable atmosphere. Golf and lake fishing nearby.
8 bedrooms No smoking in bedrooms or dining room £ Parking Open Apr-Oct

LISDOONVARNA

ORE' A TAVA HOUSE ◘◘◘
(0.5 mile from town on N67, turn left at water pump, 3rd house on left)
Ⓣ 065 74086 Ⓕ 065 74547
Attractive sitting areas, including a pretty conservatory lounge. Some bedrooms are on the ground floor - all are very pleasant..
6 bedrooms £ No smoking in dining room or lounges Parking Open mid Mar-Oct

Carraig Mhuire

KILRUSH

BRUACH-NA-COILLE ◘◘◘
Killimer Road Ⓣ 065 52250
(on Kilrush to Killimere Road)
Impressive modern house in attractive gardens facing Kilrush Wood, where you can enjoy an evening stroll in the summer.
4 bedrooms £ No smoking in bedrooms, dining room or 1 lounge Parking

OGONNELLOE

LANTERN HOUSE ◘◘◘
(on R436)
Ⓣ 061 923034 & 923123 Ⓕ 061 923139
Lovely gardens with marvellous views. Comfortable house with pretty bedrooms and a popular licensed restaurant..
6 bedrooms £ Parking Mid Feb-Oct

Bruach-na-Coille

WHERE TO EAT

RESTAURANTS

AA RECOMMENDED

THE BISTRO ❀
Temple Gate Hotel, The Square, Ennis
T 065 23300 F 065 23322
The Bistro offers a lively range of dishes from a choice of fixed-price and carte menus. Dishes such as 'real soup' and 'tangled prawns' - fresh tagliatelle covered in a basil cream sauce with large fresh prawns - reflect a relaxed and lighthearted approach to good food. There's plenty for vegetarians, too.
FIXED L ££ D ££ ALC ££

GREGANS CASTLE ❀❀
Ballyvaughan **T 065 77005**
Spacious, gracious and luxurious; dine looking out to the Burren while the pianist plays. The six-course set menu, based on local and organic produce, includes Burren lamb. Options from the carte might be Galway Bay shellfish bisque, New Quay oysters, and aromatic Barbary duck breast with stir-fried noodles and plum and honey sauce.
FIXED D £££ ALC £££

THE ORCHID RESTAURANT ❀❀
Sheedy's Spa View Hotel, Lisdoonvarna
T 065 74026 F 065 74555
The Orchid Restaurant at Sheedy's may be small but it has a big reputation. Open only for dinner. A wide choice - lots of seafood - cooked with bravado, and exceptional desserts.
ALC £££

PUBS, INNS & OTHER PLACES

BARRTRA SEAFOOD RESTAURANT
Lahinch **T 065 81280**
Bold cooking using local produce .A tiny restaurant with a big view from the cliffs.

BRANDON'S BAR & RESTAURANT
70 O'Connell Street, Ennis **T 065 218133**
Carvery lunch, full dinner menu, all-day bar food. Nightly entertainment.

BRANNAGANS RESTAURANT & BAR
Mill Road, Ennis **T 065 20211**
Continental-style dishes in lovely setting.

BRUACH NA HAILLE RESTAURANT
Roadford, Doolin **T 065 74120**
Local produce, particularly seafood, is used to good effect.

BUNRATTY CASTLE
Bunratty **T Freephone 1800 269 811**
Experience aristocratic life at a medieval banquet with the Earl of Thomond. Musical and other entertainment.

CRUISE'S PUB & RESTAURANT
Abbey Street, Ennis **T 065 41800**
Crackling fires, stone floors and open hearths. Traditional music every night.

DROMOLAND CASTLE
Newmarket-on-Fergus **T 061 368144**
Stunning setting. Extensive dinner menus including vegetarian and Taste of Ireland

DURTY NELLY'S
Bunratty **T 061 364861**
Famous pub managing to provide good food and service for the tourist crowds. .

FLAGSHIP RESTAURANT
Doolin Crafts Gallery, Doolin
T 065 74309 F 065 74511
Stone-flagged restaurant. Home-made fare from morning coffee to afternoon tea.

GARVELLO'S RESTAURANT
Clare Abbey, Limerick Road, Ennis
T 065 40011
International cuisine in elegant surroundings. Wheelchair access.

GOLDEN MOUNTAIN RESTAURANT
Shannon **T 061 364838**
Cantonese cooking, with vegetarian and seafood dishes a speciality.

J P PURTILL'S RESTAURANT
Curry Street, Kilkee **T 065 56900**
Traditional restaurant serving fresh local produce in homely surroundings.

KEYNE'S OYSTER BAR & RESTAURANT
(between Kilrush and Kilkee) **T 065 56302**
A family-run pub and restaurant offering seafood and a selection of meat dishes.

KINCORA HALL
Newtown, Killaloe **T 061 376000**
Lovely views of the Shannon and the old harbour. Fair choice of dishes.

LAZY LOBSTER
Doolin **T 065 74390**
Simple food, well-cooked. Lobsters cooked to order. Vegetarian dish always available.

MACCLOSKEY'S RESTAURANT
Bunratty Mews House, Bunratty
T 061 364082 F 061 364350
Stylish restaurant. Wide ranging menu with many adventurous dishes.

MONKS BAR
Ballyvaughan **T 065 77059**
Seafood mainly - mussels, chowder and fresh crab. Traditional music at weekends.

OLD PAROCHIAL HOUSE RESTAURANT
Kilkee **T 065 56800**
Steak and seafood.

SHAMROCK INN
Lahinch **T 065 81700**
Good cuisine for all tastes. Lively bar with Irish music, sing songs and Irish dance.

WHITETHORN RESTAURANT & CRAFTS
Ballyvaughan **T 065 77044**
Snacks, lunches and dinners. Home baking and uncomplicated food, some vegetarian.

COUNTY GALWAY

Ireland's second largest county has much to interest the visitor: the lively city of Galway with its hectic calendar of festivals and cultural events, which makes a terrific base from which to explore the county's rocky Atlantic coastline, Lough Corrib, or the Connemara National Park. The latter is famous for its tough breed of Connemara ponies, who survive the difficult terrain on a diet of brackish grass and seaweed. One of the most interesting trips is to the Aran Islands - worth a day or two of your time. Galway is another great county for outdoor activities, with angling, golf and riding all well provided for, and wonderful scope for touring, cycling and walking.

PRINCIPAL TOWNS

GALWAY

Galway rivals Limerick as the Republic's third city, with a large student population as well as a fairly big influx of tourists. It is a happening city, with innovative theatre, concerts, Irish music, convivial pubs and restaurants. It is also a major Gaelic centre, with several Irish language schools. You could catch some traditional games here, such as hurling or Gaelic football, or get involved with the Galway Races, a six-day event in July. It's a city full of character and fun, with always plenty to do.

ATHENRY

Athenry takes its name from Béal Átha An Rí (the King's Ford) and dates back 700 years ago to a Norman settlement. Both the Dominican Friary and the castle were built in 1200s, and the town today is still the bustling market town it has always been. Designated a Heritage Town, the medieval town walls are reasonably well preserved.

MUST SEE

)NNEMARA NATIONAL PARK
tterfrack T **095 41054**
is 4,942 acre/2,000-hectare area
compasses a range of habitats - heath,
gland, woodland and grassland -
cluding four peaks of the Twelve Bens
ins) mountain range. There are stunning
ews and a well-established herd of
nnemara ponies roams the park. The
itor centre provides detailed information
a variety of walks and nature trails.

LYNCH'S CASTLE
(National Monument)
Shop Street/Abbeygate Street, Galway
A 16th-century castle, now occupied by a bank but formerly the residence of the aristocratic Lynch family. One of the family, mayor at the time, condemned his own son to death for the murder of a visiting Spaniard. When no one else proved willing he carried out the sentence with his own hands - so giving rise to the expression 'lynch law'.

NORA BARNACLE HOUSE MUSEUM
Bowling Green, Galway *(close to St Nicholas)*
T **091 564743**
The smallest museum in Ireland, a perfect setting in which to take you back through the romantic mists of time. This tiny, turn-of-the-century house was the home of Nora Barnacle, companion, wife and lifelong inspiration of James Joyce. It was here in 1909, sitting at the kitchen table, that Joyce first met his darling's mother. Letters, photographs and other exhibits of the lives of James Joyce and Nora Barnacle make a visit here a unique experience. Bloomsday (16th June) readings and tour.

UNGUAIRE CASTLE
nvarra T **091 37108 or 061 360788**
unguaire Castle has stood for hundreds
years on the site of the 7th-century
ronghold of Guaire, the King of
nnaught. The castle bridges 13
nturies of Irish history from the
irmishes, battles and sieges that
aracterise its colourful past to the
erary revival of the early 20th century.
day the restored castle gives an insight
to the lifestyle of the people who lived
ere from 1520 to modern times.

ROUNDSTONE MUSICAL INSTRUMENTS
Roundstone
T **095 35875** F **095 35980**
Situated in the old Franciscan monastery at Roundstone is the craft workshop of Malachy Kearns who makes Ireland's oldest product - the bodhran (bow-rawn). It is an 18in/46cm one-sided drum made from goatskin treated by a traditional process. The drum is played with a tipper or beater while the tone is varied by pressing the back of the skin with the other hand. Visitors can see the drums being made and also decorated with handpainted designs by Anne Kearns. Bodhrans can be purchased and special designs commissioned. Seconds are available, as are smaller drums.

PANISH ARCH CIVIC MUSEUM
alway
091 567641
e arches, in the south-west quarter, date
om the days when Spain and Ireland had
ading ties. Galway City Museum at the
ch is devoted to the city's history. A large
ap of the city in 1651 can be seen in the
useum.

ROYAL TARA CHINA VISITOR CENTRE
Tara Hall, Mervue, Galway
(off N17 opposite Trappers Rest or left off N6 after Ryan's Hotel)
T **091 751301**
Royal Tara China is the country's leading manufacturer of fine bone china, cold cast bronze miniature pubs, castles and cottages, and exclusive handpainted pieces. It is situated in a magnificent Georgian mansion minutes from Galway city centre. There are free tours of the factory, where visitors can watch the creation of many exquisite pieces, which are on sale in the factory showrooms.

THOOR BALLYLEE
Gort*(0.5mile/1km off the N18, 0.5mile/1km off the N66)*
T **091 631436** F **091 565201**
This tower house is the former home of the poet William Butler Yeats, and where he completed most of his literary works. The tower has been restored to appear exactly as it was when he lived there, and has an interpretative centre with audio-visual presentations and displays of his work.

BIG OUTDOORS

COOLE NATURE RESERVE
Gort ⓣ **091 31804**
Unique matrix of habitats, with a nature trail, forest walk and lake, in the grounds of Lady Augusta Gregory's former estate. Interpretative centre, tea rooms,picnic site.

PORTUMA WILDLIFE SANCTUARY
(near Potumna town)
Forest park with 988 acres/400 hectares of walks in the former Harewood estate, bordered on the southern edges by Lough Derg. Home to a variety of animals.

TROPICAL BUTTERFLY CENTRE
Sea Winds Nurseries, Costelloe
(2 miles/3km from Rossaveal Harbour)
ⓣ **091 572210** ⓕ **091 572370**
An all-weather attraction - hundreds of free-flying butterflys in a tropical environment, plus living insects, giant spiders and small reptiles (behind glass). Coffee shop.

BEACHES
The best beaches are Silver Strand and Kinvara (both have the Blue Flag awards) .

GREAT FOR KIDS

GALWAY LEISURE WORLD
Galway Shopping Centre, Headford Road, Galway ⓣ **091 62820**
Ten-pin bowling, Laser Quest, children's indoor adventure playground, interactive video games, and health club. Restaurant and refreshments.

LEISURELAND
Salthill, Galway ⓣ **091 521455**
Water adventure pool with 213ft/65m waterslide, 82ft/25m pool, children's play area, an amusement park with crazy golf and children's rides, and a restaurant.

PETER PAN FUNWORLD
Corbett Commercial Centre, Wellpark, Galway ⓣ **091 756505**
Indoor adventure playground including a 16ft/5m free fall slide, 60ft/18m snake slide, ball pond, bouncy castle, aerial glides, scrambling nets, haunted cave and Captain Hook's Hideout.

TUROE PET FARM & LEISURE PARK
Turoe, Loughrea ⓣ **091 841580**
An attraction close to the Turoe Stone, including rare and farm animals, a display of farm machinery, a pets corner and a football pitch. Coffee shop and pinic areas.

HISTORIC & ANCIENT SITES

ALCOCK & BROWN MEMORIAL
Derrygimlagh Bog
(3.5miles/6km south of Clifden)
A cairn near the Marconi station marks the place where intrepid aviators Alcock and Brown landed after the first non-stop transatlantic flight from St John's, Newfoundland in 1919.

AUGHNANURE CASTLE
Oughterard ⓣ **091 82214**
On rocky ground close to Lough Corrib, this well preserved 16th-century tower house stands six storeys high. Remains include a banqueting hall, circular watch-tower and dry harbour.

MARCONI WIRELESS STATION
Derrygimlagh Bog
(3.5 miles/6km south of Clifden)
Only the foundations and some of the masts remain of the first transatlantic wireless station, established by Marconi. The station was destroyed during the Irish Civil War (1922-3).

TUROE STONE
(3 miles/5km north of Loughrea, nr Bullaun)
Believed to date from the first century, this large granite boulder, standing in a field, is a rare example of a decorated Celtic pillar stone, with fine La Têne sculpting.

HOMES & GARDENS

KYLEMORE ABBEY
Connemara ⓣ **095 41146**
Attractive lakeside abbey, with a Gothic chapel modelled on Norwich Cathedral, now a convent for Benedictine nuns.Well stocked craft shop. Restaurant

MUSEUMS & ART GALLERIES

DAN O'HARA'S HOMESTEAD
Connemara Heritage & History Centre, Lettershea, Clifden ⓣ **095 21246/21808**
A pre-famine farm, run as it would have been in 1840, plus a museum of Connemara history. Other attractions are the craft shop, restaurant and herd of Connemara ponies.

IRISH CRYSTAL HERITAGE CENTRE
Merlin Park, Dublin Road, Galway
ⓣ **091 757311** ⓕ **091757316**
An exhibition illustrating the art of crystal making, with demonstrations, audio-visual presentations, a boat-builders workshop, showroom and restaurant.

LACKAGH MUSEUM
Lackagh, Turloughmore ⓣ **091 797444**
(8 miles/13km northeast of Galway)
Three venues: Battle of Knockdoe Interpretative Centre; Museum & Heritage Park; Glencree Pet Farm and Pony Rides.

OCEAN'S ALIVE AQUARIUM AND MARITIME MUSEUM
Renvyle Peninsual, Connemara
ⓣ **095 43473** ⓕ **095 43911**
An aquarium and maritime museum plus an exhibition about Connemara's marine heritage, a children's playground, picnic area, tea room and craft shop.

ESSENTIAL INFORMATION

TOURIST INFORMATION

GALWAY
Victoria Place, Eyre Square
ⓣ **091 563081** ⓕ **091 565201**

AUGHRIM ⓣ **0905 73939**
CLIFDEN ⓣ **095 21163**
OUGHTERARD ⓣ **091 82808**
ⓕ **091 82811**
SALTHILL ⓣ **091 563081**
THOOR BALLYLEE ⓣ **091 31436**
TUAM ⓣ **093 24463 or 25486**

ENTERTAINMENT

THEATRES

DRUID THEATRE
7 Quay Street, Galway ⓣ **091 568617**
GALWAY PUPPET THEATRE, New Dock Street, Galway
OMNIPLEX CINEMA
Headford Road, Galway ⓣ **091 567800**
PUNCHBAG THEATRE
Quay Lane, Galway ⓣ **091 565422**
TAIBHDHEARC NA GAILLIMHE STAID LAR GAILLMHE ⓣ **091 562024**
The national theatre of the Irish language, founded in 1928.
TOWN HALL THEATRE, Court House Suare, Galway ⓣ **091 569777**

MEDIEVAL BANQUET

Dunguaire Castle
ⓣ **091 637108 or 061 360788**
A six-course banquet served twice-nightly at this 7th-century stronghold of the King of Connaught, with entertainment including songs and poems.

SHOPPING

Galway City is a great place for shopping (especially for second hand books and classy crafts). It has a large covered shopping centre with over 60 shops, good access for disabled visitors, and a crêche and baby-changing area. Galway Market held on a Saturday at St Nicholas Collegiate Church, Galway ⓣ **091 56464**

CRAFTS

ARCHWAY CRAFTS
Victoria Place, Galway (opposite Tourist Office) ⓣ **091 563693**
Woollens, ceramics, jewellery, linens.
CONNEMARA MARBLE INDUSTRIES LTD
Moycullen ⓣ **091 555102/555746**
Craftsmen and quarry owners, manufacturers and exporters of Connemara Marble, jewellery and Irish gifts. Faactory and showroom open

:ONNEMARA POTTERY
3allyconneely Road, Clifden T 095 21254
;ALWAY BLACK MARBLE
Aoycullen
8 miles west of Galway City on N59 Galway-Clifden road)
T 091 555102 or 555746 F 091 555102
:ngraved black marble jewellery by artist Aike Joyce. Factory, showroom, gift shop.
IEY DOODLE DOODLE
Eyre Street, Galway T 091 561906
paint-it-yourself pottery studio, where ou paint your own design on a piece of ottery, which is then fired for you to keep
UDY GREENE POTTERY
'ross Street, Galway T 091 561753
ecorated domestic earthenware inspired y the beauty and variety of Irish flowers.
YLEMORE ABBEY POTTERY T 095 1146
ROUNDSTONE CERAMICS
)A Park, Roundstone T 095 35874
'OUNDSTONE MUSICAL INSTRUMENTS
:oundstone T 095 35875 F 095 35980
land-made bodhrans, traditional Irish rums (see the Must See section).

SPORT & LEISURE

ACTIVITY CENTRES

ELPHI ADVENTURE CENTRE
eenane T 095 42208
;ALWAY KART RACING
iosbaun Estate, Tuam Road T 091 756844
ITTLE KILLARY ADVENTURE CENTRE
alruck, Renvyle T 095 43411

ANGLING

almon and brown trout waters, river and ough, are plentiful in the region, but sea 'out stocks have been diminished by the ffects of sea lice - check with local Tourist ffice for current fishing restrictions. The nall lakes in the Moycullen area are ood for coarse fishing.

SEA ANGLING BOAT OPERATORS

LUE WATER FISHING
rrislannan T 095 21073
AN SMITS
oolacloy, Clifden T 095 21787
OHN MONGAN
erryinver, Letterfrack T 095 43473
OHN RYAN
un Aengus, Sky Rd, Clifden T 095 21069
AT CONNEELY, Harbour View House, oundstone T 095 35854
EAN WARD
eal House, Streamstown T 095 21816

BOATING & CRUISING

ORRIB TOURS
urbo Hill, Furbo, Galway T 091 592447
aily sailings on from Woodquay.

CYCLE HIRE

HIEFTAN CYCLES Victoria Place, Merchants oad, Galway T 091 567454
CONNEELY Fishery Lodge, Toombeola, oundstone T 095 31116
UROPA BICYCLES Hunters Building, Earl's sland, Galway T 091 563355
A J FERRON Roundstone
T 095 35838
J M MANNION Bridge Street, Clifden
T 095 21160
OLIVER COYNE Cleggan T 095 44640
RENVYLE STORES Tully, Renvyle
T 095 43485

EQUESTRIAN CENTRES

CASHEL EQUESTRIAN CENTRE
Cashel Bay T 095 31082
CLEGGAN TREKKING CENTRE
Cleggan T 095 31082
CLONBOO RIDING SCHOOL
Clonboo T 091 791362
DIAMONDS
Tully, Renvyle T 095 43486
DUFFY'S CLAREGALWAY EQUESTRIAN CENTRE Claregalway
T 091 798289 or 088 583595
ERRISLANNAN MANOR
Ballyconneely Road, Clifden T 095 21134
FEENEY'S EQUESTRIAN CENTRE
Bushy Park T 091 527579 or 526553
GLEN VALLEY STABLES
Glencoft T 095 42269
HAZELWOOD RIDING CENTRE
Oranmore T 091 794275
THE POINT
Ballyconneely T 095 23685
RENVYLE HOUSE HOTEL
Renvyle T 095 43511
ROCKMOUNT RIDING CENTRE
Claregalway T 091 798147

GOLF COURSES

CONNEMARA GOLF CLUB
Balleyconneely, Clifden T 095 23502
Championship links course situated by the Atlantic Ocean in a most spectacular setting, with the Twelve Bens Mountains in the background.A tough challenge, due in no small part to its exposed location, with the back nine the equal of any in the world..Last six holes are exceptionally long.
GALWAY BAY GOLF & COUNTRY CLUB
Renville, Oranmore T 091 790500
Magnificent and challenging course, designed byChristie O'Connor Junior, on a lovely peninsula on Galway Bay.
Also:
ASHFORD CASTLE T 092 46003
ATHENRY T 091 794466
BALLINASLOE T 0905 42126
CONNEMARA ISLES T 091 572498
CURRA T 0509 45438
GALWAY T 091 522033
GALWAY BAY T 091 790500
GALWAY GOLF RANGE T 091 526737
GLENLO ABBEY HOTEL DRIVING RANGE
Bushy Park T 091 526666
GORT T 091 32244
LOUGHREA T 091 841049
MOUNTBELLEW T 0905 79259
OUGHTERARD T 091 82131
PORTUMNA T 0509 41059
TUAM T 093 28993

GREYHOUND RACING

GREYHOUND TRACK
College Road, Galway T/F 091 562273

HORSE RACING

GALWAY RACECOURSE
Ballybrit, Galway T 091 753870

Errislannan Manor

SCENIC DRIVES

THE SKY ROAD
One of the most scenic stretches of Co Galway, 8.5 miles/14km of narrow road high over Clifden Bay, circling the peninsula west of the town and opening up vast seascapes. The road is very popular with landscape painters.

WALKING

The Sky Road, the Connemara National Park and the Aran Islands are all good walking areas (see Aran Islands).
CONNEMARA WALKING CENTRE
Island House, Clifden T 095 21379

WATER SPORTS

CLIFDEN BOAT CLUB
Beach Road, Clifden T 095 21711
SAIL WEST
Carna T 095 33546
SCUBA DIVE WEST
Lettergesh, Renvyle T 095 43922

WHERE TO STAY

HOTELS

AA RECOMMENDED

SEE UNDER WHERE TO EAT FOR ALL HOTEL RESTAURANTS WITH ROSETTES

BALLINASLOE

HAYDEN'S ★★★
(on the main Dublin/Galway road N6)
T 0905 42347 F 0905 42895
Fine Georgian hotel with lovely views and gardens, owned for many generations by the same family. Good food options.
48 bedrooms £ Lift Parking

BALLYNAHINCH

BALLYNAHINCH CASTLE ★★★★
(Roundstone turning off N59, then 3 miles)
T 095 31006 or 31086 F 095 31085
By a famous salmon river in wonderful grounds. Understated elegance, comfort and a timeless qualtiy are the keynotes .
288 bedrooms ££££ Parking Tennis (hard) Closed Feb

CASHEL

CASHEL HOUSE ★★★
(turn S off N59, hotel 1 mile W of Recess)
T 095 31001 F 095 31077
Gracious country house overlooing Cashel Bay. Atmosphere of luxury and peaceful elegance. Award winning gardens .
32 bedrooms ££££ Parking Tennis No children under 5yrs Closed mid Jan-mid Feb

ZETLAND HOUSE ★★★
Cashel Bay **T 095 31111 F 095 31117**
Comfortable country house enhanced by lovely furnishings. Set in pretty gardens. Warm hospitality, superb food and service.
19 bedrooms ££££ Parking Tennis Croquet Snooker Fishing Shooting Closed Nov-early Apr

CLIFDEN

ABBEYGLEN ★★★
Castle Sky Road **T 095 21201**
F 095 21797
(0.5 mile from Clifden on the Sky Road)
Panoramic views. Friendly family-run hotel with a great atmosphere Excellent hospitality and food. Extensive grounds.
367 bedrooms inc some for non-smokers £££ Parking Leisure & sporting facilities

ARDAGH ★★★
Ballyconneely Road
(N59 1 m from Clifden, sign Ballyconneely)
T 095 21384 F 095 21314
Super family-run hotel with fine lounges taking full advantage of the impressive scenery. Award-winning restaurant
21 bedrooms ££££ Parking Pool table Closed Nov-Mar

Ardag

ROCK GLEN ★★★
T 095 21035 & 21393 F 095 21737
Converted 18th-century shooting lodge, with a leisurely feeling of well-being. Much emphasis on hospitality and superb food.
29 bedrooms ££££ Parking Croquet Snooker Tennis Putting Closed Oct-Mar

GALWAY

ARDILAUN HOUSE ★★★★
Taylor's Hill **T 091 521433 F 091 521546**
(4th left after 4th roundabout from main Dublin road)
Comfort is the keynote throughout with pleasant lounges and spacious bedrooms.Traditional standards of service
90 bedrooms (some no-smoking) £££ Lift Parking Leisure & sporting facilities

GALWAY RYAN ★★★
Dublin Road **T 091 753181 F 091 753187**
(follow signs to Galway West off N7)
Modern hotel with particularly pleasant lounge and comfortable bedrooms.
96 bedrooms (some no-smoking) ££££ Lift Parking Leisure & sporting facilities

GLENLO ABBEY★★★★
Bushypark **T 091 526666 F 091 527800**
(2.5 miles from city centre on N59)
Restored 18th-century abbey overlooking a beautiful lake in huge estate. Bedrooms are in a well designed modern wing
452 bedrooms including some for non smokers ££££ Lift Parking Leisure & sporting facilities Conference facilities Business centre

JURYS GALWAY INN ★★★
Quay Street
T 091 566444 F 091 568415
Popular modern hotel in city centre. Attractive garden bounded by river. One price room rate. Comfortable bedrooms.
128 bedrooms(some no-smoking) ££ Lift

LOCHLURGAIN ★★
22 Monksfield, Upper Salthill
T 091 529595 F 091 22399
Pleasant family-run hotel situated close to the promenade and beach. Relaxing bedrooms. French/English restaurant.
13 bedrooms (3 fmly) ££ Parking No smoking in restaurant Closed Nov-mid Ma

VICTORIA ★★★
Victoria Place, Eyre Square
T 091 567433 F 091 565880
Convenient city-centre hotel close to public car park. Atmosphere is relaxing and staff are friendly and attentive.
57 bedrooms (some no-smoking) £££ Lift

OUGHTERARD

ROSS LAKE HOUSE ★★★
Rosscahill *(on N59, Galway-Clifden rd)*
T 091 550109 & 550154 F 091 550184
Family-run modern Georgian-style house in a panoramic garden setting. Pleasant bedrooms, comfortable atmosphere.
13 bedrooms £££ Parking Tennis (hard) Closed Nov-mid Mar

RECESS

LOUGH INAGH LODGE ★★★
Inagh Valley *(after Recess take R344 towards Kylemore, hotel is in middle of Inagh valley)*
T 095 34706/34694 F 095 34708
Old shooting lodge, now a luxurious hote with friendly informal atmosphere. By a lake with lovely mountain views.
122 ££££ Parking Closed Nov-Mar

ROUNDSTONE

ELDONS ★★
T 095 35933 & 35942 F 095 35871
Colourful hotel in picturesque fishing village. Welcoming atmosphere. High standards throughout. Delicious seafood.
19 bedroom (6 in annexe) ££ Lift Closed Nov-mid Mar

ƷED & BREAKFAST ACCOMMODATION

AA RECOMMENDED

CLADDAGHDUFF

ΓON'S RESTAURANT
UEST HOUSE QQQQ
ʒaun
095 44339 /44308 F 095 44309
ɫuded house right on seashore. Luxury dern bungalow with excellent rooms. ·erb views. Good seafood restaurant.
ːdrooms No smoking in bedrooms or ʼng room ££ Open mid Mar-Oct

CLARINBRIDGE

RAUN HOUSE QQQ
dbally **T 091 796182**
ʼr village,first right, 0.5 mile off main road)
·vers are everywhere - including the e gardens. Useful base for The Burren, Aran Islands or Connemara.
ʼdrooms £ No smoking in bedrooms or ng room Parking Open mid Mar-Oct

CLIFDEN

ɿ VIEW HOUSE QQQ
ge Street **T 095 21256 F 095 21226**
ːr town on N59, opposite Esso services)
active town centre house offering good lity accomodation at a moderate cost. ıl touring base.
ıedrooms inc some for non-smokers £ smoking in dining room

ɴ RI QQQ
ːr town on N59, turn L before Statoil)
095 21625 F 095 21635
ːe guest house in quiet street close to town centre. All the rooms are ıished to the same high standard .
ɔedrooms £ No smoking in bedrooms or ng room Open Mar-Oct

.TE QQQ
ɔear, Ballyconneely Road **T 095 21159**
ɔut on Ballyconneely Rd, after 1 mile take ɾurning on R, hotel 400m from Pottery)
ɟern bungalow in a scenic location on edge of Clifden, offering excellent dards of comfort. Ideal touring centre.
drooms £ No smoking in dining room lounge Parking Open Apr-Sep

Mallmore House

FAUL HOUSE QQQ
Ballyconneely Road *(1 mile from town, turn R at Connemara Pottery and follow signs)*
T 095 21239 F 095 21998
Smart modern farmhouse in quiet road overlooking Bay. Comfortable, large bedrooms, all with good views.
6 bedrooms inc some for non-smokers No smoking in dining room or 1 lounge 28 acres sheep ponies Open mid Mar-Oct

KINGSTOWN HOUSE QQ
Bridge Street **T 095 21470 F 095 21530**
Central, close to all amenities. Pleasant house offering a warm welcome from friendly owners. Comfortable bedrooms. *8 bedrooms £ (incl dinner) No smoking in area of dining room*

MALDUA QQQQQ
Galway Road *(on N59)*
T 095 21171 & 21739 F 095 21739
Large, luxurious house with spacious bedrooms. Relax in the cleverly-built sun trap in the gardens beside a stream.
14 bedrooms £ Parking Closed Nov-Jan

MALLMORE HOUSE QQQQ
Ballyconneely Road **T 095 21460**
(1 mile from Clifden towards Ballyconneely, turn right at Connemara Pottery)
Charming house set in woodland overlooking Bay. Lovely antiques and turf fires provide warmth and atmosphere.
6 bedrooms ££ No smoking in dining room or lounges Parking Open Mar-Oct

SUNNYBANK HOUSE QQQQ
Church Hill *(on N59)*
T 095 21437 F 095 21976
Comfortable period house close to town. Pretty, spacious bedrooms, some with fine views. Lovely grounds with leisure facilities
8 bedrooms including one for non-smokers ££ No smoking in 1 lounge Parking No children under 7yrs Leisure facilities Golf & fishing nearby Open Mar-Nov

CORRANDULLA

CREGG CASTLE QQQ
T 091 791434
F 091 791434 (daytime only)
(9 miles N of Galway, signposted from N17 - just north of Claregalway village)
Lovely old castle c1648 . Enjoy the history, tranquil country living, and animated conversations around the dinner table.
7 bedrooms £ No smoking in bedrooms or in area of dining room Licenced Parking Open Mar-Oct Restricted service Nov-Feb

GALWAY

ACORN QQQ
19 Dublin Road
T 091 770990 F 091 770990
Fine modern house with comfortable well furnished bedrooms. Convenient for city.
7 bedrooms £ No smoking in area of dining room Parking No children under 10yrs

ARDAWN HOUSE QQQQ
31 College Road
T 091 568833 & 564551 F 091 563454
Friendly, hospitable hotel near city centre. Pretty bedrooms. Excellent breakfasts include home-baked breads.
6 bedrooms inc some for non-smokers No smoking in bedrooms or dining room £ Parking No children under12yrs

ASGARD HOUSE QQQQ
21 College Rd
T 091 566855 F 091 566855
Luxurious modern house near city centre. Attractive and very comfortable bedrooms.

ɑwn House

One bedroom suitable for less able.
6 bedrooms inc some for non-smokers £ No smoking in dining room or lounges Parking

ASHFORD MANOR
7 College Rd
T 091 563941 F 091 563941
Very attractive modern house with luxurious accommodation.
4 bedrooms inc some for non-smokers £ No smoking in dining room & 1 lounge Parking

ATLANTIC HEIGHTS
2 Cashelmara, Knocknacarra Cross, Salthill
(0.5 mile from Salthill Promenade on coast road to Barna)
T 091 529466 F 091 529466
On Salthill seafront, fine house with super views. Excellent bedrooms and breakfast menu with home-baking. Laundry service
6 bedrooms inc some for non-smokers £ No smoking in dining room or 1 lounge Parking

Corrib H

FLANNERY'S
54 Dalysfort Road, Salthill
T 091 522048 F 091 522048
Spacious house set in attractive gardens, with comfortable lounges. A warm welcome and tea on arrival is offered.
4 bedrooms £ Parking

KILLEEN HOUSE
Killeen, Bushypark
(on N59 midway between city & Moyculle
T 091 524179 F 091 52806
This charming 19th-century house stanc in 25 acres of grounds stretching down the shores of the loch. Inside there are lovely antique furnishings, hand-woven carpets, fine linen and exquisite crystal. bedrooms reflect the character of the house and have many comforts. You ha the choice of two sitting rooms which have a very welcoming feel.
5 bedrooms ££ No smoking in dining r Lift Parking No children under 12yrs

LAKESHORE HOUSE
134 College Road
T 091 561519 & 561920 F 091 561519
A warm welcome and comfortable roo await you. Fine views fron the back of t house over the tidal Lough Atalia.
8 bedrooms inc some for non-smokers £ No smoking in dining room or 1 lounge Parking

Asgard House

BAY VIEW
Gentian Hill, Upper Salthill
(follow coast road towards Connemara take 3rd left after Salthill, signed from main road)
T 091 522116 or 526140
Ideal as a touring centre, this modern house is situated on the edge of Salthill.
6 bedrooms No children under 5yrs Open mid Mar-Nov

BEACH HOUSE
12 Beach Court, Grattan Rd T 091 581923
Large house onsmall road parallel to Grattan Rd, overlooking the Bay. Attractive bedrooms and comfortable lounge.
6 bedrooms £ No smoking in bedrooms or dining room Parking Open Mar-Oct

CLARE HILLS
4 Threadneedle Rd, Salthill T 091 522653
Stunning views over the ocean from some of bedrooms at attractive seaside house, cleverly adapted to maximise space.
6 bedrooms £ No smoking in dining room Parking

CORRIB HAVEN
107 Upper Newcastle
T 091 524171 & 524711 F 091 524171
Close to centre,university and N9 route to Connemara. Excellent hospitality is the keyword here. Superb bedrooms.
9 bedrooms No Smoking £ Parking

FOUR SEASONS
23 College Road
T 091 564078 F 091 569765
One of a group of new luxury houses on College Road, conveniently located for the city centre. The owners have been busy upgrading the accommodation to a high standard, providing excellent levels of comfort.
7 bedrooms inc some for non-smokers £ No smoking in dining room Parking

LISDUFF
102 Fr Griffin Road T 091 588760
Attractive modern house near city centr and the seaside at Salthill. Every effort i made to make you feel welcome.
4 bedrooms £ No smoking in dining roo Parking

OCEAN WAVE
1 Cashel Mara, Knocknarra Cross, Salthill
T/F 091 5206320
(from city, pass through Salthill along coast, house a mile on right at T-junction)
6 bedrooms, inc 3 family £ Parking

Four Sea

'ary Lodge

NCALLI HOUSE
Whitestrand Avenue, Lower Salthill
R336, corner house near Ocean Wave artment Complex)
091 584159 589013 F 091 584159
coming, modern house near beach, se to city centre. Pleasant bedrooms, nfortable lounge, prettyl gardens.
edrooms £ No smoking in bedrooms, ng room or 1 lounge Parking

VERSEAS
pagh Road, Barna
st road to Barna/Spiddal, after Rusheen ing Centre on L, next R Cappagh Rd)
091 590575 F 091 590575
osing modern house in a residential a, overlooking Bay. Pretty bedrooms. ellent breakfast buffet.
drooms £ No smoking in dining room king

JTHERN HILLS
cknacarra, Salthill **T 091 528224**
acent to Galway Golf Club)
ly distinguishable white house with e lounge, pretty conservatory. Smart rooms, some overlook golf course.
drooms £ No smoking Parking

IRISE LODGE
cean Wave, Dr Colohan Road, Salthill
rance beside Cois Cuan apartments)
091 525566
urious modern house with beautifully orated bedrooms, some with front conies. Lovely sea views.
nexe bedrooms No smoking in ooms, dining room or 1 lounge Parking

ALLOW
r Griffin Road
091 589073 F 091 589175
nfortable bedrooms in large modern se. Quiet residential area near centre. ty breakfast room opens onto a patio.
drooms £ No smoking in area of dining n Parking

.A MARIA
r Griffin Road, Lower Salthill
091 589033
drooms, inc 2 family £ No smoking in ooms or dining room Parking

WEST POINT
87 Threadneedle Road, Salthill
T 091 521026 F 091 521026
Tudor-style modern house in pretty gardens close to beach. Attractive bedrooms and relaxing lounge.
6 bedrooms £ No smoking in dining room or 1 lounge Parking

WOODHAVEN LODGE
Merlin Park, Dublin Rd **T 091 753806**
Excellent bedrooms in large modern house, with two inviting lounges to relax in. Very pleasant outlook.
4 bedrooms £ No children under 12yrs

KYLEMORE

KYLEMORE HOUSE
(turn off N59 at Recess onto R344)
T 095 41143
On lakeshore with mountain views, this comfortable house has fishing rights on three lakes. Pre-book good evening meals.
6 bedrooms £ Licensed Parking No children under 10yrs Boat hire Open May-Oct

LEENANE

KILLARY LODGE
(3miles from Leaenane on Clifden rd. Turn off N59 at Maam Cross)
T 095 42276 & 42245 F 095 42314
In spectacular lake setting. Informal, relaxed atmosphere. Very attractive and comfortable throughout.. Good cooking.
20 bedrooms (9 annexe) ££ No smoking in dining room Licensed Parking Tennis Sauna Mountain biking Rock climbing Sailing Kayaking Open Mar-Oct Res Nov-Feb

MOYARD

ROSE COTTAGE
Rockfield **T 095 41082 F 095 41112**
(on the Clifden/Leenane road (N59))
Comfortable farm bungalow peacefully set amidst farmland and near a National Park.
6 bedrooms £ Parking 36 acres mixed Open Apr-Oct

ORANMORE

ASHBROOK HOUSE
Dublin Road **T 091 94196**
(just off N6, opposite yellow water tower, 6 mins drive from Galway)
Prettily decorated throughout with comfortable bedrooms. Set in one acre .
4 bedrooms Parking

OUGHTERARD

THE BOAT INN
The Square **T 091 552196 F 091 552694**
(on N59 Galway/Clifden rd in centre)
Lively place to stay. Popular guest house/ bar/bistro is located in village centre. Often live Irish music during season.
11 bedrooms ££ Licenced

LAKELAND COUNTRY HOUSE
Portacarron
(through Oughterard, pass Gateway Hotel, house on lake shore)
T 091 82121 82146
9 bedrooms No smoking in bedrooms or dining room Licensed Parking

WATERFALL LODGE
(on N59, 1st on L after Sweeneys Hotel)
T 091 552168
Idyllic location, beside river and waterfall. Elegant period house with antiques and very comfortable rooms. Very welcoming.
6 bedrooms ££ Fishing Parking

RECESS

GLENDALOUGH HOUSE
(signposted 400m off N59, 0.5 mile past Recess on Clifden side) **T 095 34669**
Superb views of mountains and lake. Spacious bungalow with comfortable and pleasant. rooms. Leisure pursuits.
6 bedrooms No smoking in bedrooms, dining room & 1 lounge Parking Golf 100 acres beef, sheep & poultry Open May-Sep

Ardmor Country House

Sunrise Lodge

SPIDDAL

ARD AOIBHINN QQQ
Cnocan-Glas T 091 553179 F 553179
(0.5 mile west of Spiddal on R336)
Fine views over Galway Bay and Aran Islands. Modern bungalow with pleasantly decoratedbedrooms. Lovley gardens.
6 bedrooms (some no-smokeing) No smoking dining room, lounges £ Parking

ARDMOR COUNTRY HOUSE QQQQ
Greenhill *(on route R336 coast road)*
T 091 553145 F 091 553596
Luxury, split-level bungalow with superb views. Excellent bedrooms and lounges, library.Pleasant gardens. Superb breakfasts
7 bedrooms £ No smoking in bedrooms, dining room or lounges Parking

UAR BEAG QQQ
Tuar Beag T 091 553422 F 091 553010
(on R337 0.5 mile west of village)
Prominent house with very good rooms, all with fine views. Breakfasts are notabl
6 bedrooms £ No smoking in bedrooms or dining room Parking

WHERE TO EAT

RESTAURANTS

AA RECOMMENDED

ABBEYGLEN CASTLE HOTEL
Castle Sky Road, Clifden
T 095 21201 F 095 21797
There are wonderful views over Clifden Bay. Good food is a priority, earning a rosette for its restaurant. There's a helipad in the grounds if you fancy dropping in for dinner.
FIXED D ££ & £££

ARDAGH HOTEL
Ballyconneely Road, Clifden
T 095 21384 F 095 21314
Splendid sea views. Local produce, particularly seafood, features in a varied and sometimes adventurous menu. Perhaps Saltlake oysters; Ardagh's famous seafood chowder, or pot roasted loin of spring lamb coated with fresh basil pesto and served with lamb jus.
FIXED D £££

BALLYNAHINCH CASTLE
Ballynahinch
T 095 31006 or 31086 F 095 31085
Fresh local produce, including game and salmon, provides the inspiration for the dishes created in the charming restaurant at Ballynahinch Castle. The hotel, at the foot of Ben Lettery, stands on the banks of the famous salmon river, the Ballnahinch.
ALC L ££ FIXED D £££ & ALC

BEDLA SEAFOOD RESTAURANT
Eldons Hotel, Roundstone
T 095 35933 & 35942 F 095 35871
The hotel is the distinctive blue and yellow painted building on the main street of the picturesque fishing village. The popular restaurant is renowned for its seafood, including fresh lobster, crab and prawns
ALC ££

CASHEL HOUSE HOTEL
Cashel, Connemara
T 095 31001 F 095 31077
Choice produce from Connemara's mountains, lakes and streams, and seafood from Cashel Bay, are served in this country house dining room. Local oysters, home-made lobster bisque, and roast Connemara lamb are among the delights on offer.
FIXED D £££

GALWAY BAY GOLF & COUNTRY CLUB
Renville, Oranmore **T 091 790500**
Superb award-wining cuisine.

LOUGH INAGH LODGE HOTEL
Inagh Valley, Recess
T 095 34706 & 34694
Superbly located overlooking the lake and with mountain views, this 19th-century shooting lodge has been skilfully restored to create a fine hotel serving good food beautifully presented.
FIXED D £££

THE RIVER ROOM
Glenlo Abbey Hotel, Bushypark, Galway
T 091 526666 F 091 527800
The dinner menu is priced according to the number of courses selected from the good variety of dishes. Starters range fro crab tar-tar with apple crisps and balsam vinegar to pigeon pie with foie gras and roasted shallots. Perhaps followed by suprême of chicken stuffed with lobster and tarragon with a creamy bisque sauc
FIXED L ££ ALC £££

ROCK GLEN MANOR
Ballyconneely Road, Clifden
T 095 21035 F 095 21737
The menu is priced according to the number of courses and offers a balance choice of dishes prepared from local produce, including oysters, suprême of wild Irish salmon with champ, chorizo, and a soya and sesame dressing.
ALC £££

ZETLAND COUNTRY HOUSE HOTEL
Cashel Bay **T 095 3111**
Both sea and garden views can be enjoyed from the dining room. Menus feature local produce; salmon, turbot an oysters predominate, but Connemara la and duckling also appear.
ALC L ££-£££ D £££

PUBS, INNS & OTHER PLACES

GALWAY CITY

RANNAGANS
per Abbeygate Street T 091 565974
oose French, Italian, Cajun, Mexican, iental, even Irish .....

FÉ KYLEMORE
re Square T 091 567121
lf-service restaurant offering freshly epared food.

TANG NOODLE HOUSE
Middle Street T 091 561443
land's only Chinese noodle house, also rving authentic soups and sauces.

LLEON
lthill T 091 521266
pen noon to midnight, seven days a eek. Fast, friendly and efficient. Air-nditioned.

BC RESTAURANT & COFFEE SHOP
Williamsgate St T 091 563087
nge of freshly prepared dishes, luding vegetarian.

OOKER JIMMY'S STEAK & SEAFOOD BAR
hmarket, Spanish Arch T 091 568351
asonably priced, good quality aightforward food. Child friendly.

OUSE OF BARDS
2 Market Street T 091 568414
th-century town house. Fresh fish and ellfish; traditional Irish fare; vegetarian.

JNTSMAN BAR & RESTAURANT
4 College Road T 091 562849
od, reasonably priced bar food.

CKSON'S RESTAURANT
am Road T 091 756269
side Trapper's Bar; specialising in afood, steak and vegetarian food.

SHMIR
Francis Street T 091 563456
ne Indian cuisine.

C BLAKE'S BRASSERIE
ay Street T 091 561826
recent arrival, in a restored 15th-century wer house.

TUS INN CHINESE RESTAURANT
anish Arch T 091 567865
gh quality food and excellent service in cosy atmosphere.

CDONAGH'S SEAFOOD HOUSE
Quay Street T 091 565001
h and chips with the freshest fish.

LT HOUSE
gh Street T 091 567866
ard-winning restaurant and bar in the art of Galway.

AXWELL MCNAMARAS
lliamsgate Street
091 565727 F 091 564379
pen from breakfast to late. Specialising vegetarian, pasta and seafood dishes.

SEV'NTH HEAV'N
Courthouse Lane, Quay Street
T 091 563838
Irish, Cajun and Tex-Mex. Lively, open noon-late, with live music.

TRATTORIA PASTA MISTA
12 Quay Street
T 091 563910
Home-made pasta and traditional Italian dishes.

TULSI RESTAURANT
3 Buttermilk Walk, Middle Street
T 091 564831 F 091 569518
Sister restaurant in Dublin, wide range of Indian dishes, tandoori a speciality.

TYSON'S SEAFOOD RESTAURANT
Rockbarton Park, Salthill
T 091 522286 F 091 527692
Notable seafood restaurant.

CO GALWAY

THE BOAT INN
The Square, Oughterard T 091 552196
Modern bistro cooking.

BOLUISCE RESTAURANT
Spiddal, Connemara T 091 553286
Fish, shellfish and Connemara lamb feature at this family-run restaurant .

CAFÉ ON THE QUAY
Kinvara T 091 637654
Dine in relaxed surroundings overlooking the harbour.

CLOONNABINNIA HOUSE HOTEL
Ross Lake, Moycullen
T 091 555555 F 091 555640
Lovely lake setting. Good use of local vegetables, seafood and Connemara lamb.

CRÉ NA CILLE
High Street, Tuam T/F 093 28232
Deservedly popular for lunches and dinners; good value menus.

CURRAREVAGH HOUSE
Oughterard T 091 552312
Small restaurant offering a single dinner sitting with a hearty six-course meal.

DESTRY RIDES AGAIN
The Square, Clifden T 095 21722
What would you expect with a name like that? A bit eccentric in decor, but the cooking is up to scratch - Mediterranean style. Wheelchair users welcome. Dinner only.

DONNELLY'S SEAFOOD BAR/RESTAURANT
Barna T 091 592487
Popular pub and restaurant, serving seafood, steak and vegetarian dishes.

DRIMCONG HOUSE RESTAURANT
Moycullen T 091555115
An exceptional range of dishes in a very welcoming restaurant.

ERRISEASK HOUSE
Ballyconneely, Clifden T 095 23553
Super food, excellent service, in a hotel tucked away on a wild coast.

FOGERTY'S RESTAURANT
Market Street, Clifden T 095 21427
A range of flavours is offered at this restaurant, from Irish to Thai.

HIGH MOORS RESTAURANT
Dooneen, Clifden T 095 21342
Superb views. Food is based on local produce, including garden vegetables.

KYLEMORE ABBEY RESTAURANT
Kylemore, Connemara T 095 41146
A busy day-time restaurant, run by nuns, offering hearty traditional meals/ snacks.

MERRIMAN INN
Main Street, Kinvara T 091 637176
Combines the rustic feel of a country haven with standards of a modern hotel.

MITCHELL'S RESTAURANT
Market Street, Clifden T 095 21867
Good food at reasonable prices in an attractive setting.

MORAN'S OYSTER COTTAGE
The Weir, Kilcolgan T 091 796113
Specialist seafood restaurant.

O'DOWD'S SEAFOOD RESTAURANT
Roundstone, Connemara T 095 35809
Seafood, steak and vegetarian options.

O'GRADY'S SEAFOOD RESTAURANT
Market Street, Clifden T 095 21450
Traditional Irish seafood restaurant, with considerable flair.

OLIVER'S SEAFOOD BAR & RESTAURANT
Cleggan T 095 44640
Pleasant premises overlooking harbour.

PADDY BURKES
Clarinbridge T 091 796226
Oysters are a speciality at pub/ restaurant.

PEACOCKES
Maam Cross T 091 552306
Good food in pleasant surroundings, next to The Quiet Man Heritage Cottage.

PORTFINN LODGE
Leenane T 095 42265
Dine in a room with a view. For seafood lovers mostly. Dinners only; closed winter.

TONY DONNELLAN'S BAR & RESTAURANT
Crow Street, Gort T 091 632157
A traditional-style restaurant with a welcoming log fire.

TY AR MOR
Barna Pier T 091 592223
French- specialising in Breton food.

WATERLILY
Bridge Street, Oughterard T 091 82737
Riverside restaurant offering Irish cooking using fresh local produce.

WESTWOOD BISTRO
Dangan, Upper Newcastle, Galway
T 091 521442
Imaginative, modern cooking,

WHITE GABLES RESTAURANT
Moycullen T 091 555744
Pretty cottage restaurant in village.

ARAN ISLANDS

The three Aran Islands, Inishmore, Inishmaan and Inisheer, out in Galway Bay, are made of the same stuff as the Burren in Co Clare - cracked sheets of limestone. Though the islands are fairly flat they appear to tilt, so that to the west of Inishmore and Inishmaan there are great cliffs plunging down into the Atlantic. This inhospitable terrain, exposed to the full force of the elements and with scant soil, supports a dwindling population of islanders who continue to fish and farm, creating fields from those materials available - sand and seaweed - and protecting them with drystone walls. Some of the most ancient remains in Ireland are to found here, including the stone-built Iron Age forts, Dún Aengus on Inishmore and DúnConchui on Inishmaan. There are several ferries and flights to the islands (details below). Inishmore is the biggest, and can be explored on foot or by cycle, minibus or pony and trap.

ESSENTIAL INFORMATION

ACCESS TO THE ARAN ISLANDS

Several ferry companies serve the Aran Islands from Galway City, Rossaveal, and Doolin (in Co Clare). Aer Arann fly tiny aircraft to all three islands. All transport services may be affected by weather and you should check schedules carefully.

AER ARANN
Connemara Regional Airport, Inverin, Co Galway **T 091 593034 F 091 593238**

DOOLIN FERRIES
Doolin, Co Clare
T 065 74455 F 065 74417

ISLAND FERRIES
Victoria Place, Galway, Co Galway
T 091 561767 F 091 568538

O'BRIEN SHIPPING
Tourist Office, Galway, Co Galway
T 091 567676 F 091 567672

WALKING

The Aran Way comprises three separate walks on each of the three islands: the Inis Mor Way (21 miles/34km), the Inis Meain Way (5 miles/8km), and the Inis Oirr Way (6.5 miles/10.5km). The highest point being Baile na mBocht at 400ft/122m.

WHERE TO EAT

PUBS, INNS & OTHER PLACES

ARAN FISHERMAN
Kilronan
For snacks or informal meals; a variety of seafood, vegetarian, meat and poultry dishes. Open all year round.

DÚN AONGHASA SEAFOOD RESTAURANT & BAR
Kilronan **T 099 61104 F 099 61225**
High above Kileaney Bay. The menu builds on the Aran heritage of seafood, using fresh, same-day fish from the Atlantic.

FISHERMAN'S COTTAGE
Inishere **T 099 75073 F 099 75073**
Local produce, including seafood and Aran lamb, served in a cosy restaurant right by the ocean.

COUNTY MAYO

Largely undiscovered by mass tourism, Mayo is a remote, sparsely populated county with a history of rural poverty and mass emigration. Its landscape of boglands, lakes and mountains makes it particularly appealing to those who want to get away from it all.

PRINCIPAL TOWN

WESTPORT

With an octagonal centre, lime trees lining either side of a canalised river, Clew Bay at its feet and a wealth of grand Georgian buildings, the planned town of Westport is very attractive to visitors and is designated a Heritage Town of Ireland. The Thursday morning market at the Octagon brings the farmers into town, and there is a frenzy of buying and selling at the clothes, produce and novelty stalls. It is even more lively when the annual Street Festival takes place in the second week of July, with free music concerts and street entertainment.

MUST SEE

ACHILL ISLAND
(reached from Mulraney on the mainland)
Reached by a short causeway, Achill is the largest of Ireland's islands. Its economy depends largely on tourism as little of its 37,065/15,000 hectares can be cultivated - it is mostly mountain or bogland covered in heather. There are weird rock formations in the cliffs flanking the 2 miles/3km beach at Keel, and the Atlantic Drive provides excellent views of the foothills and sandy beaches. Boats can be hired at Keel Harbour for shark and other big-game fishing or to enjoy the dramatic cliff scenery. Stone circles and dolmens are dotted about inland.

CLARE ISLAND
Rising to a height of some 1,640ft/500m in Clew Bay, Clare Island will appeal to walkers. It also offers fishing, sailboarding, pony trekking and diving. Clare's wildlife includes dolphins, seals and otters and it is also home to the chough, a rare, red-billed crow. A square tower near the harbour was the stronghold of Grace O'Malley, the 16th-century pirate who declared herself Queen of Clew Bay and held her own against Elizabeth 1 on a visit to London in 1575.

CONG ABBEY
Cong *(between Lough Mask and Lough Corrib)*
Completed in 1120 for the Augustinians, Cong Abbey replaced a former church built in 623 and destroyed by the Norsemen. It was founded by Turlough Mor O'Connor, High King of Ireland, whose son, Rory, destined to be the last High King, died in the abbey in 1198. The restored cloister and the monks' fishing house, built on a river platform, can still be seen. The abbey was an important ecclesiastical centre for more than 700 years, and some 3,000 people once lived there. The last Abbot of Cong died in 1829.

KNOCK SHRINE
Knock
(on the N17, 9 miles/15km south of Horan International Airport)
Pilgrims from around the world flock to Knock, where apparitions of the Virgin Mary were reported in 1879. Since then it has been regarded as the Lourdes of Ireland. A 20,000-seat circular church was built to accommodate the huge pilgrimages. It finest hour came when Pope John Paul 11 visited the site in 1979.

BIG OUTDOORS

INISHKEA ISLANDS
(2.5 miles/4km west of Mullett Peninsula)
These two low-lying islands form a sanctuary for 60 per cent of the Irish winter population of barnacle geese. There are also early Christian remains connected with St Columba.

GREAT FOR KIDS

BEACHES
There are some beautiful beaches on Achill Island. Keel and Keem beaches have Blue Flag awards.

WESTPORT HOUSE
The Quay, Westport ☎ **098 25141**
One of Ireland's most stately homes, a handsome Georgian building displaying antique silver, Waterford glass and period furniture, plus video games in the dungeons and a children's amusement park in the lakeside grounds.

HISTORIC & ANCIENT SITES

CÉIDE FIELDS
(5 miles/8km west of Ballycastle)
☎ **096 43325**
An extensive Stone-Age settlement, with tombs, 5,000-year-old dwellings, rare plants and rock formations, and an environmental interpretative centre with audio-visual presentations.

HOMES & GARDENS

ASHFORD CASTLE
Cong ☎ **092 46003**
Formerly a home of the Guinness family, this turreted castle, on the shores of Lough Corrib, is now one of Ireland's most luxurious hotels.

Ashford Castle

MUSEUMS & ART GALLERIES

FOXFORD WOOLLEN MILLS VISITOR CENTRE
Foxford ☎ **094 56756**
The story of this 19th-century working mill, from the famine years to the present day, is told in an animated presentation.

QUIET MAN HERITAGE COTTAGE & ARCHAEOLOGICAL & HISTORICAL CENTRE
Circular Road, Cong
☎ **092 46089**
A must for enthusiasts of the classic John Ford film, The Quiet Man, this visitor centre is a replica of the White-O-Mornin Cottage set in the 1920s, and is typical of an Irish country cottage of that era. Great effort has made to ensure authentic reproduction of exhibits. Audio-visual presentation and souvenirs.

The permanent exhibition upstairs details finds of interest in the surrounding area, covering archaeological and history finds from Cong and the surrounding area from 7,000 BC to the 19th century. A guide and map has been produced by an eminent historian to give an insight into the exhibition.

ESSENTIAL INFORMATION

AIRACCESS

HORAN (KNOCK) INTERNATIONAL AIRPORT

TOURIST INFORMATION OFFICES

ACHILL T 098 45384
BALLINA T 096 70848
CASTLEBAR T 094 21207
CONG T 092 46542
KNOCK T 094 88193
KNOCK AIRPORT T 094 67247
NEWPORT T 098 41895
LOUISBURGH T 098 66400
WESTPORT T 098 25711 F 098 26709

SPORT & LEISURE

ANGLING

Belmullet is charter boat angling centre, on the Erris Peninsula, where the sheltered waters of Blacksod and Broadhaven Bays provide a wide variety of sea fish. Clew Bay at Westport is another sheltered spot for successful angling.

EQUESTRIAN CENTRES

ARD AOIBHINN STABLES
Cappaduff, Tourmakeady **T/F 092 44009**

ASHFORD EQUESTRIAN CENTRE
Cong **T 092 46024 or 46507**

BARLEY HILL STABLES
Barley Hill, Bohola **T 094 84262**

BARNFIELD HOUSE EQUITATION CENTRE
Knockmore, Ballina **T 094 58175**

CLAREMORRIS EQUITATION CENTRE
Lisduff, Claremorris **T 094 62292**

DRUMINDOO STUD/EQUITATION CENTRE
Castlebar Road, Westport **T 098 25616**

KNAPPA BEG STABLES
Knappa Beg, Westport **T 098 25617**

LISBEG FARM STABLES
Gortogher, Ballina **T 096 21970**

MULRANNY RIDING CENTRE
Mulranny, Westport **T 098 36126**

TURLOUGH EQUITATION CENTRE
Turlough, Castlebar **T/F 094 22310**

GOLF COURSES

CARNE GOLF COURSE
Carne, Belmullet **T 097 82292**
A course designed around sand dunes against the backdrop of Blacksod Bay.

WESTPORT GOLF CLUB
Westport **T 098 28262 F 098 27217**
Beautiful, though challenging, course with wonderful views of Clew Bay, 365 islands and the holy mountain called Croagh Patrick, famous for an annual pilgrimage
Also:
ACHILL T 098 45172
ACHILL ISLAND T 098 43456
BALLINA T 096 21050
BALLYHAUNIS T 0907 30014
BELMULLET T 097 82292
CASTLEBAR T 094 21649
CLAREMORRIS T 094 71527
MULRANNY T 098 36262
SWINFORD T 094 51378

HORSE RACING

BALLINROBE RACECOURSE
Ballinrobe **T 092 41083**

WHERE TO STAY

HOTELS

AA RECOMMENDED

SEE UNDER WHERE TO EAT FOR ALL HOTEL RESTAURANTS WITH ROSETTES

BALLINA

DOWNHILL ★★★
T 096 21033 F 096 21338
Set in beautiful grounds. Very pleasant hotel with spacious lounges and piano bar. Good value menus. Fishing area.
50 bedrooms ££££ Parking Leisure & sporting facilities Live entertainment

CASTLEBAR

BREAFFY HOUSE ★★★
(on N60 in direction of Tuam and Galway)
T 094 22033 F 094 22276
Set in acres of woodlands. 19th-century manor house with luxurious bedrooms. Restaurant and a choice of pleasant bars.
62 bedrooms ££££ Lift Parking Conference facilities Gymnasium Croquet lawn Crazy golf Closed 23--26 Jan

WELCOME INN ★★
T 094 22288 & 22054 F 094 21766
Town-centre hotel hiding modern facilities behind Tudor frontage,. Night club/ disco sometimes or traditional music nights.
40 bedrooms ££ Lift Banqueting/ conference facilities Parking

The Olde Railway

KNOCK

BELMONT HOTEL ★★★
Main Street **T 094 88122 F 094 88532**
Very convenient pleasant hotel, near the Shrine and 10 minutes from the airport.. Do try the excellent restaurant.
49 bedrooms Banqueting facilities

WESTPORT

HOTEL WESTPORT ★★★
The Demesne, Newport Road
T 098 25122 F 098 26739
Pleasant hotel, seet in parkland with relaxing lounges, spacious restaurant, comfortable bedrooms.Leisure facilities.
1291 bedrooms (inc 6 suites) Lift Parking Leisure & sporting facilities Conference & syndicate rooms

THE OLDE RAILWAY ★★
The Mall
T 098 25166 & 25605 F 098 25090
Overlooking river. Lovely old coaching inn with atmosphere and blazing turf fires. Comfortable bedrooms. Superb food.
24 bedrooms ££ Parking Fishing & Shooting arranged Parking

BED & BREAKFAST ESTABLISHMENTS

AA RECOMMENDED

ACHILL ISLAND

GRAY'S QQQQ
Dugort T 098 43244 & 43315
Genuine hospitality. Relaxing conservatory, lounges, and bedrooms with orthopaedic beds. Self-contained villa available.
15 bedrooms (10 annexe) ££ No smoking in dining room or 1 lounge Licensed Parking Table tennis Croquet Pool Closed 25 Dec

WEST COAST HOUSE QQQ
School Road, Dooagh
(turn off N59 onto R319 onto Achill Island continue to Keel & then Dooagh, signed)
T 098 43317 F 098 43317
Smart modern house with superb views Hight standard bedrooms. Panoramic views comfortable sitting room.
5 bedrooms £ Parking No children 12yrs

Rath-a-Rosa Farmhouse

Wilmaur

KNOCK

AISHLING HOUSE QQ
Ballyhaunis Road T 094 88558
Pleasant white house, set in gardens, with comfortable bedrooms and two sitting rooms. Pre-book dinner and high tea..
5 bedrooms (1 on grond floor) Parking

WESTPORT

RATH-A-ROSA FARMHOUSE QQQ
Rossbeg T 098 25348
(on R335 Westport to Louisburgh road)
Set on hill farm with magnificent views. Spacious luxurious bungalow on shores of Clew Bay, within walking distance of pubs.
5 bedrooms £ No smoking in bedrooms or dining room Jacuzzi Parking 20 acres mixed cattle, sheep Open mid Mar–Oct

RIVERBANK HOUSE QQ
Rosbeg, Westport Harbour
T 098 25719
6 bedrooms inc 1 family room £ No smoking in dining room Parking

SEAPOINT HOUSE QQQ
Kilmeena T 098 41254
(signposted on Westport/Newport road N59,)
Large luxurious modern farmhouse on Clew Bay with comfortable bedrooms and pleasant views.
6 bedrooms £ No smoking in dining room or lounges Parking Sea angling Walking 40 acres mixed Open Apr–Oct

WILMAUR QQQQ
Rosbeg T 098 41254
(take N74 from town centre and turn right 0.5 mile after Asgard public house, signposted)
Comfortable country house on shore, where antiques and modern craftsmanshipcreate a warm atmosphere.
5 bedrooms inc some for non-smokers ££ No smoking in dining room Parking Open Apr–Sep

Call the AA Hotel Booking Service on 0990 050505 to book at AA recognised hotels and B&Bs in the UK and Ireland, or through our internet site: http://www.theaa.co.uk/hotels

CAMPING & CARAVANNING SITES

AA RECOMMENDED

KNOCK

KNOCK CARAVAN & CAMPING PARK,
Claremorris Road
T 094 88100 & 88223
Signposted Nearby town: Claremorris
3 pennants, touring caravans, motor caravans & tents.
Open March-November. Booking advisable August. Last arrival 22.00hrs. Last departure noon.
An eight-acre site with 58 touring pitches and eight statics. Electric hook up, shower, electric shaving point, launderette, hairdrier, games room, separate TV room, cold storage, children's playground, Calor Gas, Camping Gaz, battery charging, exercising area, disabled facilities.

Achill Island

WHERE TO EAT

RESTAURANTS

AA RECOMMENDED

BELMONT HOTEL
Main Street, Knock
T 094 88122 F 094 88532
Don't miss the excellent food served here, but we have no detailed information as we go to press.

THE OLDE RAILWAY HOTEL
The Mall, Westport
T 098 25166 or 25605 F 098 25090
Starters range from 'luscious white Westcoast seafood chowder' to home-made 'crubeen' sausages baked with a mustard crust and served with sweet peppers. Main courses might include glazed rack of Connemara lamb with classic Reform sauce (beetroot, ham and gherkin), and vegetarian dishes.
ALC ££

WALKING

Guided tours on the theme of The Quiet Man, John Ford's celebrated film made in 1951,from the Tourist Office in Cong.

PUBS, INNS & OTHER PLACES

ABRAKEBABRA
Pearse Street, Ballina **T 096 72936**
Hamburgers, kebabs and filled baguettes.

ARDMORE HOUSE RESTAURANT
The Quay, Westport **T 098 25994**
Seafood a speciality - oysters, lobsters and mussels - plus game in season.

ASGARD TAVERN & RESTAURANT
The Quay, Westport **T 098 25319**
Lively and homely, the restaurant over the bar offers a wide choice of quality dishes.

ASHFORD CASTLE
Cong **T 092 46003 F 092 46260**
Class, elegance, sophistication - both the food and the surroundings are luxurious.

ATOKA RESTAURANT
Valley Cross, Dugort, Achill Island
T 098 47229
Open from breakfast, every day. Full lunch and dinner menus, seafood prominent.

THE BEEHIVE
Keel, Achill Island **T 098 43134**
Very acceptable meals and snacks in this restaurant/craft shop. Home baking.

CALVEY'S
Keel, Achill Island **T 098 43158**
Lamb and beef from family farm.Seafood and noted vegetarian cooking.

CHINA COURT RESTAURANT & BAR
Bridge Street, Westport **T 098 28173**
Canton and Szechuan cooking.

DURKAN'S WEIR HOUSE & RESTAURANT
Louisburgh **T 098 66140**
Seafood restaurant, with bar food as well. Famous for its mussels and brown bread.

ECHOES RESTAURANT
Cong, **T 092 46035 or 46059** Specialising in local meat from their own butchery.

HEALY'S HOTEL
Pontoon **T 09456443 F 094 56572**
Seafood is the mainstay of the menu, with the accent on freshness.

MOUNT FALCON CASTLE
Ballina **T 096 70811 F 096 71517**
Hearty, traditional cooking. One set dinner only, with guests dining together.

NEWPORT HOUSE
Newport **T 098 41222 F 098 41613**
Georgian house on the quay. Modern icooking, using some organic produce.

QUAY COTTAGE RESTAURANT
The Quay, Westport
T 098 26412 F 098 28120
Inside it's cosy and relaxed. Imaginatively presented seafood, with choices still for carnivores and vegetarians.

RAFTERY ROOM RESTAURANT
Main Street, Kiltimagh **T 094 81116**
Home-cooked food, plus bag pipe band and historical lecture by arrangement .

The Northwestern Counties

COUNTIES DONEGAL, LEITRIM AND SLIGO

The landscape of the Northwest is quintessentially Irish, the rugged Atlantic coastline with all the splendour of fine cliffs, beaches, mountains, glens - and peat bogs - combined with the rural custom, are timeless and captivating; the scenery transformed from one moment to the next by the vagaries of the climate. But all that makes the region attractive to the visitor, makes it tough in many areas for local people to sustain a livelihood, unless through tourism. The population is ageing, emigration continues and tourism develops - for good or ill. For the time being, tourism is very seasonal, and visitors during the winter months may find many amenities closed, or services restricted.

EVENTS & FESTIVALS

March

International Folk Song & Ballad Seminar,
Inishowen, Co Donegal

June

Sligo Arts Festival,
Sligo, Co Sligo

July

Mary from Dungloe International Festival,
Dungloe, Co Donegal

August

Ballyshannon Folk & Traditional Music Festival,
Co Donegal

Carrick-on-Shannon Boat Rally & Regatta
Carrick-on-Shannon

Yeats International Summer School,
Sligo, Co Sligo

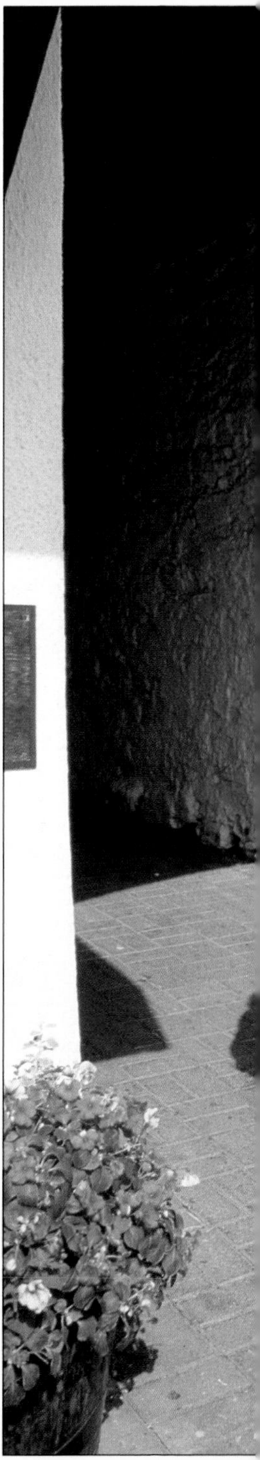

The Connemara Kitchen
Delicatessen
STOP
The
Connemara
Kitchen

COUNTY DONEGAL

Donegal is the third largest county in the Republic, after Cork and Galway, and despite its political position in the Republic, its northernmost part is actually further north than Northern Ireland. The county is, however, avowedly Nationalist, and has the largest Irish-speaking community (Gaeltacht) in Ireland - as you will notice from the road signs. Some of country's most stunning coastal scenery is to be seen here, the cliffs at Slieve League are the highest in Europe, and the wild promontories provide a vital habitat for sea birds. There are several inhabited islands off the Donegal coast, including Tory island, known for its lobsters and naive art, and Aranmore, which is more geared up for tourists.

PRINCIPAL TOWN

DONEGAL

Donegal isn't actually the county town of Co Donegal, that title has been awarded to Letterkenny, its administrative and commercial centre, but from the visitor's point of view Donegal is the more interesting town, and a useful kicking off point for the Northwestern region. It is also good for shopping (see Essential Information), and seeking out the area's most famous export - Donegal tweed.

Donegal (Dun na nGall) means 'fort of the foreigners', a reference to its history as a Viking stronghold. After the Vikings left, the town became the headquarters of Tîr Chonaill, the territory of the O'Donnell clan. 'Red Hugh' O'Donnell built a fortress and a Dominican abbey here in the 15th century. Early in the 17th century the Gaelic chieftains left Ireland in the exodus known as the Flight of the Earls, following defeat in their rebellion against Elizabeth I, and their lands and castles were appropriated by English and Scottish settlers.

MUST SEE

ARDARA HERITAGE CENTRE,
ara ⓣ 075 41704 ⓕ 075 41381
Centre offers information about the on's mountain passes, forests, lakes historical landmarks. It is an area rich olklore and archaeology, as well as a ural centre for traditional music. Ardara t the heart of Ireland's manufacturing andwoven tweed, hand-made wear and hand-loomed woollens, and e are many craft and factory shops as l as exhibitions within the Centre.

AD COIS LOCHA,
lewey
075 31699
ding, spinning and weaving nonstrations, story-telling, boat trips, an enture play area, farm tours and a craft p feature at this award-winning eside centre, where Irish is spoken.

all the AA Hotel Booking Service on 90 050505 to book at AA recognised tels and B&Bs in the UK and Ireland, or through our internet site: http://www.theaa.co.uk/hotels

NS OF DUNREE MILITARY MUSEUM,
t Dunree, Dunree, Buncrana
niles/9.5km northwest on eastern shore of gh Swilly) ⓣ 077 61817
first and only permanent and fessionally designed military museum reland. It is located a few miles thwest of Buncrana along the Inis Eoghain 100, the motoring circuit of the beautiful Inishowen Peninsula in North Donegal. The museum houses a collection of artefacts and an audio-visual display, which vividly illustrates the workings of a coastal defence battery extending back 180 years. Walks around the complex afford magnificent views.

CAVANACOR HISTORIC HOUSE & CRAFT CENTRE,
Ballindrait ⓣ 074 41143 ⓕ 074 41143
(1.5 miles/2.5km from town off Strabane/Letterkenny road)
Built in the early 1600s and commanding a view of the Clonleigh valley and the River Deele, Cavanacor House is the ancestral home of James Knox Polk, 11th President of the USA (1845-1849). The house is surrounded by 10 acres/4 ha of landscaped grounds and an old-fashioned walled garden. There is also a museum, art gallery, craft shop, tearoom, and working pottery in the fortified yard.

WATER WHEELS,
Abbey Assaroe, Ballyshannon
(cross Abbey River on Rossnowlagh Road, next turning left & follow signs)
ⓣ 072 51580
Abbey Assaroe was founded by Cistercian monks from Boyle Abbey in the late 12th century. The Cistercians excelled in water engineering and canalised the river to turn water wheels for mechanical power. The mills were restored in 1989, and include a coffee shop and auditorium. One mill powers a generator which supplies light and heat. The site occupies an unusual position overlooking the Erne Estuary and the Atlantic.

DONEGAL PARIAN CHINA
Fifteen-minute tours of the factory give the visitor an insight into the traditional methods used to produce this delicate china and porcelain. There is also the chance to buy products at factory prices. The guided tours run from Monday to Friday.

BIG OUTDOORS

RIGAL MOUNTAIN,
nlewey
negal's highest peak at 750m. Some it is an easy climb; others that the se scree and the near-perpendicular most peak can be daunting. All agree t the view is supreme.

ENVEAGH NATIONAL PARK & CASTLE,
rch Hill, Letterkenny ⓣ 074 37088
3,722 acre/9,600 ha park of mountain orland, lakes and woodland, with a tor centre and dramatically-sited castle e Homes & Gardens). Plus Ireland's last herds of red deer.

MORE GAP
niles/8km north of Buncrana)
avourite beauty spot, the Gap is ween Mamore Hill and Urris at 800ft ove sea level, affording spectacular ws of the Inishowen peninsula and the antic Ocean beyond.

GREAT FOR KIDS

UA WORLD,
ndoran ⓣ 072 41172 ⓕ 072 42168
Aqua adventure playground with tornado flume, wave pool, slide pool and rapids, adults' sauna and steam rooms, and outdoor adventure playground, plus fast food and refreshments.

BANANAS,
Unit 1, Pearse Road ⓣ 074 26644
Children's indoor adventure play area.

BEACHES
Beaches with the Blue Flag award for their superior environmental standards are Narin, near Ardara, and Marble Hill Strand, near Port-na-Blagh

LEISURE LAND,
Redcastle, Moville ⓣ 07782306
Indoor and outdoor leisure and amusement centre for children of all ages, including ball pool, rides and slides. There is a restaurant, tuck shop, souvenir shops and picnic areas.

HISTORIC & ANCIENT SITES

DONEGAL CASTLE,
Tirchonaill Street, Donegal ⓣ 073 22405
Sir Basil Brooke took over the 15th-century castle in 1610, and enlarged it into a comfortable, if well defended, Jacobean home with mullioned windows and imposing fireplaces.

HOMES & GARDENS

GLEBE HOUSE & GALLERY,
Church Hill, Letterkenny ⓣ 074 37071
(signed from Letterkenny)
A Regency House set in beautiful woodland gardens along the shore of Lough Gartan, given to the nation, along with his art collection, by the artist Derek Hill.

GLENVEAGH CASTLE GARDENS,
Church Hill ⓣ 074 37088 ⓕ 074 37072
(approximately 16km from Letterkenny)
One of Ireland's most celebrated gardens created by Henry McIlhenny from Philadelphia, including woodland gardens, an Italian terrace, a neo-Gothic conservatory and jardin potager.

MUSEUMS & ART GALLERIES

DONEGAL COUNTY MUSEUM,
High Road, Letterkenny T **074 24613**
Exhibiting artefacts dating from the Stone Age to the Donegal Railway era, in an old stone building that once formed part of the workhouse.

GLENCOLUMBKILLE FOLK VILLAGE,
Glencolumbkille T **073 30017**
A group of three traditional-style cottages spanning three centuries, each furnished according to the period it represents - 1720s, 1820s and 1920s.

LIFFORD OLD COURTHOUSE VISITORS' CENTRE,
Foyle View T **074 41228 or 41733**
A restored 18th-century courthouse, complete with damp, dark dungeons, audio-visual presentation, courtroom re enactments, clans room, coffee and gift shop.

TULLYARVAN MILL CULTURAL & EXHIBITION CENTRE,
Buncrana, Inishowen T **077 61613**
Converted from a 19th-century corn mil this visitor centre has a textile museum, wildlife display, art workshop, craft shop and café.

ESSENTIAL INFORMATION

TOURIST INFORMATION

DONEGAL
The Quay T **073 21148** F **073 22762**

LETTERKENNY
Derry Road T **074 21160** F **074 25180**

ALSO

BUNCRANA
Shore Front T **077 62600**

BUNDORAN
Main Street T **072 41350**

DUNGLOE
Main Street T **075 21297**

CRAFTS

DERRYVEAGH CRYSTAL,
2 Falcarragh Industrial Estate, Falcarragh
T **074 35788 074 35788**
Designers and manufacturers of hand-cut and mouthblown crystal. Customers are welcome to view the factory and to discuss individual requirements.

DONEGAL CRYSTAL,
The Diamond, Donegal T **073 21014**
A factory shop where engravers and cutters can be seen at work. A hand-engraving service is available.

THE GALLERY,
Dunfanaghy T **074 36224**
Housed in a mid 19th-century fever hospital, the Gallery offers an extensive range of paintings, crafts and antiques for sale.

LETTERKENNY POTTERY,
Pinehill Estate, Mountaintop, Letterkenny
(1 mile/1.5km from town on the Kilmacrenan/Creeslough road) T **074 22738**
Founded by Brian McGee, Letterkenny pottery is extremely popular in Ireland, and is notable for its colourful wax-resist decoration.

MCAULIFF'S CRAFT SHOP,
Dunfanaghy T **074 36135**
Quality Irish fashion, knitwear and other crafts, with worldwide postage service.

POTSMITHS POTTERY,
Ray Bridge, Rathmullen T/F **074 58470**
Colourful and highly original stoneware pottery. For sale in the shop adjoining the workshop overlooking Lough Swilly.

ENTERTAINMENT

ABBEY CENTRE,
Community Arts Centre, Cinema & Theatre, Tirconaill Street, Ballyshannon
T **072 51375** F **072 52832**

SPORT & LEISURE

ACTIVITY CENTRES

GARTAN OUTDOOR EDUCATION CENTRE,
Churchill, Letterkenny T **074 37032**
Daily and residential.

LETTERKENNY BOWLING CENTRE,
Ramelton Road, Letterkenny T **074 26000**
Ten pin bowling, 18-hole pitch and putt, 5-a-side all weather football, pool tables and café.

ANGLING

Donegal is renowned for its sea angling, and wreck fishing is popular, over the convoy ships destroyed during the two World Wars.

BALLYSHANNON MARINE LTD,
Kelly Business Centre
T **072 52960** *(or 072 52855 out of office hours)*
Deep sea angling in Donegal Bay.

BUNDORAN SEA ANGLING CENTRE
T **072 41526 or 072 41898**
Fully equipped and licensed boat accommodating 12 anglers.

PAT ROBINSON,
Kill, Dunfanaghy
T **074 36290** F **074 36505**
Deep sea angling, shark fishing and wreck fishing.

BOATING & CRUISING

DONEGAL COASTAL CRUISES,
Turasmara, Bunbeg Pier Office
T **075 31991 or 31340 or 31320**
Day trips to Tory Island

CYCLE HIRE

DOHERTY'S,
Main Street, Donegal T **073 21119**

HIRE & SELL CENTRE,
East End, Bundoran T **072 41526**

EQUESTRIAN CENTRES

DUNFANAGHY RIDING STABLES,
Arnold's Hotel, Dunfanaghy T **074 36208**

FINN FARM TREKKING CENTRE,
Cappry, Ballybofey T **074 32261**

GREENACRES LODGE
Rooskey Upper, Convoy T **074 47541**

INCH ISLAND STABLES,
Inch Island, Inishowen T **077 60335**

LENAMORE STABLES,
Muff T **077 84022**

LITTLE ACORN FARM,
Coast Road, Carrick T **073 39386**

STRACOMER SILVER
Strand, Bundoran T **072 41288 or 41977**

GOLF COUSES

DONEGAL GOLF CLUB,
Murvagh, Laghey T **073 34054**
A massive links course providing a worl class facility in peaceful surroundings. It a very long course with some memorab holes, including five par 5s, calling for some big hitting.

ROSAPENNA HOTEL & GOLF LINKS,
Downings T **074 55301** F **074 55128**
One of the great natural links courses enjoying a wonderfully scenic setting.
Also
BALLYBOFEY & STRANORLAR
T **074 31093**
BALLYLIFFEN T **077 76119**
BUNCRANA MUNICIPAL T **077 62279**
BUNDORAN T **072 41302**
CRUIT ISLAND T **075 43296**
DUNFANAGHY T **074 36335**
GREEN CASTLE T **077 81013**
GWEEDORE T **075 31666**
LETTERKENNY T **074 21150**
NARIN & PORTNOO T **075 45107**
NORTH WEST T **077 61027**
OTWAY T **074 58319**
PORTSALON T/F **074 59459**
REDCASTLE T **077 82073**

SCENIC DRIVES

Itineraries for good scenic drives are available in Tourist Board publications. Contact the local Tourist Office.

WALKING

There is a signposted walking trail in Donegal town, with an accompanying booklet available from the Tourist Office

WHERE TO STAY

HOTELS

AA RECOMMENDED

SEE UNDER WHERE TO EAT FOR ALL HOTEL RESTAURANTS WITH ROSETTES

nold's

BALLYBOFEY

E'S ★★★◉◉
anorlar (1 mile northeast on N15)
☎ 074 31018 🖷 074 31917
ce a coaching inn, this delightful and
ndly hotel stands on the main street.
eat here - the food is delicious.
*bedrooms £ £ Parking Leisure facilities
untain bike hire* 🗲

BUNBEG

TAN GWEEDORE ★★★
5 mile up coast from Bunbeg crossroads)
☎ 075 31177 & 31188 🖷 075 31726
ws of the ever-changing seascape are
pendous from dayrooms and some of .
cious bedrooms. Airport collection.
*bedrooms £ £ Parking Leisure &
rting facilities Closed Nov-Mar* 🗲

AVIEW ★★
☎ 075 31159 🖷 075 32238
ndly atmosphere, comfortable
ommodation, two restaurants, Irish
sic in the bar.. Use of good leisure club
sister hotel, Ostann Gweedore.
bedrooms £ Parking 🗲

DONEGAL

RVEY'S POINT COUNTRY ★★★◉◉◉
gh Eske ☎ 073 22208 🖷 073 22352
*n Donegal, take N56 then 1st right
posted Loch Eske/Harvey's Point. Hotel is
rox 10 mins drive)*
lt with peace and comfort in mind in
nderful position.Perfect place to
wind. The cuisine is quite superb.
*bedrooms (12 of which in annexe) £ £
king Tennis (hard) Fishing No children
er 10yrs Closed weekdays Nov-Mar* 🗲

ABBEY ★★★
The Diamond ☎ 073 21014 🖷 073 21014
Pleasant town-centre hotel. Welcoming
atmosphere,owner-managed. Comfortable
accommodation.
49 bedrooms £ Lift Parking 🗲

DUNFANAGHY

ARNOLD'S ★★★◉
*(on N56 from Letterkenny hotel is on right on
entering the village)*
☎ 074 36208 & 36142 🖷 074 36352
On a lovely coastline with sandy beaches.
Comfortable lounges, restaurants, some
large bedrooms with sofas. Excellent food.
*32 bedrooms £ £ Parking Tennis (hard)
Croquet Putting Closed Nov-mid Mar* 🗲

> **Call the AA Hotel Booking Service on
> 0990 050505 to book at AA recognised
> hotels and B&Bs in the UK and Ireland,
> or through our internet site:
> http://www.theaa.co.uk/hotels**

RATHMULLAN

FORT ROYAL ★★★◉◉
Fort Royal *(take R245 from Letterkenny,
through Rathmullan village, hotel is signposted)*
☎ 074 58100 🖷 074 58103
Comfortble period house in large grounds.
Lovely location with secluded sandy
beach. Good place to relax.Superb cuisine.
*11 annexe bedrooms £ £ £ £ Parking Tennis
Squash Golf-course Closed Nov-Easter* 🗲

PIER HOTEL ★
(on sea front, near harbour)
☎ 074 58178 & 58115 🖷 074 58115
Near safe sandy beach. Pleasant hotel
with friendly atmosphere. Comfortable
lounge, and delightful bedrooms.
*10 bedrooms £ Closed Nov-May Restricted
service Apr-May & Oct* 🗲

LETTERKENNY

HOTEL CLANREE ★★★
(on N13 Derry road)
☎ 074 24369🖷 074 25389
Pleasant hotel with large lounge bar and
restaurant. The ground floor bedrooms
vary in size, but all are very attractive.
66 bedrooms Parking Function room

ROSSNOWLAGH

SAND HOUSE ★★★◉◉
☎ 072 51777 🖷 072 52100
Set in crescent of safe golden sands. Well
known for superb cuisine, hospitality and
personal service. Wonderful views.
*46 bedrooms £ £ Parking Tennis (hard)
Croquet lawn Putting green Mini-golf
Surfing Canoeing Closed mid Oct-Easter* 🗲

Harvey's Point Country

BED & BREAKFAST ACCOMMODATION

AA RECOMMENDED

ARDARA

BAY VIEW COUNTRY HOUSE
Portnoo Road **T 075 41145 F 075 41858**
(half a mile outside Ardara, on Portnoo road)
Large, modern bungalow on the outskirts of a small town, overlooking the sea. Attractive and comfortable bedrooms.
6 bedrooms ££ No smoking in dining room Parking

BALLYLIFFEN

ROSSAOR HOUSE
(from Derry City take A2 towards Moville, turning off at Quigleys Point)
T 077 76498 F 077 76498
Set in mature gardens in peaceful location. Superb views. Delightful house in every sense of the word. Luxurious bedrooms
4 bedrooms £ No smoking in dining room Parking

BUNBEG

TEAC CAMPBELL
T 075 31545 & 32270 F 075 31545
Welcoming atmosphere at comfortable house near safe beach. Pretty rooms,some large and 3-bedded. Pre-book dinner.
20 bedrooms £ No smoking in dining room or 1 lounge Parking

Sandhill Ho

Mount Royd Country Home

CARRIGANS

MOUNT ROYD COUNTRY HOME
(off N13/ N14 on R236, from Derry take A40) **T 074 40163**
Pretty creeper-clad house by river. Nothing is too much trouble for friendly owners. Superb rooms. Feast of choice at breakfast
4 bedrooms £ No smoking in dining room Parking

DONEGAL

ARDEEVIN
Lough Eske, Barnesmore
(take N15 from Donegal for 3 miles, turn left at fork for Lough Eske, follow signs)
T 073 21790 F 073 21790
Comfortable house high above Lough Eske with superb views of lake and mountains. Attractive bedrooms.
6 bedrooms £ Parking No children under 9yrs Open Apr-Oct

DUNFANAGHY

SANDHILL HOUSE
Port-na-Blagh **T 074 36602 F 074 36603**
Distinctive house prominent position close to golf club and sandy beach. Bedrooms are full of charm, one for less able guests.
7 bedrooms £ No smoking in bedrooms or dining room Parking Open Feb-Nov

LETTERKENNY

CASTLE GROVE COUNTRY HOUSE & RESTAURANT
Castle Grove, Ballymaleel
T 074 51118 F 074 51384
Magnificent country house set in parklan
Luxurious bedrooms furnished with fine antiques. Relaxing lounges. Pleasant foo
8 bedrooms including some for non-smoke No smoking in dining room ££ Licensed Parking No children under 8yrs

HILL CREST HOUSE
Lurgybrack, Sligo Road
(take N14Derry, at Dryarch rdbt turn R on N13Sligo FOR1 mile, house at top on righ
T 074 22300 & 25137 F 074 25137
6 bedrooms £ Parking No smoking in dining room

PENNSYLVANIA HOUSE
Curraghleas, Mountain Top
T 074 26808 F 074 28905
Modern house in stunning setting.where personal touches add to the inviting feel
5 bedrooms ££ No smoking in the house Parking No children under 12yrs

ROSSNOWLAGH

SMUGGLERS CREEK
T 072 52366
Perched on a hilltop with superb views, Splendid inn with comfort and conviviali
5 bedrooms £ No smoking in dining roon Licensed Parking Stabling for own horses Closed mid Nov-end Dec Restricted servic Oct-Easter (closed Mon & Tue)

Castle Grove Country House & Restaur

WHERE TO EAT

RESTAURANTS

AA RECOMMENDED

RAMORE RESTAURANT
rnold's Hotel, Dunfanaghy
T 074 36208 & 36142 F 074 36352
Options from the carte might include vocado and Sheephaven crabmeat salad, llet of red snapper in herbs and butter, nd prime Irish sirloin steak, seasoned in eppercorns, flamed with Irish whiskey nd finished with a rich cream sauce.
LC £££

ORT ROYAL HOTEL
athmullan, Letterkenny
T 074 58100 F 074 58103
he good-value four-course menu is trong on seafood, and might offer fresh onegal mussels with garlic and readcrumbs, and Lough Swilly lobster nayonnaise, but fillet of beef with Dijon nustard sauce, and leek, broccoli and armesan flan are typical alternatives.
IXED ££

IARVEY'S POINT COUNTRY IOTEL
ough Eske, near Donegal
T 073 22208 F 073 22352
n a superb location on Lough Eske. Both the service and setting are smart at this lovely restaurant. The exquisite cuisine draws on French and Swiss influences with a hint of Irish .
FIXED L £ & ££ FIXED D £££

LOOKING GLASS RESTAURANT
Kee's Hotel, Stranorlar, Ballyboffey
T 07431018 F 074 31917
Ambitious and bold international-style cooking has been winning acclaim. Starters might include grilled Tinakelly black pudding on duxelle of mushroom with wild mushroom essence, followed perhaps by pan-fried monkfish with roast tomato, baked aubergine and basil-flavoured dressing.
FIXED D ££

SAND HOUSE HOTEL
Rossnowlagh
T 072 51777 F 072 52100
An imposing hotel on the beach where you can expect to dine in comfort. There are many familiar dishes, all excellent, especially fish and shellfish, from a daily-changing menu.
FIXED L ££ FIXED D £££

CRAFTS

The regional speciality is Donegal tweed, and one of the best known places to buy it is the legendary department store, Magee's, on the north side of The Diamond in Donegal town. Also worth a visit is the Donegal Craft Village, south of town (signposted from the main N15 from Ballyshannon), a complex of workshops producing a variety of high-quality crafts, including batik, ceramics, crystal, jewellery and weaving. The small town of Ardara is a centre for knitwear and tweeds, and there are plenty of shops pulling in the punters on the main street, but there are also several factory shops where prices are a bit lower, and you may have the chance to tour the works. A popular mid-summer event is the annual Weavers' Fair.

PUBS, INNS & OTHER PLACES

ABBEY RESTAURANT,
he Diamond, Donegal T/F 073 21014
he whole family is welcome, for carvery inch, snacks or dinner.

HE BELSHADE RESTAURANT,
he Diamond, Donegal T 073 22660
he restaurant at the Magee Shop, serving ood home cooking.

ASTLE GROVE COUNTRY HOUSE,
allymaleel, Letterkenny T 074 51118
ix-course dinner menu. Good choice from amiliar to more exciting dishes.

ASTLE MURRAY HOUSE,
unkineely T 073 37022 F 073 37330
heatrical location, especially at night. Set-rice dinners, with seafood to the fore.

OVE RESTAURANT,
ockhill, Port na Blagh T 074 36300
he best of local food lovingly prepared.

ANNY MINNIE'S RESTAURANT,
nnagarry, The Rosses T 075 48201
naginative cooking. Seafood, as might be xpected, and local meats. Praised puds.

RRIGAL RESTAURANT,
lain Street, Donegal T 073 21428
amous fish and chips.

HARRY'S BAR & RESTAURANT,
Bridgend T 077 68444 or 68544
Pub lunches and evening meals.

KEALY'S SEAFOOD BAR,
The Harbour, Greencastle T/F 077 81010
Seafood without frills. Flavour, freshness and quality are the bottom line here.

LE CHATEAUBRIANNE,
Sligo Road, Bundoran T/F 072 42160
Menu changes frequently to use the best of local produce. Generous portions.

THE LOBSTER POT,
Burtonport T 075 42012
Restaurant and bar located in a lovely fishing village featuring seafood.

MCNAMARAS,
Foyle Street, Moville
T 077 82010 F 077 82564
Traditional-style restaurant featuring fresh, locally caught fish.

NANCY'S PUB,
Ardara T 075 41187
Old-fashioned place where a hearty meal can be enjoyed to traditional music.

RATHMULLAN HOUSE,
Rathmullan, nr Letterkenny T 074 58188
Interesting menus, but buffet steals the show. Dinner only, and Sunday lunch.

RESTAURANT ST JOHN'S,
Fahan, Innishowen T 077 60289
Bold cooking making the most of contrasting and harmonising flavours

ST ERNAN'S HOUSE HOTEL,
Donegal T 073 21065 F 073 22098
A five-course dinner menu incorporating local produce

SMUGGLERS CREEK INN,
Rossnowlagh T 072 52366
Inn perched high on the cliffs, serving fish, but carnivores and vegetarians welcome.

TAJ MAHAL TANDOORI RESTAURANT,
22 Upper Main St, Letterkenny T 074 27554
Indian and Pakistani cooking, with some European dishes.

WEAVERS RESTAURANT,
Main Street, Carrigart T 074 55204
Specialising in fresh fish and steaks. Take your own wine.

YELLOW PEPPER BISTRO WINE BAR,
Lower Main St, Letterkenny T 074 24133
Breakfasts, snacks and lunches.From Irish dishes to exotic spiced meals.

COUNTY LEITRIM

Leitrim is Ireland's least populated, and possibly least known county. Lough Allen, the first lake on the River Shannon, cuts the county in two, with mountains to the north, and lakes, farmland and rolling drumlins to the south. For visitors, the major attractions are angling, watersports, walking and cycling.

PRINCIPAL TOWN

CARRICK-ON-SHANNON

The county town of Leitrim has a population of under 2,000. Ita is the starting point for inland cruising on the Shannon (Lough Allen) and the Shannon-Erne waterway, which was re-opened in 1994.

MUST SEE

LENCAR WATERFALL
ıst of Drumcliff)
ɔm the N16 Manorhamilton to Sligo ad you will see the 56ft/17metre-high aterfall tumbling in an unbroken leap to Glencar Lough long before the right rn that leads you to it. There are several aterfalls near by, but this is the highest. ats immortalised it in his poem The olen Child.

BIG OUTDOORS

VAN & LEITRIM RAILWAY,
omod **078 38599**
20-minute round trip on a 1950s arrow Gauge Railway to Clooncolry

ERRYCARNE WOOD
miles/3.5km north of Dromod)
mainly beech and oak wood. Picnic site d access to the Shannon.

LENFARNE DEMESNE
mile/1.5km north of Glenfarne on anorhamilton/Enniskillen road)
d woodland, now planted with Sitka d Norway spruce, which is harvested on regular basis. Picnic site and boating ay on the lake.

UGH KEY FOREST PARK
ature trails, bog gardens, deer enclosure d boating facilities.

MILLTOWN WOOD *(0.5 mile/1km NW of Manorhamilton on Lurganboy road)*
Mixed woodland with traces of an old mill race. Woodland walks and a picnic area.

HISTORIC & ANCIENT SITES

FENAGH *(near Ballinamore)*
It is believed that the small village of Fenagh was thickly populated in pre-Christian times because of the number of megalithic burial chambers.

HOMES & GARDENS

LOUGH RYNN ESTATE & GARDEN,
Mohill **078 31427**
Once the ancestral home of the Earls of Leitrim. The 1.5-hectare walled garden, designed in 1859, was originally laid out to supply the house with fruit and vegetables but now replanted in the manner of a Victorian pleasure garden. See the herbaceous borders with an orange, yellow, silver and white theme.

MUSEUMS & ART GALLERIES

KINLOUGH FOLK MUSEUM,
Barrack Street, Kinlough
(key from grocer's shop opposite)
Kinlough's Folk Museum may be small but it is crammed with fascinating items - documents, household and agricultural artefacts and a whiskey still.

TEACH DUCHAIS FOLK MUSEUM,
Drumeela, Carrigallen **049 33055**
Well worth a visit.

ESSENTIAL INFORMATION

TOURIST INFORMATION

ARRICK-ON-SHANNON
e Marina **078 20170**

GENEALOGY

E LEITRIM GENEALOGY CENTRE,
unty Library Ballinamore **078 44012**
r tracing your Leitrim ancestors.

ENTERTAINMENT

RN MILL THEATRE & ARTS CENTRE,
rrigallen **049 39612**
eatre, music and art.

SPORT & LEISURE

ACTIVITY CENTRES

LLINAMORE CANOE CENTRE
8 44860
UGH ALLEN OUTDOOR PURSUITS,
linaglera **078 43292**
ndsurfing, canoeing, hillwalking and enteering.

ANGLING

Carrick-on-Shannon is one of the best coarse angling centres in Britain or Ireland with over 40 easily accessible lakes offering roach, bream, rudd, tench, pike, eel and trout. Boats are available for hire and there are fishing maps of the area.

THE DROWES FISHERY,
Lareen Park, Kinlough **072 41208**
Five miles/eight km of one of Ireland's earliest salmon rivers, open to all anglers 1st January to 30th September.

BOATING & CRUISING

CARRICK CRAFT,
Marina, Carrick-on-Shannon **078 20236**
Two to eight-berth cruisers for leisure or angling holidays.

EMERALD STAR,
Carrick-on-Shannon **01 679 8166**
Luxury cruising on the Shannon.

MOON RIVER PLEASURE CRUISER,
Carrick-on-Shannon **078 21777**
Luxury cruising with a full bar and cabaret floor, for parties or scheduled scenic tours.

SHANNON ERNE WATERWAY LTD,
Golf Links Rd, Ballinamore **078 44855**
Cruiser, barge and day boat hire.

EQUESTRIAN CENTRES

DOHERTY'S, Leitrim Village **078 20853**
DRUMCOURA CITY FLC WESTERN RIDING CLUB, Ballinamore **078 44676**
HAYDEN'S,Mohill **078 38049**
MOORLANDS, Drumshanbo **078 41500**

GOLF COURSES

BALLINAMORE **078 44346**
CARRICK-ON-SHANNON **078 67015**

SCENIC DRIVES

North West Tourism has devised a series of tours, details from the local Tourist Information Office.

WALKING

For details on walks in the North Leitrim Glens contact the North Leitrim Glens office, Manorhamilton **072 55833.**

WHERE TO STAY

ROOSKEY

MOUNT CARMEL ◘◘

T 078 38434 38520 F 078 38434

A lovely 19th-century house standing in its own grounds beside the River Shannon. Bedrooms are simply furnished and there is a spacious combined lounge and dining room to relax in. Another dining room serving meals to non-residents. The house has a wine licence, and can offer coarse fishing and cruising.

6 bedrooms £ No smoking in dining room or lounges Parking Solarium Jacuzzi Massage Holistic healing

WHERE TO EAT

PUBS, INNS & OTHER PLACES

STANFORD'S VILLAGE INN,
Dromahair **T 071 64140**
Unpretentious pub with old-time feel to it. Straightfoward traditional cooking at reasonable prices.

CANAL VIEW HOUSE,
Keshcarrigan **T 078 42056**
Look out over the Shannon-Erne waterway and enjoy some of the best produce the region can offer (even Sligo ostrich), and some very tempting desserts.

MOUNT CARMEL
Rooskey
T 078 38434 38520 F 078 38434
An AA recommended guest house serving meals to non-residents. Wine licence only.

COUNTY SLIGO

Folklore, fine poetry and ancient remains are all part of Sligo's special magic. It is the birthplace of the poet W B Yeats, who grew up in the county, returned to it many times and was finally laid to rest here. The landscape of his childhood home, and the myths and legends of the region are all reflected in his work. The county is rich in ancient sites, the most notable at Carrowmore, the largest cemetery of megalithic tombs in Ireland.

PRINCIPAL TOWN

SLIGO

Sligo is a lively market town - one of the largest in the region - full of character and a great place for music and eating out, though not specifically touristy. A major attraction for the literary minded is the town's links with the poet Yeats, the associated local sites, and the Yeats Summer School which hold a series of courses for students from home and abroad every August.

MUST SEE

CARROWMORE
(southeast of Knocknarea Hill, on the R292)
The largest cemetery of megalithic tombs in Ireland can be seen at the top of a mountain at Carrowmore. More than 60 tombs, a variety of dolmens, passage graves and stone circles extend for 2 miles/3km. One of the dolmens dates back to 4000 BC, while the Bronze Age standing stones are thought to be from 1750 BC. T

CAVES OF KEAGH
(on the R295, 6 miles/10km S of Ballymote)
Seventeen small caves on the western side of a mountain, with traces of human occupation. The remains of cave bears, Artic lemmings, Irish elk and reindeer have also been discovered. According to legend, it was in one of these caves that Cormac Mac Airt, King of Cashel, was reared by a she-wolf.

DRUMCLIFF MONASTIC SITE,
Drumcliff,
(5 miles/8km north of Sligo)
Little is left of this 6th-century settlement except the stump of a round tower on on side of the N15 road and an elaborately carved 1,000-year-old high cross on the other. The carvings on either side of the cross depict a selection of biblical scenes from Adam and Eve to the Crucifixion.

PARKE'S CASTLE
(near Sligo, on the north shore of Lough Gill)
T 071 64149
A strongly fortified 17th-century house built by an Englishman named Parke, who undiplomatically dismantled a neighbouring castle to provide the material for his own. A video presentation relates the story. Guided tour.

IRISH FOOD

Irish food is generally hearty fare and potatoes feature heavily. Do try colcannon (potatoes with onions and white cabbage), champ (potatoes mashed with butter and chopped chives) or coddle (potatoes with bacon and onions). During the dreadful days of the Famine in the 19th century, the potato was central to the survival of many.

BIG OUTDOORS

HAZELWOOD SCULPURE TRAIL
(2 miles/3km east of Sligo)
A permanent sculture trail with 14 sculptures made of local wood.

GREAT FOR KIDS

Rosses Point beach at Mullaghmore has a Blue Flag award. Strandhill beach has sheltered beaches with excellent surfing.

HOMES & GARDENS

LISSADELL HOUSE
Drumcliffe T 071 63150
(8 miles/13km N of Sligo off Bundoran road)
Best known as the home of the remarkable Gore-Booths: Eva the poet, Sir Josslyn the horticulturalist and Constance the first woman member of the Dàil.

HISTORIC & ANCIENT SITES

SLIGO ABBEY *(National Monument)*
Abbey Street
The oldest buildings in Sligo. A Dominican friary founded by Maurice Fitzgerald in 1253, and rebuilt in 1416 after a fire.

MUSEUMS & ART GALLERIES

SLIGO ART GALLERY,
Yeats Memorial Building, Hyde Bridge, Sligo
T/F 071 45847
Contemporary and community art.

SLIGO COUNTY MUSEUM,
Stephen Street, Sligo
Collection of Yeats' works plus a permanent exhibition of modern art by Jack Yeats (brother of the poet) and othe

ESSENTIAL INFORMATION

TOURIST INFORMATION

SLIGO
Temple Street T 071 61201 F 071 60360

ENTERTAINMENT

HAWK'S WELL THEATRE,
Temple Street, Sligo T 071 61518 or 61526

SPORT & LEISURE

ANGLING

The lakes of Sligo offer good wild game and coarse fishing. Some waters are privately owned and some are under the control of local angling clubs. The coast is good for sea and shore angling, and boats can be hired at Rosses Point and Mullaghmore.

BOATING & CRUISING

SLIGO BAY CRUISES,
Ballast Quay, Sligo
T/F 071 50888 or 087 438008

WILD ROSE WATERBUS
T 071 64266 or 088 598869

EQUESTRIAN CENTRES

ARD CHUAIN EQUESTRIAN CENTRE,
Knockbrack, Corballa T 096 45084

HORSE HOLIDAY FARMS,
Grange T 071 66152

MARKREE CASTLE RIDING STABLES,
Collooney T 071 30092

OX MOUNTAIN SLOPES HORSE RIDING FARM, Corballa, Enniscrone T 096 36451

SLIGO RIDING CENTRE, Carramore, Sligo
T 071 61353 F 071 44200

WOODLANDS EQUESTRIAN CENTRE,
Loughill, Lavagh, Tubbercurry
T 071 84207 F 071 84220

GOLF COURSES

COUNTY SLIGO GOLF CLUB,
Rosses Point T 071 77186 F 071 77460
Now considered to be one of the top links courses in Ireland.

ENNISCRONE GOLF CLUB,
Enniscrone T 096 36297 F 096 36657
Another great links course, with a series c interesting holes.
Also:
BALLYMOTE T 071 83158 or 83089
STRANDHILL T 071 68188
TUBBERCURRY T 071 85971

HORSE RACING

SLIGO RACECOURSE,
Cleveragh, Sligo T 071 62484

WALKING

A signposted walking trail of Sligo begins in Stephen Street, and an accompanying booklet is available from the Tourist Office

MOUNTAIN WALKS

KNOCKNAREA MOUNTAIN (1083FT/452M
Six miles/9.5km from Sligo town and a relatively easy walk. A notice in the car park shows the route.

BENBULBEN (1730FT/527M)
Rather more of a challenge; one of Ireland's most famous mountains with a distinctive table top profile.

WHERE TO STAY

HOTELS

AA RECOMMENDED

SEE UNDER WHERE TO EAT FOR ALL HOTEL RESTAURANTS WITH ROSETTES

COLLOONEY

MARKREE CASTLE ★★★
(turn off N4 at Collooney Crossroads just north of junction with N17, 7 miles south of Sligo, hotel gates on right after 0.5 mile)
T 071 67800 F 071 67840
Magnificent castle c1640 .Owner's ancestral home.Careful restoration has transformed into lovely hotel. Superb food.
30 bedrooms £££ Lift Parking Croquet lawn

SLIGO

SLIGO PARK ★★★
Pearse Road *(on N4)*
T 071 60291 F 071 69556
Set in parkland. Pleasant hotel with excellent 'executive' bedrooms. Inviting restaurant .Good beaches, golf near
89 bedrooms including some for non-smokers £££ Parking Leisure & sporting facilities

TOWER ★★★
Quay Street
T 071 44000 F 071 46888
58 bedrooms including some for non-smokers £££ Lift Parking

SILVER SWAN ★★
(situated in the town centre)
T 071 43231 F 071 42232
Family owned hotel on riveranks in heart of Sligo. Some bedrooms have aero-spa baths. Popular bar. Exc ellent food.
29 bedrooms ££ Parking

BED & BREAKFAST ACCOMMODATION

AA RECOMMENDED

BALLISODARE

SEASHORE HOUSE QQQ
Lisduff **T 071 67827 F 071 67827**
(turn off N4 onto N59 at Ballisodare, travel 2.5 miles west, Seashore sign clearly visable)
Attractive bungalow in quiet seashore location. Comfortable lounge, sunny conservatory, garden. Lovely views.
4 bedrooms £ Parking No children under 10yrs Solarium

BALLYMOTE

CORRAN HOUSE QQQ
Sligo Road **T 071 83074**
(last house on right lon R293 to Collooney)
Near village, this comfortable house has pretty gardens and comfortable bedrooms. Area is well known angling centre.
3 bedrooms including 2 for non-smokers £ No smoking in dining room Parking

CLIFFONY

VILLA ROSA QQ
Donegal Rd, Bunduff
(1 mile past village on N15 to Donegal)
T 071 66173 F 071 66173
Pleasant house with comfortable bedrooms. Surrounding area is famous for historic folklore, walks, beautiful scenery.
5 bedrooms £ Parking Walking

DRUMCLIFF

MOUNTAIN VIEW FARMHOUSE QQQ
Carney **T 071 63290**
(N15 from Sligo to Drumcliffe, turn left after Yeats Tavern for 1 mile)
Modern farmhouse, close to Yeats's grave.. Most of the comfortable bedrooms enjoy spectacular mountain views.
5 bedrooms No smoking in bedrooms or dining room £ Parking 45 acres mixed Open Apr-Oct

SLIGO

AISLING QQQ
Cairns Hill **T 071 60704**
Pristine modern bungalow near town centre. Very comfortable bedrooms. Pleasant lounge. Mountain views.
6 bedrooms No smoking £ Parking No children under 6yrs

ATLANTA HOUSE QQ
Ballyfree, Carraroe **T 071 61521**
4 bedrooms £ Parking Open Mar-Oct

REALT NA MARA QQQQ
Sea Road, **T 071 70838 F 071 50900**
((off Strandhill Road)Take turn off N4/N15 at junction of Lord Edward Sreet/Strandhill Road, drive past bus/train station and take 2nd road on right after railway bridge)
Superb contemporary house with luxury bedrooms and sitting rooms. Charming hosts. Excellent home-baking
4 bedrooms ££ Parking Open Mar-Oct

RED COTTAGE QQQ
Donegal Road *(on N15)*
T 071 44283 F 071 43417
Friendly place with comfortable bedrooms and a split-level lounge. Tennis, squash, golf, hill-walking, beach. nearby
12 bedrooms (6 of which in annexe) Parking

TREE TOPS QQQ
Cleveragh Rd **T 071 60160 F 071 62301**
Modern house with very friendly atmosphere. Comfortable bedrooms, sitting room. Well tended gardens..
5 bedrooms Parking

TOBERCURRY

CINRAOI QQ
Ballymote Rd **T 071 85268 F 071 85268**
Pleasant bungalow near town centre. Comfortable bedrooms. Breakfast and dinner sociably served round large table.
4 bedrooms £

CRUCKAWN HOUSE QQQ
Ballymote/Boyle Rd *(signed from town square)*
T 071 85188 F 071 85239
Near golf club, which you may use. Bedrooms are attractive and comfortable. Tennis court and other facilities.
5 bedrooms Parking Tennis (hard) Leisure & sporting facilities

CAMPING & CARAVANNING SITES

AA RECOMMENDED

ROSSES POINT

GREENLANDS CARAVAN & CAMPING PARK
T 071 77113 or 45618 *Signposted*
4 pennants, touring caravans, motor caravans & tents. Open end May-August. Last arrival 20.00hrs. Last departure noon. A four-acre site with 42 touring pitches. Electric hook up, shower, electric shaver point, launderette, games room, separate TV room, cold storage, public telephone, disabled facilities.
Facilities within three miles of site: golf course, mini golf, water sports, fishing, shop

STRANDHILL

STRANDHILL CARAVAN PARK
T 071 68120 *Signposted*
2 pennants, touring caravans, motor caravans & tents. Open May-mid September. Booking advisable Jul-August. Last arrival 23.00hrs. Last departure 14.00hrs. A 10-acre site with 28 touring pitches and 12 statics. Electric hook up, shower, electric shaver point, launderette, hairdrier, games room, separate TV room, cold storage, children's playground, Calor Gas, Camping Gaz, public telephone, shop
Facilities within three miles of site: stable, fishing

WHERE TO EAT

RESTAURANTS

AA RECOMMENDED

MARKREE CASTLE ❀❀
Collooney **T 071 67800 F 071 67840**
If you want to dine in grandiose surroundings, this is for you. Mostly classic dishes, beautifully prepared, such as fillet of smoked trout with horseradish cream, sautéed duck breast with caramelised orange and ginger sauce, and chocolate marquise with praline sauce.
FIXED D £££

SILVER SWAN HOTEL ❀
Sligo **T 071 43231 F 071 42232**
A town centre hotel on the banks of the Garavogue River, with a popular bar and restaurant serving high quality cuisine.
FIXED L £-££ FIXED D ££-£££

PUBS, INNS & OTHER PLACES

BISTRO BIANCONI,
The Mall, Sligo **T/F 071 44226**
Pasta and pizza, nothing exotic, but well-prepared and fresh.

COOPERSHILL HOUSE,
Coopershill, Riverstown **T 071 65108** A small restaurant, beautifully furnished, open for a set dinner only.

COTTAGE RESTAURANT,
Castle Street, Sligo **T 071 45319**
Breakfast to supper, snacks and meals. Cajun food at weekends. Take wine.

CROMLEACH LODGE,
Castlebaldwin via Boyle **T 071 65155**
Views over Lough Arrow, some stunning dishes - they make it a real occasion.

THE EMBASSY RESTAURANT,
John F Kennedy Parade **T 071 61250**
Restaurant overlooking the Garavogue River serving wholesome Irish fare.

GLEBE HOUSE,
Collooney **T 071 67787 F 071 30438**
Generous helpings of dishes prepared with the best of local produce.

LYONS CAFÉ,
Wine Street, Sligo **T 071 42969**
Snacks and lunches, with fine home baking.

THE MOORINGS,
Rosses Point **T 071 77112**
Good views. Dine on local seafood - nothing unexpected, reasonable prices.

STRAND,
Strandhill **T 071 68140 F 071 68593**
Popular bar/restaurant, where surfers satisfy their appetites. Children welcome.

IRISH PRODUCE

Ireland is rich is home-grown produce. Rich dairy foods from cows grazing on lush Irish meadows produce a fascinatingl range of Irish cheeses. Beef, lamb and pork all benefit from the same wonderfully rich pasture land. The freshest seafood and fish are served in many speciality restaurants and the sea is never far away. You don't have to be rich to enjoy oysters here.

THE LAKELAND COUNTIES

COUNTIES CAVAN, LONGFORD, LAOIS, MONAGHAN, OFFALY, ROSCOMMON AND WESTMEATH

The focus of these small Lakeland counties is the mighty River Shannon, the longest in the British Isles, which as well as being beautiful, is a useful navigable waterway, an important wildlife habitat, and a centre of leisure activities for anglers and water sports enthusiasts. The region isn't particularly known as a tourist destination (more like part of the route), but, in addition to the big range of outdoor activities available, there are several places of interest which might well detain the discerning visitor.

EVENTS & FESTIVALS

February

Cavan International Song Contest,
Kilmore, Co Cavan

May

Belturbet Angling Festival,
Co Cavan

August

Birr Vintage Week (mid-Aug)
Birr, Co Offaly

Birr Antiques Fair
Birr, Co Offaly

Birr Georgian Cricket Match
Birr, Co Offaly

National Steam Rally,
Stradbally, Co Laois

O'Carolan Harp & Traditional Music Festival,
Keadue, Co Roscommon

September

Arva Angling Festival,
Arva, Co Cavan

Belturbet Angling Festival,
Belturbet, Co Cavan

Cootehill Angling Festival,
Cootehill, Co Cavan

Harvest Time Blues & Jazz Festival,
Monaghan, Co Monaghan

Percy French Festival,
Cavan, Co Cavan

November

Queen of the Land Festival,
Co Offaly

COUNTY CAVAN

The landscape of Co Cavan is characterised by lakes, bogs and drumlins - the small round hills that are the legacy of the last Ice Age. Actually, there are about 365 lakes attracting anglers in their droves, and in the northwest of the county are the Cuilcagh Mountains, the source of the River Shannon. Close to the border with Northern Ireland is 'bandit country' traditionally associated with cross-border smuggling and covert political activity, and the nature of the terrain makes the frontier difficult to police. It is wise to proceed with caution, here, and keep your political opinions to yourself.

PRINCIPAL TOWN

CAVAN

Cavan was devastated by British forces in 1690, and the county town we see today is unremarkable in itself, but pleasantly situated in an area of lakes and hills close to the border with Northern Ireland. An old tower marks the site of an abbey, founded in about 1300, around which the original settlement developed.

MUST SEE

ARRAIG CRAFT VISITORS' CENTRE & ASKETRY MUSEUM
ountnugent T 049 40179
od and rush basketwork in the form of ats, creels, bread baskets, shopping askets and other items are displayed. The asketry museum has an audio-visual esentation and there are emonstrations, lectures and craft orkshops. Facilities include a craft shop ad coffee shop.

LIFEFORCE MILL
Cavan T 049 62722 F 049 62923
Dating from 1846, the mill was in daily use until the 1950s. Now fully restored the mill is back at work producing Lifeforce stoneground wholemeal flour and welcoming visitors. There is a coffee shop on site, in a stone building which was demolished for a road widening project, transported and re-erected stone by stone.

BIG OUTDOORS

ÚN-A-RÍ FOREST PARK
T 042 67320
ovely forest park in the Glen of the Cabra ver.

GREAT FOR KIDS

ILL VALLEY FARM
avan T 049 61409
whole range of farm animals - cows, onkeys, horses, pigs, ducks, bantams, eep, goats and unusual fowl, plus the d farm mill, forge museum and fish.

MUSEUMS & ART GALLERIES

CAVAN COUNTY MUSEUM,
Virginia Road, Ballyjamesduff T 049 44070
Former convent of the Sisters of Poor Clare, tracing history of the county from pre-Christian times to the present day.

ST KILIAN'S HERITAGE CENTRE
Áras Chillian, Mullagh T 046 42433
Focusing on the Golden Age of learning and development in Irish history, and retracing the steps of one of Ireland's best loved saints in his hazardous travels across Europe.

ESSENTIAL INFORMATION

TOURIST INFORMATION

AVAN
rnham Street T 049 31942

CRAFTS

ARRAIG CRAFT VISITORS' CENTRE & ASKETRY MUSEUM
ountnugent T 049 40179
atural craft museum with audio visual esentation. (See Must See.)

AVAN CRYSTAL
ablin Road, Cavan T 049 31800
uided tours of the glassworks, where you n see craftspeople blowing and cutting ystal. Crystal is offered for sale in the ctory shop. Coffee shop.

SPORT & LEISURE

ACTIVITY CENTRES

UNTY CAVAN SWIMMING POOL & ISURE COMPLEX
umalee, Cavan T 049 62888 Facilities clude a 25-metre swimming pool, steam om/jacuzzi, fitness suite, aerobics room, orts hall, sunbed and restaurant.

ANGLING

There are over 365 lakes in the county, rich in *pike, bream, roach, rudd, perch, tench and eels. The best coarse angling centres are Cavan, Ballyconnell, Bawnboy, Belturbet, Cootehill, Gowna, Arva, Ballinagh, Killeshandra, Kingscourt, Blacklion and Virginia. Best centres for game fishing are Mountnugent, Ballyjamesduff, Butlersbridge, Belturbet, Ballyhaise and Kilnaleck.
* Legal restrictions apply to pike fishing, and anglers are encouraged to return all pike to the water in the interests of conservation.

BOATING & CRUISING

CRUISING ON LOUGH SHEELIN
Crover House Hotel, Mountnugent
T 049 40355
Lough cruising with views of the island and ruined castle, including sunset cruises.

TURBERT TOURS,
Deanery Banks, Belturbert T 049 22360
Cruising the River Earne and the Shannon-Erne Waterway aboard the Erne Dawn. Commentary, bar service and light refreshments.

CYCLING

ON YER BIKE TOURS
T Ciaran (Cavan) 049 31932 or 61560 & Michael (Belturbet) 049 22219
A variety of tours ranging from half a day to two weeks.

EQUESTRIAN CENTRES

KILLYKEEN EQUESTRIAN CENTRE,
Killykeen Forest Park, Cavan
T 049 61707 or 087 448563

REDHILLS EQUESTRIAN CENTRE,
Redhills T 047 55042

GOLF COURSES

BELTURBET T 049 22287
BLACKLION T 072 53024
CABRA CASTLE T 046 52372
COUNTY CAVAN T 049 31541
SLIEVE RUSSELL HOTEL, GOLF & COUNTRY CLUB T 049 26444
VIRGINIA T 049 48066

WALKING

COOTEHILL WALKING TRAILS
T 049 53039 or 52307 or 52150
Walking in 'drumlin country' to suit all levels of fitness, plus food, entertainment and accommodation.

WATER SPORTS

LAKESIDE JET SKIS,
Lakeside Manor, Lough Ramor, Virginia
T 088 596465 (weekends 049 47216)

WHERE TO STAY

HOTELS

AA RECOMMENDED

SEE UNDER WHERE TO EAT FOR ALL HOTEL RESTAURANTS WITH ROSETTES

BALLYCONNELL

SLIEVE RUSSELL HOTEL, GOLF & COUNTRY CLUB ★★★★
T 049 26444 F 049 26474
Imposing hotel set amidst simply lovely grounds. Attractive lounges and tasteful, comfortable bedrooms. Excellent food.
151 bedrooms £££ Lift Parking Leisure & sporting facilities

CAVAN

KILMORE ★★★
Dublin Road
(2 miles from Cavan on N3)
T 049 32288 F 049 32458
Set on a hillside. Very pleasant hotel features spacious lounges and comfortable bedrooms. Pleasant restaurant.
39 bedrooms ££ Parking

Call the AA Hotel Booking Service on 0990 050505 to book at AA recognised hotels and B&Bs in the UK and Ireland or through our internet site: http://www.theaa.co.uk/hotels

BED & BREAKFAST ACCOMMODATION

AA RECOMMENDED

CAVAN

HALCYON QQQ
Drumalee **T 049 318097**
(turn R off N3 immediately after cathedral, signposted 'Cootehill'. Turn R at X-roads, 'Halcyon' 100yds on left)
Lovely modern bungalow offering peace and quiet. Comfortable bedrooms, sun lounge and pretty sitting room. Garden.
5 bedrooms No smoking in dining room No children under 2yrs

WHERE TO EAT

RESTAURANTS

AA RECOMMENDED

CONALL CEARNACH RESTAURANT
Slieve Russell Hotel, Golf & Country Club, Ballyconnell
T 049 26444 F 049 26474
Attractive restaurant offering a short four-course dinner menu with dishes such as mushrooms and smoked bacon with white wine cream sauce in a puff pastry shell, poached monkfish fillets over sliced avocado with lime beurre blanc, and an 'indulgence' of chocolate mousse.
FIXED L ££ D£££

PUBS, INNS & OTHER PLACES

DERRAGARRA INN,
Butlersbridge **T 049 31003**
A fair choice of bar and restaurant food from old favourites to some more innovative dishes, with the accent on fish.

INTERNATIONAL FISHING CENTRE,
Loughdooley, Belturbet **T/F 049 26444**
Wide cross-section of diners, most here for the fishing, but locals too. French cooking and menu.

MACNEAN HOUSE & BISTRO,
Blacklion **T 072 53022 F 072 53404**
Modest outside and in, but sparkling cooking over a wide range. Food for the purist and for the family.

COUNTY LONGFORD

For centuries, Co Longford was the centre of power of the O'Farrell family, but in the 1798 Rising the combined forces of the Irish and French were defeated by the British at Ballinamuck. The Famine of the 1840s led to large-scale emigration from the area to Argentina, where Edel Miro O'Farrell, of Longford stock, became president in 1914.

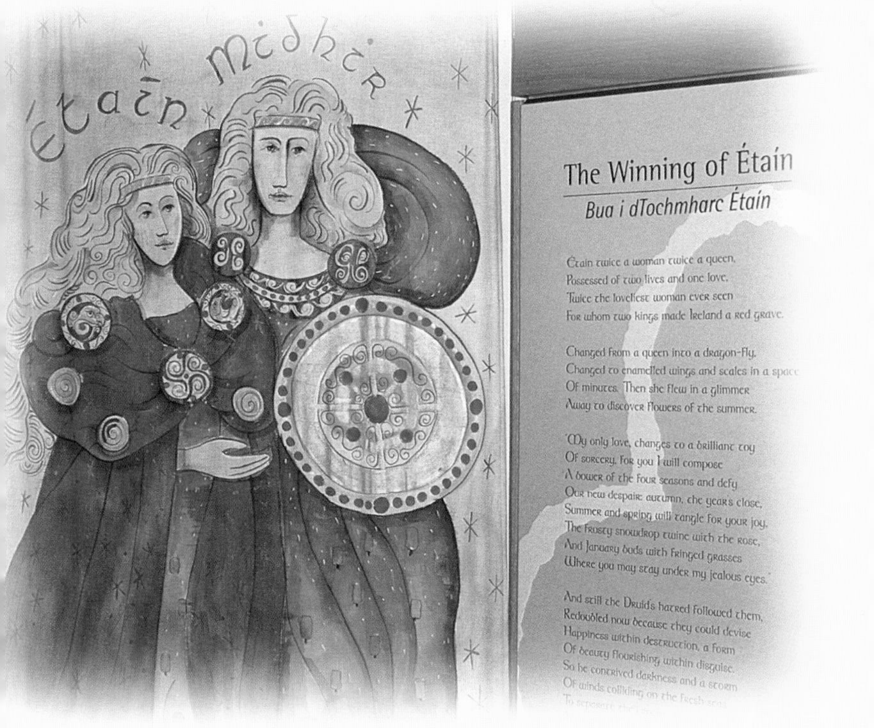

PRINCIPAL TOWN

LONGFORD

A prosperous town at the centre of an agricultural area, Longford takes its name from a fortress of the O'Farrells, of which no trace now remains.

MUST SEE

CARRIGGLAS MANOR
(8km from Longford on the N55)
T 043 45165 F 043 41026
A fine Victorian country house, built in the Tudor Gothic style for Thomas Lefroy, romantically linked in his youth to Jane Austen. The stables were designed by James Gandon, who was also responsible for the magnificent Custom House in Dublin. The stables house a costume and lace museum, a tea room and Victorian gift shop. The Manor also has delightful gardens.

HISTORIC & ANCIENT SITES

BLACK PIG'S DYKE
(2.5 miles/4km east of Longford, beginning at Lough Kinale and extending 6 miles/10km northwest to Lough Gowna)
A long series of earthworks, built to protect a network of routes, dating from somewhere between 300 BC and 300 AD, rising to 20ft/6m with a ditch on either side.

CORLEA TRACKWAY VISITOR CENTRE
Kenagh **T 043 22386**
A visitor centre intepreting the timber trackway, dating from 148 BC, found beneath the bog by turf-cutters.

GRANARD
Close to Granard is a 12th-century motte (National Monument), possibly the largest of its kind in Ireland. It is topped by a statue of St Patrick, erected in 1932.

LANESBOROUGH
This small town is home to one of Ireland's first turf-fired generating stations.

INCHCLERAUN
(6 miles/10km south of Lanesborough)
On Inchcleraun, an island in Lough Ree, are the ruins of an early monastery (National Monument), including the remains of five churches and other buildings.

ESSENTIAL INFORMATION

TOURIST INFORMATION

LONGFORD T 043 46566

SPORT & LEISURE

ANGLING

The River Shannon, near Lanesborough, is a good centre for bream, tench and roach. Lough Ree is good for trout and boats can be hired in the summer.

EQUESTRIAN CENTRES

AUGHERA HOUSE EQUESTRIAN CENTRE,
Aughera, Longford **T 043 41004**

CHEZ-NOUS RIDING CENTRE,
Arva Rd, Drumlish **T 043 24368**

GOLF COURSES

CO LONGFORD T 043 46310

WALKING

The towpath of the Royal Canal, which passes through the county to meet the Shannon, makes an interesting walking route.

WHERE TO STAY

BED & BREAKFAST ACCOMMODATION

AA RECOMMENDED

GRANARD

TOBERPHELIM HOUSE
(take the N55 from Cavan, left at Statoil, right at next junction, house on left)
T 043 86568 F 043 86568
Large Georgian country house standing at the end of a long driveway. Children are well catered for with a private playground.
3 bedrooms No smoking in 2 bedrooms or in dining room £ Licensed Parking Children's playground Bicycle hire 200 acres beef & sheep

WHERE TO EAT

PUBS, INNS & OTHER PLACES

THE VINTAGE,
Moydow **T 043 22122**
In a bit of a culinary desert, The Vintage offers some serious cooking - traditional and more wide-ranging influences. Vegetarians and families welcome.

COUNTY LAOIS

County Laois (pronounced 'leash') has the highest hills in the Lakeland region - the Slieve Bloom range, rising to 1,729ft/527m - not massive but impressive enough amid these low lying plains.Based here, the lovely countryside and pretty villages are easily explored as are the neighbouring counties of Offaly, Carlow, Tipperary and Kildare.

The Slieve Bloom Way, a long distance footpath, attracts quite a number of walkers to the county

PRINCIPAL TOWNS

PORTLAOIS

The county town of Portlaois was destroyed in the 17th century, and most of what you see today is modern, apart from the Court House and the town gate, both of which date from the early 19th century.

ABBEYLEIX

Picturesque period houses and tree lined streets characterise one of the finest planned estate towns in Ireland which was founded by the da Vesci family in the 18th century near a 12th century Cistercian monastery. There are heritage trails to follow and those keen on angling will enjoy the waters of the nearby river Nore.

MUST SEE

EMO COURT & GARDENS,
Emo
T 0502 26110
Possibly the premier attraction in the county, this fine Georgian mansion was designed by James Gandon, architect of Dublin's Custom House. Its great rotunda is lit by a lantern in the dome. The garden contains statuary, rare trees, an imposing lake, shrubs and avenues of yews.

STEAM & VINTAGE MACHINERY MUSEUM,
Irish Steam Preservation Society, The Green, Stradbally **T 0502 25444**
Steam road engines and rollers operate here during traction engine rallies and railway events, with rides on Irish Peat Board loco-hauled coaches on a narrow gauge railway. Displays portray the progess of Irish steam in Ireland.

ST FINTAN'S TREE
(3km east of Mountrath on the Portlaoise road)
This large sycamore tree on the site of the 6th-century monastery of St Fintan is a place of pilgrimage.It has a water-filled groove in one of its branches that apparently never dries out, and the water is attributed with healing properties. (The coins imbedded in its trunk are a testimony to its powers.)

HERITAGE HOUSE
Abbeyleix
T 0502 31653 F 0502 30059
The place to visit to find out about both local and county history. This award-winning interpretative centre houses excellent exhibitions, plus a coffee parlour, crafts shop as well as tourist information.

BIG OUTDOORS

SLIEVE BLOOM MOUNTAINS
Situated to the west of Portlaoise, the mountains and their beautiful valleys are best reached from Mountrath along delightful minor roads.

HISTORIC & ANCIENT SITES

BALLAGHMORE CASTLE
(3km west of Borris-on-Ossory on the N7)
T 0505 21453
A square tower fortress, carefully restored, dating from 1480. On the south wall, if you look carefully, you'll see some rather explicit fertility symbols.

LEA CASTLE
(4km east of Portarlington on the Monasterevin road, R420)
The ruin of a 13th-century castle, including the keep, two outer walls and a twin-towered gatehouse. The castle was once the stronghold of Maurice Fitzgerald, 2nd baron of Offaly.

ROCK OF DUNAMASE
(6km east of Portlaoise)
A limestone hill covered in fortifications, including an Iron-Age ring fort and 12th/13th-century keep, with clear views in all directions over the flat surrounding countryside.

TIMAHOE ROUND TOWER
(10km northeast of Abbeyleix on the R426)
A tiny village, Timahoe is notable for its large round tower, 30 metres high, with a slight tilt, and a circumference of 17m. All that remains of a 12th-century monastery.

HOMES & GARDENS

HEYWOOD,
Ballinakill **T 0502 33563**
A series of Italianate gardens designed by Sir Edwin Lutyens, set within an 18th-century park with lovely trees and a lake, thought to be one of his finest gardening achievements. Don't miss the unique Sensory Garden while you are there.

ESSENTIAL INFORMATION

TOURIST INFORMATION

PORTLAOIS T 0502 21178

SPORT & LEISURE

EQUESTRIAN CENTRES

PORTLAOIS EQUESTRIAN CENTRE,
Timahoe Road, Portlaoise **T 0502 60880**

GOLF COURSES

ABBEYLEIX T 0502 31450
THE HEATH T 0502 46533
MOUNTRATH T 0502 32558
PORTALINGTON T 0502 23115
RATHDOWNEY T 0505 46170

SCENIC DRIVES

The Carlow to Stradbally road (N80) passes through Windy Gap, one of Ireland's most famous scenic drives. Stop at the Windy Gap car park for wonderful views over the Barrow Valley.

WALKING

The 70-km way-marked trail, the Slieve Bloom Way, circles the Slieve Bloom mountains including the major features.

WHERE TO STAY

HOTELS

AA RECOMMENDED

PORTLAOISE

KILLESHIN ★★★
Dublin Rd Ⓣ 0502 21663 Ⓕ 0502 21976
(on N7, main Dublin road, on right side heading into Portlaoise)
A relaxing hotel to stay in, with well-equipped bedrooms and a comfortable lounge plus a bar, restaurant.
44 bedrooms inc some for non-smokers £ Parking Conference suite

Call the AA Hotel Booking Service on 0990 050505 to book at AA recognised hotels and B&Bs in the UK and Ireland, or through our internet site: http://www.theaa.co.uk/hotels

BED & BREAKFAST ACCOMMODATION

AA RECOMMENDED

O'Sullivan Guest House

BALLACOLLA

BALLYGOGUE BEECHES QQQQ
Ballygogue *(off N8)*
Ⓣ 0502 34025
Old country house with lovely furnishings and luxury bedrooms. Superb breakfasts - freshly baked bread, home-made mueslis.
3 bedrooms £ Parking Restricted service Oct-Feb (by arrangement only)

BALLAGHMORE

BALLAGHMORE HOUSE QQQ
Ⓣ 0505 21366
Modern farmhouse with its own fishing lake, in landscaped gardens. Comfortable rooms, decorated in warm colours.
5 rooms inc 3 family £ No smoking in 1 bedroom, dining room or 1 lounge Parking Fishing Special golfing terms 75 acres mixed

MOUNTRATH

ROUNDWOOD HOUSE QQQ
Ⓣ 0502 32120 Ⓕ 0502 32711
(take R440 towards Slieve Bloom Mountains, house is 3 miles from Mountrath)
Palladian villa, in secluded woodland, takes you back in time to an era of grace and leisure. Excellent hospitality .
10 bedrooms (4 of which in annexe) ££ No smoking in bedrooms Licenced Parking Croquet Boules

PORTLAOISE

O'SULLIVAN GUEST HOUSE QQ
8 Kelly Ville Park
(60yds from Tourist Office beside car park)
Ⓣ 0502 22774
Very welcoming family-run house with a homely atmosphere. Pleasant bedrooms. Good value.
6 bedrooms £ Parking

VICARSTOWN INN QQ
Vicarstown Ⓣ 0502 25189 Ⓕ 0502 25652
200-year-old roadside village inn, situated on the banks of the Grand Canal. Ideal centre for coarse fishing.
9 bedrooms (3 of which in annexe) including 1 for non-smokers £ No smoking in dining room Licensed Parking

WHERE TO EAT

PUBS, INNS & OTHER PLACES

BELLAMY'S RESTAURANT,
Main Street, Portlaoise
Ⓣ 0502 22303 Ⓕ 0502 60591
Reasonably priced homed-cooked food.

PRESTON HOUSE CAFÉ,
Main Street, Abbeyleix Ⓣ/Ⓕ 0502 31432
The word café doesn't prepare you for the pleasures at this charming restaurant serving homely dishes.

ROUNDWOOD HOUSE,
Mountrath Ⓣ 0502 32120
Georgian house, now a hotel. Well prepared and uncomplicated food.

WOODVIEW RESTAURANT,
Bishopswood, Durrow Ⓣ 0502 36433
Irish home cooking with vegetarian dishes available.

COUNTY MONAGHAN

Co Monaghan was once part of the old kingdom of Ulster, but these historic links were severed by Partition in 1922. It is a county of pleasant though unspectacular scenery, characterised by round drumlin hills, relics of the last ice age. The county is known for the exquisite hand-made lace it exports all over the world, with examples in Buckingham Palace and the White House. The poet Patrick Kavanagh (1906-67) was a Monaghan man, and his work reflected the tough lives of the local farming community.

PRINCIPAL TOWN

MONAGHAN

Situated close to the border with Northern Ireland, the county town has at times been a source of political ferment. One of its most famous sons, Charles Gavan Duffy, founded both the Irish Tenant League and The Nation, a nationalist newspaper - before he became Prime Minister of Victoria, in Australia. The town has some fine limestone buildings, reflecting the influence of Scots and English settlers in the 17th and 18th centuries, and the prosperity of the linen industry during the 18th and 19th centuries.

MUST SEE

PATRICK KAVANAGH RURAL & LITERARY RESOURCE CENTRE,
Candlefort T **042 78560**
(between Carrickmacross N2 & Dundalk N1)
Iniskeen, birthplace of Patrick Kavanagh, one of Ireland's foremost 20th-century poets, is a village at the heart of Irish legend and heritage. Examples of early Rock Art and stone circles testify to its ancient history. The village grew around the monastery of St Daig MacCairill, founded before 562, and its 10th-century round tower still stands, and the rolling hills have inspired poets and scholars, bards and heroes. The Centre, housed in the former parish church, chronicles the ancient history of the region and its role in developing Kavanagh's genius. There are exhibitions, an audio-visual presentation and a research library. Another attraction is Kavanagh Country Tours, Ireland's only performance tour (booking essential).

BIG OUTDOORS

ROSSMORE FOREST PARK
(3km S of Monaghan on the Newbliss road)
T **047 81968**
A 600-hectare park with low drumlin hills, small lakes and woodland walks, plus archaeological and historical points of interest.

GREAT FOR KIDS

MONAGHAN SWIMMING POOL,
Clones Road, Monaghan T **047 81325**
Swimming pool and steam room.

HOMES & GARDENS

CASTLE LESLIE,
Glaslough T **047 88109**
One of the last stately homes to be built, in 1878. Visitors can see Churchill's baby dress, Wellington's bridle, Napoleon's bed, Wordsworth's harp and the oldest working bath and WC.

HILTON PARK,
Clones T **047 56007** F **047 56033**
Pleasure grounds laid out by 'Premium' Madden in 1734 and developed by his descendant John Madden, with later restorations to capture the original style.

MUSEUMS & ART GALLERIES

MONAGHAN COUNTY MUSEUM,
1-2 Hill Street T **047 82928** F **047 71189**
This is a modern European and national prize-winning museum of local archaeology, history, arts and crafts. Special exhibitions

SAINT LOUIS HERITAGE CENTRE,
Park Road, Monaghan T **047 83529**
Tracing the history of the Saint Louis order of nuns back to the 17th century.

ULSTER CANAL STORES,
Clones T **047 52125 or 51718**
A renovated 18th-century canal warehouse with an exhibition on lace, the craft established as a 'relief scheme' during the Famine, since revived.

ESSENTIAL INFORMATION

TOURIST INFORMATION

MONAGHAN
Market House T **047 81122**

CRAFTS

CARRICKMACROSS LACE CO-OP SOCIETY
The Gallery, Carrickmacross T **042 62506**
Locally hand-made lace. Demonstrations by appointment.

CLONES LACE, MCDONALD'S,
The Diamond, Clones T **047 51051**
Exhibition of antique Clones lace, with lace for sale and demonstrations by appointment.

THE CRAFT CENTRE,
Market Street, Monaghan T **047 81346**

SPORT & LEISURE

ACTIVITY CENTRES

TANAGH OUTDOOR EDUCATION CENTRE,
Dartrey, Rockcorry T **047 81021**
Forest walking, orienteering, bird-watching, fishing, sailing, canoeing, water skiing, hill-walking, cycling.

LOUGH MUCKNO LEISURE PARK,
Castleblayney T **042 46356**
A 900-acre lake and forest area offering a wide range of activities: waterskiing, golf, fishing, tennis, windsurfing, canoeing and horse-riding.

ANGLING

Co Monaghan is renowned for its lake and river fishing with productive waters at Ballybay, Carrickmacross (famous for massive bream and rudd), Castleblayney, Clones and Monaghan.

CAR HIRE

MONAGHAN SELF-DRIVE T **047 82865**

PRACTICAL CAR HIRE T **047 84243**

CYCLE HIRE

BICYCLE SHOP, CARRICKMACROSS
Clerkins, Monaghan T **047 81113**

LOUGH MUCKNO LEISURE PARK
Castleblayney T **042 46356** F **042 46610**

M&M CYCLES Monaghan T **047 83015**

EQUESTRIAN CENTRES

CARRICKMACROSS SCHOOL OF EQUITATION T **042 61017** F **042 63724**

CASTLEBLAYNEY EQUITATION CENTRE
T **042 40418**

GREYSTONES EQUESTRIAN CENTRE
Glaslough T **047 88100** F **047 88330**

GOLF COURSES

CASTLEBLAYNEY T **042 40197**
CLONES T **047 56017**
MANNAN CASTLE T **042 63308**
MONAGHAN DRIVING RANGE
T **047 84909**
NUREMORE HOTEL & COUNTRY CLUB
T **042 61438**
ROSSMORE T **047 81316**
THADY'S DRIVING RANGE, BALLYBAY
T **042 41186**

SCENIC DRIVES

The Bragan Mountain drive in north Monaghan begins at Tydavnet village and includes some magnificent scenery.

WHERE TO STAY

HOTELS

AA RECOMMENDED

SEE UNDER WHERE TO EAT FOR ALL HOTEL RESTAURANTS WITH ROSETTES

CARRICKMACROSS

NUREMORE ★★★★❀❀
(1.5 miles south of Carrickmacross, on main Dublin/Derry road)
T 042 61438 F 042 61853
Comfortable Victorian mansion nestling snugly in lovely hills overlooking a lake. Quiet retreat with excellent facilities.
69 bedrooms ££££ Lift Parking Leisure & sporting facilities

Nuremore

MONAGHAN

FOUR SEASONS HOTEL & LEISURE CLUB ★★★
Coolshannagh *(on N2, 0.5 mile from town)*

Four Seasons Hotel & Leisure Club

FOUR SEASONS HOTEL
Coolshanagh
T 047 81888 F 047 83131
Modern single storey hotel, suitable for disabled guests, set in pleasant grounds. Good choice of food options.
44 bedrooms ££ Parking Leisure & sporting facilities

HILLGROVE ★★★★
Old Armagh Road *(turn off N2 at cathedral, continue for a quarter of a mile, on left just beyond cathedral)*
T 047 81288 F 047 84951 44
Pleasant hotel with comfortable accommodation with air conditioning. Weekly live entertainment. Restaurant.
44 bedrooms Lift Parking

WHERE TO EAT

RESTAURANTS

AA RECOMMENDED

NUREMORE HOTEL ❀❀
Carrickmacross
T 042 61438 F 042 61853
Imaginative dishes cooked with flair and confidence. There are plenty of sunny, Mediterranean flavours in dishes of sautéed rigatoni served with chorizo, sundried tomatoes and plum tomato sauce, and escalope of pink dorado with herb risotto and virgin olive oil sauce.
FIXED L ££ D £££

PUBS, INNS & OTHER PLACES

ANDY'S BAR & RESTAURANT,
12 Market Street, Monaghan
T 047 82277
There's nothing particularly fancy about the food at Andy's bar, but it is well prepared, hearty and generous. A traditional kind of place.

COUNTY OFFALY

Offaly is a typically boggy central Irish county, including Boora Bog and the Bog of Allen. It is divided from its neighbour Galway by the River Shannon, and from Laois by the Slieve Bloom mountains. It is best known as the home of Clonmacnois, one of Ireland's most important monastic sites.

PRINCIPAL TOWNS

BIRR

Designated as a Heritage Town of Ireland, Birr is Offaly's most appealing town and renowned for its annual festival in mid-August. Situated on the River Camcor, a tributary of the Shannon,the town retains much of its Georgian character and makes an excellent base for touring.

Tullamore is the county town, situated on the Grand Canal, and is home to Irish Mist liqueur. In 1785 a hot-air balloon crashed here, starting a fire that destroyed many of the town's houses.

MUST SEE

BIRR CASTLE DEMESNE
Ⓣ 0509 20336 Ⓕ 0509 21583
A magnificent landscaped park with a lake, rivers and waterfalls, withimportant plant collections, particularly magnolias A catalogue is available of the 2,650 listed plants in the collection. The Demesne is particularly colourful in spring and autumn, and is possibly best known for its formal gardens, with alleys of hornbeam and the tallest box hedges in the world. Also home to the Great Birr Telescope, built in 1844, recently restored to its former glory and open for viewing now.

BIRR VINTAGE WEEK
Ⓣ 0509 20110
If you happen to be around in mid-August, don't miss the opportunity of visiting Birr Week, one of Ireland's longest running and most successful festivals. Always a lively town, Birr goes quite mad for a festival. Annual events include a plethora of events

The Antiques Fair is perenially popular, as are the Georgian Cricket Match and a Georgian Society play..

BOG TOUR
Blackwater Works, Shannonbridge
Ⓣ 0905 74114
Organised by Bord Na Mona (the Irish Peat Board), this is an 8km tour of the Blackwater Bog aboard a train from the Clonmacnois and West Offaly Railway. Visitors can learn of the 12,000-year development of the bog from glacier to lake, to fen and to bog.

CLONMACNOIS
Shannonbridge Ⓣ 0905 74195
One of Ireland's most sacred sites, and former burial place of the kings of Connacht and Tara, this monastic settlement, founded by St Cairan in 545, contains two round towers, the remains of a cathedral, church ruins, high crosses, a 13th-century castle and over 200 grave slabs. The Nun's Chapel and the 10th-century Cross of the Scriptures are particularly noted for the quality of the mason's craft.

GREAT FOR KIDS

ASHBROOK OPEN FARM & AGRICULTURAL MUSEUM
Shannonbridge Ⓣ 0905 74166
Farm animals, donkey and cart rides through the farm, and vintage farm machinery. Coffee bar .Shop

LUSMAGH PET FARM
Banagher Ⓣ 0509 51233
An extensive range of animals, including ostriches, in a lovely setting. Nature trail.

HISTORIC & ANCIENT SITES

CLOGHAN CASTLE,
Banagher *(signposted from the village)*
Ⓣ 0509 51650
Access by guided tour to one of the oldest inhabited castles in Ireland, with battlements, a galleried great hall, a guard room and murder hole. Luxuriously furnished within.

BOATING & CRUISING

The River Shannon and the Grand Canal provide a great vantage point for visitors to Offaly. For hire details contact the local Tourist Office.

ESSENTIAL INFORMATION

TOURIST INFORMATION

BIRR Ross Row Ⓣ 0509 20110

CLONMACNOIS Ⓣ 0905 74134

TULLAMORE Ⓣ 0506 52617

CRAFTS

BUSHERTOWN CREATIVE CENTRE,
Moneygall, Birr Ⓣ 0505 45206
One to five-day courses, including embroidery, dyeing, batik and patchwork.

SPORT & LEISURE

ACTIVITY CENTRES

BIRR OUTDOOR EDUCATION CENTRE,
Roscrea Road, Birr Ⓣ 0509 20029
Canoeing, wind-surfing, sailing, orienteering, rock climbing, field studies, hill walking and camping.

KINNITTY CASTLE LEISURE CENTRE,
Kinnitty, Birr Ⓣ 0509 37318
Gymnasium with sauna, jacuzzi, steam room and solarium. Also clay pigeon shooting, archery and mountain biking.

ANGLING

THE OFFALY TOURIST COUNCIL Bury Quay, Tullamore
Ⓣ 0506 52566 Ⓕ 0506 41371
Produces a guide to fishing in Offaly's unpolluted waters.

CYCLE HIRE

EAMON & MARIE MCMANUS
Laurel Lodge, Garrymore, Shannonbridge
Ⓣ 0905 74189

EQUESTRIAN CENTRES

ANNAHARVEY FARM,
Tullamore Ⓣ 0506 43544 Ⓕ 0506 43150
BALLYSHIEL RIDING SCHOOL,
Ballyshiel, Belmont, Birr Ⓣ 0902 576366
BANAGHER EQUESTRIAN CENTRE,
Meenwaun, Banagher Ⓣ/Ⓕ 0509 51114
BARROWSIDE EQUESTRIAN CENTRE,
Treascon, Portarlington Ⓣ 0502 23082
BIRR RIDING CENTRE,
Tullamore Road, Birr Ⓣ 0509 20533
RATHMOYLE STUD,
Rhode Village
Ⓣ 0405 37006
TULLAMORE EQUESTRIAN CENTRE,
Moneyquid Stud, Killeigh, Tullamore
Ⓣ 0506 54393

GOLF COURSES

BANAGHER PITCH & PUTT Ⓣ 0509 51458
BIRR Ⓣ 0509 20082
CASTLEBARNAGH Ⓣ 0506 53384
EDENDERRY Ⓣ 0405 31072
MILLHOUSE PITCH & PUTT,
Birr Road, Roscrea Ⓣ 0505 21946/22679
TULLAMORE Ⓣ 0506 51240

WHERE TO STAY

HOTELS

AA RECOMMENDED

BIRR

OUNTY ARMS ★★★
ake N7 from Dublin to Roscrea, N62 to irr, hotel on right before the church)
0509 20791 F 0509 21234
ne Georgian house with comfortable etty bedrooms, overlooking superb ctorian walled kitchen gardens.Two staurants, a comfortable lounge and bar.
bedrooms (some no-smoking) ££ arking Funciton/conference Squash

DOOLEY'S ★★★
Emmet Square
T 0509 20032 F 0509 21332
Dating back to the era of the horse-drawn Bianconi carriages, when it was used as a staging post, this town centre hotel enjoys an excellent reputation for hospitality and cuisine. Close to Birr Castle Demesne.
18 bedrooms ££

SCENIC DRIVES

It is a pleasant drive from Birr to the village of Kinnitty, where the Slieve Bloom Mountains begin, and from Kinnitty to Mountmellick (in Co Laois).

BED & BREAKFAST ACCOMMODATION

AA RECOMMENDED

BIRR

IE MALTINGS QQQ
astle Street
0509 21345 F 0509 21345
ne-time brewery and grain store on the ver Camcor has been interestingly dapted into a guest house with a public ar, restaurant, and a fitness room.
bedrooms including some for non-nokers £ No smoking in dining room or 1 unge Licensed Parking Leisure facilities

DAINGEAN

ESKERMORE HOUSE QQ
Mount Lucas **T 0506 53079**
Pleasant house, set in 25 acres. Croquet lawn and private fishing. Children welcome.
3 bedrooms inc 2 family £ Dogs Children of all ages Parking Private fishing 25 acres beef

WALKING

The 70-km way-marked trail, the Slieve Bloom Way, circles the Slieve Bloom mountains including the major features. Details of the Birr Town Trail are available from the Heritage Centre in John's Hall, Birr.

WHERE TO EAT

PUBS, INNS & OTHER PLACES

RIDGE HOUSE,
llamore **T 0506 21704 F 0506 41338**
eaks and seafood are the specialities of is pub and restaurant.

OUNTY ARMS HOTEL,
ilway Road, Birr **T 0509 20791**
e hotel prides itself on its cooking, and uch of the produce is grown in its own rdens.

KONG LAM RESTAURANT,
Market Street, Birr **T 0509 21253**
For a bit of a change, try the Kung Po and Szechuan dishes here. The restaurant is decorated Chinese-style with elaborate embroidered wall-hangings.

THE SLÍ DALA,
Kinnity Castle, Birr **T 0509 37318**
Dine in impressive surroundings. Creative menus and extensive wine list.

THE STABLES TOWNHOUSE,
Oxmanton Mall, Birr **T 0509 20263**
Irish cooking, seafood and steaks.

THE THATCH,
Crinkle, Birr **T 0509 20682**
Not your normal bar and restaurant. Menus are ambitious and change frequently, and include a five-course dinner and very popular Sunday lunch.

COUNTY ROSCOMMON

County Roscommon, with the River Suck on its western border, and the River Shannon joining a series of loughs on its eastern border, is very much favoured by fishing enthusiasts. Otherwise its major attractions are Strokestown Park House and the Famine Museum.

PRINCIPAL TOWN

ROSCOMMON

Roscommon is a small country town with some attractive Georgian and Victorian shops in the centre and a huge Norman Castle standing in a field on the northern outskirts. During the 18th-century the town employed the notorious Lady Betty as its hangwoman for some 30 years. Sentenced to death herself, for the unwitting murder of her son, she earned her stay of execution by volunteering herself as executioner, as the town's hangman had been taken ill.

STROKESTOWN

Designated as a Heritage Town of Ireland, Strokestown is able to lay claim to having the greatest breadth to length ratio of any Irish town or village. This fame is entirely due to the second Lord Hartland,who decided to make his village thorougfare even larger than the Ringstrasse in Vienna.

ROSCOMMON

MUST SEE

LONALIS HOUSE,
astlrea T **0907 20014**
ne ancestral home of the clan O'Conor, who claim to be Europe's oldest family, acing their ancestry to AD75. Many items ssociated with the family are displayed in e19th-century mansion, including the arp of Ireland's last great bard, Turlough 'Carolan (1630-1738).

NG HOUSE,
oyle T **079 63242**
i the town centre, turn off N4 Dublin-Sligo ad at Boyle Abbey, house signposted)
uilt around 1730, the house is of unique chitectural and historical importance. It as home to the King family until 1788, hen it became a military barracks for the mous Connaught Rangers Regiment and tterly the national army. Now an award-inning attraction with several exhibitions, overing the ancient kings of Connacht nd the Gaelic way of life, the King family story 1603-1987, the triumphs of the onnaught Rangers Regiment, and eorgian abuilding techniques.

ROSCOMMON CASTLE,
Roscommon
Dating from the 13th century, though it was much altered in later years, with refined Tudor mullions added in the 16th century. The quarrelsome O'Kelly and O'Conor clans seized it periodically, but its last definitive remodelling took place at the hands of Cromwellian troops and its drum towers now stand lopped and hollow around a rectangle of neatly mown turf.

STROKESTOWN PARK HOUSE GARDEN & FAMINE MUSEUM,
Strokestown Park T **078 33712**
Built in Palladian style in the 1730s for Thomas Mahon MP, the house reflects perfectly the confidence of the newly emergent ruling class. The four-acre pleasure garden has been restored and is open to the public. The Famine Museum, commemorates the Great Irish Famine of the 1840s, when blight devastated the Irish potato crop, the staple food, and one quarter of the Irish population - in excess of two million people - either died or emigrated. Strokestown was particularly significant in that the landlord, Major Denis Mahon, was assassinated as a result of his attempts to clear two-thirds of his destitute tenants through eviction and assisted emigration to North America.

BIG OUTDOORS

OUGH KEY FOREST PARK,
oyle T **079 62363**
art of the former Rockingham Estate ating from 1617, comprising 350ha of ixed woodland and several islands of ough Key. Includes caravan park, tea om, shop and boating.

GREAT FOR KIDS

ULLYBOY ANIMAL FARM,
llyboy, Boyle T **079 68031**
entred around an 18th-century rmhouse with views of the Curlew and igna Mountains. Pony rides, animals, ayground, picnic area, gift shop, cafe

HISTORIC & ANCIENT SITES

BOYLE ABBEY,
Boyle T **079 62604**
Impressive ruins of a Cistercian abbey. The nave, with both Romanesque and Gothic arches, and the choir and transepts of the 12th-century church are still in good condition.

DOMINICAN PRIORY,
Roscommon
In the town are the ruins of a Dominican priory, last resting place of its 13th-century founder, Félim O'Conor, a king of Connaught, whose tomb is decorated with effigies of gallowglasses.

DRUM HERITAGE GROUP, DRUM MONASTIC SETTLEMENT & ST BRIGID'S HOLY WELL,
Drum T **0902 37128**
Restored site, with a Romanesque abbey and medieval church ruins. Ancient Mass Paths have been located and mapped.

FUERTY
In the graveyard are the ruins of a Franciscan church where 100 priests were killed by local tyrant Robert Ormsby, at the time of Cromwell's plundering.

MUSEUMS & ART GALLERIES

THE CLAYPIPE VISITORS' CENTRE,
Knockcroghery Village T **0903 61923**
Focusing on the unique history of the Knockcroghery Claypipe.

ESSENTIAL INFORMATION

TOURIST INFORMATION

OYLE T **079 62145**

OSCOMMON T **0903 26342**

SPORT & LEISURE

ANGLING

iere is fishing on the Rivers Shannon and Suck, and a number of loughs. Further information from the local Tourist Office.

EQUESTRIAN CENTRES

MUNSBORO EQUESTRIAN CENTRE
Munsboro T **0903 26449** F **0903 25611**

GOLF COURSES

ATHLONE T **0902 92073**
BALLAGHADERREEN T **0907 60295**
BOYLE T **079 62594**
CASTLEREA T **0907 20068**
ROSCOMMON T **0903 26382**
STROKESTOWN T **078 33303**

HORSE RACING

ROSCOMMON RACECOURSE,
Lenabane, Roscommon
T **0903 26231** F **0903 25065**

WHERE TO STAY

HOTELS

AA RECOMMENDED

BOYLE

ROYAL ★★
(turn off N4 Dublin-Sligo road for Boyle, adjacent to bridge in town centre)
T 079 62016 F 079 62016
Set beside river in town centre. Comfortable family-run hotel spacious bedrooms. Good dining options.
16 bedrooms £££ Parking

ROSCOMMON

ABBEY ★★★
Galway Rd *(on N63 opposite railway station)*
T 0903 26240 & 26505 F 0903 26021
Inviting and relaxing19th-century manor house. Bedrooms furnished in traditional period style. Restaurant. Attractive gardens.
25 bedrooms including some for non-smokers £££ Parking Closed 25-26 Dec

Call the AA Hotel Booking Service on 0990 050505 to book at AA recognised hotels and B&Bs in the UK and Ireland or through our internet site: http://www.theaa.co.uk/hotels

CAMPING & CARAVAN SITES

AA RECOMMENDED

BOYLE

LOUGH KEY FOREST PARK
T 079 62363 or 62212 *(Signposted)*
4 pennants, attractive environment, first class washing & sanitary facilities, outstanding range of sports & recreational facilities. Touring caravans, motor caravans & tents. Booking advisable three weeks before arrival. Last arrival 22.00hrs. Last departure noon. No cars by tents. A 15-acre site with 72 touring pitches. Electric hook up, shower, electric shaver point, launderette, separate TV room, children's playground, café/restaurant, public telephone, picnic area, shop, disabled facilities.
Facilities within three miles from site: golf course, boats for hire, cinema, fishing

WHERE TO EAT

PUBS, INNS & OTHER PLACES

ABBEY HOTEL RESTAURANT,
Galway Road **T 0903 26240**
Comfortable restaurant serving freshly cooked food from a fixed-price dinner menu.

ROYAL HOTEL,
Boyle **T 079 62016 F 079 62016**
Fixed-price dinner menu of well presented dishes. Bar food and a self-service buffet are also available.

COUNTY WESTMEATH

This is prime beef-rearing country, with lots of lakes and lush pastureland. Of particular scenic interest is the area north of Athlone known as Goldsmith Country.

PRINCIPAL TOWN

MULLINGAR

Mullingar is a bustling county town at the centre of a properous farming area. Of particular interest to the visitor are the town's museums and the Catholic Cathedral of Christ the King, built just before the Second World War, which has two famous mosaics by the Russian artist, Boris Arrep.

MUST SEE

ATHLONE CASTLE,
Athlone **T 0902 94603**
(on the west bank of the River Shannon)
The Anglo-Norman castle was a military post from its erection in the 13th century until 1969, when it was declared a National Monument controlled by the Office of Public Works. There is a visitor centre, and a military museum in the keep, with relics of the town and district's history.

DÚN NA SÍ HERITAGE PARK,
Moate **T 0902 81183 F 0902 81661**
A heritage theme park, incorporating a farming museum with vintage farm machinery, a portal dolmen, an Early Christian ring fort, a fisherman's cottage, picnic areas, tea rooms and a souvenir shop. It is also the base of an international folklore group, and there are monthly ceilis, and dancing, music and Irish language classes. It is also a centre for geneological research, for those tracing their Irish ancestry in the county.

FORE ABBEY & THE SEVEN WONDERS,
Fore
The ruins of St Feichin's Monastery, datin from the 7th century, are situated in the village of Fore. On the hillside, just above the old church of St Feichin, is the Anchorite Church, used by hermits until the 17th century. The last hermit in Irelar lived here until 1616. The chapel is locke but the key is obtainable from the Seven Wonders pub in the village. Associated with the abbey and St Feichin are the Seven Wonders of Fore, including the water that flows uphill, the tree that wor burn, the water that won't boil and the monastery built in a bog.

LOCKE'S DISTILLERY MUSEUM
Kilbeggan *(Dublin to Galway road, N6)*
T 0506 32134
Whiskey made by small pot still whiskey distilleries was once a widespread industry. Founded in 1757 and producing whiskey for nearly 200 years until 1953, this distillery, on the River Brosna, is the only one remaining in Ireland. Now restored by the local community as an industrial museum, optional guided tours take 45 minutes and end with a tasting. Craft enterprise centre and a café.

BIG OUTDOORS

JONATHAN SWIFT PARK,
Lilliput *(on the shores of Lough Ennell)*
An amenity park in the place that inspired the author of Gulliver's Travels. It includes a golf course, playground, and a beautifully restored Georgian house with a coffee shop.

GREAT FOR KIDS

ATHLONE LEISURE WORLD,
Grace Road, Athlone **T 0902 94766**
Computerised ten pin bowling, championship snooker tables, children's adventure playground, indoor football, indoor kart racing, and fitness gym.

GLENDEER OPEN PET FARM,
Drum, Athlone **T 0902 37147**
Pet animals including deer, Vietnamese pot belly pigs, ponies, donkeys, cows, sheep, goats, peacocks and other rare birds. Horse-drawn farm machinery, tea room and tuck shop.

IRISH PRODUCE

Bread is one of the great specialities. Irish soda bread made with buttermilk is utterly delicious. Best eaten warm and with lashings of Irish butter, it is banquet in itself. Do take the opportunity to try any number of the different breads made from potato or wheat.

HOMES & GARDENS

BELVEDERE HOUSE & GARDENS,
Belvedere, Kilbeggan Road, Mullingar
T 044 40861
The grounds extend to the shores of Lough Ennell and include a pet corner and the Jealous Wall, the greatest man-made folly in Ireland.

TULLYNALLY CASTLE & GARDENS,
Castlepollard
T 044 61159 T 044 61856
A 17th-century castle with additions, housing a fine collection of portraits, furniture and 19th-century gadgets. The house had one of the earliest central heating systems in Ireland.

MUSEUMS & ART GALLERIES

AN DÚN TRANSPORT & HERITAGE MUSEUM,
Doon, Ballinahown, Athlone **T 0902 3010**
A private collection of restored cars, pen farthing and pre and post-war cycles, far implements, and a model railway and cal car working display. Gift and coffee shop

ECCLESIASTICAL MUSEUM,
Cathedral of Christ the King, Mullingar
T 044 48338
A small museum over the sacristy housi the vestments of St Oliver Plunkett.

MILITARY MUSEUM & BARRACKS,
The Columb Barracks **T 044 48391**
A fascinating display of military artefacts and an interesting section devoted to the old IRA.

ESSENTIAL INFORMATION

TOURIST INFORMATION

'HLONE & DISTRICT TOURISM
Church Street ☎ 0902 73966

ASTLE VISITOR CENTRE,
Peter's Square ☎ 0902 94630

ASSON VILLAGE
ach de Faoite ☎ 0902 85119

LBEGGAN
cke's Distillery Museum ☎ 0506 32134

NNEGAD
nnegad Visitor Centre, Galway Road
☎ 044 75682 or 75610

ULLINGAR
dland East Regional Tourism, Dublin Road
☎ 044 48650

GENEALOGY

N NA SÍ HERITAGE PARK,
ate ☎ 0902 81183 Ⓕ 0902 81661
n Na Sí has been designated as the search centre for Co Westmeath by the h Geneological Project, and it has a 'y computerised database.

CRAFTS

NNEGAD VISITORS CENTRE,
lway Road, Kinnegad
044 75682 or 75610
Visitor Centre incorporating the Tourist ormation Point, coffee shop, bureau de ange and a craft shop selling many ally produced items.

LLINGAR BRONZE & PEWTER CENTRE
llingar
urs of the workshops to see the ancient ft of pewter making, and the ftsmanship of bronze and pewter lpturing. Showroom, shop and coffee op.

SPORT & LEISURE

ANGLING

ere are over 20 lakes, rivers and etches of canal to choose from offering vide range of species. Loughs Sheelin, vel and Ennell are good for brown trout; er Inny, the Royal Canal and the eever Loughs for coarse fishing, and for p try Gaulmoylestown Lake.

BOATING & CRUISING

M V ROSS BOAT TRIPS,
Jolly Mariner Marina, Athlone
☎ 0902 72892
Up to 90 passengers on a 90-minute cruise on the Shannon, including bar, coffee shop and commentary.

THE VIKING SHIP,
Rosanna Cruises, The Strand, Athlone
☎ 0902 73383
Cruises to Lough Ree or Clonmacnois on a real-life Viking ship, with a chance to arm-wrestle with Odin, Thor and Eric, or meet great King Turgesius and his wife Ota at the rudder.

COACH TOURS

PADDY KAVANAGH MINIBUS SERVICE
☎ 0902 74839
Visits to sites of interest in the region.

CYCLE HIRE

IRISH CYCLE TOURS
Ballykeeran, Athlone ☎ 0902 85309

EQUESTRIAN CENTRES

DILGER HORSES,
Lacken, Multyfarnham ☎ 044 71271

HARBOUR LODGE STABLES
Harbour Road, Kilbeggan ☎ 0506 32310

LADESTOWN HOUSE RIDING SCHOOL & TREKKING STABLES
Ladestown House, Lough Ennell, Mullingar
☎ 044 48218

MULLINGAR EQUESTRIAN CENTRE,
Athlone Road, Mullingar ☎ 044 48331

GOLF COURSES

GLASSON GOLF & COUNTRY CLUB,
Glasson, Athlone ☎ 0902 85120
An 18-hole championship standard course designed by Christy O'Connor Junior. Outstanding holes include the Par 3 15th which has both tee and green situated in Killiure Bay.

MULLINGAR ☎ 044 48366
The wide rolling fairways between mature trees provide parkland golf at its very best. The course, designed by the great James Braid, offers a tough challenge and annually hosts one of the most important amateur events in the British Isles - the Mullingar Scratch Cup.

Also:
BALLYMORE PITCH & PUTT ☎ 044 56270
DELVIN CASTLE ☎ 044 64315
MOATE ☎ 0902 81271
MOUNT TEMPLE ☎ 0902 81841

GREYHOUND RACING

BALLINDERRY, MULLINGAR
☎ 044 48348

HORSE RACING

KILBEGGAN RACECOURSE
☎ 0506 32176 Ⓕ 0506 32125

SCENIC DRIVES

THE GLASSON TRAIL
Begin at the Tourist Office, in the 'Village of Roses', then around the Killinure Peninsula taking in Portlick, Bethlehem and places associated with Oliver Goldsmith.

THE GOLDSMITH TRAIL
This trail links the places in counties Westmeath and Longford associated with the writer Oliver Goldsmith.

LOUGH REE TOURIST TRAIL
Beginning at Athlone Castle, the trail leads the visitor to the most beautiful locations in the Lakelands.
Other trails include:
Clonmacnois Trail, the Fore Trail and the Belvedere Trail. Full details from Tourist Offices.

WALKING

Athlone and Mullingar both have signposted walking tours, starting at the Market house in Mullingar and the Tourist Office in the castle at Athlone.

ATHLONE WALKING TOURS
☎ 0902 72466
Heritage walks around Athlone town centre, by appointment only.

WATER SPORTS

LOUGH REE SAILING CLUB
(5km north of Athlone)
☎ 0902 75976

LOUGH OWEL SAILING CLUB
Mullally ☎ 044 42561

THE IRISH PUB
The Irish pub is not just for drinking, but the very social centre of many communities, both rural and urban, and are full of conviviality and atmosphere. It s usually not too long before someone starts singing in soft and mellifluous tones or music starts to play.

IRISH WHISKEY
Try the well-known Bushmills, or any other local brand on offer, either neat or with a splash of good Irish water. If this seems too strong, try Irish coffee, first invented to warm up long haul air passengers at Shannon Airport; or one of the creamy liqueur conncoctions which always seem to slip down so easily

IRISH BEER
Try the local lager, Harp, which is brewed by Guinness. If your prefer something similar to English bitter, then ask for Smithwicks Ale. Guinness Ireland's distinctive 'nectar' of rich black liquid with its 'foamous' creamy head (as James Joyce called it), is brewed from a basic recipe of Irish-grown barley, soft Irish water, hops and a strain of yeast.

WHERE TO STAY

HOTELS

AA RECOMMENDED

SEE UNDER WHERE TO EAT FOR ALL HOTEL RESTAURANTS WITH ROSETTES

HODSON BAY ★★★
Hodson Bay
(from N6 take N61 to Roscommon. Take right turn - hotel 0.5 mile on Lough Ree)
T 0902 92444 F 0902 92688
Lovely historic hotel with comfortable bedrooms. Most of which have excellent views. Waterside location. Superb food.
97 bedrooms £££ Lift Parking Leisure facilities

PRINCE OF WALES ★★★
(in centre of town, opposite Bank of Ireland)
T 0902 72626 F 0902 75658
Pleasant and friendly staff are the hallmark of this modern town centre hotel. Excellent food .
73 bedrooms including some for non smokers ££ Parking

ROYAL HOEY ★★
Mardyke Street
T 0902 72924 & 75395 F 0902 75194
A tradition of warm hospitality is upheld at this family-run town centre hotel, where rooms are most comfortable. All day foo
38 bedrooms including some for non-smokers ££ Lift Parking

Hodson B

BED & BREAKFAST ACCOMMODATION

Temple Country House

MULLINGAR

CROOKEDWOOD HOUSE QQQQQ
Crookedwood
(signposted 8 miles W of Mullingar on N4)
T 044 72165 F 044 72166
Restored old rectory with superb accommodation in lovely rual setting. Renowned food in restaurant.
8 bedrooms including some for non-smoke £££ No smoking in area of dining room Licensed Tennis (hard) Closed 2 wks Jan

ATHLONE

RIVERVIEW HOUSE QQQQ
Galway Road, Summerhill
(on N6 1.25 mile from Athlone town centre)
T 0902 94532
Three archways distinguish this pleasant house near town centre. Excellent, pretty rooms with breakfast room opening on to the gardens. Useful for anglers.
5 bedrooms including some for non-smokers £ No smoking in dining room Parking Closed mid Dec-Jan

GLASSON

BENOWN HOUSE QQQ
T 0902 85406
Modern house set in pretty village. Thoughtful touches throughout. Home-baked breakfasts. Garden.
6 bedrooms £ No smoking in dining room Parking

MOATE

TEMPLE QQQQ
Horseleap *(0.5 mile off N6, signposted)*
T 0506 35118 F 0506 35118
Built on the site of an early monastery, this lovely Georgian farmhouse offers very comfortable accommodation. Relax by the fire and join in the chat. Pre-book dinner.
4 bedrooms ££ No smoking in dining room Licensed Yoga room Massage therapy Children's play room 96 acres cattle & sheep Open Mar-Oct Activity Packages (golf, riding, cycling, walking) can be arranged

Hilltop House

LLTOP HOUSE ◘◘◘◘
lvin Road ⓣ 044 48958 ⓕ 044 48013
ke 2nd exit off Mullingar by-pass road N4, low N52 for Delvin, Hilltop sign is 1 mile m exit roundabout)
arming south-facing country house in rious gardens with comfortable rooms. cellent breakfast menu. Pre-book dinner.
edrooms including some for non-smokers No smoking in dining room or lounges rking Restricted service Nov-Feb

STREAMSTOWN

WOODLANDS ◘◘
Horseleap ⓣ 044 26414
(from Dublin take N6 and continue through Kilbeggan to Horseleap, turn right at filling station. Farm 2.5 miles signposted)
Attractive large house in a sylvan setting, conveniently located off the Mullingar/Athlone road.
6 bedrooms No smoking in 1 lounge 120 acres mixed Open Mar-Oct

Call the AA Hotel Booking Service on 0990 050505 to book at AA recognised hotels and B&Bs in the UK and Ireland, or through our internet site: http://www.theaa.co.uk/hotels

CAMPING & CARAVAN SITES

AA RECOMMENDED

ATHLONE

DSON BAY CARAVAN & CAMPING PARK
pennants, touring caravans, motor avans & tents. Open mid May-mid ptember. Booking advisable bank hols d last week July/first week August. Last ival 22.30hrs. Last departure noon. No gs.
wo-acre site with 32 touring pitches d two statics. Electric hook up, shower, electric shaver point, launderette, hairdrier, games room, separate TV room, cold storage, children's playground, Calor Gas, Camping Gaz, battery charging, toilet fluid, public telephone, barbeque area, picnic area, disabled facilities.
Facilities within three miles of site: stable, golf course, mini golf, water sports, boat hire, cinema, fishing, shop

BALLYKEERAN

LOUGH REE CARAVAN & CAMPING PARK
ⓣ 0902 78561 or 74414
Signposted
2 pennants, touring caravans, motor caravans & tents. Open April-September. Booking advisable bank holidays. A five-acre site with 40 touring pitches and 2 statics. Electric hook up, shower, electric shaver point, public telephone, shop

WHERE TO EAT

RESTAURANTS

AA RECOMMENDED

SCALE RESTAURANT ❀❀
dson Bay Hotel, Athlone
0902 92444 ⓕ 0902 92688
e carte menu offers a varied choice, h starters such as sautéed lambs' neys Dijonnaise, and pan-fried Athlone ck pudding with cabbage and bacon. An excellent seafood selection includes Ballinskellig's Bay lobster, and supreme of wild Irish salmon, while typical entrees might be rack of lamb roasted with fresh garden herbs, or roast free-range duckling with citrus fruits and ginger sauce.
ALC £££

PRINCE OF WALES HOTEL ❀
Athlone
ⓣ 0902 72626 ⓕ 0902 75658
A spacious and comfortable hotel restaurant offering very good quality cooking.
FIXED L £ D ££

PUBS, INNS & OTHER PLACES

ACK KETTLE,
in Street, Kilbeggan ⓣ 0506 32148
and restaurant food, featuring Irish oking, steaks and seafood.

NLON'S RESTAURANT,
Dublingate Street, Athlone
0902 74376
ely town centre restaurant serving good h cooking, both traditional and modern.

OOKEDWOOD HOUSE,
okedwood, Mullingar ⓣ 044 72165
stomers come a long way to enjoy local at, game and venison. Vegetarians will be disappointed either.

R GREEN RESTAURANT,
h Street, Ballymore ⓣ 044 56559
interesting menu with a range of ernational influences.

GLASSON VILLAGE RESTAURANT,
Glasson near Athlone ⓣ 0902 85001
Good seafood - you might find Lough Ree eels on the menu. Tempting meat and poultry dishes too.

THE GRAMBY,
Dominick Street, Mullingar
ⓣ 044 40280
Irish and continental cuisine - steaks a speciality

GROGAN'S & NANNIE MURPH'S,
Glasson near Athlone ⓣ 0902 85158
A bar that's a bit more adventurous in the food department than normal.

LEFT BANK BISTRO,
Bastion Street, Athlone ⓣ 0902 94446
The name says it - informal, but quite exciting. The influences include Irish, Oriental and Mediterranean.

LITTLE INDIA,
2 Dublin Bridge, Mullingar ⓣ 044 40911
North Indian cooking.

NALLY'S
9 Oliver Plunkett St, Mullingar ⓣ 044 48635
A reasonably priced family-run restaurant.

POLLARD ARMS,
The Square, Castlepollard ⓣ 044 61194
A traditional-style restaurant specialising in steaks and local seafood.

RESTAURANT LE CHÂTEAU,
Abbey Lane, Athlone ⓣ 0902 94517
Duck, game and seafood feature on the menus here. Despite being rather hidden away, it attracts locals and visitors.

WINEPORT RESTAURANT,
Glasson near Athlone ⓣ 0902 85466
Beautiful setting, attentive service, and cooking that strives to be interesting and varied.

Northern Ireland

BELFAST, ANTRIM, ARMAGH, DOWN, FERMANAGH, LONDONDERRY AND TYRONE

The visitor to Northern Ireland is bound to entertain some anxiety about the Troubles that have beset the province for so many years. Incidents of political bigotry and sectarian violence inform our image of the area, and yet the day-to-day reality is quite different. As a tourist you are, statistically speaking, safer than you would be in many another holiday destination - crime rates here are actually rather low. The North of Ireland, like the South, is a generally peaceful place, aside from a few specific trouble spots. Do be aware of sensitive areas, such as Derry, Armagh and Newry, and keep to designated car parks. Some towns actually have marked control zones, where cars should not be left unattended and illegal parking could cause a security alert.

The main tourist attractions in Northern Ireland are its natural features: the Mountains of Mourne, the Glens of Antrim, the Giant's Causeway and the Lakes of Fermanagh. It is a popular region for fishing and walking, with the long-distance Ulster Way marking a path through the loveliest scenery in all six counties.

Visitors, wherever you are from, will particularly appreciate the warmth and extraordinary hospitality of the local people - Catholic or Protestant - so proud of all that is good in the North and so anxious for you to enjoy it.

EVENTS & FESTIVALS

February

Derry Festival, *County Londonderry*

March

Belfast Musical Festival

Derry Festival, *County Londonderry*

Fermanagh Feis, *County Fermanagh*

Newry Drama Festival

Newry & Mourne Arts Festival

Opera Northern Ireland Spring Season, *Belfast*

St Patrick's Day Parade, *(March 17th), Armagh City, County Armagh & other locations*

April

City of Belfast Spring Flower Show

May

Apple Blossom Festival, *Armagh*

Ballyclare May Fair, *(3rd week in May),*

Belfast Civic Festival

Belfast Marathon

Erne Boat Rally, *County Fermanagh*

Fermanagh Classic Fishing Festival,

Florence Court Craft Fair, *Florence Court, County Fermanagh*

Lisnaskea Feis, *County Fermanagh*

Lord Mayor's Show, *Belfast*

May Day Fair, *Holywood, County Down*

Newry Agricultural Show,

Royal Ulster Agricultural Society Show, *Belfast*

June

Armagh Show

Carnival Parade *Belfast*

Enniskillen Horse Show,

Fermanagh County Fleadh

Garden Party Concerts, *Belfast*

Kilbroney Vintage Car Rally, *Rostrevor, County Down*

The Proms, *Belfast*

Shankhill Festival, *Belfast*

South Armagh Festival & Folklore Week,

Taste Fest, *Belfast*

Vintage Rally, *Drumcill, County Armagh*

July

City of Belfast International Rose Trials *(July-September)*

Fiddler's Green International Folk Festival, *Rostrevor, County Down*

International Maiden of Mourne Festival, *Warren Point, County Down*

Lady of the Lake Festival, *Irvinestown, County Fermanagh*

National Balmoral Showjumping Championships, *Belfast*

Orangeman's Day (12th)

South Armagh Festival & Folklore Week, *County Armagh*

August

Bank Holiday Festival & Raft Rac

Bangor, County Down

Folk Festival *Belfast*

Enniskillen Agricultural Show,

Erne Vintage Car Rally, *County Fermanagh*

Feilé An Phobail, *Belfast*

Fiddler's Green International Fol Festival, *Rostrevor, County Down*

Florence Court Craft Fair

Game & Country Fair, *Gosford Forest Park, County Armagh*

rgian Festival, *Armagh*

rnational Maiden of Mourne ival, *Warren Point, County Down*

d of Glendurragh Festival, *County Fermanagh*

Lammas Fair, *astle, County Antrim*

ptember

ects Literary Festival, *r, County Down*

of Belfast Flower Show

ast Opera Festival

October

Antiques & Fine Art Fair, *Enniskillen, County Fermanagh*

Arts Festival, *Armagh*

Apple Week, *Armagh*

Belfast Antiquarian Book Fair

Festival at Queen's University, *Belfast*

Eddie Duffy Traditional Music Festival, *Derrygonnelly, County Fermanagh*

Royal Ulster Academy Annual Exhibition, *Belfast*

Ulster Antiques & Fine Art Fair, *Belfast*

November

Fashion Awards, *Belfast*

Keady Fair (crafts, antiques & finals of Bard of Armagh), *Armagh*

Orchard County Craft Fair, *Armagh*

William Kennedy Festival of Piping, *Armagh*

December

Cinemagic Film Festival, *Belfast*

Traditional Mummers Festival, *Enniskillen, County Fermanagh*

BELFAST

Belfast is the capital city of Northern Ireland, though the province has been ruled directly from Westminster since 1972, and Stormont, the grand former parliament building is now the administrative base. The city is quite a bit smaller than Dublin, and has few sights of specific interest, but the atmosphere is great, with a large student population, lively pubs, plenty of restaurants, a successful sports scene and an acclaimed annual arts festival, at Queen's University. Security measures are necessarily in evidence, but are borne by the locals with great good humour, and detract little from the visitor's experience of the city.

MUST SEE

LFAST CASTLE,
rim Road BT15 5GR
5 miles/4km from city centre, take Antrim o Glengormley, turn L to Innisfayle Park)
01232 776925 F 01232 370228
e Scottish baronial-style castle, with its at square six-storey tower and baroque ircase, was built in 1870 by the 3rd rquis of Donegal. It was presented to city by the Earl of Shaftesbury in 1934, d restored in the 1980s. It is used for all es of functions and is open daily for als and refreshments. The castle stands the lower wooded slopes of Cave Hill, area popular for walks and picnics. If are feeling energetic, the climb to the of the hill is worth it for the views.

OWN LIQUOR SALOON,
Great Victoria Street, Belfast 2
01232 249476
p back in time in this ornately orated former railway hotel with cative gas lighting, fine wood panelling, hly decorated tiles and glass. A popular dezvous and one of Belfast's finest torian buildings, now owned by the ional Trust.

BELFAST ZOO,
Antrim Road BT36 7PN
(6 miles/9.5km north of Belfast on A6)
T 01232 776277 F 01232 370578
Set in a dramatic setting on the face of Cave Hill, the 50-acre/20ha zoo offers spectacular views and attractions such as the award-winning primate house (gorillas and chimpanzees), penguin enclosure, free-flight aviary, African enclosure, and underwater viewing of sealions and penguins. Don't miss the rare spectacled bears, red pandas or free-ranging lemurs.

ULSTER MUSEUM,
Botanic Gardens BT9 5AB
(M1/M2 to Balmoral exit)
T 01232 383000 F 01232 383003
Not just a place for a rainy day, the Ulster Museum is both a national museum and an art gallery. The collections are Irish and international in origin and cover antiquities, art, botany and zoology, geology and local history (including industrial archaeology). Among the fascinating displays are the Dinosaur Show; Made in Belfast, Armada Treasures, and Irish Flora & Fauna. A new gallery, Early Ireland spans the Ice Age to the early Bronze Age. The temporary exhibitions are always worth a visit, as are the films and Sunday afternoon events. Visit even in a heatwave.

ART GALLERIES

CHES GALLERY,
olywood Road, T 01232 459031
temporary Irish artists.

L GALLERY,
delaide Park
artists, including graphics.

EHILL GALLERY,
Old Cavehill Road T 01232 776784
temporary Irish artists.

IN GALLERY,
Lisburn Road T 01232 668522
blished Irish artists.

DERESKY GALLERY,
niversity Road T 01232 235245
temporary Irish artists.

GEE GALLERY
Ormeau Road, Established artists.

E OXFORD STREET, Contemporary art.

MEAU BATHS,
Ormeau Avenue T 01232 321402
temporary art and bookshop.

M CALDWELL GALLERY,
radbury Place,
temporary Irish artists.

LOW BLUE GALLERY,
cher Crescent, Contemporary art.

BIG OUTDOORS

BELVOIR PARK FOREST
(South Belfast)
A haven for birdwatchers, this is the headquarters of the Royal Society for the Protection of Birds, and has its own visitor centre.

CAVE HILL COUNTRY PARK
(4 miles/6.5km north of Belfast)
At the top of the hill is MacArt's Fort, ancient earthworks where in 1798 Wolfe Tone and the United Irishmen asserted Irish independence. Belfast Castle is situated on the lower slopes.

COLIN GLEN FOREST PARK,
Stewartstown Road T 01232 614115
(5 miles/8km west of the city)
A 200-acre/81ha park at the foot of Black Mountain, with nature trails, ponds and a river, plus a visitor centre with an audio-visual presentation.

DIXON PARK,
Upper Malone Road T 01232 320202
Home of the International Rose Trials, which take place from July to September, the park has over 20,000 rose bushes and is a must for all those who love roses.

LAGAN VALLEY REGIONAL PARK
T 01232 491922
This is the place to walk in Belfast, as the park includes ten miles/16km of towpaths between Belfast and Lisburn. The start is near Belfast Boat Club, Stranmillis, and ends upstream from Moore's Bridge, Hillsborough Road, Lisburn.

MINNOWBURN BEECHES
(on B205 3.5 miles/5.5km south of the city at Shaw's Bridge)
Beautiful woodland and walks to Edenderry village and the Giant's Ring.

ORMEAU PARK,
Ormeau Road
One of the largest parks in the city, with trees, parkland, two children's playgrounds, bowling greens and sports pitches.

GREAT FOR KIDS

DUNDONALD ICE BOWL,
Old Dundonald Road T 01232 482611
Indianaland, an indoor adventure playground for the under 12s, as well as ten-pin bowling, ice-skating and hockey.

THE O-ZONE LEISURE CENTRE,
Ormeau Embankment T 01232 458024
Indoor laser adventure playground, part of the Belfast Indoor Tennis Arena complex.

STREAMVALE OPEN DAIRY FARM,
Ballyhanwood Road T 01232 483244
(near Dundonald Ice Bowl)

The chance to see milking time and maybe bottle feed a lamb. There is also a nature trail, pony rides, a picnic area, shop and café.

HISTORIC & ANCIENT SITES

CITY HALL,
Donegall Square, Belfast 1 **T 01232 320202**
When Queen Victoria gave Belfast city status in 1888, work began in on the ornate City Hall, which is built in the classical style with a high dome based on St Paul's Cathedral in London.

GIANT'S RING
(near Edenderry village, south Belfast. Approach via Ballynahatty Road)
A huge circular Bronze-Age enclosure nearly 200ft/61m in diameter, with a dolmen in the centre, bordered by banks 20ft/6m wide and 12ft/3.5m high. Interestingly, it was used as a race course in the 18th century.

ST ANNE'S CATHEDRAL,
Corner Donegall & York Streets, Belfast 1
T 01232 328332
An Anglican basilica in neo-Romanesque style began in 1899 and completed about 80 years later. Lord Edward Carson, opposer of Home Rule, is buried in the unusually high nave.

SINCLAIR SEAMAN'S CHURCH,
Corporation Square, Belfast 1
Sailors have worshipped here since 1853. Sermons are preached from a pulpit which is built like a ship's prow, and the organ has port and starboard navigation lights.

STORMONT,
Belfast 9 *(6 miles/10km east of the city, off the Newtownards road)*
The former Northern Ireland Parliament building (now administrative offices) is not open to the public, but people can wander in the parklands, which line the 1 mile/1.5km drive.

HOMES & GARDENS

BOTANIC GARDENS,
Stranmillis Road BT7 1JP
T 01232 324902 F 01232 237070
Dominated by the elegant domed glass and cast iron Victorian Palm House, these pleasant gardens include a Tropical Ravine where many of the plants enclosed are a century old.

GROVELANDS,
Stockmans Lane BT9 7JA
T 01232 381996 F 01232 391216
A must if you are interested in gardening. The Horticultural Training Centre is open to the public and visitors may look round the enclosed garden.

MALONE HOUSE-BARNETT DEMESNE,
Upper Malone Road BT9 5BP
T 01232 681246 F 01232 682197
A 19th-century Georgian mansion overlooking the River Lagan, restored in 1983 after a fire. It is owned by the city council, used for various functions, and houses a restaurant and art gallery.

MUSEUMS

FERNHILL HOUSE, THE PEOPLE'S MUSEUM,
Glencairn Road **T 01232 715599**
(2 miles/3km west of city)
The history of the Shankhill area, Home Rule and World War I. A quite fascinatin place, featuring the contents of a local terraced house.

LAGAN LOOKOUT CENTRE,
Donegall Quay **T 01232 315444**
Overlooking Belfast's River Lagan, the centre focuses on the city's social and industrial history.

ROYAL ULSTER RIFLES MUSEUMS,
Waring Street **T 01232 232086**
Exhibits include uniforms, medals, photgraphs and equipment.

RUC MUSEUM,
Knock Road **T 01232 332288**
The history of the Irish Constabulary fro its formation in 1822.

ULSTER LINEN HALL LIBRARY,
17 Donegall Square North **T 01232 3217**
Belfast's oldest library founded in 1788 'improve the mind and excite a spirit of general enquiry'. It has an important Iris collection of over 20,000 volumes, a reading room and café.

ESSENTIAL INFORMATION

TOURIST INFORMATION

ST ANNE'S COURT,
North Street **T 01232 246609**

ACCESS

AIR ACCESS

BELFAST CITY AIRPORT,
Sydenham Bypass, **T 01232 457745**
Accessible by coach from from Europa Bus Centre, Glengall Street, Belfast

BELFAST INTERNATIONAL AIPORT T 01849 422888

BUS ACCESS

CITYBUS *(Belfast area only)* **T 0246485**
ULSTERBUS T 01232 333000

RAIL ACCESS

CENTRAL STATION,
East Bridge Street, Belfast **T 01232 899411**

SEA ACCESS

NORSE IRISH FERRIES
(Liverpool-Belfast) **T 01232 779090**

ISLE OF MAN STEAM PACKET COMPANY
(Isle of Man-Belfast) **T 01624 661661**

SEACAT *(Stranraer-Belfast by catamaran)*
T 0345 523523

STENA LINE *(Stranraer-Belfast)*
T 0990 707070

GENEALOGY

The places to go for tracing your Belfast ancestry:

FAMILIA,
Wellington Place **T 01232 235392**

PUBLIC RECORD OFFICE,
Balmoral Avenue **T 01232 255905/6**

SHOPPING

Belfast has a conveniently compact city centre, with a large pedestrianised area and covered arcades. Shops are generally open 9am-5.30pm, with late night shopping until 9pm on a Thursday. Best buys for souvenirs are local crafts, high quality Irish linens and hand-knitted garments. The university area is good for interesting gifts and secondhand books.

CRAFTS

BROOKFIELD CRAFT CENTRE
Crumlin Road **T 01232 745241 or 746431**
Jewellery, knitwear, sculpture, hurley sticks and traditional Irish bodhrans.

CRAFTWORKS
Bedford House, Bedford Street
T 01232 244465
Wide range of ceramics, clocks, jewelle hand-painted silk, hand-woven garmen linen, wood, baskets,fishing flies.

CHINACRAFT
24 Queen's Arcade **T 01232 230766**
Irish china and glass, including Beleek, Tyrone, Tara, Galway and Waterford.

COPPER MOON
The Spires, Howard Street **T 01232 235**
Contemporary crafts and jewellery, wooden games, paintings and cards.

HALLS
Queen's Arcade **T 01232 320446**
Specialises in Celtic jewellery, Donegal tweeds, Aran jumpers and carved compressed peat figures.

IRISH LINEN STORES
Fountain Centre, College St
T 01232 322727
The place to go for Irish linen.

STEENSONS
Bedford Hse, Bedford St **T 01232 2482**
Jewellery made from precious metals featuring Irish designers.

STER WEAVERS DISPLAY
ntgomery Road
nodern linen-weaving factory with a
op and tours for visitors.

'ID EARTH,
Dublin Road T **01232 245787**
ntemporary crafts.

CKER MAN,
negall Arcade, Castle Place
01232 243550
twear, jewellery and other crafts.

ENTERTAINMENT

CINEMAS

IEWORLD, Kennedy Centre

RZON, Ormeau Road

VIE HOUSE, Glengormley

EEN'S FILM THEATRE,
University Street T **01232 244857**
es) 01232 244857 (day)

GIN MULTIPLEX,
blin Road T **01232 245700**

RKGATE MOVIE HOUSE,
k Street T **01232 755000**

TRADITIONAL MUSIC PUBS

ou want a taste of traditional music in
os, these are the ones to go to:

KE OF YORK, off Lower Donegall Street

RIGLE INN, Ormeau Road

ONT PAGE, Donegall Street

RCULES, Castle Street

TY DALY'S, Ormeau Avenue

LLY'S CELLARS, Bank Street

CHEN BAR, Victoria Square

ERPOOL BAR, Donegall Quay

ODEN'S, Smithfield

'S BAR, Prince's Dock Street

BINSONS,Great Victoria Street

TTERDAM BAR, Pilot Street

THEATRES

BELFAST CIVIC ARTS THEATRE,
Botanic Avenue T **01232 316900**

CRESCENT ARTS CENTRE,
University Road T **01232 242338**

CULTÚRLANN MACADAM FIAICH,
Falls Road T **01232 239303**
Irish language arts centre housing a bookshop and secondary school. Venue for regular concerts and exhibitions .

GRAND OPERA HOUSE
Great Victoria Street T **01232 249129**

GROUP THEATRE
Bedford Street T **01232 329685**

KING'S HALL
Balmoral T **01232 665225**

LYRIC THEATRE
Ridgeway Street T **01232 381081**

OLD MUSEUM ARTS THEATRE
College Square North T **01232 233332**

ULSTER HALL
Bedford Street T **01232 323900**

WATERFRONT HALL
Lanyon Place T **01232 334400**

SPORT & LEISURE

ACTIVITY CENTRES

BELFAST INDOOR TENNIS ARENA & THE O-ZONE LEISURE CENTRE,
Ormeau Embankment T **01232 458024**

COACH TOURS

CITYBUS TOURS
T **01232 458484**
A varied programme of tours, from the historic buildings in Belfast city to the coastline of the southeast of Belfast and surrounding areas.

CYCLE HIRE

MCCONVEY CYCLES
467 Ormeau Road T **01232 491163**

EQUESTRIAN CENTRES

LAGAN VALLEY EQUESTRIAN CENTRE
170 Upper Malone Road, Dunmurray BT17 9JZ T **01232 614853**

GOLF COURSES

MALONE GOLF COURSE
240 Upper Malone Road, Dunmurry, Belfast BT17 9LB T **01232 612758**
Two parkland courses, extremely attractive with a large lake, mature trees and flowering shrubs. Very well maintained and offering a challenging round.

BELVOIR PARK GOLF COURSE,
73 Church Road, Newtownbreda BT8 4AN
T **01232 491693**
Undulating parkland course, not strenuous to walk, but is certainly a test of your golf, with tree-lined fairways and a particularly challenging finish at the final four holes.

Also:
BALMORAL T **01232 381514**
CLIFTONVILLE T **01232 744158**
DUNMURRY T **01232 610834**
FORTWILLIAM T **01232 370770**
KNOCK T **01232 483251**
MOUNT OBER T **01232 401811**
ORMEAU T **01232 641069 or 640999**
SHANDON PARK T **01232 401856**

WALKING

Walking tours, departing from the Tourist Information Centre in North Street, offer a tour of the old town, and a pub tour T **01232 246609.**

Other tours include:
BELFAST CITY CENTRE & LAGANSIDE WALK T **01232 491469**
BELFAST TOWN AND GOWN
T **01232 491469**
THE BLACKSTAFF WAY T **01232 672351**
Wends through the heart of the city following the Blackstaff River
THE C S LEWIS TRAIL T **01232 672351**
Links places in Belfast and North Down most closely associated with the writer

WHERE TO STAY

HOTELS

AA RECOMMENDED

SEE UNDER WHERE TO EAT FOR ALL HOTEL RESTAURANTS WITH ROSETTES

AA ★★★★ RATING

CULLODEN ✿
Bangor Road Holywood BT18 0EX *(on A2)*
T 01232 425223 F 01232 426777
One of Northern Ireland's foremost hotels. luxurious mansion set in large landscaped grounds with fabulous views.
874 bedrooms including some for non-smokers ££££ Lift Parking Leisure & sporting facilities

EUROPA HOTEL
Great Victoria Street BT2 7AP
T 01232 327000 F 01232 327800
Close to concert complex Stylish lounges and very comfortable bedrooms Good range of restaurants.
184 bedrooms including some for non-smokers ££££ Lift Hairdressing & beauty salon Business & conference centre

STORMONT
587 Upper Newtonards Road BT4 3LP
T 01232 658621 F 01232 480240
Overlooking Stormont Castle, this busy hotel has comfortable accommodation and a choice of bars and restaurants.
109 bedrooms including some for non-smok ££££ Lift Parking 24-hour room service Confex centre Banqueting facilities

AA ★★★ RATING

HOLIDAY INN GARDEN COURT
15 Brunswick Street BT2 7GE
(from M2 follow city centre signs to Oxford St, turn right to May St, Brunswick St is 4th on left) **T 01232 333555 F 01232 330070**
Popular city centre hotel with good range of accommodation,bars and pretty restaurant. Car park nearby
76 bedrooms including some for non-smokers £££ Lift Beauty salon

JURYS BELFAST INN
Fisherwick Place, Great Victoria Street BT2 7AP **T 01232 533500 F 01232 533511**
(at the intersection of Grosvenor Road and Great Victoria Street, beside the Opera House)
Smart hotel with spacious bedrooms, bars and restaurants.
190 bedrooms including some for non-smokers ££ Lift

LANSDOWNE COURT
657 Antrim Road BT15 4EF
T 01232 773317 F01232 370125
Bright and pleasant hotel near the airpc with good bedrooms. Bar and restaurar
25 bedrooms £££ Parking Banqueting & meeting rooms Licve entrtainment

MALONE LODGE
60 Eglantine Avenue BT9 6DY
T 01232 382409 F 01232 382706
Bright, modern hotel in a quiet setting. Comfortable lounge,. Good value meals
33 bedrooms £££ Lift Parking

AA ★★ RATING

BALMORAL
Blacks Road, Dunmurry BT10 0ND
T 01232 301234 F 01232 601455
Modern hotel with comfortable bedrooms.
44 bedrooms ££ Parking

RAYANNE COUNTRY HOUSE ✿✿
60 Desmesne Road BT18 **T 01232 425859**
Elegant Victorian house, with much charm.
6 bedrooms, all no smoking ££ Parking

RENSHAWS
75 University Street BT7 1HL
T 01232 333366 F 01232 333399
Near university. Bistro/bar & restaurant
20 bedrooms (some no-smoking) Continental breakfast Lift

FORTE POSTHOUSE BELFAST KINGSWAY,
Dunmurry BT17 9ES *(6 miles SW of Belfast)*
T 01232 612101 F 01232 626546
Quiet modern hotel in substantial gard
82 bedrooms (somer no-smoking) Lift Parking Function/banqueting facilities

HOLIDAY INN EXPRESS BELFAST
106a University Street BT7 1HP
T 01232 311909 F 01232 311910
Budget-price but smart bedrooms.
114 bedrooms (some no-smoking) ££ Continental breakfast Lift Parking

BED & BREAKFAST ACCOMMODATIO

AA RECOMMENDED

MALONE QQQ
79 Malone Road BT9 6SH
(exit M1 at Balmoral, enter Stockmans Lane, turn left after 5th set of traffic lights, hotel after 3rd set of traffic lights) **T 01232 669565**
Located on the south side of the city, this Victorian villa with bright accommodation and a comfortable lounge.
8 bedrooms ££ Parking No children 12yrs

CAMERA QQ
44 Wellington Park BT9 6DP
(located 0.5 mile from Queen's University, follow University Road leads into Malone Road, then take second turning on the right)
T 01232 660026 F 01232 667856
Victorian house with a variety of bedrooms and a comfortable lounge
9 bedrooms, some family ££

Call the AA Hotel Booking Service o 0990 050505 to book at AA recognis hotels and B&Bs in the UK and Irela or through our internet site: http://www.theaa.co.uk/hotels

WHERE TO EAT

RESTAURANTS

AA RECOMMENDED RESTAURANTS

BARNETT RESTAURANT ❀
Malone House, Malone Road BT19 5PB
T 01232 681246 F 01232 682197
The daily changing set-dinners offer a short choice of imaginative dishes. Typical dishes are cucumber soup with ginger, Cajun chicken with mango salsa, and pistachio tart with rum cream.
FIXED L ££ D ££

CULLODEN ❀
Bangor Road BT18 0EX
T 01232 425223 F 01232 426777
A former bishop's palace, overlooking A spring meal began with pan-fried scallops, followed by loin of lamb with a wild mushroom crêpe. The dessert, a poached white peach in a brandy snap basket, was served with praline cream.
ALC £££ FIXED L £££ D £££

DEANES ❀❀❀
38-40 Howard Street BT1 6PD
T 01232 560000
Alively street-level brasserie and more formal first-floor restaurant with highly contemporary decor. The cooking has a strong oriental, mainly Thai slant, with extensive use of exotic oils as dressings drizzled around the plate. The earthy tones of risotto of wild mushrooms with roast foie gras and pigeon breast were underlined by the subtle use of truffle oil and jus of star anise.
FIXED L £££ D £££ ALC (Brasserie) ££

RAYANNE COUNTRY HOUSE ❀❀
60 Desmesne Road, BT18 9EX
T 01232 425859F 01232 423364
Everything here is freshly cooked with care and the flavour of quality ingredients shines through. Dishes enjoyed include confit of duck with orange and passion fruit sauce, fillet of spring lamb with a crust of garlic crumbs, tarragon jus, fresh tarragon and cucumber, and a good choice of home-made desserts
ALC £££

ROSCOFF ❀❀❀
Lesley House, Shaftesbury Square BT2 7DB
T 01232 331532 F 01232 312093
Hot chefs don't come much hotter than Jeanne and Paul Rankin, who have jointly put Belfast on the gastronomic map.along the way. Much is made of Paul's eclectic style, and a visit to the airy, modern restaurant can take in dishes sourced from the Wolfgang Puck schooll of pizza-making (spiced chicken with grilled red onion and aubergine, to Australasian ideas such as a starter of cold oysters with soba, ginger and mirin. Roux brothers-style roast chump of lamb, crusty on the outside with caramelised juices, was meltingly pink and tender within, and wonderfully sauced with garlic cream infused with rosemary.
FIXED L ££16.95 D £££

PUBS, INNS & OTHER PLACES

ANTICA ROMA,
7 Botanic Avenue **T 01232 311121**
Smart Italian restaurant with an intriguing ancient Roman interior.

BENGAL BRASSERIE,
339 Ormeau Road, **T 01232 640099**
Good range, including daily specials and authentic vegetarian dishes.

CAFÉ SOCIETY
Donegal Square East **T 01232 439525**
Imaginative dishes using the fresh ingredients, many of them locally sourced.

CROWN LIQUOR SALOON
46 Great Victoria Street **T 01232 249476**
Extraordinarily decorative Victorian pub, now owned by the National Trust.

ILLERS COFFEE SHOP,
31-235 Saintfield Road **T 01232 701409**
Traditional home baking and wholesome cooking at lunchtime.

THE MAD HATTER,
2 Eglantine Avenue **T 01232 683461**
Quality home cooking served for breakfast, lunch and afternoon tea, with a tea garden for summer use.

MANOR HOUSE CANTONESE,
43-47 Donegall Passage **T 01232 238755**
A family-run Cantonese restaurant offering a truly extensive menu.

MIZUNA,
99 Botanic Avenue **T 01232 230063**
Innovative menus, drawing on wide cultural influences, using local produce.

NICK'S WAREHOUSE,
35-39 Hill Street **T 01232 439690**
A lively bar and restaurant on offering an interesting menu of freshly cooked dishes.

SKANDIA RESTAURANT,
50 Howard Street **T 01232 240239**
A family-friendly, unlicensed restaurant, with special children's menus.

SPERANZA,
16 Shaftesbury Square **T 01232 230213**
Cheerful Italian restaurant offering mainly pizzas and pasta. Family-friendly

VILLA ITALIA,
39 University Road **T 01232 328356**
Pizzas, pasta and a range of Italian dishes. Children welcome, with colouring sheets and crayons provided.

WELCOME RESTAURANT,
22 Stranmallis Road **T 01232 381359**
A Chinese restaurant complete with pagoda roof. and an extensive menu.

LOCAL FOOD

Foodstuffs to look out for are dulse, a kind of edible seaweed, Coleraine cheese, fadge potato bread, and 'yellow man' sweeties.

COUNTY ANTRIM

The distinguishing features of the county - among Northern Ireland's major tourist attractions - are the Causeway Coast and the nine Glens of Antrim, cutting through the hills that range between Ballycastle and Larne. The one sight that you simply cannot go home without visiting is the fantastic Giant's Causeway, an extraordinary natural rock formation set against a stunningly beautiful cliff-lined coast, which was first brought to public attention in 1692 by the Royal Geographical Society and is of such wonder and importance that it was designated a World Heritage Site in 1987.

Those interested in American history will find the childhood homes of two American presidents here.

PRINCIPAL TOWNS

Belfast, capital of Northern Ireland, is County Antrim's main urban centre, and the county's other towns, such as Ballycastle, Ballymena, Ballymoney, Larne and Portrush are relatively small. Antrim Town has a good shopping centre but, like the rest of inland Antrim, has few sites of particular interest to tourists.

MUST SEE

CARRICK-A-REDE ROPE BRIDGE & .ARRYBANE VISITORS CENTRE
'east of Ballintoy on B15)
T 012657 62178 or 31159
\ shaky rope bridge suspended 80ft/24m ıbove the sea, bridging the 60ft/18m gap ɔetween the cliffs and a small rocky sland. It owes its existence to the salmon :hat regularly make a dash through the :hasm and get netted for their efforts, and he fishermen who need access to the :ommercial fishery on the southeast side ɔf the island. The bridge has been put up ›very spring and taken down every ɪutumn for about the last 300 years. From 'he Larrybane car park, where there is a \ational Trust Information Centre, the 'rust have made a clifftop path to the ›ridge and the views are lovely.

'HE GIANT'S CAUSEWAY,
iiant's Causeway Centre, 44 Causeway Road, :arrickfergus BT57 8SU *(2 miles/3km north f Bushmills on B146)*
T 012657 31855 F 012657 32537
'his dramatic rock formation is ındoubtedly one of the wonders of the ıatural world. It comprises a series of ›romontories, the most spectacular :onsisting of about 37,000 polygonal olumns of dark basalt, packed together ke a child's building blocks. Most of the olumns are hexagonal, forming a oneycomb pattern, but some have five, even or even ten sides, measuring about 12in/30cm across and reaching a height of up to 39ft/12m. The most popular legend associated with the Causeway relates the tale of the giant Finn MacCool, who, it is said, built it so that he could walk over to Scotland.

At the top of the cliffs, there is a visitor centre with an exhibition, audio-visual show and tourist information. There are also craft and souvenir shops, a National Trust tea room and a restaurant. Ulsterbus provides a minibus service to the stones and there are guided walks, picnic tables and special facilities for the less able.

HILDEN BREWERY,
Hilden, Lisburn
T 01846 663863
Not only real ale buffs will enjoy visiting this working brewery, situated in the courtyard of Hilden House, the 19th-century former home of the Barbours, one of the great Irish linen families. The brewery produces award-winning real ales and visitors are invited to brewery tours and an exhibition on brewing, so there is much of interest. There is also a restaurant in the courtyard.

RISH LINEN CENTRE & LISBURN 1USEUM,
Aarket Square, Lisburn BT28 1AG
01846 663377 F 01846 672624
'his imaginative centre, next to Lisburn Auseum, tells the story of the Irish linen ndustry, past and present. Individual ıctory scenes are re-created and a series f creative hands-on activities describe the nen manufacturing processes. A highlight f the exhibition is the handloom weaving vorkshop. You can buy linen items in the hop on the ground floor.

KNIGHT RIDE,
Heritage Plaza, Carrickfergus
T 01960 366455 F 01960 350350 (Tourist Information Centre)
You don't have to be a child to enjoy this monorail themed ride. You will be whizzed through a thousand years of the town's history, including the Vikings, King William, King Fergus and the Titanic, with special sound and smell effects. Don't miss the walk-through exhibition with a scale model of the town. There is a gift shop.

OLD BUSHMILLS DISTILLERY,
Bushmills BT57 8XH
(on the Castlecatt road)
T 012657 31521 F 012657 31339
Make a point of visiting the oldest whiskey distillery in the world, which was first granted a license in 1608. Nowadays there are guided tours, showing the whiskey making process, tasting sessions, a coffee shop and two shops.

BIG OUTDOORS

ALLYCASTLE FOREST
? miles/3km south of Ballycastle, car park on rumavoley Road)
easant forest on the slopes of Knocklayd ountain, with wonderful views across e town to Rathlin Island and Scotland.

ALLYBOLEY FOREST,
ff main Larne to Ballymena road)
though on the routeof the Ulster Way, ɔu can reach this impressive pine forest / less strenuous efforts.There is a servoir too.

ALLYPATRICK FOREST
' miles/8km from Ballycastle on main 'ushendall road)
Peatland conifer forest with a delightful five-mile/eight km forest drive with views of Ballycastle and Rathlin Island.

CARNFUNNOCK COUNTRY PARK,
Coast Road, Larne
T 01574 260088 or 270541
Woodland walks, lovely gardens, a maze in the shape of Northern Ireland, a nine-hole golf course, children's activity centre, craft shop, café, camping and caravanning facilities.

GLENARIFF FOREST PARK
(off main Ballymena to Cushendall road)
Forest including the well known and beautiful Glenariff Waterfall Walks, horse-riding routes, tea room, picnic and barbecue areas, camping and caravanning, and facilities for the less able.

GLENARM FOREST
(off Altmore Street)
A mixed forest on the banks of the Glenarm River.

PORTGLENONE FOREST
(1 mile/1.5km from Portglenone on Ballymena road)
Mixed forest with walks by the River Bann. Catch the bluebells in May.

RANDALSTOWN FOREST
(Staffordstown Road, 1 mile west of Randalstown)
This forest is a National Nature Reserve including a deer enclosure with a herd of wild fallow deer and a wildfowl hide on Lough Neagh shore.

RATHLIN ISLAND
Less than an hour by ferry from Ballycastle. Great for bird-watching. There is a beach, diving centre, Boathouse Centre with various exhibitions, campsite, pub, restaurant and guest house.

SHANE'S CASTLE,
Antrim *(on A6 Randalstown Road)*
A castle with a chequered history, finally gutted by fire in the 1922 troubles. Part of the estate is open to the public, including rare breeds, a deer park, nature trail and butterfly area.

SLIEVEANORRA FOREST
(lying between Newtown Crommelin, Amoy and Cushendun)
An extensive pine forest around Slieveanorra. If you climb to the top you will be rewarded with views from the Western Isles to the Mountains of Mourne.

TARDREE FOREST
(west of main Doagh to Ballymena road)
A mixed conifer forest affording views over the county and Lough Neagh. It includes a geological reserve in the rhyolite quarry.

GREAT FOR KIDS

BEACHES
Portrush is a large resort with two long sandy beaches, which have won international awards for their water quality. Plenty of seaside attractions.

DUNLUCE CENTRE,
Portrush **T 01265 824444**
Hi-tech interactive fun for the family, including the Myths & Legends Theatre; Earthquest, a portrayal of local wildlife, and Turbo Tours movies, where you feel as well as see the action!

LESLIE HILL OPEN FARM,
Ballymoney **T 012656**
An open farm with plenty of animals, pony and trap rides, a walled garden and tea room.

LOUGHSIDE OPEN DAIRY FARM,
17 Island Road Lower, Ballycarry *(on B90)*
T 01960 353312
Highland cattle, ponies, donkeys and Jacob sheep populate this farm, and there's a pets' corner and bird sanctuary. Other facilities include an adventure playground and miniature train.

MAUD'S ICE CREAM FACTORY,
Gleno Glen **T 01574 272387**
Located at Gleno glen - also known for its lovely waterfall and village. There are 15-minute factory tours, to see the ice cream being made, and a café with a huge range of flavours. How could you miss this?

WATERTOP OPEN FARM
(on A2 6 miles/9km southeast of Ballycastle)
Working farm, plus pony trekking, fishing and boating. Facilities for less able visitors.

WATERWORLD,
The Harbour, Portrush **T 01265 822001**
A fun pool with a pirate theme, including slides, water canons, swings, a rope bridge and a scramble net. There is also a health suite, restaurant and sea water aquarium.

HISTORIC & ANCIENT SITES

ANTRIM ROUND TOWER,
Antrim *(north of town)*
T 01232 235000 F 01232 310288
The tower stands among lawns and trees but was once surrounded by monastic buildings. Antrim was an important early monastery, probably 6th century, closely linked with Bangor.

BONAMARGY FRIARY
(on A2 0.5 mile/8km east of Ballycastle)
Reasonably intact ruins of the 16th-century friary, where the extremely penitent 'black nun' is buried under the main walkway, where people will forever tramp over her humbled form.

DUNLUCE CASTLE,
Portballintrae *(off A2)*
T 012657 31938 F 01232 318288
Picturesque ruins of a 16th-century castle perched on a rocky crag high above the sea. A cave below provides a secret entrance from the sea. Displays and audio-visual show.

BALLYLUMFORD DOLMEN
Ballylumford
(on B90 on northwest tip of Island Magee)
T 01232 235000 F 01232 310288
Incorporated in the front garden of a house in Ballylumford Road are the remains of this huge 4-5,000-year-old single chamber Neolithic tomb, also known as the Druid's Altar.

BONAMARGY FRIARY
Ballycastle **T 01232 235000**
(east of town, at golf course)
Founded by Rory MacQuillan around 1500 and later passed on to the MacDonnels, Earls of Antrim. Remains include the friary gatehouse, church and cloister.

CARRICKFERGUS CASTLE
Carrickfergus **T 01960 351273**
(on the north shore of Belfast Lough)
Best preserved Norman castle in Ireland, imposingly placed on a rocky headland overlooking Belfast Lough. Exhibits, banqueting suite, visitors' centre, shop,cafe

CARRICKFERGUS TOWN WALLS
Carrickfergus
T 01232 235000 F 01232 310288
Carrickfergus was enclosed with stone walls from 1611 onwards and more than half the circuit is still visible, often to its full height of four metres to the wall walk.

CRANFIELD CHURCH
Churchtown
(3.75 miles/6km southwest of Randalstown)
T 01232 235000 F 01232 310288
The small medieval church is situated on the shores of Lough Neagh. Beside it is a famous holy well.

DUNEIGHT MOTTE & BAILEY,
Lisburn, *(2.3 miles/3km south beside river)*
Impressive Anglo-Norman earthwork castle with high mound-embanked enclosure, making use of the defences of an earlier pre-Norman fort.

HARRYVILLE MOTTE,
Balymena *(north bank of the River Braid)*
T 01232 235000 F 01232 310288
On a ridge to the south of the town, this Norman fort, with its 40ft-high/12m motte and rectangular bailey, is one of the finest examples of Norman earthworks left in Northern Ireland.

OLDERFLEET CASTLE,
Larne **T 01232 235000 F 01232 310288**
A 16th-century tower house, the last surviving of three which defended Larne.

PATTERSONS SPADE MILL,
Templepatrick **T 01849 433619**
(2 miles/3km southeast on A6)
The last remaining water-driven spade mill in Ireland. It has been completely restored by the National Trust and is now back in production.

TEMPLETOWN MAUSOLEUM,
Templepatrick
Situated in the graveyard of Castle Upton, this splendid family mausoleum is in the shape of a triumphal arch and was designed by Robert Adam.

HOMES & GARDENS

ANTRIM CASTLE GARDENS,
Antrim **T 01849 428000**
A restored 17th-century Anglo-Dutch water garden in a 37-acre/15ha site by the Sixmilewater River. Amongst its features are a raised terrace, formal parterre, wilderness area, ornamental pond and cascade.

THE ANDREW JACKSON CENTRE,
Boneybefore, Carrickfergus
T 01960 366455
Andrew Jackson emigrated to America in 1765. In 1829 he was elected 7th President of the USA. You can step back in history and see his cottage restored to its period style, complete with earth floor.

ARTHUR COTTAGE,
Dreen, Cullybackey **T 01266 880781**
The cottage, situated northwest of the village, is where the family of Chester Alan Arthur, 21st President of the USA, once lived. Interpretative centre, refreshments and souvenirs on site.

THE BALLANCE HOUSE,
118A Lisburn Road, Glenavy BT29 4NY
T 01846 648492
The birthplace of John Ballance (1839-93), Prime Minister of New Zealand, Liberal politician and reformer. Exhibits on emigration, pioneer life and Maori culture. Tea room and gift shop.

BENVARDEN GARDEN,
Dervock, Ballymoney
T 012657 41331 F 012657 41955
Estate dating from the 1630s, with landscaping and trees mostly from the early 1800s. There is a walled garden, cobbled stable yard and small museum.

MUSEUMS & ART GALLERIES

ALLYCASTLE MUSEUM,
astle Street, Ballycastle T 012657 62024
oused in the 18th-century workhouse, e museum focuses on the Glens of ntrim - fact and folklore - with an teresting range of exhibits.

ARRICKFERGUS GASWORKS,
ish Quarter West, Carrickfergus
T 01960 351438
preserved coal-fired gasworks, built in 855 to light the local street lamps. xhibits include an audio-visual esentation, gas-powered items and iginal machinery.

ORD FARM PARK & MUSEUM,
arne T 01960 353264
ear Duff's Corner on the way to Ballylumford)
small museum in a rural location, owing old farm implements, fishing araphernalia. and other local artefacts. Wool from the farm's sheep is used for spinning demonstrations.

HERITAGE FARM PARK,
Leslie Hill, Ballymoney BT53 6QL
(1 mile/1.5km northwest of Ballymoney on MacFin Road)
T 012656 66803 F 012656 66803
An 18th-century estate with a fine house, farm buildings, museum, rare breeds, horse-drawn machinery, a working forge, walled garden, adventure playground, and pony rides.

LARNE & DISTRICT HISTORICAL CENTRE,
Old Carnegie Library, Victoria Road, Larne
T 01574 279482
Fascinating local history exhibits including a reconstructed country kitchen, milk house and smithy from the 1900s. Wheelchair accessible.

LARNE INTERPRETATIVE CENTRE,
Narrow Gauge Road, Larne
T 01574 260088
The story of the building of the Antrim Coast Road, one of the country's finest scenic drives, featuring a model. Wheelchair accessible.

RAILWAY PRESERVATION SOCIETY
near Whitehead Railway Station, Whitehead
T 01960 366455
A collection of Irish Standard Gauge steam locomotives to delight the enthusiast. Open some Sundays in summer, when one engine is in steam for short rides.

US RANGERS CENTRE,
Boneybefore, Carrickfergus
T 01960 366455
An exhibition dedicated to the American GIs, located in the grounds of the Andrew Jackson Centre (see Homes & Gardens). Exhibits include photographs, uniforms and documents.

ESSENTIAL INFORMATION

TOURIST INFORMATION

ALLYCASTLE
eesksburn House, 7 Mary Street BT54 6QH
T 012657 62024 F 012657 62515

ALLYMENA
-15 Bridge Street BT43 5EJ
T 01266 44111 F 01266 46296

ARRICKFERGUS
eritage Plaza, Antrim Street BT38 7DG
T 01960 366455 F 01960 350350

ARNE
arrow Gauge Road BT40 1XB
T/F 01574 260088

ACCESS

ACCESS BY SEA

RGYLL & ANTRIM STEAM PACKET OMPANY *(Campbeltown-Ballycastle)*
T 0345 523523

&O EUROPEAN FERRIES *(Cairnryan-Larne)*
T 01574 274321

SHOPPING

est buys for souvenirs are locally oduced crafts, including knitwear, ramics, glass, baskets and jewellery; hiskey and blackthorn sticks.

SPORT & LEISURE

ACTIVITY CENTRES

ALLYEARL COURTYARD THEATRE & ART GOLF CENTRE
eatre with a varied programme of amatic and artistic events, combined th a 9-hole golf course and driving range.

ANGLING

Game, sea, coast and rock angling are all available, with a huge range of species to fish for. Check out the rivers Bush, Carey, Glensheck, Margy and Roe for brown trout, seatrout and salmon. Brown trout can also be fished in the River Agivey and Dungonnell and Altnahinch reservoirs.

COACH TOURS

In high season the Bushmills Bus offers a scenic tour from Coleraine to the Giant's Causeway.

EQUESTRIAN CENTRES

ASHFIELD RIDING CENTRE,
9 Middle Road, Islandmagee, Larne BT40 3SL
T 01960 372609 or 382729

BRAMLEY HOLLOW EQUESTRIAN CENTRE,
16 Mulaghcarton Road, near Maghaberry, Lisburn BT28 2TE T 01846 621259

DRUMAHEGLIS RIDING SCHOOL,
89 Glenstall Road, Ballymoney BT53 7NB
T 01265 665500 F 01265 54268

GALGORM PARKS RIDING SCHOOL,
112 Sand Road, Ballymena BT42 1DN
T 01266 880269

KILOAN RIDING CENTRE,
40 Killyless Road, Cullybackey, Ballymena BT42 1HB T 01266 880031

LOUGHAVEEMA TREKKING CENTRE,
Watertop Farm & Family Activity Centre, 188 Cushendall Road, Ballycastle BT54 6RL
T 012657 62576 or 63785

LUSK EQUESTRIAN,
48 Knockany Road, Lisburn BT27 6YB
T 01846 638407 F 01846 638981

GOLF COURSES

MASSERENE,
51 Lough Road BT41 T 01849 428096

ROYAL PORTRUSH T 01265 822311
Considered one of the best six courses in Britain,with views to Scotland when clear
Also:
ALLEN PARK T 01849 429001
BALLYCASTLE T 01265 762536
BALLYCLARE T 01960 322696
BALLYMENA T 01266 861487
BUSHFOOT T 01265 731317
CAIRNDHU T 01574 583324
CARRICKFERGUS T 01960 363713
CUSHENDALL T 012667 71318
GALGORM T 01266 46161
GARRON TOWER T 012667 71210
GRACEHILL T 012657 51209
GREENISLAND T 01232 862236
LAMBEG T 01846 662738
LARNE T 01960 382228
LISBURN T 01846 677216
RATHMORE G T 01265 822996
WHITEHEAD T 01960 353631

SCENIC DRIVES

The Antrim Coast Road from the Newtownabbey lough shore, past Whitehead and Islandmagee to Larne, and onward through some delightful villages - Glenarm, Carnlough, Cushendall and Cushendun - and up to Torr Head to see the Scottish coast just 13 miles away, or Fair Head for views of Rathlin Island

WALKING

The Ulster Way is a 560-mile/900km marked route that does a circuit of the six counties of Northern Ireland and Donegal. Probably the most spectacular section is in County Antrim, taking in the Glens of Antrim and the Causeway Coast.

WHERE TO STAY

HOTELS

AA RECOMMENDED

SEE UNDER WHERE TO EAT FOR ALL HOTEL RESTAURANTS WITH ROSETTES

BALLYGALLY

BALLYGALLY CASTLE ★★★
274 Coast Road BT40 2QR
T 01574 583212 F 01574 583681
Atmospheric castley with lovely sea views and gardens. More recent wing includes lounge, restaurant and some bedrooms.
30 bedrooms ££ Conference/function rooms

BALLYMENA

ADAIR ARMS ★★★
1 Ballymoney Road BT43 5BS
T 01266 653674F 01266 40436
Popular with locals, choice of restaurants and the the piano can be heard on many an evening in the ounge and bar.
40 bedrooms £££

COUNTRY HOUSE HOTEL ★★★
20 Doagh Road, Kells BT42 3LZ
(from M2 junct 5, take A57 to Larne, turn left for Doagh and take B59 to Ballymena. Hotel 6 miles on the right)
T 01266 891663 F 01266 891477
Hospitable modern hotel in quiet countryside with comfortable bedrooms, restaurant, conservatory and lounges..
39 bedrooms £££ Leisure, conference and banqueting facilities

GALGORM MANOR ★★★★
BT42 1EA **T 01266 881001**
F 01266 880080
(1 mile outside Ballymena on A42, between Galgorm & Cullybackey)
Splendid mansion in large tranquil grounds with charming bedrooms. Excellent restaurant.
23 bedrooms ££££ Clay pigeon shooting Archery Equestrian Centre Banqueting & conference facilities 85 acres

CARNLOUGH

LONDONDERRY ARMS★★★
20 Harbour Road BT44 0EU
T 01574 885255 F 01574 885263
Coaching inn, with lovely views ,a friendly atmosphere and comfortable bedrooms. Once owned by Sir Winston Churchill.
35 bedrooms ££

CARRICKFERGUS

DOBBINS INN ★
6-8 High Street BT38 7AP
T 01960 351905 F 01960 351905
Nautical theme throughout .Versatile coffee shop/bistro plus dining room. Pleasant accommodaton.
13 bedrooms ££

CUSHENDALL

THORNLEA HOTEL ★★
6 Coast Road BT44 0RU *(centre of village)*
T 012667 71223 F 012667 71362
Good value holiday accommodation, convenient for hiking routes and an outdoor activity centre.
13 bedrooms ££

NEWTOWNABBEY

CHIMNEY CORNER★★★
630 Antrim Road BT36 4RH *(off M2 at Sandyknowes onto A6, hotel 1 mile on left)*
T 01232 844925 & 844851
F 01232 844352
Busy hotel, built around an old inn, with bright bedrooms and an attractive restaurant.
63 bedrooms ££ Leisure facilities Bicycles

PORTBALLINTRAE

BEACH HOUSE ★★
The Sea Front BT57 8RT
T 012657 31214 F 012657 31664
Very popular family-run resort hotel with fine sea views. Wide range of meals.
32 bedrooms ££ Pool table Table tennis

PORTRUSH

CAUSEWAY COAST ★★★
36 Ballyreagh Road BT56 8LR
(on A2 between Portrush & Portstewart, opposite Ballyreagh Golf) (Best Western)
T 01265 822435 F 01265 824495
Modern hotel where some bedrooms hav fitted kitchens. Popular wine bar offers an informal option to the dining room.
21 bedrooms £££ Snooker Pool

3ED & BREAKFAST ACCOMMODATION

AA RECOMMENDED

:aireal Manor

CUSHENDALL

AIREAL MANOR
) Glenravel Road, Glens of Antrim,
artinstown BT43 6QQ
n A43, 6 miles north of Ballymena)
012667 58465 F 012667 58465
xcellent accommodation. Chauffeur
ervice to the proprietor's restaurant in the
unning Glenariffe Glen.
bedrooms £

LARNE

ERRIN GUEST HOUSE
Prince's Gardens BT40 1RQ *(access via A2)*
01574 273269 & 273762
01574 273269
istine house.with boldly decorated
edrooms. .Enjoy the rose garden in
armer months.
bedrooms £

MANOR GUEST HOUSE
23 Older Fleet Road, Harbour Highway BT40 1AS **T 01574 273305**
(2 minutes walk from Larne Ferry Terminal & Harbour Train Station)
Charming lounge and bedrooms are furnished with antiques; one has a four-poster bed. .
8 bedrooms £ Secure car parking

LISBURN

BROOK LODGE FARMHOUSE
79 Old Ballynahinch Road, Cargacroy BT27 6TH *(M1 exit 6, Ballynahich A49, 3.5 miles)*
T 01846 638454
Delightful modern farmhouse with a welcoming atmosphere. Light, airy but compact bedrooms. Hearty breakfasts.
6 bedrooms £ 65 acres mixed farming

Manor Guest House

Derrin Guest House

CAMPING & CARAVAN SITES

AA RECOMMENDED

BALLYCASTLE

LVER CLIFFS HOLIDAY VILLAGE,
Clare Road BT54 6DB
012657 62550 *(0.25 miles west off A2)*
pennants, touring caravans, motor
ravans & tents.
pen March-October, booking advisable
ly-August. Last arrival 20.00hrs. Last
parture 17.00hrs.
typical large seaside site with a
vimming pool and bar. Close to the
ach and River Glenshek. A 2-acre site
th 50 touring pitches and 250 static.
n beds, sauna and snooker. Electric
ok up, shower, electric shaver point,
nderette, indoor swimming, games
room, cold storage, licensed bar, children's playground, Calor Gas, Camping Gaz, battery charging, toilet fluid, café/restaurant, public telephone, fast food/takeaway, picnic area, shop on site, disabled facilities. *Facilities within three miles of site: stables, golf, course, boats for hire, fishing*

CUSHENDALL

CUSHENDALL CARAVAN CAMP,
62 Coast Road BT44 0QW
T 012667 71699 *Signposted*
3 pennants, touring caravans, motor caravans & tents. Open March-October, booking advisable peak periods. Last arrival 23.00hrs. Last departure 14.00hrs. A pleasant site next to the beach and sailing club on the A2, one mile south of town. A one-acre site with 14 touring pitches and 55 statics. Shower, electric shaver point, launderette, hairdrier, Calor Gas, public telephone, barbeque area, picnic area, shop on site. *Facilities within three miles of site: stable, gol course, mini golf, watersports, boats for hire, fishing*

CUSHENDUN

CUSHENDUN CARAVAN PARK,
14 Glendun Road BT44 0PX
T 01266 74254
Signposted
2 pennants, touring caravans, motor caravans & tents.
Open March-October, booking advisable July-August. Last arrival 22.30hrs. Last departure 12.30hrs.
A small touring site with mostly level pitches next to a larger static site. From A2 take B52 for one mile, clearly signed. A 0.5-acre site with 15 touring pitches and 50 static. Shower, hairdrier, tennis court, games room, separate TV room, children's playground, battery charging, toilet fluid, public telephone, shop on site.
Facilities within three miles of site: stable, golf course, boats for hire, fishing

LARNE

CURRAN CARAVAN PARK,
131 Curran Road
T 01574 260088
Signposted
3 pennants, touring caravans, motor caravans & tents.
Open April September, booking advisable at peak times.
A tidy and very clean council site ideal for the ferry. Site on A2, a quarter of a mile from the ferry, and clearly signed. A 3-acre site with 40 touring pitches. Bowling & putting greens. Electric hook up, shower, children's playground, public telephone, barbeque area, picnic area, dog exercise area on site.
Facilities within three miles of site: golf course, mini golf, boats for hire, cinema, fishing, launderette, shop

PORTBALLINTRAE

PORTBALLINTRAE CARAVAN PARK,
Ballaghmore Avenue BT57 8RX
T 012657 31478
Signposted Nearby town: Bushmills
2 pennants, touring caravans, motor caravans & tents. Open April-September, booking advisable Easter & July-August. Last arrival 20.30hrs. Last departure 14.00hrs.
Very tidy site, popular for Giant's Causeway. In Portballintrae village clearly signed from A2. Quarter of a mile from Bushmills distillery. A 12-acre site with 53 touring pitches and 150 statics. Electric hook up, shower, electric shaver point, launderette, cold storage, children's playground, Calor Gas, public telephone, dog exercise area on site, disabled facilities.
Facilities within three miles of site: stable, golf course, boats for hire, fishing

WHERE TO EAT

RESTAURANTS

AA RECOMMENDED

GALGORM MANOR
Ballymena BT42 1EA
T 01266 881001 F 01266 880080
A listed manor house set by the impressive River Maine, and surrounded by an 86-acre estate. The elegant dining room certainly reflects the gracious living of a bygone era. a spring meal comprised a tartlet of sweet and sour tomatoes, fillet of salmon in a herb crust, and vanilla crème brûlée.
ALC £££ FIXED PRICE L ££ D £££

RAMORE
The Harbour, Portrush BT56 8DF
T 01265 824313 F 01265 823194
Vibrant restaurant overlooking Portrush Harbour where you can view the maritime goings-on or keep your eyes on the chefs at the open-plan grill. Fish from the quay is the main attraction, with dishes such as glorious seared scallops set atop little mounds of lobster and pea risotto, and grilled turbot with Dublin Bay prawns, puff pastry and creamy garlic sauce.
Phone for details

PUBS, INNS & OTHER PLACES

BUSHMILLS INN HOTEL,
25 Main Street, Bushmills
T 012657 32339 F 012657 32048
Local Bushmils whiskey is often featured in dishes on the dinner menu..

FALSTAFFS,
66 Main Street, Ballyclare **T 01960 352336**
Good range of hot dishes, salads, sandwiches and home baking..

THE LAUREL INN,
99 Caryduff Road, Temple Baillies Mills, Lisburn **T 01846 638422**
Imaginative modern cooking, featuring seafood and game in season.

MCGEOWN'S OF GLENARVY,
22 Main Street, Glenarvy
T 01849 422467 01849 453967
Village pub providing good home-cooked bar food and a sophisticated restaurant menu. 20 mins from Belfast.

MORELLI'S OF PORTSTEWART,
53-58 The Promenade, Portstewart
T 01265 832150
A seafront café with an extensive range of hot dishes and an irresistable display of ice creams.

NATIONAL TRUST TEA ROOM,
Giant's Causeway Visitors' Centre, Bushmills
Wholesome soups and home-baked specialities.

THE OLD BANK HOUSE
9 Church Street, Ballymoney
T 01265 662724
Striking surroundings for some wholesome modern cooking served in hearty portions.

SWEENEY'S WINE BAR,
6B Seaport Avenue, Portballintrae, Bushmills
T 012657 32405 F 012657 31279
Overlooking the bay, with a conservatory to take full advantage of the view. Open for both lunch and dinner.

THE TEA SHOP RESTAURANT,
21 Main Street, Ballymoney
T 012656 62435 F 012656 62026
Healthy eating,, based on local produce,. at this tea shop/restaurant. No smoking.

TOP OF THE TOWN,
77 Fountain Street, Antrim **T 01849 428146**
Lovely old world pub well known for the quality of its home-cooked food. Garden.

WYSNERS LICENSED RESTAURANT,
16 Ann Street, Ballycastle
T 012657 62372 F 012657 62372
A good-value family restaurant using fresh produce, including locally caught fish.s

COUNTY ARMAGH

County Amargh is predominantly Catholic, close to the border, and generally fiercely nationalistic, and the sense of conflict and unease with the British 'occupation' is more apparent here than in other parts of Northern Ireland. This undoubtedly deters many a would-be tourist, which is a shame as the county is scenically beautiful and has many historically significant sites and places of interest well worth visiting.

Armagh has long been known as the Orchard County, with a long tradition of apple growing centred around the village of Loughgall. The apple industry is a major employer in the area, and these days the Bramley is the king of the crop. The local community celebrates its favourite fruit in the annual Apple Blossom Festival in May

PRINCIPAL TOWN

ARMAGH CITY

While County Armagh is mainly Catholic, the city of Armagh is predominantly Protestant, and has been the scene of conflict for centuries. Many battles have been fought here, and the town has been burnt down and re-built on several occasions. Both Protestant and Catholic Cathedrals are named for St Patrick, who founded a monastery and church here in around 445, and Amargh remains a major ecclesiastical centre. A feature of the town is the number of buildings constructed in pink, yellow or red sandstone, known as 'Armagh marble ', a material favoured by the 18th-century architect Francis Johnson. Look out for his work on Armagh's main thoroughfare, The Mall.

MUST SEE

ARMAGH PLANETARIUM & SCIENCE CENTRE,
College Hill BT61 9DB *(on main Armagh-Belfast road)*
T 01861 523689 or 524725
F 01861 526187
A trip to the outer limits of the universe, including the Star Theatre, a multi-media environment equipped with the latest technology and featuring a virtual reality digital system; the Hall of Astronomy; and the new Eartharium building,. Surrounding the Planetarium is the Astropark, a 25-acre/10ha park devoted to explaining scale in the universe. Wheelchair access and hearing loop system in theatre.

NAVAN CENTRE,
Killylea Road, Armagh BT60 4LD
(2 miles/3km west on A28)
T 01861 525550 F 01861 522323
Navan is one of Europe's most important Celtic sites, the seat of the ancient kings of Ulster and the setting for the legends of the mythical CúChulainn. The Centre unveils the history and archaeology of Navan Fort in a stunning visual and interactive display. Facilities include a shop, refreshments, wheelchair access and hearing loop system.

PALACE STABLES HERITAGE CENTRE,
Palace Demesne, Armagh BT60 4EL
T 01861 529629
A place to really get you imagination into gear. This restored Georgian building, set around a cobbled courtyard, houses a heritage centre where you can experience 18th-century stable life, both in the Tack Room and the Coachman's House. The exhibition A Day in the Life uses audio-commentary, life-like models and spectacular murals. Other attractions are the hayloft, ice house, servants' tunnel, education room, audio-visual theatre, craft shop and restaurant. A sensory garden and children's adventure play area are situated in the historic woodland surrounding the 18th-century palace.

ST PATRICK'S TRIAN,
English Street, Armagh BT61 7BA
T 01861 521801
This complex in the centre of the city illustrates the development of Armagh from prehistoric times to the present day, and also reveals Armagh's importance as a world ecclesiastical centre. Other attractions within the development are the Land of Lilliput (based on Gulliver's Travels and a real hit with the children), the Craft Courtyard, Pilgrim's Table Conservatory Restaurant and educational facilities. Wheelchair accessible.

BIG OUTDOORS

GOSFORD FOREST PARK,
Gosford Road, Markethill **T 01861 551277**
Once the demesne of Gosford Castle, with some of Jonathan Swift's favourite walks. There's a deer park, traditional poultry breeds, ornamental pigeons, a walled garden and nature trail.

LOUGH NEAGH DISCOVERY CENTRE,
Oxford Island **T 01762 322205**
(exit 10 from M1)
An award-winning Centre telling the story of Lough Neagh's history and wildlife. The lovely island is a birdwatcher's delight with over 5 miles/8km of walks with viewing hides.

PEATLANDS PARK
(exit 13 from the M1, 6.5miles/11km east of Dungannon, County Tyrone)
T 01762 851102
Learn the inside story of the peat boglands which are over 10,000 years old. To prevent erosion, you will go across the bog by narrow-gauge railway, which was originally used for carrying turfs.

GREAT FOR KIDS

THE LAND OF LILLIPUT
St Patrick's Trian, English Street,
Armagh BT61 7BA **T 01861 521801**
You really cannot avoid taking the children to this wonderful fantasy land based on Jonathan Swift's Gulliver's Travels, complete with a talking 20ft/6m giant. (See St Patrick's Trian in MUST SEE)

TANNAGHMORE ANIMAL FARM & MUSEUM
Armagh **T 01762 343244**
Meet and handle a variety of traditional farmyard animals and poultry, many of them now rare breeds. Everyone should enjoy the museum of farming life.

HISTORIC & ANCIENT SITES

ARMAGH FRIARY
(on the southeast edge of town)
T 01232 235000 F 01232 310288
Just inside the gates of the former Archbishop's Palace are the remains of the longest friary church in Ireland (163ft/50m). Dating from 1263, it was destroyed in the mid-16th century.

KILLEVY CHURCHES
Camlough **T 01232 235000**
F 01232 310288
(3 miles/4.5km south, on the lower slopes of Slieve Gullion)
The ruins of two churches (10th and 13th-century), standing back to back and sharing a common wall, on the site of a 5th-century nunnery, with a path to a nearby holy well.

KILNASAGGART INSCRIBED STONE
Jonesborough *(1.25 miles/2km south)*
T 01232 235000 F 01232 310288
A granite pillar stone dating back to the 8th century, with numerous crosses and a long Irish inscription carved on it.

MOYRY CASTLE,
Newry **T 01232 235000 F 01232 310288**
(7.5 miles/12km south)
A tall, three-storey keep built by Lord Mountjoy, Queen Elizabeth's deputy, in 1601, to secure the Gap of the North which was the main route into Ulster.

TYNAN VILLAGE CROSS
T 01232 235000 F 01232 310288
Worth making a detour to see, if you are interested in such things. Although this carved High Cross, 11ft/3m tall, was broken in two for many years, it was skilfully mended in 1844. The carvings depict Adam, Eve and the serpent entwined around an apple tree.

HOMES & GARDENS

RDRESS,
nnaghmore, Portadown BT62 1SQ
01762 851236
farmhouse made mansion by architect eorge Ensor, who married a local girl in 760. Fine plasterwork, period furniture nd paintings, plus pleasant gardens and arming exhibit.

RGORY,
errycaw Road, Moy BT71 6NA
4 miles/6.5km northeast)
018687 84753 F 018687 89598
Regency house, built on a hillside verlooking the Blackwater River, with eriod furniture, bric-a-brac, and acetylene ghting installed in 1906. Lovely roses and walled garden.

DERRYMORE HOUSE,
Bessbrook BT35 7EF T 01693 830353
(off the A25 Newry to Camlough road)
This National Trust property is a pretty thatched cottage, built in 1776 by Newry's representative in the Irish Commons, and surrounded by a lovely estate laid out by John Sutherland.

MUSEUMS & ART GALLERIES

ARMAGH COUNTY MUSEUM,
The Mall, Armagh BT61 9BE
T 01861 523070 F 01861 522631
A museum, art gallery and library housed in a 19th-century schoolhouse. It features a collection of local folkcrafts and natural history exhibits.

ROYAL IRISH FUSILIERS MUSEUM,
Sovereign House, The Mall, Armagh
T 01861 522911
The history of the regiment from 1793 to 1968. Exhibits include a uniform from the Peninsular War and a Christmas card from Adolf Hitler, dated 1943.

LOCAL FOOD

Foodstuffs to look out for are dulse, a kind of edible seaweed, Coleraine cheese, fadge potato bread, and 'yellow man' sweeties.

ESSENTIAL INFORMATION

TOURIST INFORMATION

RMAGH
ld Bank Building, 40 English Street
01861 521800

GENEALOGY

RMAGH ANCESTRY,
2 English Street, Armagh BT 61 7BA
01861 521802 F 01861 510033
or tracing your Armagh Ancestry.

SHOPPING

rmagh is an attractive city for shopping, ith a good mix of multiple and dependent stores, and some picturesque obbled streets to explore.

ENTERTAINMENT

RMAGH CITY FILMHOUSE
01861 511033

SPORT & LEISURE

ACTIVITY CENTRES

CRAIGAVON GOLF & SKI CENTRE
(off the M1, Belfast to Dungannon, junction 10)
T 01762 326606
An attractive woodland setting for an artificial ski slope, three golf courses, a floodlit driving range and two putting greens. There is also a fitness suite, golf shop and restaurant.

CRAIGAVON WATERSPORTS CENTRE
(off the main Lurgan to Portadown road, roundabout 3)
T 01762 342669 F 01762 346018
Mobile 0378 980555
Activities including snorkling, jet-skiing, windsurfing, water-skiing, canoeing, sailing and orienteering, with expert instruction in a sheltered environment.

ANGLING

There are fishing opportunities on the Keady Lakes, Lowry's Lough, Marlacoo Lake, the Portadown to Newry Canal, Seaghan Reservoir and Shaw's Lake.
ARMAGH ANGLING CLUB T 01861 522428

EQUESTRIAN CENTRES

LIME PARK EQUESTRIAN CENTRE,
5 Lime Kiln Road, Maghaberry, Moira BT67 0JD
T 01846 621139 F 01846 621139

RICHHILL EQUESTRIAN CENTRE,
38 Annareagh Road, Richhill BT61 9JT
T 01762 871258

COACH TOURS

In season, a courtesy coach service operates in Armagh City, to take visitors to all the main tourist attractions.

GOLF COURSES

ASHFIELD T 01693 868180
COUNTY ARMAGH T 01861 525861
EDEMORE T 01846 611310
LURGAN T 01762 322087
PORTADOWN T 01762 355356
SILVERWOOD T 01762 326606
TANDRAGEE T 01762 841272

WHERE TO EAT

PUBS, INNS & OTHER PLACES

HE ARCHWAY COFFEE LOUNGE,
Hartford Place, Armagh T 01861 522532
n attractive coffee house, centrally tuated in a Victorian archway on the Mall

HE FAMOUS GROUSE COUNTRY INN,
allyhagan Rd, Loughgall T 01762 891778
idway between Armagh and Portadown, is inn offers a choice of food

HOBBS CAFÉ
Armagh
A downstairs café and upstairs restaurant, providing a good choice of food at reasonable prices.

THE NAVAN CENTRE,
81 Killylea Rd, Armagh T 01861 525550
,Excellent coffee shop open to the public within an award-winning attraction

THE OLD THATCH
(Alexander's of Markethill)
3 Keady St, Markethill T 01861 551261
Thatched cottage coffee shop within a department store, providing morning coffee, hot lunches, and afternoon tea.

THE WHEEL & LANTERN COFFEE SHOP,
17-21 Market St, Armagh T 01861 522288
A department store coffee shop where beams and oak furniture create a comfortable old world atmosphere.

COUNTY DOWN

The Mountains of Mourne are the crowning glory of County Down, with 15 summits within a 25 mile/40km circuit, all over 2,000ft/610m, the highest being Slieve Donard at 2,782ft/848m. Roads circle the mountains, providing an ever-changing panorama for the motorist, but no road crosses the central area, known as 'the wilderness', which is perfect for walking. The county enjoys relatively good, dry weather and its seaside resorts are popular with visitors from nearby Belfast. They also attract a high proportion of retired residents. Many of the county's other attractions centre around Strangford Lough, an important wildlife habitat, 15.5 miles/25km long and averaging about four miles/six km wide, cut off from the sea by the narrow Ards Peninsula, except for a half mile/one km strait - the Narrows - at Portaferry.

PRINCIPAL TOWN

DOWNPATRICK

The town takes its name from its association with Ireland's patron saint. St Patrick's was blown ashore at Strangford Lough and built his first church at the fort of Rath Celtchair, the earthwork that can still be seen to the southwest of Down Cathedral. The town experienced another flowering in the 17th and 18th centuries, and there are some fine Georgian buildings on English, Irish and Scottish Streets, and the central Mall. The streets are so named because of the division into ethnic ghettoes that took place during the 17th century.

MUST SEE

EACHES

ome of the county's best loved beaches clude Ballyholme, Crawfordsburn, elen's Bay and Newcastle, where in ddition to traditional seaside attractions, ou might also find wind-surfing and a nge of other watersports. At Newcastle, e Tropicana Pleasure Beach has a eated outdoor pool with giant slides. arrenpoint is another family favourite, nd Ballyhornan and Coney Island in the ecale District. Tyrella Beach (see BIG UTDOORS) is one of the most ectacular beaches, with its vast expanse sand. There are safe waters at Millisle, allywalter, Ballyhalbert and Cloughey, nd facing south there's Rostrevor, and the ue Flag beach at Cranfield.

CASTLE ESPIE,
Ballydrain Road Comber BT23 6EA
(3 miles/5km south of Comber, 13 miles/21km southeast of Belfast. Signed from the A22 Comber-Killyleagh-Downpatrick road)
T 01247 874146 F 01247 873857)
Located on the shores of Strangford Lough, Castle Espie is home to the largest collection of wildfowl in Ireland. New hides (wheelchair accessible) enable visitors to watch the splendour of migratory waders and wildfowl. Beautiful landscaped gardens, a taxidermy collection and fine paintings by wildlife artists can also be seen. Visitors, especially children, are encouraged to feed the birds, many of which are rare and endangered. Facilities include a restaurant and shop.

DOWN COUNTY MUSEUM & ST PATRICK HERITAGE CENTRE,
The Mall BT30 6AH
T 01396 615218 F 01396 615590
The museum occupies the old county gaol, built between 1789 and 1796. The St Patrick Heritage Centre, in the former gatehouse, tells the story of Ireland's patron saint. Did you know that there are no snakes in Ireland, thanks to St Patrick? In the recently restored governor's residence there are galleries relating to the human and natural history of County Down.

RUMENA CASHEL,
astlewellan
.25/3.5km miles southwest)
01232 235000 F 01232 310288
here are many stone ring forts in orthern Ireland, but few as well eserved as Drumena. Dating back to arly Christian times, the fort is 98ft/30m diameter and has an 36ft/11m cessible underground stone-built assage, probably used as a refuge and r storage.

EXPLORIS,
The Rope Walk, Castle Street, Portaferry BT22 1NZ *(A20 or A2 or A25 to Strangford Ferry Service)* **T 012477 28062 F 012477 28396**
Northern Ireland's only public aquarium, situated in Portaferry on the shores of Strangford Lough, housing some of Europe's finest displays. The Open Sea Tank holds 246 tons/250 tonnes of sea water and the Shoal Ring, where visitors are surrounded by hundreds of shoaling fish, is 20ft/6m in diameter. You can take a journey from Strangford Lough through the neck of the Lough - the Narrows - and out into the Irish Sea without any risk of seasickness! The complex includes a park with a duck pond, picnic area, children's playground, caravan site, woodland, tennis courts and bowling green. Refreshments, shop, and facilities for the less able.

REY ABBEY,
allywalter
n east edge of village)
01232 235000 F 01232 310288
a lovely parkland setting are the tensive ruins of a Cistercian abbey, unded in 1193 by Affreca, daughter of e King of the Isle of Man. The abbey was urnt down in 1572, and then used as a arish church - look out for the many 7th- and 18th-century memorials. The bey now has a beautiful medieval-style erb garden and a visitors' centre.

JORDAN'S CASTLE,
Ardglass
T 01232 235000 F 01232 310288
Still an important fishing port, Ardglass was once the the busiest seaport in Northern Ireland. Between the 14th and 15th centuries a ring of tower houses and fortified warehouses was built to protect the port. Jordan's Castle, a late 15th-century, four-storey tower house, situated in the centre of town, is one of these. It was besieged in the early 1600s and held for three years. In the early 20th century it was bought, repaired and filled with bygones by a Belfast solicitor.

MAYPOLE,
High Street/Shore Street Intersection, Holywood
The tradition of the maypole in Holywood dates from before 1700, when a Dutch ship ran aground on the nearby shore. The crew, celebrating their deliverance, erected the ship's broken mast in the town, on the eve of May Day, and proceeded to dance around it. The mast has been replaced several times, but the dancing continues to this day, during the May Day Fair.

OUNT STEWART HOUSE, GARDEN & EMPLE OF THE WINDS,
eyabbey, Newtownards BT22 2AD
miles/8km southeast off A20)
012477 88387 or 88487
012477 88569
is 18th-century house on the shore of rangford Lough was the home of the ewart family (later Marquesses of ndonderry). The house is the work of ree architects - James Wyatt in the 780s, George Dance and Vitrusvius orrison in the19th century. The gardens, nong the very best of the National ust's, are inspired. Many rare and sub-opical trees thrive, while by the shore is e Temple of the Winds, built in 1782 for e first Marquess. Refreshments, shop, cilities for the less able.

ULSTER FOLK & TRANSPORT MUSEUM,
Cultra, Holywood BT18 0EU *(on A2)*
T 01232 428428 F 01232 428728
The museum, in the grounds of Cultra Manor, is in two parts. The Folk Museum, which covers a 137-acre/55.5ha site, has a wonderful collection of rural and urban buildings, taken from their original settings all over Ulster and reconstructed at the Museum. They include farmhouses, cottages, watermills, a small town with shops, a school, churches, printer's workshops, a bank and terraced houses, re-creating the Ulster landscape of the 1900's. In the rural area there are farm animals native to Ireland and fields cultivated using traditional farming methods.

The second part, the Transport Museum, exhibits all forms of transport, including the popular Titanic exhibition and the spectacular Irish Railway Collection. There is a shop, refreshments and facilities for the less able.

SILENT VALLEY,
Head Road, Annalong
T 01232 746581 or 741166 ext 309
Two dams, in a dramatic mountain setting, gather water in two reservoirs currently providing up to 30 million gallons of water a day to consumers in Down and Belfast. Visitors' centre, restaurant, craft shop and conference centre.

STRUELL WELLS,
Downpatrick *(1.5 miles/2.5km east)*
T 01232 235000 F 01232 310288
Pilgrims come to collect the healing waters from these holy drinking and eye wells, which are fed by a swift underground stream. Nearby are the ruins of an 18th-century church and even more interesting, the single-sex bathhouses.

BIG OUTDOORS

CRAWFORDSBURN COUNTRY PARK,
Bridge Road South, Helen's Bay BT19 1LD
T 01247 853621
On the southern shores of Belfast Lough, featuring 2 miles/3.5km of coastline, two beautiful beaches, a wooded glen with a waterfall, a Countryside Centre, restaurant and waymarked trails.

DELAMONT COUNTRY PARK,
Downpatrick **T 01396 828333**
Woodland and parkland with a visitor centre, gardens, a playground and tea rooms. There is access to Strangford Lough and boat trips are available.

KILBRONEY PARK
(0.5/1km mile from Rostrevor Village on the A2 to Kilkeel) **T 016937 38134**
Beautiful parkland encompassing a landscape of mountain, valley and sea lough.

MARINE PARK, Annalong
Facilities for boat launching, regardless of the tide, a herb garden, Marine Park Trail, café and Visitors' Centre. Footbridge to Annalong village.

THE MOURNE WALL
A 22-mile/35km drystone wall built 1904-22 to enclose the Silent Valley, which was dammed to create a huge reservoir. The wall links the main peaks of the Mourne Mountains.

MURLOUGH NATURE RESERVE
(southeast of Dundrum on main Dundrum to Newcastle Road) **T 013967 51467**
A rich wildlife habitat of sand dunes, heathland and woodland surrounded by the estuary and sea.

QUOILE COUNTRYSIDE CENTRE,
5 Quay Road, Downpatrick BT30 7JB
T 01396 615520
Seasonal displays and information on the Quoile Pondage and other nature reserves in the county.

REDBURN COUNTRY PARK,
Old Holywood Road **T 01247 811491**
(signposted from Jackson's Road) Holywood
An 80-acre/32ha park of mixed woodland and parkland extending from the Holywood hills to the shore of Belfast Lough, with wonderful views of the city.

SCRABO TOWER,
Scrabo Country Park, 203A Scabo Road, Newtownards BT23 4SJ *(1 mile/1.5km west)*
T 01247 811491 F 01247 820695
The 135ft/41m tower is at the centre of the park around the slopes of Scrabo Hill. Wonderful walks and spectacular views of the county and Stranford Lough.

TYRELLA BEACH & CONSERVATION AREA,
Killough Road, Downpatrick
T 01396 851228 or 828333
A beautiful wide, clean and safe sandy beach, with car-free zones, sand dunes and a visitor centre.

WARD PARK, Bangor
(entrances on Castle Street & Hamilton Road)
Tennis **T 01247 457177** Bowling
T 01247 458773
A 37-acre/15ha town park with ponds, islands, wildfowl, a mini-menagerie of hamsters, guinea pigs and fancy poultry, a playground, putting green, bowls and tennis.

WILSON'S POINT, Bangor
A vantage point from which to see the ferryboats, tankers and container ships on the move in Belfast Lough.

GREAT FOR KIDS

ARK OPEN FARM,
296 Bangor Road, Newtownards
T 01247 812672 or 820445
Rare breeds and a variety of interesting animals, including pygmy goats, Jacob's sheep and miniature horses, plus a pets' corner and pony rides.

COCO'S ADVENTURE PLAYGROUND,
27A Central Promenade, Newcastle
T 03967 26226
Assault course, slides, free fall, ball pools and soft play areas, with a snack bar.

DOWNPATRICK & ARDGLASS RAILWAY COMPANY,
Market Street, Downpatrick **T 01396 83014**
Steam engine trips on a restored 0.5 mile/1km section of the BCDR Downpatrick-Ardglass branch line on Sundays in summer.

MUSEUM OF CHILDHOOD,
Central Avenue, Bangor **T 01247 471915**
A modest but absorbing collection of bygone toys, clothes and prams, cots and cradles.

PICKIE FAMILY FUN PARK,
Bangor **T 01247 274430**
Traditional seaside fun and games, including a railway, adventure playground, paddling pool, giant swan rides in the lagoon, entertainment arena and café.

SEAFORDE BUTTERFLY HOUSE,
Seaforde **T 01396 811225**
Hundreds of free-flying exotic butterflies, plus insects, parrots and reptiles (the latter safely behind glass). There are also beautiful gardens and a maze.

SLIEVENALARGY OPEN FARM,
5 Largy Road, Kilcoo, Newry
T/F 013967 70083
Farm animals in danger of extinction. Other attractions include pony rides, mountain walk, nature trail, children's play area, picnic site and farm shop.

THRILLS & SPILLS,
7-9 Dock Street, Warrenpoint
T 016937 52852
Assault course, slides, free fall and ball pools.

HISTORIC & ANCIENT SITES

DLEY'S CASTLE,
angford
5 miles/2.5km west by the shore of angford Lough)
01232 230560 F 01232 310288
15th-century tower house on Strangford ugh offering lovely views from its top or. The internal fittings are complete.

NALONG CORN MILL,
nalong Harbour **T 013967 68736**
e of Ulster's last working watermills, erating until the 1960s, powered by a ft/4.5m waterwheel and a 1920s arshall 'hot-bulb' 20hp engine

WN CATHEDRAL,
e Mall, English Street, Downpatrick
01396 614922
e 12th-century cathedral is situated on e historic Hill of Down. Next to the thedral is what is believed to be the ave of St Patrick, Patron Saint of Ireland.

JNDRUM CASTLE,
wcastle *(4 miles/6.5km north)*
01232 235000 F 01232 310288
is medieval castle, one of the finest in land, occupies a strategic position erlooking Dundrum Bay, offering visitors e views over the sea to the Mountains Mourne.

REENCASTLE,KILKEEL
miles/6.5km southwest)
01232 235000 F 01232 310288
13th-century royal fortress, with a lourful history, standing on the shores of rlingford Lough with fine views of the ourne Mountains.

LLSBOROUGH FORT,
lsborough
01846 683285 F 01232 310288
ilt on an Early Christian site, the existing t dates from 1650. Ornamented in the th century, and set in a forest park with ake and pleasant walks.

CH ABBEY, DOWNPATRICK
.75 miles/1.25km northwest off A7)
01232 235000 F 01232 310288
autiful riverside ruins of a Cistercian bey founded around 1180. Look out for e tall, pointed, triple east window.

GANANNY DOLMEN,
omara **T 01232 235000**
01232 310288
miles/6.5km south)
eatrically situated on the slopes of eve Croob, this tall tripod dolmen with huge capstone is the most graceful of orthern Ireland's Stone-Age monuments.

LOUGHINISLAND CHURCHES
Downpatrick
(4 miles/6.5km west)
T 01232 235000 F 01232 310288
A remarkable group of three churches on an island in the lough, accessible by a causeway, dating from the 13th century onwards.

MAGHERA CHURCH,
Newcastle **T 01232 235000**
F 01232 310288
(2 miles/3km northwest)
The stump of a round tower, blown down in a storm in the early 18th century, survives from the early monastery, with a ruined 13th-century church nearby.

MOUND OF DOWN
(on the Quoile Marshes, from Mount Crescent)
T 01232 235000 F 01232 310288
A hill fort from the Early Christian period, conquered by Anglo-Norman troops in 1177, who then built an earthwork castle on top. This was the first town, preceeding Downpatrick.

NARROW WATER CASTLE,
Warrenpoint *(1 mile/1.5km northwest)*
T 01232 235000 F 01232 310288
Both picturesque and complete in detail, this 16th-century battlemented tower house is surrounded by a wall and juts out into the river estuary it was built to defend.

SKETRICK CASTLE,
Killinchy *(3 miles/5km east on western tip of Sketrick Islands)*
T 01232 235000 F 01232 310288
A badly ruined tall tower house, probably 15th century. The ground floor rooms include a boat bay and prison. An underground passage leads from the bawn to a freshwater spring.

STRANGFORD CASTLE,
Strangford
T 01232 235000 F 01232 310288
A three-storey tower house built in the 16th century, overlooking the small double harbour of Strangford.

HOMES & GARDENS

CASTLE WARD,
Strangford BT30 7LS
(0.5 miles/1km west of village on A25)
T 01232 235000 F 01232 310288
The marked diversity of styles in the house reflects the incompatible tastes of the 1st Viscount of Bangor and his wife. It overlooks Strangford Lough and has a richly planted garden.

MARINE GARDENS,
Bangor
A beautiful stretch of coastland, with panoramic views of Bangor Bay and the hills of Antrim. A focal point is the ornate bandstand, dating from 1891.

ROWALLANE GARDEN,
Saintfield BT24 7LH
(1 mile/1.5km south on A7)
T 01238 510131 F 01238 511242
An exotic 50-acre/20ha garden started by the Rev John Moore in 1860 and continued by his nephew. Exquisite plants from all over the world.

MUSEUMS & ART GALLERIES

BALLYCOPELAND WINDMILL,
Donaghadee
(1 mile/1.5km west on B172)
T 01247 861413 F 01232 310288
The only complete working windmill in Northern Ireland, dating from the late 18th century, fully operational until 1914. There are additional displays in the Miller's House and drying kiln.

BRONTË HOMELAND INTERPRETIVE CENTRE
(off B10, 8.5 miles/14km southeast of Banbridge) **T 018206 31152**
Patrick Brontë, father of the three famous sisters, was incumbent at Drumballyroney school and church before moving to Yorkshire. It has now been preserved as an interpretive centre.

NORTH DOWN HERITAGE CENTRE,
Bangor Castle, Bangor
T 01247 271200 or 270371
Occupying castle outbuildings, with exhibitions on the Early Christian monastery, the Scottish settlers and seaside nostalgia. There is a gift shop, restaurant and facilities for the less able.

ROUTE 66,
94 Dundrum Road, Newcastle
T 013967 25223 F 013967 23302
Ireland's only American automobile and memorabilia museum.

SOMME HERITAGE CENTRE,
Newtownards **T 01247 823202**
The First World War through the experiences of the 10th and 16th Irish and the 36th Ulster Divisions, including a trench system and audio-visual recreation of the battle of the Somme.

ESSENTIAL INFORMATION

TOURIST INFORMATION

BANBRIDGE
Gateway Tourist Information Centre (off A1)
T 018206 23322

BANGOR
34 Quay Street **T 01247 270069**

DOWNPATRICK
74 Market Street **T 91396 612233**

KILKEEL
6 Newcastle Street **T 016937 62525**

NEWCASTLE
Newcastle Centre, Central Promenade
T 013967 22222

NEWRY
Newry Tourist Office, Town Hall BT35 6HR
T 01693 68877 F 01693 68833

WARRENPOINT
Warrenpoint Tourist Office, Town Hall, Church Street BT34 3HM
T 016937 53022 F 016937 53022

GENEALOGY

ULSTER ANCESTRAL RESEARCH,
Mrs C F Macnaghten BA, Ballyvester House, Donaghadee BT21 0LL
T 01247 882218 F 01247 882218
Trace your ancestors with the help of Mrs Macnaghten, for a fee.

CRAFTS

If you wish to visit one of the craft workshops, then it is generally advisable to phone ahead and make an appointment.

ALGAN ARTS,
32 Ballyalgan Road, Crossgar BT30 9NQ
T 01396 831199
Ancient Irish sites, fairy thorn trees and holy wells featuring in original etchings, lithographs, woodcuts, prints and cards.

ARDA JEWELLERY,
80 Station Road, Saintfield BT24 7EN
T 01238 511764 F 01238 511717
Contemporary silver and gold jewellery - commissions welcome - plus a range of greetings cards and framed prints.

BALLYTRIM ANGORAS,
10 Ballytrim Road, Killyleagh BT30 9TH
T 01396 828057
Angora goat farm producing home-grown mohair, dyed and made up into garments and rugs.

CELTIC CLAYS,
9 Downpatrick Road, Ardglass BT30 7SF
T 01396 841543
Hand-thrown pottery with Celtic motifs.

CELTIC CRAFTS GALLERY,
45 Dromara Road, Dundrum BT33 0NS
T 013967 51327
An extensive range of crafts and gifts with a Celtic theme, featuring gold and silver jewellery made in the workshop.

CONEY ISLAND DESIGN,
41 Killough Road, Coney Island, Ardglass BT30 7UG **T 01396 841673**
Hand-painted tiles and ceramic animal sculptures.

CREATIVE WOODTURNING,
31 Drumaness Road, Ballynahinch BT24 8LT
T 01238 563863
A range of turned pieces in native woods - all from fallen and dead trees.

THE FERGUSON LINEN CENTRE,
Scarva Road, Banbridge **T 018206 23491**
The sole manufacturers of Double Damask Linen offer tours of the centre, where you can see the various stages of production.

FRANCES M DONNAN,
'Brena', 35 Shore Road, Killyleagh BT30 9UE
T/F 01396 828355
Ceramic sculptures, with sheep and goats a speciality.

KILKEEL KNITWEAR,
44 Newry Road, Kilkeel BT34 4DU
T 016937 65717 F 016937 63241
Knitwear made to order.

LOCH RURAY HOUSE,
Contemporary Design Gallery, 8 Main Street, Dundrum BT33 0LU
T 013967 51544 F 013967 51601
A designer linen studio selling the work of many top Irish designers. There is also a tea room where light lunches are served.

THE LOG CABIN,
51 Central Promenade, Newcastle BT33 0HH
T 013967 25027
Patchwork and quilting specialists.

RICHCRAFT WOODTURNING,
Ricky Richardson, 31A Green Road, Conlig BT23 3PZ
T 01247 463322 or 468788
Hand-made occasional furniture and wooden giftware.

STRANGFORD BLACKTHORN,
32 Drumroe Road, Strangford
T 01396 881226
Traditional Irish walking sticks, and a range of other products manufactured from locally harvested blackthorn.

TIEVESHILLY ORIGINAL KNITWEAR,
37 Caragh Road, Crossgar BT30 9AG
T 01396 830958
Knitwear reflecting the subtle tones of the Irish landscape, with over 200 shades

TURNIP HOUSE KNITWEAR,
4E Causeway Road, Newcastle BT33 0DL
T/F 013967 26754
Hand framed designer knitwear inspired by Celtic ornament and landscape colours

SPORT & LEISURE

ACTIVITY CENTRES

BANGOR CINEPLEX,
Valentine Road, off Castle Park Road
T 01247 454729
A four-screen cinema, children's adventu play area, 16-lane computerised tenpin bowling alley and a bistro.

TOLLYMORE MOUNTAIN CENTRE,
Bryansford, Newcastle BT33 0PT
T 013967 22158 F 013967 26155
Courses in mountain-walking, rock climbing, canoeing and orienteering.

ANGLING

BALLYGRANGEE FLY FISHERY,
Mountstewart Road, Carrowdore
T 012477 88883
Fly fishing for large rainbow trout, all yea tackle available for hire.

FISHERY & TROUT FARM,
Church Road, Holywood **T 01232 425592**
Game fishing, with day permits Monday Saturday.

RINGDUFFERIN ESTUARY (GIBSON FLY FISHERY),
34 Ringdufferin Road, Toye, Killyleagh
T/F 01396 828321

M V PURPLE HEATHER & M V WHITE HEATHER
North Pier, Bangor **T 01247 455321**
Fishing trips for all the family, skate and dog fishing on a Friday night, herring fishing off Blackhead, and traditional dee sea fishing. Disabled people welcome.

BOATING & CRUISING

LEISURE SAILING CRUISES
5 Coastguard Villas, Newcastle BT33 0QT
T 013967 228822 Mobile 0860 353526
Sightseeing, entertainment, meals and s training.

M V WHITE HEATHER
Bangor **T 01247 455321**
Sea cruises and trips to the 140m Gobbi Cliffs, Rockport Reef to see the seals anc wildlife, Copeland Isle, Groomsport and Carrickfergus.

NELSON'S BOATS,
146 Killaughey Road, Donaghadee BT21 0B
T 01247 883403 Mobile 0378 893920
Sea fishing trips and pleasure cruises to Copeland Islands. Also activity cruises or restored former lifeboat.

STRANGFORD CHARTER,
Sketrick Island, Whiterock, Killinchy
T 0831 189909 F 01238 541564
Luxurious 32ft/10m cabin cruiser licensed f 12 passengers

CAR HIRE

LOW COST CAR & VAN HIRE,
12 Church Street, Bangor BT20 3HT
T 01247 271535

CYCLE HIRE

MIKE THE BIKE,
53 Frances Street, Newtownards
T 01247 811311
Bikes delivered to your door.

EQUESTRIAN CENTRES

BALLYKNOCK RIDING SCHOOL,
38 Ballyknock Road, Hillsborough BT26 6EF
T 01846 692144

BIRR HOUSE RIDING CENTRE,
81 Whinney Hill, Holywood BT16 0UA
T 01232 425858

BRENTFORD RIDING SCHOOL,
Brentford, Ballydrain, Comber
T Killinchy 541259

EAST HOPE EQUESTRIAN CENTRE,
71 Killynure Road West, Carryduff BT8 8EA
T 01232 813186

LESSANS RIDING STABLES,
126 Monlough Road, Saintfield BT47 7EU
T 01238 510141

MILLBRIDGE RIDING CENTRE LTD,
Ballystockart, Comber BT23 5QT
T 91247 972508

MOUNT PLEASANT TREKKING CENTRE,
15 Bannonstown Road, Castlewellan BT31 9BG
T 01396 778651 F 01396 770030

MOURNE TRAIL RIDING CENTRE,
96 Castlewellan Road, Newcastle
T 013967 24351

NEWCASTLE RIDING CENTRE,
35 Carnacaville Road, Castlewellan BT31 9HD
T 01396 722694

PENINSULAR EQUESTRIAN ACADEMY,
4 Cardy Road, Grey Abbey, Newtownards
BT22 2LS
T 01247 788681

GOLF COURSES

ROYAL BELFAST,
Station Road, Craigavad BT18 0BP
T 01232 428165
An attractive course on the shores of Belfast Lough, comprising wooded parkland on undulating terrain, which provides a pleasant, challenging game.

Also:
ARDGLASS T 01396 841219
BANBRIDGE T 018206 62211
BANGOR T 01247 270922
BLACKWOOD T 01247 852706
BRIGHT CASTLE T 01396 841319
CARNALEA T 01247 270368
CLANDEBOYE T 01247 271767
CROSSGAR T 01396 831523
DONAGHADEE T 01247 883624
DOWNPATRICK T 01396 615947
HELEN'S BAY T 01247 852815
HOLYWOOD T 01232 423135
KILKEEL T 01693 65095 or 62296
KIRKISTOWN CASTLE T 01247 771233
LISBURN T 01846 677216
MAHEE ISLAND T 01238 541234
MOURNE T 013967 23889
RINGDUFFERIN T/F 01396 828812
ROYAL COUNTY DOWN T 013967 23314
SCRABO T 01247 812355
SPA T 01238 562365
TEMPLE T 01846 639213
WARRENPOINT T 01693 753695

HORSE RACING

DOWNPATRICK RACECOURSE,
Downpatrick BT30 7EY **T 01396 612054**

SCENIC DRIVES

MOUNTAINS OF MOURNE
Details of scenic drives through the Mournes are available from Tourist Information Centres in Newcastle and Downpatrick.

BRONTË DRIVE
The Brontë Homeland Interpretive Centre (see Museums & Art Galleries) marks the beginning of an 8 mile/13km scenic signposted drive, which includes Patrick Brontë's birthplace at Emdale.

COASTLINE DRIVE
There is a rocky coastline drive from Bangor North Pier to Kingsland. Start from Tower House and take the Seacliff Road past The Long Hole.

TOURS

THE IRISH LINEN TOUR
T 018206 23322
Starting at Banbridge Gateway Tourist Information Centre and taking in a visit to a water-powered scutching mill, the Irish Linen Centre and a local linen factory.

TIME TRACKS HERITAGE TOURS,
PO Box 87, Newry BT34 1TX
Weekend and day tours focusing on Irish heritage and culture.

WALKING

THE MOURNE WALL WALK
Follow the 22-mile/35km drystone wall that links the main Mourne peaks and encloses the Silent Valley. For information on walking in the Mourne Mountains contact the Mourne Countryside Centre, 91 Central Promenade, Newcastle
T 013967 24059.

NORTH DOWN COASTAL PATH
A lovely coastal walk from Holywood to Portavoe.

WATER SPORTS

BALLYHOLME YACHT CLUB,
Seacliff Road, Bangor **T 01247 271467**

BANGOR MARINA,
Bangor **T 01247 453297**
Ireland's largest haven for pleasure craft.

BANGOR SEA SCHOOL
T 01247 460081
Day or weekend courses to suit all levels

COCKLE ISLAND BOAT CLUB,
Groomsport **T 01247 464431**

DONAGHADEE SAILING CLUB,
Donaghadee, BT21 0QB

DOWN CRUISING CLUB,
Rose Cottage, Ballyminstagh, Comber
BT23 6AB

DOWN YACHTS, SAIL TRAINING & YACHT CHARTER,
Bangor & Stranford Lough, Terry Anderson, 37 Bayview Road, Killinchy BT23 6TW
T 0238 542210
RYA recognised practical cruising school.

DV DIVING,
138 Mountstewart Road, Newtownards, BT22 2ES **T/F 01247 464671**
RIB diving for groups or individuals in Belfast Lough, Strangford Lough and the Irish Sea, including a wide range of courses.

FRANK SMYTH SEA SCHOOL & YACHT CHARTER T 0247 460081

HOLYWOOD YACHT CLUB,
T 01232 423345

NEWTOWNARDS SAILING CLUB,
98 James Street, Netowanrds BT23 0PY

NORSEMAID SEA ENTERPRISES LTD,
152 Portaferry Road, Newtownards BT22 2AJ
T 01247 812081 F 01247 820194
Air and technical diving onboard a 59ft/18m dive vessel along the coast of County Down, including wreck and scenic diving. IANTD facility for technical dive training.

PORTAFERRY SAILING CLUB,
25B Pascali Drive, Rose, Newtownards

ROYAL NORTH IRELAND YACHT CLUB,
Holywood **T 01232 428041**

ROYAL ULSTER YACHT CLUB,
101 Clifton Road, Bangor **T 01247 270568**

SKETRICK MARINE CENTRE,
Sketrick Island, Whiterock, Killinchy BT23 6QH
RYA Sailing and powerboat courses for beginners and improvers.

WHERE TO STAY

HOTELS

AA RECOMMENDED

SEE UNDER WHERE TO EAT FOR ALL HOTEL RESTAURANTS WITH ROSETTES

Clandeboye Lodge

BANGOR

CLANDEBOYE LODGE ★★★
10 Estate Road, Clandeboye BT19 1UR
T 01247 852500 F 01247 852772
Genuine hospitality, delicious food and luxury accommodation are all to be found here.
3 bedrooms ££££ Petanque court Conference & banqueting facilities

MARINE COURT ★★★
18-20 Quay Street BT20 5ED
T 01247 451100 F 01247 451200
Overlooking the marina, this smart hotel offers cheerful accommodation and a choice of eating options.
51 bedrooms ££££ Lift Conference rooms Gym Swimming pool Sauna Spa

ROYAL HOTEL ★★★
Seafront BT20 5ED
T 01247 271866 F 01247 467810
A popular hotel with harbour views. Comfortable bedrooms, three small bars, a bistro and restaurant.
50 £££ Lift

CRAWFORDSBURN

OLD INN ★★★
15 Main Street BT19 1JH
T 01247 853255 F 01247 852775
Ancient hostelry with inviting bars and restaurants. Many of the pretty bedrooms are furnished with antiiques.
334 bedrooms ££££

HILLSBOROUGH

WHITE GABLES ★★★
14 Dromore Road BT26 6HS
T 01846 682755 F 01846 689532
Friendly, personal service is one of the strengths at this modern hotel with well equiped bedrooms
31 bedrooms £££ Conference rooms

NEWCASTLE

ENNISKEEN HOUSE★★
98 Bryansford Road BT33 0LF
(from Newcastle town centre follow signs for Tollymore Forest Park, hotel 1 mile on left)
T 013967 22392 F 013967 24084
Beautifully situated hotel where tradition both in the decor and in the standards of serviceis the byword here.
12 bedrooms ££ Lift

SLIEVE DONARD ★★★
Downs Road BT33 0AH
T 013967 23681 F 013967 24830
Impressive Victorian hotel with relaxing lounges and a panelled restaurant..Many bedrooms overlook the sea or mountains
134 bedrooms ££££ Leisure & sporting facilities Function & conference facilities

PORTAFERRY

PORTAFERRY ★★★
10 The Strand BT22 1PE *(situated on Lough Shore opposite ferry terminal)*
T 012477 28231 F 012477 28999
Pleasant setting with comfortably modern bedrooms, pleasant lounges and exquisite food
14 bedrooms £££

BED & BREAKFAST ACCOMMODATION

AA RECOMMENDED

Beech Hill

ANNALONG

THE SYCAMORES QQQ
52 Majors Hill BT34 4QR
(from Newcastle turn off at church on main road (A2) going through Annalong, turn right at church and continue until sign for 'The Sycamores')
T 013967 68279
Pretty house with mountain views. Expect a warm welcome and a hearty breakfast.
3 bedrooms £

Edenvale House

DOWNPATRICK

HAVINE FARM QQ
51 Bally Donnel Road, Ballykilbeg BT30 8EP
T 01396 851242
Warm home-from-home atmosphere. Smallishbut comfortable bedrooms.
3 bedrooms 125 acres beef & sheep

HOLYWOOD

BEECH HILL QQQQQ
23 Ballymoney Rd, Craigantlet BT23 4TG
(1.5 miles from bridge at Ulster Folk Museum, turn right up Ballymoney Road. House on left)
T 01232 425892 F 01232 425892
Brimming with style. Luxury bedrooms, comfortable lounge and conservatory .
3 bedrooms ££ No children under 10 Croquet Boules

NEWTOWNARDS

EDENVALE HOUSE QQQQQ
130 Portaferry Road BT22 2AH
(between Newtownards and Greyabbey, 2 miles from Newtownards on A20)
T 01247 814881 F 01247 826192
Excellent house in seven acres. Wonderful views from the sunroom. Good breakfasts.
3 bedrooms ££ Croquet

PORTAFERRY

THE NARROWS QQQ
8 Shore Road BT22 1JY
(follow A20 & continue to shore & turn left, The Narrows is then on the left)
T 012477 28148 F 012477 28105
Charming house with good views. Restaurant often uses local produce.
13 bedrooms, incl some family & interconnecting rooms ££ Lift

CAMPING & CARAVAN SITES

AA RECOMMENDED

CASTLEWELLAN

CASTLEWELLAN FOREST PARK,
Dept of Agriculture, Forest Service BT31 9BH
T 01396 778664 *Signposted*
3 pennants, touring caravans, motor caravans & tents.
Open all year, booking advisable weekends and July-August. Last arrivals 22.00hrs. Last departure 16.00hrs.
Attractive forest park site, situated down a long drive with views of the castle. Site broken up into smaller areas by mature trees and shrubs. Off A25 in Castlewellan; turn right at Upper Square and turn into Forest Park, clearly signed. A 5-acre site with 90 touring pitches. Lake, arboretum, fishing on site. First Aid. Electric hook up, shower, electric shaver point, café/restaurant, public telephone, fast food/takeaway, barbeque area, picnic area, dog exercise area on site, shop, disabled facilities.
Facilities within three miles of site: stable, fishing

NEWCASTLE

TOLLYMORE FOREST PARK
T 01396 722428 *Signposted*
3 pennants, touring caravans, motor caravans & tents. Open mid March- mid November (restricted service mid Nov-mid March). Last arrival 21.00hrs. Last departure 17.00hrs.
Popular site with family field and large tent area. From A2 at Newcastle take B180, and site clearly signed on right. A 7.5-acre site with 100 touring pitches. Electric hook up, shower, electric shaver point, launderette, Calor Gas, Camping Gaz, café/restaurant, public telephone, barbeque area, picnic area, mobile shop, shop, disabled facilities.
Facilities within three miles of site: stable, golf course, mini golf, watersports, boats for hire, cinema, fishing

WHERE TO EAT

RESTAURANTS

AA RECOMMENDED

CLANDEBOYE LODGE HOTEL
10 Estate Road, Clandeboye, Bangor BT19 1UR
T 01247 852500 F 01247 852772
This restaurant has a lovely setting within the Gothic-style country lodge, set in acres of landscaped grounds and woodland. The weekly menus point to plenty of imagination and flair in the kitchen. The climax of one meal was a dish of superbly light sautéed scallops served with an intriguing sauce based on dry sherry, tarragon and crème fraîche.
FIXED D ££

PORTAFERRY HOTEL
10 The Strand, Portaferry BT22 1PE
T 012477 28231 F 012477 28999
The dining room has wonderful views, of a little ferry running back and forth. The fixed-price menu offers a good choice, with seafood figuring strongly alongside prime Ulster beef, Mourne lamb and local game. Typical dishes are Strangford scallops, pan-roasted with bacon and glazed apple on a saffron sauce; baked fillet of hake with tempura vegetables on spiced champ with soya and black bean sauce.
FIXED L ££ D £££

SHANKS ❀❀❀
The Blackwood, Crawfordburn Road, Bangor BT19 1GB
T 01247 853313 F 01247 853785
Tacked on to the side of a golf clubhouse, the award-winning, Conran-designed interior of this restaurant is a triumph of style over location.Impressive levels of technical skill are demonstrated in dishes such as a perfectly creamy, textured saffron risotto with langoustines, mussels and julienne of chirizo, exquisitely presented on a plate dotted with pesto. A modern classic, confit of duck leg, with grilled potato gnocchi, grilled fennel, and rosemary scented lentils in balsamic vinegar and spinach, was served in Ulster trencherman-sized portions. Puddings are superb.
ALC £££ FIXED L ££

Shank.

PUBS, INNS & OTHER PLACES

ADELBODEN LODGE RESTAURANT, BAR & BISTRO,
38 Donaghadee R, Groomsport
T 01247 464288
Splendid sea views, home-style food, excellent bread, plus vegetarian menu.

BALLOO HOUSE,
1 Comber Road, Killinchy T 01238 541683
Local ingredients are used at this former coaching inn with various dining options.

THE BRASS MONKEY,
16 Trevor Hill, Newry T 01693 63176
A lovely old bar with stone floors and a spiral staircase. Popular for its steaks.

THE BUCK'S HEAD,
77 Main Street, Dundrum T 013967 51868
A friendly 18th-century pub with a conservatory and beer garden.

CASTLE ESPIE COFFEE ROOM,
Castle Espie
Views of the nature reserve and Strangford Lough. Good food, including lunch.

COFFEE PLUS,
Market House, New Street, Donaghadee
T 01247 882641
In a pretty village setting, serving morning coffee, light lunches and afternoon tea.

THE CUAN,
The Square, Strangford T 01396 881222
Delightful village setting. Bar snacks during the day ,choice of menus in the evening,

DUFFERIN ARMS COACHING INN,
35 High St, Killyleagh T 01396 828229
Good food and music. Near the Castle by the shores of Strangford Lough.

GILBERRY FAYRE,
92 Banbridge Rd, Gilford T 01762 832098
A former school house, attractively converted serving wholesome food

GRACE NEILL'S,
33 High St, Donaghadee T 01247 882553
Acknowledged as Ireland's oldest pub, dating from 1611. Good quality pub food.

HALLS MILL INN,
Banbridge Road, Laurencetown, Gilford
T 018206 25565
Bar snacks,high tea served daily.The restaurant features County Down ostrich.

HARRY'S BAR,
7 Dromore St, Banbridge T 018206 62794
Traditional-style pub with home-style food and 14 draft ales. Tempting desserts.

HEATHERLEA TEA ROOMS,
94-96 Main Street, Bangor T 01247 453157
Good range of home-baked goodies and freshly cooked lunches.

THE HILLSIDE,
21 Main St, Hillsborough T 01846 682765
17th-century pub/restaurant in a pretty village setting,. Imaginative cooking

KNOTT'S CAKE & COFFEE SHOP,
49 High St, Newtownards T 01247 819098
Cakes and coffee as the name promises. Popular range of hot meals at lunchtime.

LISBARNETT HOUSE,
Lisbane, Killinchy T 01238 541589
Old post house, also known as 'Dick's'. Choice of bars and lounge/dining area.

OLD INN,
11-15 Main St, Crawfordsburn
T 01247 853255
Dates from 1614. Choice of menus, prepared from locally supplied produce.

OLD PRIORY INN,
13 High Street, Holywood T 01232 428164
Lunch menu served until 5pm, a free crêche at Sunday lunch time.

OLD SCHOOLHOUSE INN,
100 Ballydrain Rd, Comber T 01238 541182
On the Ulster Way near Strangford Lough. Features fresh seasonal produce

PERCY FRENCH,
Downs Road, Newcastle T 013967 23175
In the grounds of Slieve Donard Hotel, wonderful mountain and sea views.

ROMAS,
4 Regent St, Newtownards T 01247 812841
Once a blacksmith's. Home-made wheaten bread used in sandwiches.

ROSEMARY JANE TEA ROOM
Vegetarian options and a range of home-made soups, salads and puddings.

SEAFORDE INN,
24 Main Street, Seaforde T 01396 811232
A country inn featuring local produce. where possible

SULLIVANS,
Sullivan Place, Holywood T 01232 421000
Open for morning coffee, lunch, afternoon tea; full restaurant service in the evening .

TOURIST TROPHY LOUNGE,
101-103 Mill Street, Comber
T 01247 874554
Evokes the 1920s-1930s era, when the Tourist Trophy motor races took place.

VILLA TOSCANA,
Toscana Park Waste Circle Road, Bangor
T 01247 473737
Large Italian restaurant,extensive menu of popular dishes, including pizza and pasta.

THE YELLOW DOOR,
Bridge Street, Gilford T 01762 831543
Good service is a priority. Dishes are basec on local produce, particularly fish.

COUNTY FERMANAGH

One of Ireland's smallest counties, predominantly Catholic, close to the border and generally nationalistic. It is known for two dramatic events in recent history: the IRA Remembrance Day bombing at Eniskillen in 1987 when 11 people lost their lives and 61 were injured, and the hunger strike of MP Bobby Sands, campaigning for political recognition of IRA prisoners, who died after 66 days without ever taking his seat at Westminster.

The River Erne flows through Fermanagh and into the 50 mile/80km Lough Erne, which divides into two sections with the town of Eniskillen at its narrowest point. Not surprisingly fishing and water sports are among the county's major attractions.

PRINCIPAL TOWN

ENNISKILLEN

Enniskillen, the county town of Fermanagh, is small and attractively situated on an island where the two parts of Lough Earne reach their narrowest part. It makes a good base from which to explore the surrounding lakes and islands. As a point of literary interest, both Oscar Wilde and Samuel Beckett attended school in the town.

MUST SEE

BELLEEK POTTERY,
Belleek BT93 3FY
T 013656 58501 F 013656 58625
Known worldwide for its fine Parian china, Ireland's oldest and most historic pottery was started in 1857 by the Caldwell family. Although the Caldwells originally used felspar from the Castle Caldwell estate, today it is imported mainly from Norway. Visitors can see the delicate porcelain being hand-crafted and visit the museum where pieces dating back over 100 years are exhibited. There is also a shop, display area and restaurant

CASTLE COOLE,
Enniskillen BT74 *(1.5 miles/2.5km SE A4)*
T 01365 322690 F 01365 325665
One of the finest classical mansions in Northern Ireland and no expense was spared when it was built .Vast amounts of Portland stone were imported, together with an Italian expert in stonework. The house is filled with beautiful Regency furniture - don't miss the sumptuous state bed in scarlet silk.

CROM ESTATE,
Newtownbutler*(3 miles/5km west)*
T 013657 38174 F 013657 38174
About 1,350 acres of woodland, parkland and wetland on the shores of Upper Lough Erne, and one of Northern Ireland's most important native conservation areas, with international significance.

DEVENISH ISLAND,
Enniskillen T 01232 235000
This island, two miles/three km downstream from Enniskillen, was once the site of a 6th-century monastery founded by St Molaise - one of the 12 apostles of Ireland . Look out for the elaborately carved north chancel door and a pretty 15th-century cross in the graveyard. Admission includes ferry c

ENNISKILLEN CASTLE,
Enniskillen T 01365 322711
Dating back to the 15th century, this impressive castle, overlooking the River Erne, houses two museums and a heritage centre. The keep, now the Museum of the Royal Inniskilling Fusiliers is surrounded by massive stone-built barracks, and a turreted, fairytale, 17th-century water gate. This popular family attraction includes displays of Fermanagh's history, wildlife and landscape with audio visual programme Lifesize models in darkened vaults show life in the castle in the 15th and 17th centuries. Shop.

MARBLE ARCH CAVES,
Enniskillen, Marlbank Scenic Loop BT92 1EW
(off A4 Enniskillen-Sligo road)
T 01365 348855 F 01365 348928
A magical cave system - one of Europe's finest - under the Mountains of Cuilcagh. Visitors are given a tour through a wonderland of stalagmites, stalactites, underground rivers and lakes, starting with a boat trip on the lower lake. The streams that disappear into the mountain feed the caves and then emerge at Marble Arch, a huge 30ft/9m detached limestone bridge. Shop and refreshments.

BIG OUTDOORS

CASTLE ARCHDALE COUNTRY PARK
(off the B82, 3 mile/5km south of Kesh)
T 013656 21588
Situated on the shores of Lower Lough Erne, the park has picnic areas, walks, natural history exhibits, agricultural implements, boat and cycle hire, pony trekking and a ruined castle.

CASTLE CALDWELL FOREST
(4 miles/6.5km from Belleek at the western end of Lower Lough Erne)
Forest featuring castle ruins, the Fiddler's Stone, nature trails, lough and woodland wildlife, wildfowl hide and picnic sites.

ELY LODGE FOREST
(9 miles/4.5km from Enniskillen on main Belleek road)
Near Carrickreagh Viewpoint, the forest has a jetty, lakeshore trails & picnic area.

FLORENCE COURT FOREST PARK
(8 miles/13km from Enniskillen on the road to Swanlinbar)
Park with forest trails, duck pond, restored sawmill, pleasure grounds and views of Benaughlin mountain.

LOUGH NAVAR FOREST
(signposted off the A46, 5 miles/8km northwest of Derrygonnelly) T 013656 41256
Red deer and wild goats roam. A steep path (part of the Ulster Way) leads to one of the best views in Ireland, across Lough Erne to counties Donegal and Sligo.

MARBLE ARCH FOREST
(near Marble Arch Caves. Entrance off main Florence Court to Blacklion road)
Forest with nature trails, a waterfall and a walk along the Claddagh Glen.

HISTORIC & ANCIENT SITES

CASTLE BALFOUR,
Lisnaskea T 01232 235000
F 01232 310288
Dating from 1618 and refortified in 1652, this is a T-plan house with vaulted rooms. It was badly burnt in the early 1800s and has remained in ruins.

EXPLORE ERNE,
Erne Gateway, Corry, Belleek BT93 3FU
T 0136565 8866 F 0136565 8833
The story of Lough Erne, part of the most extensive inland waterway in Western Europe; its history and mythology, customs and traditions, and how it has influenced the lives of local people in their work and leisure. Video presentations in English, French and German.

THE JANUS STATUE, Boa Island
(0.5 mile/1km from the west end bridge)
Boa Island, at the north of Lough Erne, is connected at either end by bridges to the shore. The Janus figure in Caldragh cemetery, very striking to look at, is believed to be 2,000 years old.

MONEA CASTLE,
Enniskillen T 01232 235000
(6 miles/10km northwest)
A fine example of a plantation castle, still with much of its enclosing bawn, built around 1618. Of particular interest is the stone corbelling, giving additional support to the turrets.

TULLY CASTLE,
Derrygonnelly T 01232 235000 *(3 miles/5km N of west shore of Lower Lough Erne)*
Ruins of a Scottish-style stronghouse with an enclosing bawn overlooking Lough Erne. It was destroyed and most of its occupants slaughtered by the Maguires in the 1641 Rising.

WHITE ISLAND CHURCH,
Castle Archdale Bay T 01232 235000
(ferry from marina)
Roofless 12th-century church with eight carved stone figures, part Christian and part pagan, whose significance has been the subject of great debate.

HOMES & GARDENS

LORENCE COURT
nniskillen BT92 1DB 01365 348249
8 miles/13km southwest via A4 & A32)
n 18th-century mansion, gutted by fire in 955, but miraculously restored. There are leasure grounds and parkland full of fine ees, including the mother of all Irish ews. National Trust. Craft Fairs are ometimes held here.

MUSEUMS & ART GALLERIES

BICYCLE MUSEUM,
Main St, Brookeborough 013655 31206
An unusual and fascinating collection of some 80 bicycles dating from 1870 onwards.

OLD BARN FAMILY MUSEUM,
Carrybridge Rd, Tamlaght 01365 387278
Over 1,000 items collected over 250 years including farming implements, books, letters, coins, stamps, guns, swords, birds' eggs, fossils and other curios.

ROSLEA HERITAGE CENTRE,
Monaghan Road, Roslea 013657 51750
A restored cut-stone building showing an exhibition on the Irish famine and a selection of McMahon spades and other artefacts.

ESSENTIAL INFORMATION

TOURIST INFORMATION

NNISKILLEN
ermanagh Tourist Information Centre, Vellington Road BT74 7EF
T 01365 323110 F 01365 325511

GENEALOGY

OSLEA HERITAGE CENTRE,
Monaghan Road, Roslea 013657 51750

CRAFTS

RDESS CRAFT CENTRE *(near Kesh)*
01365 631267
raft courses for resident and non-resident tudents. Spinning and weaving classes

HE BUTTERMARKET,
nniskillen Craft & Design Centre, Down treet, Enniskillen BT74 7DU
01365 324499
craft shop and gallery selling a wide ange of gifts; craft workshops and a offee shop serving traditional fare.

ERMANAGH CRYSTAL,
Main Street, Belleek 013656 58631
ee craftspeople at work producing hand-ut Fermanagh Crystal.

RISH HAMMERSLEY POTTERY,
Market Yard, Irvinestown 013656 21934
ee ornamental creamware being made y skilled craftspeople. Visitors' Centre, ntroductory video, shop, museum, and he chance to decorate your own piece.

O TINNEY STUDIO,
ullycleagh Lodge, Ballinamallard
01365 388626
between Enniskillen & Irvinestown)
ward-winning artist welcomes callers at er studio (phone for times) to view her aintings and traditional hand-painted urniture, which are available for sale.

SPORT & LEISURE

ACTIVITY CENTRES

ASTLE ENTERTAINMENT CENTRE,
aceview, Enniskillen 01365 324172
hree-screen cinema, 10-lane 10 pin owling, game zone virtual reality driving, kiing,motorcycling,fast, food restaurant.

CORRALEA ACTIVITY CENTRE
01365 386668
Canoeing, windsurfing, caving, abseiling and mountain-biking with qualified instructors. Surf boards and bikes for hire.

SHARE HOLIDAY VILLAGE,
Smiths Strand, Lisnaskea BT92 0EQ
T 013657 22122 F 013657 21893
Purpose-built for less able guests. Day visit opportunities include cruises on replica Viking ship, and a range of land and water activities, such as canoeing, windsurfing and banana skiing.

ANGLING

There is superb fishing to be had in County Fermanagh on the rivers and lough shores, and many anglers come to the county every year to participate in the various competitions, or simply for pleasure. Lough Melvin is particularly renowned - boasting its own species of trout.

BOATING & CRUISING

MV KESTREL,
Enniskellen 01365 322882
Departing from Round 'O' Quay for 1hour 45 minute cruises of Lower Lough Erne, stopping off at Devenish Island.

VIKING VOYAGES ON UPPER LOUGH ERNE,
Share Holiday Centre, Lisnaskea
013657 22122
Cruises in a replica Viking Longship. Tours last approx 1 hour 30 minutes..

CYCLE HIRE

CORRALEA ACTIVITY CENTRE
01365 386668

CYCLE-OPS,
Mantlin Road, Kesh 013656 31850

LAKELAND CANOE CENTRE,
Castle Island, Enniskillen 01365 324250

MCCYCLE TOURS
2 Brookeborough Road, Maguiresbridge

EQUESTRIAN CENTRES

ASHBROOKE RIDING SCHOOL,
Brookeborough 01365 53242 or 53204

DRUMBONEY RIDING STABLES,
Lisnarick BT94 1NB 013656 21892

FLORENCE COURT RIDING CENTRE,
Derreens East 01365 348330 or 338441

LAKEVIEW RIDING CENTRE,
Leggs, Belleek
013656 58163

ULSTER LAKELAND EQUESTRIAN CENTRE,
Necarne, Irvinestown 013656 21919

GOLF COURSES

CASTLE HUME,
Belleek Road, Enniskillen 01365 327077

ENNISKILLEN,
Castle Coole 01365 325250

SCENIC DRIVES

Fermanagh District Council Tourist Information Centre, Enniskillen, has details of two scenic drives, the Lower Lough Erne Scenic Drive and the Lower Lough Erne and Lough Navar Scenic Drive, both of which offer superb lough views.

WALKING

There is a Heritage Trail around the county town of Enniskillen, details from the Tourist Information Centre.

WATER SPORTS

LAKELAND CANOE CENTRE,
Enniskillen 01365 324250 /322411 (eves)
Campsite and equipment hire, including bikes, caving helmets, lights, tents, canoes, sailboards, sailing boats and jet skis. Ferry service from Lakeland Forum Jetty.

WHERE TO STAY

HOTELS

AA RECOMMENDED

ENNISKILLEN

KILLYHEVLIN★★★
BT74 6RW *(2 miles south, off A4)*
T 01365 323481 F 01365 324726
Impressive hotel, good levels of comfort and lakeside views. Some holiday chalets with private jetties.
43 bedrooms £££

RAILWAY ★
BT74 6AJ
T 01365 322084 F 01365 327480
Practical family-run hotel with a railway theme.Popular with locals. All-day food.
19 bedrooms £

IRVINESTOWN

MAHONS★★
Mill Street BT741GS *(on A32 midway between Enniskillen and Omagh)*
T 013656 21656 F 013656 28344
Popular hotel combining old and modern. Pretty bedrooms, lounges and restaurant.
18 bedrooms ££ Solarium Pool table

BED & BREAKFAST ESTABLISHMENTS

AA RECOMMENDED

ENNISKILLEN

TULLYHONA FARM GUEST HOUSE ❀❀❀
Marble Arch Road, Florence Court BT92 1DE
T 01 365 348452
Peacxeful house with cheeful bedrooms.
4 bedrooms(4 fmly) £ No smoking Children's activities Parking

DROMARD HOUSE ❀❀❀❀
Tamlaght BT74 4HJ T 01 365 387250
Pleasant Victorian house near the University. Good value accommodation
4 bedrooms £ No smoking Parking

Dromard House

CAMPING & CARAVANNING

LISNASKEA

LISNASKEA CARAVAN PARK
BT92 0NZ T 01365 721040
Signposted. From A34 turn onto B514 for Lisnaskea, and site signed half a mile before town. Nearby town: Enniskillen

2 pennants, touring caravans, motor caravans & tents.
Open April-September, booking advisable July-August. Last arrival 21.00hrs. Last departure noon.
A 4-acre site with 43 touring pitches.

Electric hook up, shower, electric shaving point, cold storage, children's playground, public telephone, dog exercise area on site, disabled facilities.
Facilities within three miles of site: stable, golf course, boats for hire, fishing, shop

WHERE TO EAT

PUBS, INNS & OTHER PLACES

BLAKES OF THE HOLLOW,
6 Church Street, Enniskillen T 01365 322143
Fine pub in the centre of Enniskillen which has been in the Blake family since 1929.

THE HOLLANDER,
5 Main Street, Irvinestown T 01365 621231
Warm welcome and good home-made food in both the bar and restaurant.

LE BISTRO,
Erneside Shopping Centre, Enniskillen
T 01365 326954
Serves freshly cooked dishes prepared from the best available ingredients.

LUSTY BEG ISLAND,
Kesh T 01365 632032
A phone call summons free ferry to the Island. Inn serves home-style bar food

MULLIGAN'S BAR & RESTAURANT,
33 Darling St, Enniskillen T 01365 322059
Family-friendly place. Wide choice of food, including Ulster and international dishes.

THE SHEELIN,
Bellanaleck, near Enniskillen T 01365 348232
Thatched bar and restaurant.Wholesome evening meals and Sunday lunches.

WILLOW PATTERN PANTRY,
Clareview, 89 Crevenish Road, Kesh
T 013656
On a dairy farm overlooking Lower Lough Erne. Home baking and local specialities

COUNTY DERRY/ LONDONDERRY

County Derry/Londonderry has a history of bitter religious and political division, violence and conflict. However visitors are as safe here as in any other part of Northern Ireland, though it is sensible to be circumspect about airing political opinions in sensitive areas. While the town of Derry is mainly Catholic - with a vociferous Protestant minority - other towns further inland are staunchly Protestant. The main attraction in the county is the walled town of Derry itself, situated on a curve in the River Foyle, where there is much for the visitor to explore.

PRINCIPAL TOWN

DERRY/LONDONDERRY

The predominantly Catholic population prefers the name Derry. The 'London' bit comes from the time when James I gave the city to the livery companies of London as a gift. Derry is home to the notorious Bogside district, where the Catholic/Protestant divide is most clearly evident - as you can see from the wall slogans alone. It was here that 13 Catholics were killed during a civil rights march on 'Bloody Sunday' in 1972.

For all its political tensions, Derry is a fascinating city to visit. Its massive 17th-century walls have never been breached - though not for want of trying. The longest siege in British history took place here in 1688, when the Protestant apprentice boys stole the keys of the city and locked the gates against the Jacobites. Over 7,000 of the 30,000 people crammed within the walls died from starvation or disease, yet still they would not capitulate. After 105 days, James' troops retreated in the face of William's forces. To this day, the Loyalists celebrate the actions of the apprentice boys in their marches.

MUST SEE

CITY WALLS,
Derry
T 01232 235000 F 01232 310288
The finest and most complete city walls to be found in Ireland. The walls, 26ft/8m high and up to 29.5ft/9m thick, are mounted with ancient canon, and date back to the 17th century. The walled city is a conservation area with many fine buildings. Visitors can walk round the city ramparts - a circuit of one mile/1.5km.

MOUNT SANDEL,
Coleraine *(1 mile/1.5km southeast)*
T 01232 230560 F 01232 310288
This 200ft/61m oval mound overlooking the River Bann is believed to have been fortified in the Iron Age. Nearby is the earliest known inhabited place in Ireland, where post holes and hearths of wooden dwellings, and flint implements dating back to 6,650BC have been found. The fort was a stronghold of de Courcy in the late 12th century and was refortified for artillery in the 17th century.

TULLAGHOGE FORT,
Cookstown *(2 miles/3km south)*
T 01232 235000 F 01232 310288
This large hilltop earthwork, planted with trees, was once the headquarters of the O'Hagans, Chief Justices of the old kingdom of Tyrone. Between the 12th and 16th centuries the O'Neill Chiefs of Ulster were also crowned here - the King Elect was seated on a stone inauguration chair new sandals were placed on his feet and he was then anointed and crowned. The last such ceremony was held here in the 1590s; in 1600 the stone throne was destroyed by order of Lord Mountjoy.

MUSSENDEN TEMPLE,
Bishop's Gate & Black Glen, Mussenden Road, Castlerock
T 012658 48728
Spectacularly placed on a cliff edge overlooking the Atlantic, this perfect 18th-century rotunda was modelled on the Temple of Vesta at Tivoli. Frederick Hervey, Bishop of Derry and 4th Earl of Bristol, had the temple built as a summer library for his cousin, but sadly she died before its completion, so he studied there himself. The temple, with its magnificent views of the Antrim and Donegal coasts, is only a part of the Bishop's Downhill demesne; visitors entering by the Bishop's Gate can enjoy a beautiful glen walk up to the headland where the temple stands. It is now a National Trust property.

BIG OUTDOORS

BANAGHER GLEN
(W of Dungiven) T 015047 60304
A beautiful woodland walk of some three miles/five km to Altnaheglish Reservoir.

BENONE STRAND
(off A2, 12 miles/19km north of Limavady)
A seven-mile/11km strand against a backdrop of cliffs and sand dunes.

NESS WOOD COUNTRY PARK
(7 miles/11km southeast of Derry)
T 015047 22074
Lovely woodland walks with a path leading to Ulster's highest waterfall.

PORTSTEWART STRAND
A two-mile/three km strand with sand dunes, in the care of the National Trust.

ROE VALLEY COUNTRY PARK
(off the B192, 1 mile/1.5km S of Limavady)
T 01504 722074
Ulster's first hydroelectric power station, bulit 1896, and old water mills for linen production are features. Visitors' centre.

GREAT FOR KIDS

ADVENTURE CASTLE,
Brunswick Superbowl, Derry T 01504 37199
Indoor adventure play area for children up to 11 years old.

BANANAS,
Derry T 01504 373731
Indoor adventure play area for children .

BEACHES
Portstewart has all the traditional seaside attractions. Castlerock and Downhill are quieter alternatives. Lovely Benone Strand was the North's first Blue Flag beach.

OPEN ANIMAL FARM,
46 Leitrim Road, Castledawson
(1 mile north)
A range of animals, from goats, rabbits, guinea pigs, Shetland ponies, Jacob and Soya sheep to rare fowl breeds.

HISTORIC & ANCIENT SITES

BANAGHER CHURCH,
Dungiven T 01232 235000
(2 miles/3km southwest)
Impressive ruins of the church founded by St Muiredach O'Heney in 1100, who is said to have endowed his large family with the power of bringing good luck.

DUNGIVEN PRIORY,
Dungiven T 01232 235000
(southeast of town overlooking the River Roe)
The priory, of which extensive ruins remain, dates from 1150 and the church contains one of Ireland's finest medieval tombs, belonging to Cooey na Gall O'Cahan who died in 1385.

MAGHERA CHURCH,
Maghera T 01232 235000
(eastern approach to town)
A 6th-century monastery founded by St Lurach, later a bishop's see and finally a parish church. The cross-carved stone to the west of the church is thought to be the grave of the founder.

ROUGH FORT,
Limavady
(1 mile/1.5km west off the A2)
An Early Christian Rath in the care of the National Trust.

ST COLUMB'S CATHEDRAL,
Bishop Street Within, Derry T 01504 2673
Stained glass windows in the cathedral illustrate scenes from the seige of Derry (1688-9), and an audio visual presentatic tells the story of the siege as well as the history of the cathedral.

HOMES & GARDEN

BELLAGHY BAWN,
Castle Street, Bellaghy T 01648 386812
Restored fortified house dating from 161 Inside there are local history exhibits, an work by local boy Seamus Heany and other contemporary Northern poets.

ARHART CENTRE & WILDLIFE ANCTUARY,
llyarnet, Derry ☎ **01504 354040**
.5 miles/2km beyond Foyle Bridge)
ttage with exhibits on Amelia Earhart, e first woman to fly the Atlantic solo in 932, landing in the field here.

EZLETT HOUSE,
stlerock, Coleraine BT51 4TN
miles/8km W on Coleraine/Downhill coast d) ☎ **01265 848567**
low thatched cottage built around 1690 th an interesting cruck truss roof, nstructed from arches of curved timbers, filled with clay, rubble and other ailable material. National Trust

RINGHILL,
oneymore, Magherafelt BT45 7NQ
mile/1.5km from Moneymore on B18)
016487 48210
17th-century manor house, in the hands the National Trust, incorporating a costume museum. There are also gardens and woodland walks to enjoy.

THE WILSON DAFFODIL GARDEN,
University of Ulster Campus, Coleraine
A rare collection of Irish-bred daffodils - a wonderful sight in April.

MUSEUMS & ART GALLERIES

FIFTH PROVINCE,
Butcher Street, Derry ☎ **01504 373177**
The history of the Celts, genealogical research and a restaurant.

FOYLE VALLEY RAILWAY MUSEUM,
Foyle Road, Derry BT48 6SQ
☎ **01504 265234** Fax **01504 377633**
A fascinating collection of relics from the four railway companies that served Londonderry, and the story of the people who ran the railways and those who use the trains.

GARVAGH MUSEUM & HERITAGE CENTRE,
Main Street, Gavagh ☎ **012665 58216**
Featuring displays of farming equipment, Stone-Age relics from the Bann Valley, an eel fishing boat and a jaunting car.

HARBOUR MUSEUM,
Harbour Square, Derry ☎ **01504 377331**
Museum of maritime Derry, featuring a replica of the 30ft/9m curragh that took St Columba to Iona in 563AD.

PLANTATION OF ULSTER VISITOR CENTRE,
50 High Street, Draperstown ☎ **01648 28113**
Telling the story of the Plantation and the Flight of the Earls.

TOWER MUSEUM,
Union Hall Place, Derry ☎ **01504 372411**
History of Derry from pre-historic times to the present day, with artefacts, theatrical displays. Wide range of AV programmes.

ESSENTIAL INFORMATION

TOURIST INFORMATION

OLERAINE
ailway Road ☎ **01265 44723**
01265 51756

MAVADY
Connell Street ☎ **015047 22226**

NDONDERRY
Bishop Street ☎ **01504 267284**

ACCESS

AIR ACCESS

TY OF DERRY AIRPORT,
rport Road, County Derry
01504 810784

GENEALOGY

FTH PROVINCE,
itcher Street, Derry
01504 373177

CRAFTS

ERRY CRAFT VILLAGE,
ipquay Street
ty centre)
omplex of craft workshops. Coffee shop.

SPORT & LEISURE

ACTIVITY CENTRES

RESCENT LEISURE COMPLEX,
rtstewart Strand ☎ **01265 832847**

ICROLIGHT FLYING,
hadowey ☎ **01265 868002 or 823793**

LSTER GLIDING CLUB,
llarena
015047 50301 (w/ends) or 301206 (eves)

ILD GEESE SKY DIVING,
hadowey ☎ **012665 58609**

ANGLING

Tourist Information Centres provide details on permits and so forth for coarse and game anglers. For sea angling, boats are available for hire from Portstewart.

CAR HIRE

AVIS CAR HIRE,
City of Derry Airport ☎ **01504 811708**

DESMOND MOTORS,
173 Strand Road ☎ **01504 360420**

VEHICLE SERVICES,
Campsie ☎ **01504 810832**

CYCLE HIRE

CAR & HOME SUPPLIES,
Coleraine ☎ **01265 42354**

CYCLE CENTRE,
Coleraine ☎ **01265 52655**

EQUESTRIAN CENTRES

BALLYLAGAN EQUESTRIAN CENTRE,
Aghadowey ☎ **01265 868463**

CULMORE RIDING SCHOOL,
130 Culmore Road, Derry ☎ **01504 359248**

HILL FARM RIDING & TREKKING CENTRE,
47 Altikeeragh Rd, Castlerock
☎ **01265 848629**

ISLAND EQUESTRIAN CENTRE,
49 Ballyrashane Rd, Coleraine
☎ **01265 42599**

GREENACRES,
Coleraine ☎ **01265 57359**

MADDYBENNY RIDING CENTRE,
Atlantic Rd, Coleraine ☎ **01265 823394**

TIMBERTOP RIDING CENTRE,
Aghadowey ☎ **01265 868788**

GOLF COURSES

BENONE TOURIST COMPLEX,
☎ **015047 50555**
BROWN TROUT ☎ **01265 868209**
CASTLEROCK, ☎ **01265 848314**
CITY OF DERRY ☎ **01504 46369**
FOYLE ☎ **01504 352222**
KILREA ☎ **012665 40119**
MANOR ☎ **012665 40661**
MOYOLA PARK ☎ **01648 468468**
PORTSTEWART ☎ **01265 832015**
RADISSON ROE PARK HOTEL
☎ **015047 60105 or 22212**

WALKING

Information on the best local walking routes is available from the Tourist Information Centre, these include guided walks in the city of Derry, and the Columban Heritage Trail, linking the sites in the city associated with the saint. Visitors to Derry can also walk the city ramparts - a circuit of one mile/1.5km.

WATER SPORTS

CUTTS WATER-SKI CLUB,
Coleraine ☎ **01265 44013**

SKI SUPREME,
Coleraine ☎ **01265 55700**
Surf Board Hire:

TROGGS,
Portstewart ☎ **01265 833361**

OCEAN WARRIOR,
Portstewart ☎ **01265 836500**

WHERE TO STAY

HOTELS

AA RECOMMENDED

Radisson Roe Park Hotel & Golf Resc

AGHADOWEY

BROWN TROUTCOUNTRY INN ★★
209 Agivey Road BT51 4AD
T 01265 868209 F 01265 868878
Family-run inn with cheerfully decorated bedrooms. Hearty home-cooked fare
17 bedrooms ££ Gymnasium 9-hole golf course

LIMAVADY

RADISSON ROE PARK HOTEL & GOLF RESORT ★★★★
BT49 9LB **T 015047 22222 F 01547 22313**
Set in parkland with spacious, cheerful bedrooms .Choice of bars and restaurants. Award-winning food. Super leisure club
64 bedrooms ££££ Lift Sport, leisure & conference facilities Beauty salon

LONDONDERRY

EVERGLADES ★★★★
Prehen Road BT47 2PA *(1 mile from city centre)*
T 01504 346722 F 01504 349200
Stylish hotel beside River Foyle with lovely bedrooms and smart rooms.
65 bedrooms Conference/banqueting fac

TRINITY HOTEL ★★★
22-24 Strand Road BT48 7AB
T 01504 271271 F 01504 271277
Smartly designed contemporary hotel with pleasant bedrooms . Bars and restaurant offer both Irish and international fare.
40 bedrooms ££ Lift Conservatory

MAGHERA

ARDTARA COUNTRY HOUSE ★★
8 Gorteade Road BT46 5SA
T 01648 44490 F 01648 45080
Charming country house set in lovely grounds. Pretty conservatory & lounges.
8 bedrooms £££ Sports facilities No children under 12 years

BED & BREAKFAST ESTABLISHMENTS

AA RECOMMENDED

CASTLEROCK

CRANFORD HOUSE
11 Circular Road, Castlerock BT51 4XA
T 01265 848669
Near Golf Club and beach. Comfortable bedrooms and sitting room. Excellent breakfast choices.
3 bedrooms, inc 1 family £ No smoking in bedrooms Parking

COLERAINE

GREENHILL HOUSE QQQQQ
24 Greenhill Road, Aghadowey BT51 4EU
(from Coleraine take A29 for 7 miles turn left onto B66 for approx 300yds, house on right)
T 01265 868241 F 01265 868365
Lovely Georgian house with good views. Cheerful bedrooms and traditional lounge. Enjoyable home-cooking.
6 bedrooms £ Mar-Oct

PORTSTEWART

STRANDEEN QQQQ
63 Strand Road, Portstewart BT55 7LU
T/F 01265 833159
Delightful house with sea views. Bright, airy bedrooms and elegant lounge/dining room. Superb Irish breakfasts
3 bedrooms (1 fmly) £ Parking Private fishing No smoking house

Strande

CAMPING & CARAVANNING

CASTLEROCK HOLIDAY PARK,
24 Sea Road, **T 01265 848381**
From the A2 to Castlerock turn right before the railway station into site; signposted.
3 pennants, touring caravans, motor caravans & tents. Open Easter-October, booking advisable July-August. Last arrival 21.00hrs. Last departure noon.
A mainly static site at the seaside with a tidy touring area, 2 minutes from the beach. A 2-acre site with 40 touring pitches and 210 statics.Electric hook up, shower, electric shaving point, games room, children's playground, Calor Gas, Camping Gaz, battery charging, toilet fluic public telephone, fast food/takeaway.
Facilities within three miles of site: stable, golf course, boats for hire, fishing, shop

COUNTY TYRONE

The main features of County Tyrone for the visitor are the unspoilt countryside, the wild Sperrin Mountains (where you can still try your hand at panning for gold), a number of prehistoric sites and the celebrated history parks. The mass emigration from Tyrone to the United States forged strong links with the country, which remain to this day and are reflected in the massive Ulster-American Folk Park, one of the finest museums of its kind in Ireland and certainly a must see.

PRINCIPAL TOWN

OMAGH

Omagh, the county town, is attractively situated at the confluence of the rivers Camowen and Drumragh. It has few sights of particular interest itself, but is an ideal base for exploring the area and is well provided with shops and restaurants.

MUST SEE

ULSTER AMERICAN FOLK PARK,
Omagh BT78 5QY
(5 miles/8km northwest)
T 01662 243292
An outdoor museum tracing the history of Ulster's links with America and the emigration of Ulster residents during the 18th and 19th centuries. The 70-acre/28ha site is divided between the Old and the New World. The Old World is centred around the restored farmhouse of Thomas Mellon, who emigrated to Pennsylvania in 1818, and later founded the Mellon Bank of Pittsburgh. Log houses and outbuildings in the New World are all appropriately furnished, and there's the cottage of John Joseph Hughes, who emigrated from Augher in 1817, became the first Catholic Archbishop of New York and initiated the building of St Patrick's Cathedral there in 1858. Further information is provided in the visitor centre, through exhibits and audio-visual presentations, and demonstrations of Old and New World crafts. A special feature is the Emigration Gallery area, complete with dockside buildings and emigrant ship. There is a café, shop and facilities for the less able.

ULSTER HISTORY PARK,
CULLION BT79 7SU
(7 miles/11km on B48)
T 016626 48188 F 016626 48011
Set in 35 acres, the History Park tells the story of the settlement of Ireland with the aid full scale models of homes and monuments from the Stone Age which you can see, touch and enter. Buildings include Megalithic tombs, a rath, crannog, monastic settlement, and a 17th-century plantation manor house. The Vistiors' Centre houses exhibitions and a 20-minute audio-visual presentation. Facilities include a café, shop, picnic facilities and access for the less able.

SPERRIN MOUNTAINS
The Sperrin Mountains, bounded by the towns of Omagh, Magherafelt, Cookstown and Strabane, are gently contoured, with Sawel the highest at only 2,240ft/683m. The range extends about 40 miles/64km from east to west, and you can drive for 200 miles/322km through the valleys to be delighted by the ever changing scenery

BIG OUTDOORS

BENBURB VALLEY PARK,
10 Main Street, Benburb **T 01861 549752**
Parkland by the Blackwater river featuring the ruined 17th-century castle (see Ancient & Historic Sites) and a limestone gorge surrounded by trees.

DRUM MANOR FOREST PARK,
Cookstown *(4 miles/6.5km west on A505)*
Park including a café, shrub garden, walled butterfly garden, a lovely arboretum, lakes, a heronry and a nature trail, plus self-guided trail for wheelchair users.

GORTIN GLEN FOREST PARK,
Omagh **T 016626 48217**
(7 miles/11km north on B48)
A five-mile/8km scenic forest drive with pull-in spots to enjoy the views, and trails which also lead to viewing points. There is a visitor centre, resident wildfowl, sika deer enclosure and a café.

PARKANAUR FOREST PARK,
Dungannon **T 01868 759664**
(4 miles/6.5km west off A4)
Look out for daffodils and rhododrenrons in spring, and the herd of white fallow deer. Plus a Victorian garden, wishing well, old archway, exhibition and lecture halls.

GREAT FOR KIDS

ALADDIN'S KINGDOM,
Mountjoy Road, Omagh **T 01662 251550**
Children's indoor adventure playground, with soft play area, spiral glide, crawl tunnels, mountain climb, rope bridges, haunted house, aerial gliders and pendulum swings.

ALTMORE OPEN FARM,
32 Altmore Road, Pomeroy
T 01868 758977
A 176-acre/71 ha sheep farm with rare breeds of farm animals and poultry, and information on the Sperrin Mountains. Pony trekking and fishing in the summer.

HISTORIC & ANCIENT SITES

ARDBOE CROSS,
Ardboe **T 01232 235000**
(off B73 on western shore of Lough Neagh)
The best High Cross in Northern Ireland, marking the site of an ancient monastery. It has 22 sculptured panels, many biblical, stands over 18ft/5.5m high and dates from the 10th century.

BEAGHMORE STONE CIRCLES & ALIGNMENTS,
Beaghmore **T 01232 235000**
Impressive ritualistic stones discovered in the 1930s, dating from the Bronze or even Neolithic Ages, including three pairs of stone circles, a single circle and stone rows (alignments).

BENBURB CASTLE,
Benburb **T 01232 235000**
Ruins of a 17th-century castle - three towers and massive walls - dramatically set on a cliff-edge 120ft/37m above the River Blackwater. There are attractive walks down to the river.

CASTLECAULFIELD,
Castlecaulfield **T 01232 235000**
Built on the site of an ancient fort in 1619 badly burnt in 1641, repaired and occupied by the Caulfield's until 1670. St Oliver Plunkett and John Wesley both preached in its grounds!

MOUNTJOY CASTLE,
Magheralamfield
(3 miles/5km southeast off the B161)
Ruins of an early 17th-century brick and stone fort, with four rectangular towers, overlooking Lough Neagh. It was built by Lord Mountjoy during his campaign against Hugh O'Neill.

HARRY AVERY'S CASTLE,
Newtownstewart **T 01232 235000**
(0.75 miles/1.25km southwest)
Hilltop ruins of a Gaelic stone castle c14th century, built by one of the O'Neill chiefs. Oldest surviving Irish-built castle in North.

TULLAGHOGE FORT, Cookstown
(2.5 miles/4km southeast off B162)
Headquarters of the O'Hagans, chief justices of Ireland, who crowned the O'Neill kings from 12th-17th century. Take the path from the car park and be rewarded by the view!

HOMES & GARDENS

US GRANT ANCESTRAL HOMESTEAD & VISITOR CENTRE,
Dergenagh, Ballygawley Road, Ballygawley
(off A4, 3 miles/5km on Dergenagh road)
T 016625 57133 F 01868 767911
The ancestral home of Ulysses S Grant,

18th President of the USA, restored to the style of a mid 19th-century smallholding. Visitor centre, audio-visual theatre, shop and café.

WILSON ANCESTRAL HOME, Dergalt, Strabane ☎ **01662 243292**
A simple thatched house in the Sperrin Mountains which was home to the grandfather of Woodrow Wilson, the 28th President of the USA. Still with some of its original furniture.

MUSEUMS & ART GALLERIES

AN CREAGAN VISITOR CENTRE
(off A505 at Creggan, Omagh)
☎ **016626 70795**
The archaeology and history of the local area, plus bog trails. The centre is accessible to the less able and has a restaurant.

BENBURB VALLEY HERITAGE CENTRE, Milltown Road, Benburb ☎ **01861 549752**
Display of machinery from the linen industry housed in a 19th-century weaving factory beside the old Ulster Canal. Also a scale model of the Battle of Benburb and a café.

CASTLEDERG VISITOR CENTRE, 26 Lower Stabane Rd, Castlederg
☎ **016626 70795**
Local history presented on video. Model of Fort Alamo Fort in Texas, where Davy Crockett made his last stand. (The Crocketts hail from this area.)

COACH & CARRIAGE MUSEUM, Blessingbourne, Fivemiletown
☎ **013655 21221**
An extensive collection of coaches dating from 1790 to 1910, also some horse-drawn farm machinery.

CORNMILL HERITAGE CENTRE, Lineside ☎ **01868 748532**
(off Dungannon road), Coalisland
The story of Coalisland's industrial history told through old photographs and personal reminiscence.

DONAGHMORE HERITAGE CENTRE, Pomeroy Road, Donaghmore *(400yds/366m from high cross)* ☎ **01868 767039**
A converted National School housing local artefacts, photographs and documents.

GATEWAY CENTRE & MUSEUM, Grange Court Complex, 21 Moyle Road, Newtownstewart ☎ **016626 62414**
Exhibits of artefacts, agricultural implements, photographic equipment and military history. Featuring a traditional farmhouse kitchen. Café

GRAY'S PRINTING PRESS, 49 Main Street, Strabane ☎ **01504 884094**
The print shop is all that remains of Strabane's once thriving printing and publishing industry. It is a National Trust property housing three 19th-century presses and a printing museum.

KINTURK CULTURAL CENTRE, 7 Kinturk Rd, Cookstown ☎ **01868 748532**
(10 miles/16km east, off A73 - follow signs for Ardboe)
History of fishing and the eel industry on Lough Neagh, with displays of boats and equipment. Boat trips available.

SPERRIN HERITAGE CENTRE, 274 Glenelly Road, Cranagh, Gortin
(9 miles/14.5km east of Plumbridge on B47)
☎ **016626 48142**
Exhibitions on the natural history of the Sperrins and gold mining, including audio-visual presentations. Also, try your luck at panning for Iron pyrite and gold. Craft shop and café.

WELLBROOK BEETLING MILL, Corkhill, Cookstown ☎ **01868 748532**
(4 miles/6.5km west of Cookstown, 0.5 miles off A505)
An 18th-century water-powered linen mill restored by the National Trust. Beetling was the process of beating the linen with hammers (beetles) to achieve a smooth, slightly shiny finish.

ESSENTIAL INFORMATION

TOURIST INFORMATION

COOKSTOWN
48 Molesworth Street ☎ **016487 66727**

KILLYMADDY
Killymaddy Tourist Amenity Centre, Ballygawley Road, Dungannon
☎ **01868 767259**

OMAGH
Market Street ☎ **01662 247831**

STRABANE
Abercorn Square ☎ **01504 883735**

GENEALOGY

HERITAGE WORLD FAMILY CENTRE, 26 Market Street, Dungannon
☎ **01868 724187**
Over eight million computerised records and full coverage of the Irish counties. Exhibition on the Irish Famine.

CRAFTS

Craft products to look out for are bagpipes, jewellery, knitwear, pottery, turfcraft, tweeds and Tyrone Crystal

TYRONE CRYSTAL, Killybrackey, Coalisland Road, Dungannon
☎ **018687 25335**
Tours of the factory where you can see all the stages of glass production, including blowing, marking, cutting and finishing. There is also a craft shop and coffee shop.

SPORT & LEISURE

ACTIVITY CENTRES

BALLYNAHATTY FAST TRACK KARTING CLUB, 3 Edergole Avenue, Omagh
☎ **01662 250170**

ANGLING

The River Foyle is said, locally, to be one of salmon fishing's best kept secrets and believed to be the equal of the Dee, Tay or Spey. Certainly the Foyle and its tributaries provide some excellent angling.

FOYLE SPORTING AND ANGLING COMPANY, Grange Court, 21-27 Moyle Road, Newtownstewart ☎/Fax **016626 61877**

EQUESTRIAN CENTRES

DERGMONEY RIDING SCHOOL, Dergmoney House, Dublin Road, Omagh
☎ **01662 2336**

EDERGOLE EQUESTRIAN CENTRE, 70 Moneymore Road, Cookstown BT80 8PY
☎ **01648 762924**

S A KIRK,
2 Tullymran Road, Strabane

M P LAFFERTY,
Clady Vrney, Strabane

MOY RIDING SCHOOL,
131 Derrycaw Road, Moy ☎ **01868 784440**

TERMON EQUESTRIAN CENTRE, 60 Termonbeg, Carrickmore, Omagh
☎ **01662 761782**

GOLF COURSES

DUNGANNON ☎ **018687 22098 or 27338**
FINTONA ☎ 01662 841480
STRABANE ☎ **016626 59599**
18-hole course and 17-bay covered driving range, golf tuition and shop.
KILLYMOON ☎ **01648 763762**
NEWTOWNSTEWART ☎ **01662 661466**
OMAGH ☎ **01662 241442**
STRABANE ☎ **01504 382007**

SCENIC DRIVES

GORTIN GLEN FOREST PARK, Omagh ☎ **016626 48217**
(7 miles/11km north on B48)
A five-mile/8km scenic forest drive with pull-in spots to enjoy the views.

WALKING

There is good walking country in the Sperrin Mountains, contact the Tourist Information Centre for details.

WHERE TO STAY

HOTELS

AA RECOMMENDED

OMAGH

ROYAL ARMS★★
51 High Street BT78 1BA
T 01662 243262 F 01662 245011
Old family-run hotel with pleasant bedrooms. Popular, good value food options plus heavily-beamed restaurant.
19 bedrooms Snooker Function rooms Theatre Golf & Fishing can be arranged

BED & BREAKFAST ACCOMMODATION

AA RECOMMENDED

DUNGANNON

COHANNON INN (LODGE)
212 Ballynakilly Road BT71 6HJ
(400yds from junct 14 on M1)
T 01868 724488 F 01868 724488
Comfortable, good value modern accommodation. All day food available in the adjacent inn until 9-30pm.
50 bedrooms £

GRANGE LODGEQQQQQ
7 Grange Road BT71 7EJ*(1 mile from M1 junct 15 on A29 Armagh, take sign for 'Grange' then first right & first house on right)*
T 01868 784212 F 01868 723891
Excellent hospitality and food .Splendid drawing room with paintings and antiques. Very pretty bedrooms.
5 bedrooms ££ 20 acres No children under 12 years Closed 21 Dec-9 Jan

Grange Lodg

WHERE TO EAT

PUBS, INNS & OTHER PLACES

THE COURTYARD,
56A William Street, Cookstown
T 016487 65070
Agricultural bygones are a feature of the decor at this coffee shop, and the country theme is reflected in the style of the food.

MELLON COUNTRY INN,
134 Beltany Road, Omagh
T 016626 61224
This country inn is situated opposite the Ulster American Folk Park, and offers bar food with a lunchtime buffet, and an extensive restaurant menu.

NUMBER 15 COFFEE SHOP & RESTAURANT,
15 Church Street, Dungannon
T 018687 53048
All day breakfast, morning coffee, lunch and afternoon tea are served at this establishment, over Murray Richardsons Book Shop.

ROSAMUND'S COFFEE SHOP,
Station House, Augher
T 016625 48601
A converted Clogher Valley Railway Station House serving simple, wholesome food, including Clogher Valley Cheddar. Local crafts are also offered for sale.

ROYAL ARMS,
51-53 High Street, Omagh
T 01662 243262 F 01662 244860
A listed building dating from 1887, convenient for the Ulster American Folk Park and the Ulster History Park, the inn offers a range of menus for families or more formal dining.

SUITOR GALLERY GIFTS & TEA ROOM,
Balleygawley Roundabout, Ballygawley
T 016625 68653
A converted barn in an orchard setting, selling crafts and serving a range of home baked fare, and where a simple lunch of home-made soup and bread may be enjoyed.

VISCOUNTS RESTAURANT,
10 Northland Row, Dungannon
T 01868 753800 F 01868 753880
A converted church hall with a medieval theme, offering meals through from breakfast to dinner, including lunch and bar suppers.

DUBLIN & THE EASTERN COUNTIES

DUBLIN

Cumberland Lodge

Bed & Breakfast Accommodation pages 28-29

Glenveagh Townhouse

Bed & Breakfast Accommodation pages 28-29

Raglan Lodge

Bed & Breakfast Accommodation pages 28-29

Morehampton Lodge

Bed & Breakfast Accommodation pages 28-29

CARLOW

Greenlane House

Bed & Breakfast Accommodation page 61

THE SOUTHEASTERN COUNTIES

WEXFORD

Churchtown House
Bed & Breakfast Accommodation
pages 87-88

Mount Auburn
Bed & Breakfast Accommodation pages 87-88

CORK & THE SOUTHWESTERN COUNTIES

CORK

Kieran's Folkhouse Inn

Bed & Breakfast Accommodation pages 104-105

THE WESTERN COUNTIES

CLARE

GALWAY

Lochlurgain

Hotels page 138

Victor

Hotel page 138

Killeen House
Bed & Breakfast Accommodation
pages 140-141

Atlantic Heights
Bed & Breakfast Accommodation
pages 140-141

Beach House
Bed & Breakfast Accommodation
pages 140-141

THE NORTHWESTERN COUNTIES

DONEGAL

Teac Campbell

Bed & Breakfast Accommodation page 158

THE LAKELAND COUNTIES

WESTMEATH

Crookedwood House

Bed & Breakfast Accommodation pages 190-191

BELFAST & NORTHERN IRELAND

ANTRIM

A

B

C

D

F

G

H

L

M

N

O

S

U

V